W9-ANT-813

# Not to the Swift

The Old Isolationists
in the Cold War Era

# Not to the Swift

## The Old Isolationists
## in the Cold War Era

### Justus D. Doenecke

The race is not to the swift, nor the battle
to the strong, nor yet bread to the wise, . . .
but time and chance happeneth to them all.

—Ecclesiastes 9:11

LIBRARY
BRYAN COLLEGE
DAYTON, TN. 37321

*Lewisburg*
*Bucknell University Press*
*London: Associated University Presses*

66623

© 1979 by Associated University Presses, Inc.

Associated University Presses, Inc.

Cranbury, New Jersey 08512

Associated University Presses
Magdalen House
136–148 Tooley Street,
London, SE1 2TT, England

Doenecke, Justus D.
Not to the swift.
Bibliography: p.
Includes index.
1. United States—Foreign relations—1945–1953.
2. United States—Politics and government—1945–1953.
3. United States—Neutrality.     I. Title.
E813.D57          327.73          76–1030
ISBN 0–8387–1940–6
ISBN 0–8387–2289–X (paperback)

PRINTED IN THE UNITED STATES OF AMERICA

# Contents

For Carol
*and for*
Sylvia and Pinkus Sugarman
Ellen and Forrest McDonald

# Preface

Four days after the Pearl Harbor attack, the National Committee of America First voted to close its doors. Local chapters soon followed. With the Japanese air strike, and with Germany's subsequent declaration of war, active opponents of American intervention suddenly found their work terminated. Most isolationists undoubtedly agreed with Senator Burton K. Wheeler (Dem.–Mont.) that the only thing to do was to "lick hell out of them," although they seldom regretted their opposition to United States involvement. General Robert E. Wood, AFC national chairman and board chairman of Sears Roebuck, wrote Colonel Charles A. Lindbergh, whose fame as an aviator helped to make him America's First's most popular speaker: "I am sure we were right and I am sure that history will prove we were right."[1]

Entry into World War II was merely the beginning of more intense international involvements. Within five years after the conflict ended, the United States had become the financial and political mainstay of a new international organization, underwriter of a foreign aid program unprecedented in all of modern history, linchpin of a military alliance that spanned the Atlantic, and the main combatant in an Asian war fought thousands of miles from its shores.

Many isolationists, however, continued to oppose such global activity. Isolationist legislators often stayed on in Congress, particularly in the House, and played leading roles in Cold War debates. Isolationist businessmen, scholars, and publicists remained vocal on issues of foreign policy, frequently serving as a mainstay of the Republican Party. In so doing, many of them provided strength for the conservative and nationalist wings of the Grand Old Party. And in all this activity, "old" isolationists sought ways of preserving the nation's autonomy amid new realities of atomic weapons, large-scale Soviet expansion, and a Communist ideology that appeared to possess ecumenical appeal for deprived peoples.

This book tells their story. After a quick overview of American isolationism, it begins in 1943 with their opposition to unconditional surrender and ends in 1954 with attempts to prevent the United States from intervening in Indochina. From Pearl Harbor to the middle of 1943, much of

9

their protest had been muted. After 1954 many were too old, or politically too impotent, ever again to make concerted opposition.

During the most heated years of the Cold War, such naysayers continually stressed certain themes. They deplored the inroads made upon the war-making power of Congress and feared the new alliance system. They claimed that the administration of President Harry S. Truman was conjuring war scares in order to secure appropriations. They questioned whether the Soviet Union posed a military threat to Western Europe. They argued that foreign aid could only foster domestic disintegration and "statism," while doing little for recipient peoples. Some old isolationists —and not just the liberals among them—stressed that the country might be engaging in imperialism, warned against underwriting reactionary regimes, and feared that America itself could end up as a garrison state.

In addition, many old isolationists promoted the belief that United States entry into the Second World War had only in an indirect sense been provoked by enemy attack. On a more fundamental level, they claimed, it had been caused by the machinations of President Franklin D. Roosevelt. They made strong and impassioned efforts to obtain the presidentical nomination for Senator Robert A. Taft (Rep.–Ohio) and, at times, General Douglas MacArthur, thereby hoping that at least one major party would oppose, and oppose with vigor, the burgeoning international commitments. They were often among those who argued that the Communist seizure of China, and the American defeat in Korea, had been caused by a treason reaching to the very highest levels of the government.

Much of this crusading was to no avail. Even when the Republican Party—which contained most of the congressional isolationists—assumed control of Congress in 1946 and of the presidency in 1952, isolationism formed little part of American foreign relations. Within the very ranks of the GOP there was strong support for Truman diplomacy, and there were those who suggested that Senator Arthur H. Vandenberg (Rep.–Mich.) had more influence in forming national policy than the Secretary of State. In short, isolationism—as traditionally defined and traditionally understood— had failed.

There is, however, far more to this tale, for during the first decade of the Cold War, the fundamental nature of isolationism was significantly altered. Cold War isolationism, like its predecessors of two world wars, could still be defined in terms of aloofness from European conflicts and retention of the free hand. Yet its focus became concentrated less and less upon withdrawal from the world's passions and battles, and more and more upon the most hazardous of commitments on the Asian continent. Genuine "outsiders," such as commentator Lawrence Dennis, essayist Garet Garrett, and historians Harry Elmer Barnes and William L. Neumann, called in vain for a return to a more consistent and cautious ideology. Garrett in fact asked as he addressed himself to the "loss" of China, a popular isolationist theme, "How could we lose China or Europe, since they never belonged to us?" Still and all, such people remained "a minority within a minority."[2]

In the short run—that is, the 1940s, 50s, and 60s— the interventionists won almost all the major battles. Indeed, by 1972 the United States was maintaining 2,000 military bases in thirty-three countries, had Military Assistance Advisory groups functioning in fifty nations, and disbursed nearly four billion dollars a year for arms and aid. Defense installations were located in 363 congressional districts, or five-sixth of the total.[3]

In 1965, however, the administration of Lyndon B. Johnson committed the nation to a full-scale war in Vietnam, a conflict that lasted over a decade, involved 15,300 casualties, and was priced at $57.7 billion. The war overheated the nation's economy to such a degree that by the middle of the 1970s the full cost was not yet tallied. Given the intense domestic reaction to the conflict, pundits now claim to see a new isolationism at work, and today more than one commentator suspect that a cautious public and Congress will not allow the United States to assume "world leadership" for the foreseeable future.

This study considers some dozen Senators, some ninety Congressmen, and well over a hundred publicists and business leaders active during both the debate of 1939–1941 and the formative years of the Cold War. Before Pearl Harbor these individuals deemed it more important to stay out of the European conflict than to see Britain victorious over the Axis. In the interest of brevity, I will refer to such people as "old isolationists," "veteran isolationists," and "World War II isolationists."

Focus upon those individuals who reacted to both major conflicts is deliberate. By concentrating upon the response of the same group to entirely different events, one can better understand the nature of isolationism itself, as well as the specific issues surrounding both global controversies. Particularly because the ideology of American isolationism changed during the Cold War, it is necessary to stress the continuity of the historical actors. Therefore, I have omitted discussion of politicians active only after 1941—Senator Kenneth S. Wherry (Rep.–Neb.), Congressman Howard Buffett (Rep.–Neb.), and Senator Forrest Donnell (Rep.–Mo.) come to mind—as well as such polemicists as columnist Westbrook Pegler or such serious writers as novelist Louis Bromfield.

Although the main narrative concerns those old isolationists who opposed Cold War bipartisanship, it does not cover them alone. Noninterventionism before Pearl Harbor encompassed far more than the latter-day followers of Taft and MacArthur, and no account can be faithful to the divergent course of World War II isolationism that totally neglects other groups. The followers of Senators Vandenberg and Henry Cabot Lodge (Rep.–Mass.), for example, forsook their past anti-interventionism to back Truman foreign policy. Such pacifists as the journalist Oswald Garrison Villard, once editor of the *Nation*, cooperated with isolationists on certain issues. And no account can neglect the activities of Frederick J. Libby, a peace lobbyist for many years close to the isolationists.

Defining *isolationism* has long been a problem. The so-called isolationists themselves were almost unanimous in hating the term. Professor Edwin M. Borchard of Yale, for example, found the designation "essentially dishonest." Reliance on it, he continued, involved a transparent dismissal of those who preferred not to enter European or Asian wars. Taft once commented that the label *isolationist* was given to "anyone who opposed the policy of the moment." Colonel Robert R. McCormick, publisher of the *Chicago Tribune,* made his point even stronger: "Every traitor calls a patriot an isolationist."[4]

Isolationists continually denied that they were isolationists. General Wood commented that, to the best of his knowledge, there had "never been a real isolationist." By this the General meant that he fully realized that the United States could not live totally divorced from other countries. Lindbergh expressed this aspect of isolationism well when he said that he favored "a policy not of isolation, but of independence." Senator Wheeler remarked that America "always sought to trade with other people, helped them out in case of disaster, and married a lot of our rich girls off to some good for nothing European royalty." The *Chicago Tribune* referred to kindred spirits as *nationalists,* and commentator Lawrence Dennis preferred the term *neutralists*.[5]

Scholars of isolationism are as wary of the conventional label as are foes of intervention themselves. They find it a loaded term and one possessing such emotional connotations that dispassionate analysis is indeed difficult. Wayne S. Cole defines isolationists as people who opposed intervention in European wars and who believed in America's unimpaired freedom of action. They often differed from pacifists—those people who refused to sanction any given war—in being strident nationalists and in endorsing strong military preparations. Some isolationists, Cole notes, welcomed certain forms of imperialism and were not averse to military action in Latin America or Asia. Another historian, Manfred Jonas, finds two strands dominant in American isolationism: "unilateralism in foreign affairs and the avoidance of war." In discussing the former point, Jonas notes that the isolationists ever sought to maximize the options open to the country. At no time did isolationists seek literally to "isolate" the United States from either the world's culture or its commerce.[6]

If the word *isolationist* is slippery and misleading, the term *internationalist* is equally so. Unlike the word *isolationist,* the word *internationalist* usually bears a positive connotation. To be an internationalist is to adhere to a far-sighted "large policy" designed to punish "aggression" and to "preserve" the "world community." If used in the purest sense, a genuine internationalist seeks a global community of interest so great that all nations—including the United States—would sacrifice sovereignty in order to preserve it. Common usage of the term, however, denotes a belief that the United States and the rest of the world—and, in particular, Western Europe—are interdependent. Hence, those people usually called internationalists long maintained that domination of the European continent by any single hostile power would alter the balance of power, and alter it so radically that American security would be threatened. In 1941 the internationalists argued that a British victory was more important than keeping the United States out of war.[7]

In describing the administration's Cold War policies, I use the term *interventionist,* thereby hoping to avoid the image of mutuality and shared decision-making that the term *internationalist* evokes.[8] During the Cold

War, the administration would often use the rhetoric of "internationalism" to promote unilateral ends. For example, the United States helped foster the veto within the United Nations Security Council in order to preserve the complete sovereignty of the great powers. Both the Truman Doctrine and the Marshall Plan were designed and initiated in Washington, and the practical workings of the North Atlantic Treaty Organization and of the United Nations action in Korea rested in American hands.

Most attempts to explain isolationism stress ethnic, geographic, economic, and party ties. Historians, for example, note that isolationists often lived in the Middle West, were likely to be employed in small businesses or farms, and frequently belonged to the Republican Party. They find isolationism particularly strong among such ethnic groups as German and Irish-Americans. Such emphases, while valuable, can neglect the nature of their reasoning and the rationale of their arguments. Thomas N. Guinsburg has noted that most studies accept the isolationists "as a shadowy 'given,' while generally denouncing the fruits of their labors." "The historian," Guinsburg writes, "must seek to understand why the isolationists responded as they did; he must, to use Walter Lippmann's term, examine the world outside and the pictures in their heads."[9] The task is an obvious one: to place the ideology of the old isolationists within the context of their own time, and thereby to reveal both their dreams and their fears.

# NOTES

1. Burton K. Wheeler and Paul F. Healy, *Yankee from the West* (Garden City, N.Y.: Doubleday, 1962), p. 36; Robert E. Wood to Charles A. Lindbergh, December 12, 1941, Box 3, the Papers of Robert E. Wood, Herbert Hoover Presidential Library, West Branch, Iowa.

2. Garet Garrett, "Marks of Empire," *Freeman* 2 (April 21, 1952): 469.

3. Barbara W. Tuchman, "The Citizens versus the Military," *Daily Press New Dominion*, September 24, 1972.

4. Edwin M. Borchard to F. J. Libby, July 31, 1942, the Papers of the National Council for the Prevention of War, Swarthmore College Peace Collection (hereafter cited as the "NCPW Papers"); Robert A. Taft, address to the Ohio Society of New York, November 10, 1947, *Congressional Record*, p. A4251 (hereafter cited as *CR*); Robert R. McCormick, *Chicago Tribune*, November 2, 1950.

5. R. E. Wood to E. J. Bermingham, February 28, 1951, Box 15, Wood Papers; Lindbergh in Wayne S. Cole, *Charles A. Lindbergh and the Battle Against American Intervention in World War II* (New York: Harcourt Brace Jovanovich, 1974), p. 87; B. K. Wheeler to R. E. Wood, April 21, 1944, Box 7, Wood Papers.

6. Wayne S. Cole, *An Interpretive History of American Foreign Relations*, rev. ed. (Homewood, Ill.: Dorsey, 1974), pp. 321–22; Manfred Jonas, *Isolationism in America, 1935–1941* (Ithaca, N.Y.: Cornell University Press, 1966), pp. 4–7. Quotation is from p.15.

7. Cole, *Interpretive History*, p. 323.

8. For the general argument that "internationalists" have seldom sought a surrender of American sovereignty, see Manfred Jonas, "Internationalism as a Current in the Peace Movement: A Symposium," in Charles Chatfield, ed., *Peace Movements in America* (New York: Schocken, 1973), pp. 174–77.

9. Thomas N. Guinsburg, "Hiram Johnson: Paragon of Interwar Isolationism," paper delivered at the Duquesne History Forum, Pittsburgh, November 1, 1973, p. 1, and "Senatorial Isolationism in America, 1919–1941," Ph.D. diss., Columbia University, 1969, p. iv. For a summary of the various theories attempting to explain isolationist behavior, see Justus D. Doenecke, *The Literature of Isolationism: A Guide to Non-Interventionist Scholarship, 1930–1972* (Colorado Springs, Colo.: Ralph Myles, 1972), pp. 8–12, and idem, "Isolationists of the 1930s and 1940s: An Historiographical Survey," in Robert W. Sellen and Thomas A. Bryson, eds., *American Diplomatic History: Issues and Methods* (Carrollton, Ga.; West Georgia College Studies in the Social Sciences, 1974), pp. 5–40. For the dilemma of relevance, see Doenecke, "The Isolationist and a Usable Past: A Review Essay," *Peace and Change* 5 (Spring 1978), 67–73.

# Acknowledgments

Without the generosity of others, this book could never have been written. Forrest and Ellen McDonald and James T. Patterson gave untold hours to this manuscript. Their questions were probing, their criticism trenchant. Thomas M. Campbell, Robert W. Sellen, Leo Ribuffo, Leonard Liggio, George H. Mayer, and James G. Moseley, Jr., have made perceptive comments on the entire work. Various chapters have been read critically by the following historians: Eugene Davidson, Robert H. Ferrell, Raymond G. O'Connor, Warren F. Kuehl, Bruce Bartlett, Lawrence S. Kaplan, and Wayne S. Cole. To a man, they have taken time out of a busy schedule to come to my aid, as has—at a later time—Martin L. Sherwin.

My gratitude must also extend to Murray Rothbard, Laszlo Deme, Ronald Radosh, James J. Martin, David Riesman, Elmer Berger, Lloyd C. Gardner, Charles Chatfield, Barton J. Bernstein, and Arthur Schlesinger, Jr., all of whom encouraged me to embark upon this research several years ago and who have been more than kind in offering suggestions. Two of my former professors, Arthur S. Link and Charles S. Blackton, have given their usual strong support. Research has been expedited through the magnanimity of Kenneth S. Templeton, Jr., and the Institute for Humane Studies, John Barcroft and the National Endowment for the Humanities, Walter Muir Whitehill and the John Anson Kittredge Educational Fund, and the Harry S. Truman Library Institute. The faculty and administration of New College of the University of South Florida have given me two academic leaves in order to complete this project.

Librarians and archivists have gone out of their way to make research a pleasure. The author is particularly indebted to Gene M. Gressley of the University of Wyoming, Martin Schmitt of the University of Oregon, Archie Motley of the Chicago Historical Society, Philip Brower of the General Douglas MacArthur Memorial Library, Rosemary Little of Princeton University, Dennis Bilger of the Harry S. Truman Presidential Library, and Robert Wood of the Herbert Hoover Presidential Library. Pat Bryant of New College deserves special mention. The author is also grateful to the staffs of the Hoover Institution on War, Revolution and Peace; the State Historical Society of Wisconsin; the Ohio Historical Society; the Swarthmore College Peace Collection; the Manuscripts Division of the Library of Congress; the Houghton Library of Harvard University; the Butler Library of Columbia University; and the libraries of Cornell University, Ohio Wesleyan University, Manatee Junior College, Eckerd College, and the Tampa campus of the University of South Florida.

Permission to quote directly from manuscript collections has generously and graciously been given by Miriam Vagts and William Beard concerning Charles A. Beard; by Mrs. Eugene Davidson concerning Sterling Morton; by Thomas D. Flynn concerning John T. Flynn; by Senator Robert A. Taft, Jr. concerning his father; by Faith Ward Libby concerning Frederick J. Libby; by Robert H. Barnes and Mrs. Henry Cannon Tilford, Jr. concerning Harry Elmer Barnes; by Doris Neumann concerning William L. Neumann; by Lawrence Dennis concerning his own letters; and by Felix Morley concerning his correspondence.

Several old isolationists and pacifists have been willing to chat about a bygone era, and I must thank Page Hufty of Palm Beach; Frank Cullen Brophy of Phoenix; George Morgenstern, Henry Regnery, and R. Douglas Stuart, Jr. of Chicago; Lawrence and Dora Dennis of New York City; Felix Morley of Gibson Island, Maryland; the late William L. Neumann of Towson, Maryland; and Frank D. Waldrop, Gladys MacKenzie, James Finucane, and the late General Bonner Fellers of Washington, D.C. Dean Clarence Manion of South Bend, Indiana, corresponded with me concerning aspects of Cold War isolationism.

My greatest support of all has been my wife, who has labored with me in every step of this project.

# Not to the Swift

The Old Isolationists
in the Cold War Era

# 1
# An Ideology under Stress:
# An Introduction to Modern
# Isolationism

Isolationists have not fared well in the judgment of history. According to the Authorized Version of the American past, a wise and courageous President Roosevelt realized as early as 1937 that the rise of Japan and Germany threatened the safety and security of the United States. Hence, during the next four years, the Chief Executive carefully and skillfully led the nation toward participation on the side of the Allied Powers. Despite his ability, and despite his charismatic hold on many Americans, he found the undertaking a most difficult one: a large proportion of the population, led by ignorant, prejudiced, and singularly obtuse people, flatly opposed intervention, and not until the Japanese attacked Pearl Harbor did its opposition dissolve.

Most of the isolationists, the story goes on, temporarily and reluctantly "saw the light" after Pearl Harbor, and a minority of the more "enlightened," led by Senator Vandenberg, was instrumental in assisting Presidents Roosevelt and Truman conduct both World War II and the Cold War. Many old isolationists, however, soon went back to sheer obstruction, thereby endangering the United States in its struggle with the Soviet Union.

This Authorized Version, like many another chapter in American history, is merely an account told by the winners of a complex and bitter battle. Some historians, writing in a later time, claim that Roosevelt was weak as well as deceptive. Up to the very eve of the Japanese attack, he was —like his country—a "reluctant belligerent," and one never fully committed to United States involvement.[1] The Revised Standard Version has not yet been extended to the isolationists, and it is not the purpose of the present book either to plead their case or to justify their beliefs and their behavior. Instead, this work delineates who the old isolationists were, what they believed, and what they did during the Cold War years. For this to be accomplished, even though the emphasis in the study is on the years 1943 to 1954, some background must be filled in.

19

Before and during World War II, interventionists undertook a vicious propaganda war against isolationists. Acting out of misguided patriotism, or in a deliberate effort to discredit Roosevelt's foes, or because of sheer malice, ardent interventionists attempted to link the isolationists as a group to the Axis enemy. To read John Roy Carlson's sensationalistic *Under Cover* (1943), subtitled "My Four Years in the Nazi Underworld of America," one would think of the isolationists as part of a treasonous fifth column. To peruse Rex Stout's *Illustrious Dunderheads* (1942), one would suppose that leading noninterventionist Congressmen continually spewed "the Nazi line." A sheer scanning of the headlines of the New York tabloid *P.M.* would lead a person to conclude that the entire nation was ridden with subversive agents.[2]

And if the isolationists were not seen as outright Fascists, they often found themselves branded as anti-Semites, lunatics, and people whose stupidity or naiveté came close to subversion. Henry R. Luce's *Life* and *Time* led the reader to suspect that many—perhaps the bulk of isolationists—longed for a Hitler victory; a reading of Walter Winchell's columns would discover such taunts against America First as "in union there is stench"; and a devotee of columnist Drew Pearson would find lavish use of the label *anti-Semitic*. Then, after the war was over, interventionists continually paraded the voting records of their isolationist opponents, without—of course—offering a word of explanation of the reasoning behind noninterventionist sentiments. Even liberal positions on domestic issues seldom protected those who had led the fight against American entry into World War II.[3]

The factual basis for such attacks was indeed slight. Only an infinitesimally small number of isolationists were pro-Fascist. Certain professional anti-Semites—the fundamentalist clergymen Gerald L. K. Smith and Gerald Winrod—remained in isolationist ranks during the Cold War. A few isolationist publicists, such as lobbyist Merwin K. Hart and radio broadcaster Upton Close, would use the term *Zionist* to describe the whole range of Fair Deal foreign and domestic policy, but these two people usually drew upon standard isolationist arguments. Ironically, if the noun *Zionist* were taken in the strictest sense, one would find many isolationists—particularly in Congress—endorsing the goal of a Jewish homeland in Palestine.[4]

When World War II came to an end, scholars commenced a more serious examination. Some argued that isolationism was rooted in such ethnic groups as German and Irish-Americans, although the great majority of isolationists came from Anglo-Saxon backgrounds. Others saw isolationism grounded in middle-western Populism, although it was later noted that the Mississippi Valley had long possessed a heritage of overseas expansion and imperialism. Still others asserted that isolationism was a form of ethnocentrism, with an insecure and xenophobic "in-group" projecting its fears and self-hatreds upon all "outsiders." Driven by an "authoritarian personality," the isolationists were striking out blindly against a world they never made. Particularly during the period of "McCarthyism," when social scientists exhibited a fear of unruly masses, such sociological and psychological explanations were much in vogue.[5]

Undoubtedly the isolationist movement included many xenophobes, people who could find representation in such isolationist Congressmen as Clare E. Hoffman (Rep.–Mich.) and John E. Rankin (Dem.–Miss.). Hoffman, a thin man with the homey twang and physical features of comedian Will Rogers, combined his anti-interventionism with hostility toward minority groups (Jews in particular, he implied in 1945, possessed disproportionate power), New Dealers, and the "Communistic" Congress of Industrial Organizations. Reared in the countryside of Cass County, Michigan, he would spice his rhetoric with such comments as "The farmers won't stand for this. They'll get their pitchforks and come to town." Rankin was a small, wiry, white-haired man who stood to the left of the New Deal on such issues as public power and monopolies. During the Great Debate of 1939 to 1941, he consistently voted for Roosevelt's foreign-policy proposals. His personal comments about administration intervention, however, were far less enthusiastic, for in 1941 he accused "Wall Street and a little group of our international Jewish brethren" of fomenting war and asked former President Herbert Hoover to give a series of isolationist speeches in the South. He often declared that "white Gentiles" were being persecuted and opposed the repeal of the Chinese Exclusion Act on the grounds that "Japs" would flood the country after the war.[6]

However, even when debate was at its most heated, responsible commentators realized that the virulent sentiments of a Hoffman or a Rankin were held by only a small minority within isolationist ranks. One can push the theme of "alienation" itself only so far, for not all isolationists stood outside the nation's dominant economic and cultural institutions. Many isolationists, particularly among the leadership, possessed a far broader background. Robert A. Taft graduated first in his class at Harvard Law School, Harry Elmer Barnes wrote over thirty scholarly books, columnist Felix Morley had been editor of the *Washington Post* and president of Haverford College. Listed in the noninterventionist ranks in 1940 were a novelist who won the Nobel Prize, one of the world's leading physiologists, the most respected historian in the United States, the president of the University of Chicago, two distinguished authorities on international law, America's foremost architect, the head of the CIO, and the co-founders of one of the country's most successful advertising firms. (Their names respectively: Sinclair Lewis, Anton J. Carlson, Charles A. Beard, Robert M. Hutchins, Philip Jessup, Edwin M. Borchard, Frank Lloyd Wright, John L. Lewis, Chester Bowles, and William Benton.) Student contributors and supporters of the newly formed America First Committee included two future presidents and one future vice-presidential candidate—John F. Kennedy, Gerald R. Ford, and R. Sargent Shriver.[7]

Economic and geographical interpretations are more sound. Isolationist spokesmen of the Middle West and the Great Plains, as one historian has noted, often represented "the owners of small farms and small businesses —the group in society that considered itself buffeted by big business, big labor and big government." For such people, large-scale intervention could mean only further erosion of an individualist and rural ethic. Many isolationists from farm areas realized that war would bring few military contracts to their home districts, while draining both manpower and political strength to the city. The government, in a sense, would be supporting urban and industrial areas at the expense of the farmer. Such agrarian voices as Senator Gerald P. Nye (Rep.–N. D.) claimed that interventionists were taxing farmers in order to build battleships and munitions. These appropriations, said Nye, indicated hidden subsidies for both steel manufacturers and shipbuilders, with the overseas investments of Wall Street speculators being guarded at the expense of the country's true producers.[8]

Congressional voting patterns often lend support to the "rural interpretation" of American isolationism. One example of the rural-urban dichotomy can be found in 1947 during the debate over the Truman Doctrine. Although the voting in Congress was limited to a specific appropriation—aid to Greece and Turkey—both supporters and opponents of the bill realized that broad issues, and ones involving general containment of the USSR, were at stake. Many of the bill's opponents, as in the case of those who fought Roosevelt's interventionist proposals of 1939–1941, came from rural areas between the Appalachians and the Rockies. A closer look, however, shows that those old isolationists representing cities—even if these cities were located in the Middle West—were beginning to back Truman's foreign policy. Cincinnati and Columbus, Ohio; Flint and Grand Rapids, Michigan; St. Louis, Missouri; Knoxville, Tennessee; and even Bismarck, North Dakota, had Representatives who voted for America's first major Cold War commitment.[9]

Hence the rural explanation, while often illuminating, is inadequate. Patterns are seldom neat. Such Republican Senators as Arthur Capper and Clyde Reed, both from the agricultural state of Kansas, voted for the Greek-Turkish appropriation; Congressmen from such areas as suburban Cleveland, suburban Detroit, Harrisburg, Fort Wayne, and Racine opposed the bill.[10] Congressman Daniel A. Reed of Dunkirk, New York, criticized the appropriation while his fellow upstate Republican, John Taber of Auburn, favored it. Both were extremely conservative on domestic issues, usually believed in slashing foreign appropriations, and harbored strong suspicions of urban America.

Explanations therefore cannot be limited to factors of demography and urbanization. To account for the behavior of even the "rural" isolationists, environment must be placed in an ideological framework. Geography alone is a cogent but insufficient explanation.

What the isolationists ultimately shared was not social caste or geographical location. Instead, what they possessed in common was an ideology with roots deep in the country's past. As far back as the eighteenth century, American colonists—influenced by such prophets as the Tory theorist Henry St. John, Viscount Bolingbroke—believed that British commercial and political rapaciousness was corrupting their rural society.

Admittedly, the colonists themselves were building their own "cities in the wilderness" and engaging in wanton speculation for lands ranging from Georgia to Maine; however, they continually and ardently preached that American "innocence" was ever superior to European "corruption." Such travelers as John Dickinson and Charles Carroll portrayed England as enveloped in a Hogarthian nightmare of fixed elections, squalid slums, and dissipated living. Benjamin Franklin compared the extremes of "Poverty and Misery" in Europe to "the happy Mediocrity" of self-employed "Cultivators" on Pennsylvania farms. Jefferson, himself thoroughly at home in the salons of Paris, feared that the effete aristocratic values of Europe had already corrupted the eastern seaboard of his nation. It was better, he wrote a friend, that his grandson not be educated in Philadelphia, for people might "acquire there habits and partialities which do not contribute to the happiness of their after life."[11]

To the colonists, the American Revolution was more than a political event; it symbolized a break from a European ethos as well as from European rule. Thomas Paine, in describing America as the "asylum for mankind," merely secularized and updated the *Arbella* sermon of Puritan leader John Winthrop, who in 1631 had hoped that the Massachusetts Bay experiment would embody "the city on a hill" described by Jesus in Matthew 5. And if in reality Americans did use their new-found freedom to slaughter Indians and enslave blacks, they perceived themselves as establishing an Edenic utopia.

Frederick Jackson Turner's seminal paper of 1893, with its stress upon the rejuvenating role of the frontier, was no mere academic hypothesis. In many ways, the Wisconsin professor was simply articulating what his countrymen had believed for two hundred years. Democrats Andrew Jackson and Thomas Hart Benton, as well as Whigs Henry Clay and William Henry Harrison, had propounded the doctrines that the yeoman embodied republican virtue and that the woods and the prairies of the West offered perennial rebirth.[12]

Certain symbols soon took on a life of their own. Despite an occasional yearning for Old World sophistication, the people of the new nation usually preferred the simple to the complex, the "natural" West to the "artificial" East, the "frontier" to "civilization." The "American" virtues of plain speaking and unadorned living surpassed the "European" values of sophistication and luxury; the "honest" toil of the farmer was preferable to the "dishonest" speculation of the banker, the merchant, and the broker; and intuitive "wisdom" was more reliable than formal "knowledge." And if commerce, finance, and even factories ever became necessary, they must, and indeed could, be so tempered by rural surroundings and an agrarian ethos that they would actually help to tame the primitive wilderness. The "machine" would help create the American "garden," thereby fulfilling the early promise of the republic.[13]

In developing this ideology, the isolationist perspective has always played a crucial role. Continental and commercial expansion—the building of farms and the selling of goods— would guarantee America's prosperity. Ideological expansion, centering on America's democratic values and the tenets of Protestant Christianity, would prevent civil and spiritual decay. Ensnarement in foreign alliances, however, would invariably create deterioration of the "pure" values Americans had long treasured.

Intervention abroad possessed other threats as well, threats that affected the physical as well as the ideological environment. Quite obviously, major commitments overseas would so mobilize, standardize, and regiment the nation that the "old America" could never be restored. Ahead lay only impersonal and squalid cities, ugly factories, and conflict between classes. Few isolationists went so far as Louis Taber, National Grange master and national committeeman for America First, who defined cities as places "where there were slums and dirt, and noise, and filth and corruption and saloons and prostitutes." By 1941, however, more than one isolationist was firmly convinced that the war would submit the United States to such social strain that the country might not survive.[14]

Some fears concerning World War II were quite tangible. Elitist commentator Lawrence Dennis predicted that returning veterans and a suddenly unemployed managerial class would seize control. Advertising executive Chester Bowles, a liberal on domestic policy and AFC national committeeman, feared Communist uprisings, class war, and Fascist repression. Colonel Lindbergh commented: "God knows what will happen here before we finish it [World War II]—race riots, revolution, destruction."[15]

A common ideological base does not mean that all isolationists were similarly motivated. Cold War isolationism, like its forerunners of World Wars I and II, was composed of several diverse elements. In other words, it drew from both the political left and right. During the Cold War, the ranks of the isolationists contained such varied groups as Congressmen from rural areas, midwestern manufacturers, right-wing publishers, freelance writers, anarchist philosophers, and oldtime liberals and progressives. A few prominent pacifists—such as Frederick J. Libby and Oswald Garrison Villard—occasionally cooperated with the isolationists, working together so closely on some issues that the efforts of both groups could be seen as one.

Even before World War II, conservative isolationists had outnumbered more liberal ones, and by 1935 much isolationism was rooted in a more general opposition to the Roosevelt administration. For both Old Guard conservatives and former progressives, the New Deal smacked of paternalism, subsidies to special interests, class warfare, and a broker state. The only New Deal measures that many isolationists supported were those designed to discipline Wall Street and the New York Stock Exchange. Intervention, such conservatives believed, would hasten the most destructive trends of Roosevelt's domestic program, with war thrusting powerful and despotic labor unions and a federal "octopus" upon the country. The independent businessman would lose his autonomy, and the days of the open shop, low taxes, and "free enterprise" would be gone forever. Fiscal solvency, clean and limited government, rural and small-town values, economic individualism, a self-determined foreign policy—all appeared interconnected and all appeared beyond recall.[16]

Conservative isolationists were particularly strong in Congress, the business world, and the press. Sitting in the House and Senate, such individuals—contrary to legend—did not cast one negative vote after another, extending from relief appropriations in the 1930s to social security increases in the 1950s, merely in order to tally a "distinguished record of total sterility." Instead, they were engaged in a rear-guard effort to preserve a rural arcadia from the inevitable onslaughts of modernity.

Daniel A. Reed, in many ways, typifies this background. Reed was born in 1875 on a farm in Sheridan, New York. After working his way through Cornell, he entered private law practice, was employed by the state's liquor enforcement bureau, and coached football for several colleges. From 1913 to 1920, Reed served as a publicist for the Chamber of Commerce of Flint, Michigan, where he preached the gospel of private property and business efficiency. In 1918 he was elected to Congress as an example of "the American success story," and he remained in the House until his death in 1959. As Congressman, he sought to preserve an America of small businesses and family farms against unionization, big government, and an impending industrialism that was altering the character of his own district. On the one hand, Reed strongly opposed New Deal welfare legislation. (When a reporter told him that he had voted against more bills than any other Congressman, Reed—who had been looking rather glum—brightened immediately. He replied, "I did?", and walked off beaming!). On the other, he fought chainstores, banks, and taxes upon small concerns. Both the Great Depression and World War II, Reed believed, were caused by tyrannical industrialists and financiers seeking to preserve their holdings.[17]

In the Senate, no isolationist received more respect than Robert A. Taft. An intellectual who wore rimless glasses and spoke in a metallic voice, Taft lacked broad national appeal but was literally worshiped by his followers. The Ohio Republican was so often seen as the leader of the party's right-wing faction that reporters gave him the title "Mr. Conservative." Most historians emphasize that Taft represented a midwestern state and that he frequently voiced suspicion of eastern monopolists, mass circulation magazines, and Wall Street speculators. The small businessman, the Senator genuinely believed, was the key to the nation's progress.

Yet Taft, in many ways, lacked the supposed narrowness and crude gregariousness that the popular mind so often associates with the heartland. More than is commonly supposed, Taft drew his ideas from both East and Middle West, while remaining somewhat aloof from the cultural milieu of either section. He was born the son of a president and educated in a battery of eastern schools—Taft preparatory school, Yale University, Harvard Law School. He served overseas with Herbert Hoover's American Relief Administration, endorsed United States membership in the League of Nations and the United Nations, and fervently believed—as did his father before him—that international law could resolve major disputes among nations. His domestic voting record was more liberal than that of most congressional conservatives, and he was more given to compromise on such issues as the Truman Doctrine, the Marshall Plan, and troops to Europe. For all of Taft's own relative moderation, however, his foreign-policy views reinforced, rather than converted, those of more dogmatic persuasion. Like John C. Calhoun a century earlier, Taft appeared far from unwilling to restrain his more extreme followers.[18]

Certain kinds of businessmen composed another conservative element. These people were particularly strong in mining, service concerns, retailing, and light-goods manufacturing. Since the 1920s they had believed that the American interior contained such an abundance of resources that the country could avoid European commitments. An economic axis of agriculture and industry, the linking, so to speak, of Duluth grain elevators and Pittsburgh steel mills, would insure national self-sufficiency. The *Chicago Tribune* spoke for many midwestern businesses when it said in 1929, "The other sections of the country, and particularly the eastern seaboard, can prosper only as we prosper. We, and we alone, are central to the life of the nation." "Isolationist" companies, often family controlled, were able to bypass Wall Street financing; their goods, circulating freely within the country's expansive boundaries, needed no government subsidizing.[19]

General Robert E. Wood typified this group. A short, sharp-featured man, Wood had been board chairman of Sears Roebuck from 1939 to 1954. Sears was a Chicago-based firm, long serving an agrarian and small-town clientele. As Sears's top executive, Wood pioneered in developing retail outlets and was active in establishing branches in Latin America. His continued law suits against monopolies were often more effective than the anti-trust crusades of the Department of Justice. Resentful of the economic power of the Northeast, Wood—a Republican—backed Roosevelt for president in 1932. The West and the South, he once said, received "skimmed milk"; the East always got the "cream." At first Wood supported much of the New Deal and served with such government agencies as the National Recovery Administration and the Works Progress Administration. Yet the honeymoon with Roosevelt did not outlive the President's second term, for Wood opposed Roosevelt's pump priming, court packing, and deficit spending.

From the time that he earned his first bars at West Point, the General was a strong nationalist. He could boast of a military career that included the Philippine insurrection, the building of the Panama Canal, and the famous Rainbow Division of World War I. Wood, however, fought United States entry into World War II, and, while chairman of the America First Committee, continually maintained that intervention would ruin the nation's capitalist economic system.[20]

Conservative isolationists received support among segments of the American press. If industrialists could supply the financing and Congressmen the votes, newspapers could offer both the vehicle and much of the rationale for the isolationist ideology. Foremost here was the *Chicago Tribune,* owned by Colonel Robert Rutherford McCormick. Educated at Ludgrove, a British preparatory school located in Middlesex; Groton in Massachusetts (where he developed a lifetime hostility toward the eastern elite); and Yale, "Bertie" McCormick assumed control of the *Tribune* in 1910. The Bull Mooser and Chicago alderman soon turned the editorial page into a forum for personal crusades. He attacked the greater part of New Deal legislation, beginning with the "Fascistic" NRA. As with many other conservatives, McCormick made an exception for the Securities and Exchange Commission, which he saw as a vehicle to police a predatory Wall Street.

Something of an eccentric, McCormick found British imperialism far more dangerous than the teachings of Marx and he continually warned against the wiles of "Perfidious Albion." Senator Taft once quipped to a *Tribune* journalist, "I hope that you got the Colonel off safely to Europe, where I trust he will not start a war with the British."[21] In 1940 the Colonel was a minority among his fellow isolationists in opposing any aid to Britain. Ironically, McCormick physically resembled nothing so much as a tall, handsome, British gentleman, an image to which he added by speaking with a slight English accent.

The archetype of a militant nationalist, the Colonel long supported universal military training, a large navy, and a bellicose foreign policy. During the 1930s he hoped that China would repel the Japanese invasion. He grew increasingly apprehensive about Roosevelt's interventionism, however, and began to fear that the President would push the country into war, doing so by means of conscription and large fleets. By 1940 he was opposing the draft and the construction of an offensive navy as well. McCormick's staunch isolationism applied to Asia as well as to Europe, for he fought any measure that might result in conflict with Japan.[22]

If the isolationists of the right feared that intervention would lead to the demise of American capitalism, those of a more leftist persuasion claimed that wars always retarded social reform. A regimented, militarized country, acting in a futile quest to impose its way of life upon the rest of the world, would inevitably lose sight of domestic injustice. Isolationist survivors among liberals were by no means so numerous as those on the right, particularly as the Cold War became increasingly heated. Yet there was always a vocal minority of liberals, both in the Congress and outside, who opposed direct participation in both World War II and the Cold War.

In the Senate, such liberalism was represented by William Langer (Rep.–N. D.). The son of German immigrants from Prague and a graduate of Columbia University Law School, Langer had faced many stormy periods in Dakota politics. At one time he was removed as state governor by the North Dakota Supreme Court. He was always a staunch liberal on domestic issues, backing a Fair Employment Practices Commission, opposing the establishment of the Subversive Activities Control Board, and continually seeking increased social security, public housing, and federal aid to education. Never a party regular, Langer supported Truman's reelection in 1948 and traveled with his whistle-stop campaign four years later. Although opposed to Truman's foreign policy, Langer agreed with the President's advocacy of high farm supports and domestic welfare measures.

Vehemently anti-British, Langer envisioned himself as a modern "Paul Revere." In fact, when Winston Churchill visited the United States in 1952, Langer requested that the minister of Boston's Old North Church put two lanterns in the belfry. He believed that his state of North Dakota amounted to little more than a colony of Wall Street. The Dakota farmer, Langer claimed, toiled long hours to grow the premium wheat that "outside" millers and speculators forced him to sell "cheap." When, in turn, the farmer tried to buy the machinery needed to grow more wheat and to capture more of the market, he was at the mercy of farm-implement manufacturers. Langer's biographer has written, "Under such conditions there was little hope for a higher standard of living. Someone else, always an outsider, profited from the labor and resources of North Dakota. In this respect the people of North Dakota were kindred to the colonists of the rest of the world." Langer's anger would show forth in frequent and lengthy filibusters, made in a curious whistling tone, and watched in half-bemused, half-fearful amazement by his Senate colleagues.[23]

Senator Robert M. La Follette, Jr. (Prog.–Wis.) was another isolationist liberal, one whom both Congress and the public held in much greater respect. The son of one of the country's most prominent reformers, the short, diffident, personable "Young Bob" entered the Senate in 1925 upon his father's death. Like "Old Bob," Robert possessed a critical intelligence and a studious mind; unlike "Old Bob," he avoided barbed polemics. *New York Times* correspondent Allen Drury found La Follette approaching his ideal of the model public servant—"a man who works tirelessly and consistently and honestly, through many defeats, toward the goal of a better society for his fellow men."

A strong defender of Roosevelt, whom he endorsed for three terms, "Young Bob" could be more radical than the New Deal. In 1936, for example, he advocated government ownership of railroads, power plants, and munitions factories, and sought as well a federally owned central bank. If by 1945 he had broken with Roosevelt over intervention, he continued to seek appropriations for New Deal agencies.

La Follette's isolationism stemmed from his liberalism. War, he believed, was caused by imperialism and power politics, and no peace that perpetuated an unjust status quo, or that violated principles of self-determination, could last. In 1929 La Follette had urged President Hoover to withdraw the Marines from Nicaragua. In 1932 he sought a one-year moratorium on naval construction. During the thirties he backed the neutrality acts while calling for a war referendum and heavy taxation on war profits. In 1940 he helped line up Senators to speak for America First, although he personally found the group too conservative for closer affiliation. In Wilson's time, his father had stressed the evils of bankers and munition makers; twenty years later, "Young Bob" maintained that it was the weakening of the reform impulse that was causing Roosevelt to intervene abroad.[24]

If conservative isolationists possessed a voice in the *Chicago Tribune,* more liberal ones found one in the *Progressive,* a weekly partly owned by the Wisconsin senator. Founded as *La Follette's Magazine* in 1914 and retitled the *Progressive* in 1929, it had been the personal voice of Robert M. La Follette, Sr., a man who combined his isolationism with strong doses of social reform. The list of contributors—Lincoln Steffens, Jane

Addams, Louis D. Brandeis, Senator George W. Norris (Rep.–Neb.), Senator Hiram Johnson (Rep.–Calif.)—embodied a veritable *who's who* of American progressivism. In June 1940 Philip La Follette, former governor of Wisconsin, and his brother "Young Bob" assumed direct ownership, buying out the interest of its interventionist editor William J. Evjue. They hired a young, peppery New Yorker, Morris Rubin, to replace him. Rubin, only five years out of the University of Wisconsin and possessing the slimmest of budgets, was able to recruit many noninterventionists of the left to write for the journal. Although the *Progressive* received generous support during the war years from isolationist manufacturer William H. Regnery, it faced bankruptcy and closed in October 1947. Four months later it was transformed from a weekly to a monthly, with Rubin as both editor and publisher. Such contributors as reformer Oswald Garrison Villard and Socialist leader Norman Thomas assured that the *Progressive* would continue its traditional role, opposing interventionism while supporting labor, consumers, and minorities.[25]

Despite the rich diversity among conservative and liberal isolationists, both groups agreed that intervention would spread two major perils of the Old World: British imperialism and Russian Bolshevism. America, they maintained, could not afford to be the unwitting agent of either colonial despotism or revolutionary terror.

From the time of Jefferson to the time of Blaine, the United States had regarded Britain with the greatest of suspicion. Not all statesmen, of course, were so vocal as Townsend Harris, whose parents had supposedly raised him up to offer prayers, fear God, and hate the British.[26] To many isolationists, however, England was ever conspiring to rescue its domestic plutocracy and archaic empire. So long as it maintained domination over much of the globe, it would be oppressing billions of subject peoples and attempting to hoard the bulk of the world's wealth.

In 1940 and 1941 isolationists were particularly fearful that their countrymen might fall prey to British wiles. Margaret Sanger, the prominent advocate of birth control, warned in 1941 that the British were invading America not with "redcoats" but with charm, flattery, and "diplomacy" to "the Nth degree." In the eyes of the revisionist historian Charles Callan Tansill, England, repeating its machinations of World War I, was again trying to entice the United States into conflict. The cause of England, isolationists insisted, had no affinity with that of America. The liberal Keep America Out of War Congress recalled John Bull's indifference to the fate of Weimar Germany and Loyalist Spain. Wheeler denied that Britain was fighting Hitler because the *Führer* was a foe of democracy; rather, said the Montana Senator, England was merely responding to Nazi military aggression. Journalist John T. Flynn, chairman of the New York chapter of America First, went so far as to predict that —regardless of the war's outcome—the British would be controlled by the socialistic Labor Party, a group that possessed "the making of a genuine fascism."[27]

Isolationists often focused upon the evils of the British Empire. Advertising executive Chester Bowles indicted British activity in India, Ireland, and South Africa. As with every other nation, the British—Bowles commented—have been cruel and ruthless. Essayist Albert Jay Nock used the newly published autobiography of Jawaharlal Nehru to assail British rule in India, while former Senator Rush D. Holt (Dem.–W. Va.) pointed to concentration camps constructed to imprison the Boers. Colonel McCormick suspected that Rhodes Scholars were part of a grand design to return the American colonies to Mother England. Scholarship recipients were, he said, little better than Benedict Arnold! Even during World War II, Philip La Follette found a clash of interest between the United States and Great Britain, for the United States, unlike England, opposed new colonial efforts.[28]

Few isolationists, of course, wanted to see Britain defeated. Many spokesmen of the America First Committee, for example, desired a negotiated peace, wherein England would retain its navy and colonies while Germany secured its economic control of Western Europe. Such leading congressional isolationists as Senator Taft, Senator Wheeler, and Representative Hamilton Fish (Rep.–N.Y.) favored a British triumph. On a more informal level, Mrs. Robert E. Wood, wife of America First's national chairman, participated in benefits for the British War Relief Society. Yet, if isolationists had little desire to prevent a British victory, they had still less to risk American troops in order to accomplish it.[29]

The Union of Soviet Socialist Republics presented a newer threat. After the Hitler-Stalin Pact of August 1939, Russia had become unpopular among the interventionists. It is doubtful, however, whether their hatred of Russia ever exceeded that of the isolationists. From the conservative backers of Representative Fish, who led a House investigation of domestic Communism in 1931, to the Socialist Party followers of Norman Thomas, who found their party sabotaged by Communists in 1935, anti-interventionists found both Russia and its official ideology anathema. Essayist Anne Morrow Lindbergh, wife of the famous aviator, called Russia the one great foe of "European" civilization. Senator Bennett Champ Clark (Dem.–Mo.) accused the Russians of seeking the "cruel extirpation of all religion." Journalist Freda Utley went so far as to comment that Nazi Germany might be "a little more likely to bear the seed of a better ordered world than Stalin's bastard socialism."[30]

The continued waging of the European war, maintained many isolationists, would inevitably result in Communist domination of the Continent. Early in September 1939 Taft declared that "apparently, Russia proposes to sit on the side-lines and spread Communism through the nations of Europe, both the defeated and the victorious." On November 27 of the same year, Fish predicted that stalemate would permit "the Communist vulture" to "sweep down on the bloody remains of Europe." In October 1940 General Wood claimed that another year of conflict would bring about "Communism in all Europe," a "species of National

Socialism in England," and the "end of capitalism all over the world."
Peace lobbyist Frederick J. Libby wrote an antiwar editorial in October
1940 entitled "Only Stalin Could Win."[31]

Germany's invasion of Russia, launched in June 1941, merely increased
isolationist anxiety. Flynn asked, "Are we going to fight to make Europe
safe for communism?" The Keep America Out of War Congress declared
that—more than ever—the conflict was not worth "one American penny,
one American man, or one American hour." Lindbergh preferred to see
the United States allied to Germany than to enter the war supporting "the
cruelty, the godlessness, and the barbarism that exist in Soviet Russia."
The *Chicago Tribune* echoed its "sister" newspaper, the *New York Daily
News,* in predicting that the defeat of Hitler ("the bulwark against
Bolshevism") might force the United States into a new war against Russia.[32]

During World War II, isolationists continued to reveal hostility toward
the Soviet Union. Senator Edwin C. Johnson (Dem.–Colo.) proposed a
resolution demanding the independence of Eastern Europe. Otherwise, he
said, American ideals of "justice and freedom" would be "pure flimflam."
Taft found Roosevelt's "appeasement" rooted in the naive hope that Stalin
would "turn out to have an angelic nature." In 1944 Vandenberg asserted
that the Atlantic Charter had "already been torn to shreds—so far as its
promises to little countries are concerned." Russia and Britain, he suggested,
had already agreed upon the spoils. More and more isolationists were
siding with the Paulist priest James Gillis, editor of *Catholic World,* who
found "the greatest potential menace to permanent peace" lying in the
Soviet Union.[33]

In recent years it has become increasingly fashionable to portray the
isolationists as prophets. Parallels are made to "New Left" critics, with
even the once-maligned Taft now praised for his protests against America's
"moral and economic imperialism."[34] While such belated tribute no doubt
contributes to a more balanced picture, the questions historians ask must,
in the long run, be different ones. One can no more responsibly isolate
elements in the isolationist world view, pulling out the favorable ones
and dismissing the rest, than one can selectively clip a person's thought
in the middle of a sentence. It is difficult to separate perceptive warnings
concerning presidential war making or economic imperialism from comments expressing either McCarthyism or brinkmanship. Far more often
than not, these tendencies can be found in the same person.

Both the rational and the frenzied arguments, the points of perception
and the points of hysteria, reveal a group caught in the severest kinds of
social stress. One study, dealing with the ideology of the American Revolution, has shown that the colonial leaders genuinely believed in a worldwide
"conspiracy against liberty."[35] Such an attitude could equally be ascribed
to many isolationists. If their cognition was not always in tune with reality,
their sense of injury was nonetheless real.

During the Cold War more than ever, the twin plagues of the Old

World—revolution and imperialism—appeared to threaten the New. To put the themes in terms of the Puritan jeremiad, the covenanted people were becoming "like among the nations"—that is, they were finally facing the same "degeneration" that Europe had long known. And again, one did not have to share the domestic conservatism of John T. Flynn to agree that the "forces . . . eating away the foundations of European civilization" were now repeating "their work of destruction upon us."[36]

## NOTES

1. Robert A. Divine, *Roosevelt and World War II* (Baltimore, Md.: The Johns Hopkins University Press, 1969), and *The Reluctant Belligerent: American Entry into World War II* (New York: Wiley, 1965); James MacGregor Burns, *Roosevelt: The Soldier of Freedom, 1940–1945* (New York: Harcourt Brace Jovanovich, 1970).

2. John Roy Carlson [pseud. Avedis Derounian], *Under Cover: My Four Years in the Nazi Underworld of America* (New York: Dutton, 1943); Rex Stout, *The Illustrious Dunderheads* (New York: Knopf, 1943); James A. Wechsler, "The Life and Death of P.M.: Part I," *Progressive* 13 (March 1949): 9–12; "Part II" (April 1949): 15–17.

3. W. A. Swanberg, *Luce and His Empire* (New York: Scribner's, 1972), p. 187; Bob Thomas, *Winchell* (Garden City, N.Y.: Doubleday, 1971), p. 165; Oliver Pilat, *Drew Pearson: An Unauthorized Biography* (New York: Pocket Books, 1973), p. 184. For efforts before Pearl Harbor to link isolationism with subversion, see Geoffrey S. Smith, *To Save a Nation: American Countersubversives, the New Deal, and the Coming of World War II* (New York: Basic Books, 1973).

4. For general descriptions of both Gerald L. K. Smith and Gerald Winrod, see Ralph Lord Roy, *Apostles of Discord: A Study of Organized Bigotry and Disruption on the Fringes of Protestantism* (Boston: Beacon, 1953), pp. 26–34, 60–70, and Leo Ribuffo, "Protestants on the Right: William Dudley Pelley, Gerald B. Winrod and Gerald L. K. Smith," Ph.D. diss., Yale University, 1976, chap. 3 and 4. For biographical profiles of Upton Close [pseud. Josef Washington Hall] and Merwin K. Hart, see respectively *Current Biography, 1944* (New York: H. W. Wilson, 1945), pp. 99–100 and *1941*, pp. 367–69. Various congressional statements sympathetic to Zionism are found in Reuben Fink, *America and Palestine* (New York: American Zionist Emergency Council, 1944). For example, of some 171 isolationists in the House in 1941, some 77 had by 1944 made statements to which official Zionist organizations could point with approval. Similarly, of 40 Senate isolationists, some 22 made such statements.

5. The ethnic factor is stressed in Samuel Lubell, *The Future of American Politics*, 3d ed., rev. (New York: Harper, 1965), pp. 131–55. The "populist" thesis is advanced in Ray Allen Billington, "The Origins of Middle Western Isolationism," *Political Science Quarterly* 60 (March 1945): 44–64, and challenged in William G. Carleton, "Isolationism and the Middle West," *Mississippi Valley Historical Review* 33 (December 1946): 377–90. Sociological and psychological explanations are found in Bernard Fensterwald, Jr., "The Anatomy of American 'Isolationism' and Expansion," *Journal of Conflict Resolution* 2 (June 1958): 111–39 (December 1958): 280–307; Daniel Bell, ed., *The Radical Right* (Garden City, N.Y.: Doubleday, 1963); and Edward A. Shils, *The Torment of Secrecy* (Glencoe, Ill.: Free Press, 1956).

6. Accounts of Clare E. Hoffman may be found in *Current Biography, 1949*, pp. 276–78, and obituary, *New York Times*, November 5, 1967, p. 86. His comment on Jews can be found in *CR*, March 14, 1945, p. 2229. For a sketch of John E. Rankin, see *Current Biography, 1944*, pp. 555–58. The comment concerning Jews is found in *CR*,

June 4, 1941, pp. 4726–27. The suggestion concerning a Hoover tour is found in notes of Fred Burdick interview with Rankin, June 13, 1941, Box 73, the Papers of Herbert Hoover, Hoover Presidential Library, West Branch, Iowa.

7. Entry of John F. Kennedy, large contributors file, the Papers of the America First Committee, Library of the Hoover Institution on War, Revolution and Peace, Stanford University (hereafter cited as "AFC Papers"); account of Gerald R. Ford in Ruth Sarles, "A Story of America First" (unpublished manuscript; undated and on deposit with AFC Papers), p. 50; Robert A. Liston, *Sargent Shriver: A Candid Portrait* (New York: Farrar, Straus, 1964), p. 37.

8. The historian cited is Joan Lee Bryniarski, "Against the Tide: Senate Opposition to the Internationalist Foreign Policy of Presidents Franklin D. Roosevelt and Harry S. Truman, 1943–1949," Ph.D. diss., University of Maryland, 1972, p. 151. For material on Nye, see Wayne S. Cole, *Senator Gerald P. Nye and American Foreign Relations* (Minneapolis, Minn.: University of Minnesota, 1962), pp. 124–32, and for a general interpretation, see Guinsburg, "Senatorial Isolationism," pp. 265–66. For a comparative evaluation of the class that supplied much of the isolationist social base, see Arno J. Mayer, "The Lower Middle Class as Historical Problem," *Journal of Modern History* 47 (September 1975): 406–36.

9. The Congressmen representing these cities were, respectively: William E. Hess, John M. Vorys, William W. Blackney, Bartel J. Jonkman, Walter C. Ploeser, John Jennings, Jr., and Charles R. Robertson. All were Republicans.

10. The Congressmen were respectively: George H. Bender, George A. Dondero, John C. Kunkel, George W. Gillie, and Lawrence H. Smith. All were Republicans.

11. Bernard Bailyn, *The Ideological Origins of the American Revolution* (Cambridge, Mass.: Belknap Press, 1967), pp. 49–51, 89–91; Paul W. Conner, *Poor Richard's Politicks: Benjamin Franklin and His New American Order* (New York: Oxford University Press, 1965), pp. 32–33; Charles S. Sanford, *The Quest for Paradise: Europe and the American Moral Imagination* (Urbana, Ill.: University of Illinois Press, 1961), p. 128.

12. John William Ward, *Andrew Jackson: Symbol for an Age* (New York: Oxford University Press, 1955).

13. Henry Nash Smith, *Virgin Land: The American West as Symbol and Myth* (Cambridge, Mass.: Harvard University Press, 1950); Leo Marx, *The Machine in the Garden: Technology and the Pastoral Ideal in America* (New York: Oxford University Press, 1964).

14. Transcript of interview with Louis Taber, 1952, Oral History Collection, Butler Library, Columbia University, p. 367. The sense of loss rooted in the coming of a bureaucratic society is described in Otis L. Graham, Jr., *An Encore for Reform: The Old Progressives and the New Deal* (New York: Oxford University Press, 1967), pp. 24–91.

15. Lawrence Dennis, *The Dynamics of War and Revolution* (New York: Weekly Foreign Letter, 1940), p. xxx; Chester Bowles to R. Douglas Stuart, Jr., July 15, 1941, Box 18, AFC Papers; entry of April 25, 1941, *The Wartime Journals of Charles A. Lindbergh* (New York: Harcourt Brace Jovanovich, 1970), p. 478.

16. For endorsements of New Deal restrictions on Wall Street by conservative isolationists, see Frank Gannett to O. G. Villard, September 19, 1938, the Papers of Oswald Garrison Villard, Houghton Library, Harvard University; Joseph Borkin, *Robert R. Young: The Populist of Wall Street* (New York: Harper and Row, 1969), p. 4; Samuel B. Pettengill, *Smoke Screen* (New York: Southern Publishers, 1940), p. 80.

17. Peter B. Bulkley, "Daniel A. Reed: A Study in Conservatism," Ph.D. diss., Clark University, 1972, gives the fullest account of the Congressman's life. For Reed's exchange with the reporter, see p. 158.

18. For the most comprehensive and perceptive life of Taft, see James T. Patterson, *Mr. Republican: A Biography of Robert A. Taft* (Boston: Houghton Mifflin, 1972). But

see also Ronald Radosh, *Prophets on the Right: Profiles of Conservative Critics of American Globalism* (New York: Simon and Schuster, 1975), pp. 119–96.

19. Cole, *Interpretive History,* p. 322; "The Central States" (editorial), *Chicago Tribune,* April 14, 1929. For an elaboration of isolationist economic perception, see Justus D. Doenecke, "Power, Markets, and Ideology: The Isolationist Response to Roosevelt Policy, 1940–1941," in Leonard Liggio and James J. Martin, eds., *Watershed of Empire: Essays on New Deal Foreign Policy* (Colorado Springs, Colo.: Ralph Myles, 1976), pp. 132–64.

20. Accounts of General Wood may be found in *Current Biography, 1940,* pp. 933–35; obituaries in *New York Times,* November 7, 1969, p. 35, and *Chicago Tribune,* November 7, 1969; "The General's General Store," *Time* 59 (February 25, 1952): 84–94; Irving Pflaum, "The Baffling Career of Robert E. Wood," *Harpers* 208 (April 1954): 63–73; "General Robert E. Wood, President," *Fortune* 17 (May 1938): 66–69, 104–10. The most thorough life of Wood can be found in Justus D. Doenecke, "General Robert E. Wood: The Evolution of a Conservative," *Journal of the Illinois State Historical Society* 71 (August 1978), 162–175.

21. R. A. Taft to W. Trohan, July 1, 1948, Box 14, the Papers of Walter Trohan, Hoover Presidential Library.

22. The best studies of McCormick and his views are Jerome E. Edwards, *The Foreign Policy of Col. McCormick's Tribune, 1929–1941* (Reno: University of Nevada Press, 1971), and Frank C. Waldrop, *McCormick of Chicago: An Unconventional Portrait of a Controversial Figure* (Englewood Cliffs, N.J.: Prentice-Hall, 1966); but see also Walter Trohan, *Political Animals: Memoirs of a Sentimental Cynic* (Garden City, N.Y.: Doubleday, 1975), pp. 1–21.

23. For biographies of Langer, see *Current Biography, 1952,* pp. 326–28, and Glenn H. Smith, "Senator William Langer: A Study in Isolationism," Ph.D. diss., University of Iowa, 1968. The quotation is from Smith, p. 140. Langer's speaking style is described in Allen Drury, *A Senate Journal, 1943–1945* (New York: McGraw-Hill, 1963), entry of November 30, 1944, p. 301.

24. For biographies of Senator Robert M. La Follette, Jr., see *Current Biography, 1944,* pp. 368–72; Alan E. Kent, "Portrait in Isolationism: The La Follettes and Foreign Policy," Ph.D. diss., University of Wisconsin, 1956; and Arthur M. Schlesinger, Jr., *The Politics of Upheaval* (Boston: Houghton Mifflin, 1960), pp. 104–7. The quotation from Drury is found in *Senate Journal,* entry of July 19, 1945, p. 466.

25. For material on the *Progressive,* see William B. Hesseltine, "Forty Years the Country's Conscience," *Progressive* 13 (December 1949): 6–14; Charles H. Backstrom, "The Progressive Party of Wisconsin, 1943–1946," Ph.D. diss., University of Wisconsin, 1956, pp. 98–101; and Kent, "Portrait," pp. 306–8. The *Progressive* was recommended by the America First Committee, although the AFC did claim that its endorsement was of necessity restricted to foreign policy. See AFC Bulletin, #77. Among the anti-interventionists contributing to the *Progressive* were journalists Oswald Garrison Villard, William Henry Chamberlin, and Frank C. Hanighen, clergyman John Haynes Holmes, aviation writer Al Williams, and cartoonist Daniel R. Fitzpatrick. Isabel Bacon La Follette, wife of Philip, was associate editor until 1947 and contributed a weekly column.

26. Thomas A. Bailey, *The Man on the Street: The Impact of American Public Opinion on Foreign Policy* (New York: Macmillan, 1948), p. 214.

27. Margaret Sanger to America First Committee, June 7, 1941, Box 51, AFC Papers; Frederick L. Honhart III, "Charles Callan Tansill: American Diplomatic Historian," Ph.D. diss., Case Western Reserve University, 1972, p. 101; "Cooperate—But Not for Foreign War" (leaflet) (New York: Keep America Out of War Congress, 1938); Burton K. Wheeler, "America Beware!", NBC radio address, *Scribner's Commentator* 10 (June

1941): 91–92; Richard C. Frey, Jr., "John T. Flynn and the United States in Crisis, 1928–1950," Ph.D. diss., University of Oregon, 1969, p. 218.

28. C. Bowles to P. La Follette, September 28, 1939, the Papers of Philip La Follette, Wisconsin State Historical Society, Madison, Wisconsin; review by Albert Jay Nock, *Scribner's Commentator* 10 (August 1941): 87–91; Rush D. Holt, "Is Churchill Good Enough for Roosevelt?," *Scribner's Commentator* 10 (July 1941): 36; McCormick in Waldrop, *McCormick of Chicago,* pp. 237–39; Philip La Follette to I. La Follette, October 13, 1943, Philip La Follette Papers.

29. For attitudes toward the British of America First leaders, Wayne S. Cole, *America First: The Battle against Intervention, 1940–1941* (Madison: University of Wisconsin Press, 1953), pp. 35–50. For Taft, Wheeler, and Hamilton Fish, see Jonas, *Isolationism in America,* p. 240. For Mrs. Wood, see *Chicago Daily News,* February 5, 1941.

30. Anne Morrow Lindbergh, "A Prayer for Peace," *Reader's Digest* 36 (January 1940): 5; Bennett Champ Clark in "Should America Fight to Make the World Safe for Communism?" (leaflet) (Chicago: America First Committee, 1941); Freda Utley, *The Dream We Lost: Soviet Russia Then and Now* (New York: John Day, 1940), p. 298.

31. Taft, *Congressional Digest* 18 (October 1939): 235; Fish speech as reprinted in Hamilton Fish, *The Red Plotters* (New York: Domestic and Foreign Affairs, 1947), p. 37; Wood, "Our Foreign Policy," address to the Chicago Council on Foreign Relations, October 4, 1940, in *Vital Speeches* 7 (December 15, 1940): 133; Frederick J. Libby, "Only Stalin Could Win," *Peace Action* 7 (October 1940): 1–3.

32. Flynn in "Should America Fight to Make the World Safe for Communism?"; statement of Mary Hillyer, June 25, 1941, materials of the Keep America Out of War Congress, Socialist Party collection, Duke University Library; Charles A. Lindbergh, address in San Francisco, July 2, 1941, *CR,* p. A3283; "What Are Our War Aims as to Russia?" (editorial), excerpt from *New York Daily News* in *Chicago Tribune,* January 21, 1941.

33. Edwin C. Johnson in John L. Gaddis, *The United States and the Origins of the Cold War, 1941–1947* (New York: Columbia University Press, 1972), p. 150; Taft, speech of June 8, 1944, *CR,* p. A2901; Arthur H. Vandenberg to Monroe Shakespeare, March 18, 1944, in Arthur H. Vandenberg, Jr. and Joe Alex Morris, eds., *The Private Papers of Senator Vandenberg* (Boston: Houghton Mifflin, 1952), p. 92; Vandenberg, diary entry, May 26, 1944, *Private Papers,* p. 103; Father James Gillis, "Getting Wise to Russia," *Catholic World* 160 (October 1944): 1.

34. Henry W. Berger, "Senator Robert A. Taft Dissents from Military Escalation," in Thomas G. Paterson, ed., *Cold War Critics: Alternatives to American Foreign Policy in the Truman Years* (Chicago: Quadrangle, 1971), p. 172.

35. Bailyn, *Ideological Origins;* Gordon S. Wood, "Rhetoric and Reality in the American Revolution," *William and Mary Quarterly* 23 (October 1966): 3–32.

36. The twin plagues of imperialism and revolution are described in the Wilson period in N. Gordon Levin, Jr., *Woodrow Wilson and World Politics: America's Response to War and Revolution* (New York: Oxford University Press, 1968). Flynn's comment is found in his book *The Road Ahead: America's Creeping Revolution* (New York: Devin-Adair, 1949), pp. 9–10.

2

# The Lost Victory, 1943-1945

The "destruction" to which Flynn referred was not long in coming. At the core of the isolationists' beliefs was an intense love of country, however varied their conceptions of it might have been. The label *superpatriot* had not yet entered the vocabulary as a term of derision, and had it been used to describe the isolationists in 1941, most of them would have worn it proudly. Virtually no isolationists, however, became overnight converts to interventionism, or suddenly and trustingly embraced the leadership of Franklin D. Roosevelt. Indeed, they kept a wary eye upon him at all times, lest wartime commitments bind the United States to a perpetual system of "entangling alliances" that would facilitate the expansion of Soviet Communism and the bolstering of the British Empire. As early as May 1942 Herbert Hoover commented that America could not reconcile any crusade for liberty with such disparate and destructive partners.[1]

Even when World War II was at its height, many isolationists freely attacked the administration without reprisals from the voters. In 1942 most anti-interventionists in Congress carried their districts as strongly as ever. They claimed that Roosevelt had as yet brought no victories. In addition they were undoubtedly aware that their constituencies were not yet ready to repudiate their own isolationist sentiments.[2]

Certain old isolationists took advantage of their opportunity to assail Roosevelt's war leadership. Wheeler, Vandenberg, and Senator Henrik Shipstead (Rep.–Minn.) backed the demands of Senator Albert B. ("Happy") Chandler (Dem.–Ky.) for a "Japan first" strategy. Several isolationists, including Langer and Taft, claimed that the indictment of some twenty-six "native fascists" for sedition was, in reality, a "political purge" of dissenters. Some isolationists opposed the Fulbright Resolution, a proposal calling for international peace-keeping machinery. It was, said Congressmen Reed, "a wild and reckless plunge in the dark." Others, such as Vandenberg, criticized diplomacy by executive agreement. The Michigan Senator believed that entry into the relatively innocuous United Nations Relief and Rehabilitation Administration by such means could have only one meaning: the President and State Department were deliberately intending to bypass the Congress.[3]

Yet, from the viewpoint of most old isolationists, successes were few, failures many. Three major conferences, in particular, were troubling: the Casablanca conference between Churchill and Roosevelt in January 1943; the Yalta conference—held in the Crimea among Roosevelt, Churchill, and Stalin—in February 1945; and the San Francisco conference, in session from April to June of 1945. In each of those meetings one group of isolationists or another saw its worst anxieties confirmed.

At Casablanca Roosevelt and Churchill agreed in principle to the opening of a "second front" by invading Sicily and Italy, named Dwight D. Eisenhower supreme commander of Allied forces in North Africa, and made several other strategic decisions. They then jointly declared that the war would continue until the "unconditional surrender" of the enemy had been achieved, a manifesto more portentous than all the military aspects of the conference combined.

At first old isolationists offered little criticism of "unconditional surrender." Frederick J. Libby opposed it on the grounds that German hegemony in Western Europe was as inevitable as United States domination of the Americas, but he was almost alone in his opposition. For about a year after the Casablanca Conference, most old isolationists were either silent or expressed tacit approval. In August 1943 Vandenberg endorsed the policy, and in November retired diplomat William R. Castle, national committeeman of America First, claimed that British statesman Lord Vansittart was correct in seeing Germany itself, not Hitler, as the real enemy.[4]

It was only in January 1944, when Russia began its offensive into Eastern Europe, that isolationists strongly attacked unconditional surrender. Socialist leader Norman Thomas asserted that such demands would create Axis intransigency. Senator Wheeler blamed the policy for "blowing Europe and our own boys to bits without rhyme or reason." Vandenberg now found it crucial to distinguish between the surrender of governments and of peoples.[5]

Several veteran isolationists harbored similar anxieties regarding Asia. Taft told the new president, Harry Truman, in April of 1945 that peace terms for Japan should include its continued control of Formosa. Hoover hoped that Japan could retain its form of government and maintain its authority over both Formosa and Korea. The ultra-rightist radio broadcaster Upton Close asserted that destruction of Japanese power would, of necessity, result in Russian domination of all Asia. Unconditional surrender, warned columnist Felix Morley, would make Soviet control of Manchuria and Korea inevitable, thereby violating "that earlier triumph of American statemanship known for almost half-a-century as the Open Door." Journalist Frank Hanighen claimed that Russian control over Manchuria, China's richest area, signified that the United States had already lost the Pacific war.[6]

Far more old isolationists complained about Yalta. At the Crimean Conference, the Big Three made preliminary plans for the occupation of Germany, refined provisions for the new United Nations organization made several months earlier at Dumbarton Oaks, and—in a secret protocol—obtained the promise of the USSR to enter the Pacific War in return for concessions in Manchuria. The diplomats also agreed to conduct free elections inside the liberated countries, pledging secret ballots and universal suffrage for the highly contested nation of Poland. Leaders from the Western-backed government-in-exile, located in London, would join the Soviet-controlled Lublin regime; Poland would give Russia hundreds of square miles on its eastern borders while being permitted to administer highly developed German lands to the west. At first glance it appeared as if much of the Yalta agreements embodied a Wilsonian peace. The language of the agreement, however, was deliberately vague, and it soon became obvious that the Russians had no intention of sharing Poland's government with non-Communists.

Staunch conservatives, of course, were among Yalta's first critics. The Crimean treaty, so the editors of a new newsletter entitled *Human Events* argued, was far more unjust than Versailles; indeed, it was a "new Munich." (One editor, William Henry Chamberlin, might have forgotten, or conveniently overlooked, the fact that he had endorsed the original Munich agreement. England and France, he had written before war broke out, had been wise to renounce "interference" in Eastern Europe.)[7]

*Human Events* was founded by men disillusioned with American intervention. Felix Morley, son of a Haverford professor and himself a graduate of the Pennsylvania college, had served as a volunteer ambulance worker overseas in 1915–16, written for the *Socialist Call,* and, while a Rhodes scholar, become editor of the *New Oxford,* a labor magazine. A journalist during the 1920s and 1930s, he won the Pulitzer Prize for his *Washington Post* editorials. Morley was a strong internationalist, heading the Geneva office of the League of Nations Association of the United States, writing a pro-League history entitled *The Society of Nations* (1932), and opposing the neutrality acts. By 1941, however, he was an ardent foe of Roosevelt's foreign and domestic policies. He declined an invitation to serve on the national committee of America First, but found himself increasingly in sympathy with its aims. While president of Haverford College, he spoke before a major America First gathering in Washington and helped Herbert Hoover and Alfred Landon, Republican standard-bearer in 1936, draft a petition opposing further steps toward American involvement.[8]

Morley's colleague Frank Hanighen combined an Omaha boyhood with a Harvard degree, foreign reporting for the *New York Evening Post* and the *New York Times,* and the co-authorship of the popular tract *Merchants of Death* (1934). More of a genuine isolationist than Morley, Hanighen had worked for such anti-interventionist journals as *Common Sense, Uncensored,* and the *Progressive,* and had briefly been on the staff of the

America First Committee. Contributing editor William Henry Chamberlin, an anarchist by the time he finished Haverford (where he was one class behind Morley), enthusiastically covered the Soviet "experiment" for the *Christian Science Monitor*. Soon disillusioned with Russian Communism, he remained long enough to gather material for a series of books on the USSR. His history of the Russian Revolution, published in 1935, remains a classic, both in brevity and balance. Closer to the liberal isolationists than to America First, Chamberlin addressed a major assembly of the socialist-pacifist Keep America Out of War Congress.[9]

The newsletter was launched with a $3,000 gift from the conservative Joseph N. Pew, Jr., vice-president of the Sun Oil Company, and received financial support from several leaders of the America First Committee. The eight-page Washington weekly began publication on February 2, 1944, with 117 subscribers. Starting in a modest fashion, it was produced in Hanighen's H Street apartment. His bedroom served as the business office. The title *Human Events* was suggested by Morley and came from the Declaration of Independence. Like the august Jefferson, the editors believed that America must maintain a "separate" as well as an "equal" station among "the powers of the earth." An initial statement of policy combined domestic conservatism with nonintervention: "True liberalism will survive neither subordination to a despotic bureaucracy at home, nor entanglement in any Balance of Power system directed from abroad." The United States, founded as "a nation unique among the nations," was now imperiled by centralized government at home and permanent military alliances overseas. Indeed, "all forms of imperial rule—capitalist as well as fascist or communist"—were suddenly threatening the republic.[10]

The initial issue set the tone, with Chamberlin predicting conflict between England and Russia. He cited the warning of South African premier Jan Christian Smuts: "Russia is the new colossus on the European continent."[11]

Such anxieties were far from limited to conservatives, for prominent liberal isolationists found themselves as apprehensive as the editors of *Human Events*. To them also the Crimean Conference signified "the great betrayal." Morris Rubin claimed that Yalta revealed the triumph of brute force. Sidney Hertzberg, editor of *Common Sense* and long a Socialist, commented, "We have kicked . . . millions of desperate men and women in the face." *Progressive* columnist Milton Mayer spoke for more than his fellow pacifists in referring to the "Bottom-of-the-Atlantic Charter"; pro-Administration apologists, he said, had been living "on the flat of their backs" for years.[12]

For both conservatives and liberals among the old isolationists, Poland's fate indicated that a brutal peace lay ahead. Vandenberg saw Poland as "the acid test" of Allied "good faith." The Michigan Senator was undoubtedly aware of his state's large Polish constituency, with Detroit alone having more Poles than any other city except Warsaw and Chicago. Thomas admitted that the Polish government, long known for its anti-Semitism and despotism, was far from perfect, and he did not find its expansive borders of 1939 particularly sacrosanct. For the Socialist leader, however, the central issue involved Allied policy toward conquered peoples. Taft went so far as to deny the reactionary nature of Poland's old regime; the central European state, he said, possessed "a great percentage of small farms than England or France."[13]

Several critics argued that Soviet anxieties over security were exaggerated. Former Democratic Congressman Samuel B. Pettengill, conservative syndicated columnist ("The Gentleman from Indiana") and adviser to America First, denied that so small a country as Poland could possibly threaten Russia. Senator La Follette predicted that Russia, like France in the 1920s, would find no genuine protection in a ring of satellite states; instead, it would learn, and learn the hard way, that genuine peace and "domination from the outside" were mutually exclusive.[14]

In some ways, Yalta was only the beginning. After the conference articulate old isolationists found conditions within Europe worse than ever. Essayist Henry Beston compared the spread of "Red Eurasia" to the barbarian invasions of the Dark Ages. For the first time since the Bronze Age, he told readers of *Human Events*, "Asia" was no longer "at bay." And even if some areas faced no direct danger of "Asian" conquest, the Continent faced tremendous upheaval. Anxieties rampant at the end of World War I were again voiced. The very first sentence of Chamberlin's book *America: Partner in World Rule* (1945) read: "Large-scale war is the most effective imaginable instrument for revolutionary change." Upon returning from Europe late in the spring of 1945, Wheeler predicted that once the American army withdrew, most European states would face revolution, counterrevolution, and "some form of communism." (At one point the Montana Senator hinted of possible war between Russia and the West.)[15]

Nor was revolution the only danger. Devastation, some old isolationists believed, must lead to chaos and autarchy, with Europe compelled to abandon its capitalistic system. In February 1945 Morley claimed that the "utterly exhausted" Continent would find itself forced to adopt varied state controls. Given the extent of Russian military penetration, popular support of Bolshevism would be automatic, "needing no impetus from Moscow." Hoover, noting the victory of the British Labor Party in August 1945, saw "communism or creeping socialism" sweeping the Old World.[16]

In 1944 and 1945, isolationists offered various solutions that, they hoped, could avoid future Yaltas. Several urged their nation to foster a United States of Europe. Rubin reasoned that such a body, modeled on the federal system of Switzerland, could wipe out artificial economic barriers and thereby permit needed economic integration. Federation, Wheeler declared, possessed the added advantage of integrating a disarmed Germany into the European economy.[17]

Several isolationists opposed continued talk of unconditional surrender and Germany's dismemberment. Morley noted that the Russians were skillfully exploiting the German generals who composed Moscow's "Free

Germany Committee," and he called upon the West to use the German underground more effectively. Wheeler asked the Allies to revive the tactic of Woodrow Wilson's Fourteen Points by stating peace terms to the German people.[18]

In addition, a few isolationists sought more strategic use of American aid. Taft suggested that a more stringent application of lend-lease might reverse Russian policies. Villard drew upon his knowledge of World War I to demand a Supreme Allied Council devoted exclusively to food. Relief, he said, could prevent anarchy and collapse.[19]

One prominent isolationist, Senator Vandenberg, hoped that the United States could alleviate Soviet anxieties over Germany, and thereby free Eastern Europe from Russian occupation. Vandenberg proposed a "hard-and-fast treaty" among the Big Three, centering on the permanent disarmament of the Reich; if Stalin refused to cooperate, America might have to look to its own defenses.[20]

It remains doubtful whether such recommendations could have had much effect. The Continent was too demolished to benefit immediately from a United States of Europe, and it would take several years for European production to reach the level at which it could gain from economic integration. The United States did drastically reduce lend-lease to Russia and tabled its request for a six billion dollar loan but, far from coercing the Soviets, it only made them more intransigent. The Russians themselves balked at Vandenberg's proposal when, in February 1946, it was formally advanced by Secretary of State James F. Byrnes. Unconvinced that such a treaty brought benefits. Russia preferred to keep a free hand in Germany. Proposals for the abandonment of unconditional surrender contained more rhetoric than substance; such a policy might have halted much of the Soviet advance but would have necessitated cooperation with the German military. Those German generals prominent in the resistance leadership would undoubtedly have demanded Allied acquiescence to the Reich's 1939 boundaries and total autonomy in both foreign and domestic policy. It remains doubtful whether the American public would have tolerated such magnanimity.[21]

In reality, proposals advanced by isolationist critics could have done little to change European power relations, much less push Russia back to its prewar boundaries. Hoover envisioned the new United Nations organization as a court of appeals for any nation "still held in subjection," but was under no illusion that the Russians could be forced to leave occupied lands. "Nothing you or I can do," he told former Governor Alfred Landon of Kansas, "will set them free." Commenting on Poland, Vandenberg wrote a friend, "We confront a condition and not a theory."[22]

Old isolationists found themselves taking increasing refuge in declarations and manifestoes, asking the great powers to renounce imperialism, territorial aggrandizement, and other features of power politics. Continual isolationist references to the Atlantic Charter (a declaration to which they had been singularly indifferent in 1941) might embarrass the administration at Big Three conferences and hence prevent some "concessions" to the British and the Russians. Reporter Drury, noting that Wheeler had introduced a resolution reaffirming the Charter, commented: "Idealism coincides neatly with political warfare."[23] Similar motivations no doubt help to explain the persistent talk of self-determination for such countries as Poland, for isolationist voices had been conspicuously silent about these areas before Pearl Harbor.

If old isolationists had no real alternative to the peace symbolized by Yalta, they still saw the need for greater propaganda and research facilities. Frederick J. Libby, executive secretary of the National Council for the Prevention of War, took the lead. Although the NCPW itself was a peace society and Libby a Quaker pacifist, the body had openly backed many isolationist political leaders. Research, speech writing, publicity, informal liaison—the NCPW supplied all of these to a degree shunned by such traditional pacifist groups as the Fellowship of Reconciliation and the War Resisters League. If the NCPW was "nonpartisan," in the sense of not acting as the overt agent of a political party, it was hardly nonpolitical.

The organization itself was born in 1922 in order to promote the Washington Disarmament Conference. It reached the height of its power during the 1930s, when it fostered the neutrality acts and the Ludlow Amendment. While it listed many religious and civic organizations among its sponsors, Libby himself always maintained firm control. A graduate of Bowdoin College and Andover Seminary, Libby had served as a Congregationalist pastor, an instructor at Phillips Exeter Academy, and a relief administrator for the Quakers. Tenacious and wiry, Libby has been described as "a small man, built close to the bone as a Maine fence hugs the land, but [whose] personality and energy were expansive. He was generous with his friendship even to those with whom he differed, although he never willingly gave up a vote in a political fight, whether to the Navy League or within his own organization." He was equally at home with Colonel Charles A. Lindbergh and pacifist leader A. J. Muste, with Wall Street lawyer John Foster Dulles and the maverick Senator Glen H. Taylor (Dem.–Idaho). During the debates of 1940 and 1941, Libby lent his staff to the America First Committee, presided over the business meetings of the Keep America Out of War Congress (which he had helped organize in 1938), and testified against the sending of convoys to Europe.[24]

Increasingly fearful about the postwar order, Libby was quick to attack the proposed "enslavement" of Germany and the Polish settlement. Yalta merely permitted American representatives to give "their silent blessing to the most cruel and ruthless purges now going on." Libby predicted a "great debate on which the future peace of the world will hang," and in March 1945 he used the occasion of Roosevelt's public report on the Big Three conference to propose a research bureau. William H. Regnery, a textile manufacturer who had given generously to America First and who had carried the NCPW through the difficult war years, immediately offered help. Libby consulted prominent isolationists for advice and finally prevailed upon Phoebe Morrison, research assistant to international law professor Edwin M. Borchard, to direct the new organization. In August 1945 the Foundation for Foreign Affairs received its charter.[25]

Initial aspirations were high. Regnery hoped that the new organization would publicize "the frauds and deceits practiced upon the people of the nation for making them war-minded." In short, he declared, it should expose the "futility and the stupidity of wars." Borchard, a member of the corporation, envisioned the group as counteracting "the propaganda work done by the Carnegie Endowment." Miss Morrison wanted the foundation to rival services offered by such groups as the Foreign Policy Association and the Institute of Pacific Relations. The story of the founding of the FFA remains important, not because of the group's subsequent—and often innocuous—career, but because it reveals that at least several old isolationists realized the immensity of the task facing them. They were outside of any policymaking or opinion-forming elite and they fully realized it.[26]

By word and by deed, varied anti-interventionists—the Morleys and the Libbys—had expressed the disillusionment soon felt by many other Americans. In a sense, their opposition to Yalta merely echoed their warnings of 1940 and 1941. Wheeler asserted that the war had produced only one result: "We have substituted Stalin for Hitler." In 1945, isolationist attention focused upon the specific terms of the agreement and, in particular, the Polish settlement. Only later would Yalta take on symbolic meaning, revolving around Roosevelt's supposed mental deterioration and the trial of Alger Hiss. Even in 1945, however, isolationist outrage reflected far more than mere right-wing reaction to the activities of "That Man," for liberal and socialist isolationists too were finding the war a futile crusade. Senator La Follette remarked concerning the Crimean conference, "The proof of the pudding would be in the eating thereof." He was not speaking with optimism.[27]

The United Nations Charter appears to offer similar threats. In the temporary euphoria that accompanied V-E and V-J days, several old isolationists—a minority, to be sure—were cautiously hopeful concerning the new world organization. Senator Charles W. Tobey (Rep.–N. H.) called for enforcing "international morality upon any aggressor nation." Senator Alexander Wiley (Rep.–Wis.), though still defending his prewar opposition to what he called "reckless intervention," claimed that the UN was evidence that the country was keeping "faith with her dead sons." (Wiley also asserted that the promotion of international music could help bring about peace!) Ex-Congressman Hamilton Fish, who had led the House isolationists in 1941, hoped that the UN would be given "a fair and decent chance," and financier Joseph P. Kennedy offered one of his properties —the Whitelaw Reid Mansion on New York's Madison Avenue—as the new UN headquarters.[28]

A few veteran isolationists spoke with all the fervor of a religious conversion. Senator Edwin C. Johnson went so far as to say that the UN was "the last great hope for avoiding World War III." Senator George D. Aiken (Rep.–Vt.) found the deliberations at San Francisco as momentous as those of the Constitutional Convention of 1787. Congresswoman Frances

P. Bolton (Rep.–Ohio) claimed that the pacifistic visions of Chinese philosopher Lao-tse might finally be fulfilled.[29]

Such endorsements were not so sweeping as they appeared, and the most publicized "conversion," that of Senator Vandenberg, might not have been any conversion at all. By 1945 Vandenberg—according to the conventional wisdom—had abandoned his isolationism to become the Republican leader in bipartisan planning. Evidence includes his major address of January 1945, his participation at the San Francisco conference in 1945 and at varied foreign ministers' meetings in 1946, and his steering of Truman's foreign policy through Congress during the early Cold War years.

The early record of Arthur H. Vandenberg, however, places him squarely in a conservative nationalist tradition, and it is questionable whether he ever left it. The son of a harnessmaker and the keeper of a boardinghouse, Vandenberg had worked his way through the University of Michigan. As editor of the *Grand Rapids Herald,* he endorsed American possession of the Philippines, the Roosevelt Corollary to the Monroe Doctrine, and the Open Door policy. During World War I, Vandenberg made eight hundred speeches for Liberty Loans while branding all isolationists and pacifists as traitors. He was indeed such a partisan of the Allies that he kept Austrian violinist Fritz Kreisler from appearing in Grand Rapids. Once the war was over, he insisted upon American entry into the League of Nations and endorsed the Palmer raids. "Communism," he wrote, "deserves nothing from us but uncompromising quarantine." Although he was an ardent backer of Harding and Coolidge (he coined the slogan, "With Harding at the helm, we can sleep nights"), Vandenberg harbored suspicions of Eastern financial power and sought government regulation of Wall Street.

Entering Congress in 1928, Vandenberg opposed much of the New Deal and established a reputation as a leading conservative. During the 1930s, he criticized the recognition of Russia, was a major participant in the Nye munitions inquiry, and fought Roosevelt's interventionist proposals. War, he claimed, would lead to regimentation; lend-lease alone involved "the suicide of the Republic."[30]

During World War II he defended his prewar isolationism, favored the ultra-nationalist General MacArthur as his presidential choice, and attempted to protect congressional war-making powers. When Secretary of State Cordell Hull mentioned that the proposed world security organization would be built on the Big Four alliance, the Michigan Senator was delighted: "The striking thing about it," he recorded in his diary, "is that it is so *conservative* from a nationalist standpoint."[31]

The words *conservative* and *nationalist* well represented Vandenberg's position. Wartime "appeasement" of Russia, he believed, must stop. At the San Francisco conference, Vandenberg spent much of his time—not in fostering "international community" *per se*—but in curbing Russian ambitions. He was unsuccessful in preventing the seating of White Russia and the Ukraine, but took satisfaction in seeing the Lublin government denied admission to the conference. By making room in the Charter for regional agreements, he was able to receive international sanction for

United States influence in the Western Hemisphere. Never letting up, Vandenberg expressed the hope that the "new peace league" could drive Russia out of Poland, sought Western press access for what he (long before Churchill) called the "iron curtain," and opposed any "Monroe Doctrine" for the USSR in Central Europe.[32]

In sum, Vandenberg was not a penitent isolationist at all; he remained an ardent nationalist who found himself suddenly involved in a world arena. No doubt personal vanity (he could strut sitting down, one commentator said) played a role in his transformation, as did export pressures from General Motors—an enterprise vital to his state.[33] His anti-Soviet tenets persisted throughout, and few "conversions" have been made with so many previous assumptions intact. A militant nationalism was by no means opposed to Vandenberg's brand of interventionism.

Not many critics of the United Nations Charter supported Senators William Langer and Henrik Shipstead in demanding its outright rejection, or in voting against its ratification on July 28, 1945. Most Senators, realizing that the Charter drew great popular support, were content to play a waiting game. As one anonymous Senator from the Middle West commented, "Hell, I'm the biggest isolationist that ever lived, but I'm sure as hell not going to vote against the Charter." Villard feared that an America that refused to enter the United Nations would be blamed for any possible failure. "If it collapses," he said, "our approving will make no difference. If any good comes out of it, so much the better." Charles A. Beard, denying that the new organization altered fundamental power relationships, could only remark caustically: "The children will cry if they do not get their charter."[34]

More often than not, old isolationists were suspicious of the new international body. The war, they noted, had swept away traditional institutions. The old order was dying throughout the world, and no international organization could maintain it. Flynn predicted continual "ideological wars and wars of liberation." Borchard saw "the line between us and anarchy . . . very thin." Outright foes of the charter were even more blunt. Langer asserted that "the present revolutionary situation in Europe" of necessity accelerated Russian expansion. Taking a slightly different tack, Shipstead denied that either Russia or America could maintain permanent hegemony.[35]

Many opponents did not argue that the Charter was too idealistic; instead they claimed that it was the most cynical of documents. And, in attempting to prove their case, they could point to one administration proclamation after another. Upon returning from the Moscow Conference of October 1943, Secretary Hull had promised the country that there would "no longer be need for spheres of influence, for alliances, for balance of power." Now, with the appearance of the Charter, the day of reckoning was at hand. To many old isolationists, the fundamental structure of the UN could only belie administration promises. For, like the Yalta accords, the Charter appeared to guarantee the rule of the strong over the weak.[36]

Isolationists hammered at the power of the new Security Council.

Wheeler predicted that the new body would serve to "underwrite tyranny." Shipstead accused the Big Five of giving themselves "the power to freeze indefinitely the status quo." Flynn claimed that England, France, and Russia—three of the Security Council's five permanent members—had long records of aggression. "Practically everybody," he continued, "is restrained from making war, by this Charter, but the warmakers." Such isolationists found the veto privilege given to the five permanent members particularly disturbing. To Morley, it implied one law for the strong, another for the weak. Imagine, he said, a municipal court in the United States announcing that "because it is never easy to convict a rich criminal . . . ,no offense committed by a millionaire should be indictable."[37]

Several veteran isolationists warned their country against committing American troops to an international police force. Although the UN Charter had permitted the Security Council "to take urgent military measures" in order to maintain "international peace and security," Congress lacked formal control over the American delegate to the Council. Congress in fact was merely called upon to appropriate the funds for any UN move, and later, in 1950, found itself backing a major UN "police action" without having authorized it. Villard, in commenting upon the Dumbarton Oaks provisions for Security Council representatives, warned against delegating the country's war-making authority to "one man's will." Wheeler demanded specific congressional authority for any use of American troops. Professor Borchard cited the Supreme Court ruling in *Missouri* vs. *Holland* (1920) to claim that congressional war powers might be undermined by treaty law. In December 1944 Taft offered amendments in the Senate to curb the discretion of the American representative, but received only six supporting votes.[38]

Although isolationists worried most about Russia, some in their ranks scrutinized the activities of other European powers. Senator La Follette pointed to Britain's "curious operations" in Italy and Greece (where it was engaged in bolstering rightist regimes), to Churchill's affirmation of friendship for "the Fascist government of Spain," and to France's three-day bombardment of Damascus. The *Chicago Tribune* found the British strafing of Indonesian nationalists, and the exploitation of Africa and Asia by "the rubber barons of the Netherlands and the colonial capitalists of France," clear evidence that Charter supporters belonged "in an insane asylum."[39]

To such isolationists, the danger was obvious: as Wheeler claimed, America might be "holding the draw strings of an international grab bag while Britain and Russia connive or fight for the spoils." At this prospect, the isolationists balked. Flynn found himself quite willing to let the Russian experiment "succeed on its own energy," but did not want the USSR living "on the energy of the capitalist system which she is trying to destroy." Senator La Follette was no more willing to have the United States enforce British rule over Burma, India, and Malta than to see Soviet domination of Eastern Europe. Senator Hugh A. Butler (Rep.–Neb.) questioned whether Iraq, Egypt, or "a harassed and suppressed Greece" could any more oppose Britain in the General Assembly than could Poland or Yugoslavia vote against the Soviet Union.[40]

Several isolationists on the extreme right advanced arguments that were far less cogent and that at times approached hysteria. Congresswoman Jessie Sumner (Rep.–Ill.) predicted that the "new world supergovernment" would occupy the United States "in the same way the Southern States were conquered in the Civil War." Merwin K. Hart, president of the National Economic Council, suspected that a Communist-dominated France and China would use Security Council machinery to violate the Monroe Doctrine. (To adapt Voltaire's oft-quoted remark about the Holy Roman Empire, Hart's organization was neither national nor economic nor a council: it had no popular membership, devoted itself to attacking inter-ventionism, "Zionism," and social welfare legislation, and was led entirely by Hart himself.) Representative Frederick C. Smith (Rep.–Ohio) feared that America would permanently underwrite foreign prosperity, while Shipstead warned that the United States would be subject to "a controlled plan of world economics." One isolationist, Mrs. Agnes Waters, harangued the Senate Foreign Relations Committee for ten minutes about secret efforts to "make of this nation a feeding trough for 'have nots' of the world." Head of an obscure organization called the National Blue Star Mothers of America, she was forcibly removed by two policemen.[41]

Some isolationists offered alternatives. One first thinks of the remedies suggested by the more obtuse among their ranks. Congressman John E. Rankin, undoubtedly betraying his anti-Semitism, said he preferred an atomic monopoly to "some super government to be run by a gang of long-nosed internationalists." Clare E. Hoffman thought that the United States should act as a football referee, siding with the weaker nation and sending the offender back "to the showers." Colonel McCormick suggested that the countries of the world file application for American statehood.[42]

It would be misleading, however, to see all isolationist alternatives as irresponsible. Isolationists suggested, for example, that the UN increase the power of its General Assembly, and increase it at the expense of the Security Council. Flynn called for ending the Council's monopoly of force; all nations, he said, should be recognized as sovereign equals. (The New York journalist spoke vaguely of the use of collective force by such a league.) Borchard not only sought to eliminate the veto, but desired that the Assembly possess powers equal to those of the Security Council. All efforts to "enforce" peace should be scrapped, he said, and the UN should address itself to fundamental economic problems. Morley supported efforts by Canada and Australia to abolish the veto; such a move could turn "the league of victors proposed at Dumbarton Oaks into a real international organization."[43]

Isolationists also advocated greater regionalism. Wheeler declared that if England and Russia accepted a United States of Europe, he would do all he could to foster American participation in a world organization. Such a body could guarantee Russia's legitimate interests and territory on the basis of international law. (Given such criteria, Russia would undoubtedly have been forced back to its 1939 boundaries.) Langer went even further, calling for an entire globe subdivided into a number of regions. If each region possessed the raw materials and markets to make it self-sufficient, it would lose all impulse to make war. The Dakota Senator found the United States, Russia, China, and Brazil the logical hubs for these regions, because they alone had the resources to survive independently. Hoover suggested that the Western Hemisphere, Europe, and Asia, if so organized, might resolve major controversies before Security Council intervention was necessary. All such proposals could enable the United States to avoid many foreign commitments, while leaving it in control of its own region.[44]

Quite a different set of isolationist alternatives concerned international law. Hoover pushed for codification of such political rights as free elections, civil liberties, equality of trade, and freedom of the seas. Wheeler and La Follette sought a world bill of rights. In addition, Wheeler wanted internationally supervised plebiscites in all liberated countries and a UN political council empowered to enforce the Atlantic Charter. Taft hoped that the International Court of Justice could assume the function that the UN charter assigned to the Security Council. If a country defied the decrees of the court, it would face economic and—ultimately—military sanctions.[45]

But the isolationists, out of power and often in public disfavor, could actually offer few viable options. On the one hand, few citizens would support a retreat to "Fortress America" and overt atomic diplomacy. On the other hand, trust in international law—always a favorite Taft alternative—was equally illusory. Such codification, and such tribunals, were far too weak to serve as the primary international mechanism of the postwar world. Regionalism was also spurious, for only the American and Soviet blocs could be really self-supporting.

Elimination of the veto would violate the very free hand that so many anti-interventionists treasured. Few of the isolationists who criticized the veto offered an alternative, and some, such as Taft, reluctantly supported the mechanism. This device, said the Ohio Senator, could protect the United States from becoming the victim of majority rule. Despite such obvious problems, isolationist protests against the veto might force attention to the "hypocrisy" of the Charter. To speak of equal voting rights for all countries was a "safe" form of opposition, for there was little likelihood of its coming to pass. In addition, elimination of the veto would probably benefit, not threaten, the nation. Many isolationists were undoubtedly aware that a clear majority of the countries in the General Assembly, as it was composed in 1945, would usually side with the United States. The absence of a veto could help universalize American standards of "international justice" and "equity," while preserving national sovereignty.

In 1944 and 1945 many Americans shared the uneasiness of the more vocal isolationists. If public opinion surveys can be trusted, people believed that both Britain and Russia were acting in an increasingly truculent manner, and they strongly opposed such behavior. Even some interventionists voiced fears concerning a concert of powers. When preliminary drafts of Dumbarton Oaks were first released to the press, Republican presidential candidate Thomas E. Dewey accused the Big Four of attempting to subject the rest of the world to its will. America, said the New York Governor, should avoid such rank imperialism and should champion full rights for all nations.[46]

Anxieties over an isolationist resurgence would usually cause such interventionists to hold back. The official Republican critique was far less biting than that of the isolationists. Politically, the Republicans could not afford the "isolationist" label, for the party's image as "spoiler" of League ratification in 1919 appeared to bode ill for future success. In 1944, unlike 1942, the Democrats were able to pin such a tag upon their opponents and made strong congressional gains.[47]

Isolationist apprehension often went deeper than partisanship. World War II was confirming their worst fears. It had placed Soviet armies in central Europe and in Manchuria and had left two devastated continents ripe for revolution. Unconditional surrender assured that Germany and Japan would be in no condition to help "stabilize" Europe and Asia; Yalta appeared to confirm Soviet domination over Eastern Europe; the United Nations Charter seemed to promise continued American enforcement of an unjust peace. Liberal isolationists placed more stress upon the betrayal of Wilsonian peace aims; conservative isolationists put more emphasis upon the loss of social order. For both groups, the world of autonomous, democratic nation-states—living together in peace and security—was farther away than ever. And, as both groups realized, the United States would face even greater and more hazardous involvements in the years to come.

# NOTES

1. Herbert Hoover, cited in Richard E. Darilek, "A Loyal Opposition in Time of War: The Republican Party and the Politics of Foreign Policy from Pearl Harbor to Yalta," Ph.D. diss., Princeton University, 1973, p. 73.

2. Ibid., pp. 55–56, 75–76, 86–89; Richard Polenberg, War and Society: The United States, 1941–1945 (Philadelphia: Lippincott, 1972), pp. 187–92.

3. For the "Asia-first" strategy, see Roland Young, Congressional Politics in the Second World War (New York: Columbia University Press, 1956), pp. 149–52. For the sedition case, see William Langer, CR, September 8, 1944, pp. 7620–26, and "Political Purges File–1944," Box 680, the Papers of Robert A. Taft, Library of Congress. For Daniel A. Reed, see CR, September 17, 1943, p. 7623. For Vandenberg, see Darilek, "Loyal Opposition," p. 122.

4. F. J. Libby to F. Gannett, April 20, 1943, Box 13, the Papers of Frank Gannett, Cornell University Library; Vandenberg in Darilek, "Loyal Opposition," p. 170; William R. Castle to R. E. Wood, Box 19, November 15, 1943, Wood Papers.

5. Norman Thomas, in Murray Seidler, Norman Thomas: Respectable Rebel, 2d ed. (Syracuse, N.Y.: Syracuse University Press, 1967), p. 216; Burton K. Wheeler, CR, January 6, 1945, p. 85; A. Vandenberg to R. L. Buell, March 11, 1945, in Private Papers, p. 91.

6. Taft in Patterson, *Mr. Republican*, p. 301; Hoover memo on conversation with President Truman, May 28, 1945, Box 139, Hoover Papers; Upton Close in *Closer-Ups* 1 (July 30, 1945): 2; Felix Morley, "What Unconditional Surrender Means," *Human Events* 2 (June 27, 1945), and "Manchuria and the Open Door," *Human Events* 2 (September 5, 1945); Frank Hanighen, "The Far Eastern Dilemma," *Human Events* 2 (August 15, 1945).

7. Morley, "For Yalta, Read Munich," *Human Events* 2 (February 21, 1945); William Henry Chamberlin, "Yalta is Mr. Roosevelt's Munich," *Progressive* 9 (March 5, 1945): 1. For Chamberlin's endorsement of the Munich conference, see his *Confessions of an Individualist* (New York: Macmillan, 1940), pp. 252–53.

8. For biographical profiles of Morley, see F. Morley to H. J. Miller, June 2, 1950 (in the possession of Kenneth Templeton, Jr.); back of pamphlet by Morley, "Humanity Tries Again" (Chicago and Washington: Human Events, 1946). Morley's relation to America First is found in R. E. Wood to F. Morley, December 24, 1940, F. Morley to R. E. Wood, January 4, 1941, the Papers of Felix Morley, Hoover Presidential Library. For the petition of Republican leaders, see Donald R. McCoy, *Landon of Kansas* (Lincoln: University of Nebraska Press, 1966), pp. 471–73.

9. For the career of Hanighen, see obituary, *New York Times*, January 11, 1964, p. 22. Chamberlin's life can be found in his own *Confessions of an Individualist* and in Robert H. Myers, "William Henry Chamberlin: His Views of the Soviet Union," Ph.D. diss., Indiana University, 1973. For Chamberlin's participation in the KAOWC rally, see "Peace Congress Meets in Capital," *Christian Century* 58 (June 11, 1941): 790–91.

10. Morley, "An Adventure in Journalism," and "Human Events: A Statement of Policy," in *A Year of Human Events* (Chicago: Human Events, 1945), 1: viii, x; and Morley, "The Early Days of Human Events," *Human Events*, 34 (April 27, 1974): 26, 28, 31. In 1945 Morley, Hanighen, and publisher Henry Regnery each owned one-third of the stock, and five years later, Morley—who strongly opposed Hanighen's Cold War militancy—resigned and sold his stock back to the company. Among the isolationists helping to launch *Human Events* were such America First Committee leaders as General Wood, Colonel Lindbergh, J. Sanford Otis, Sterling Morton, Colonel McCormick, General Thomas Hammond, Isaac Pennypacker, Clay Judson, William Regnery, Morris Leeds, and Edwin S. Webster, Jr. See undated list of informal sponsors, Box 18, the Papers of John T. Flynn, University of Oregon Library.

11. Chamberlin, "Stalin, Pravda and Churchill," *Human Events* 1 (February 2, 1944).

12. Morris Rubin, "Where Do We Go from Yalta?," *Progressive* 9 (February 26, 1945): 1; Sidney Hertzberg, "The Curse of Realism: An Editorial," *Common Sense* 14 (March 1945): 4; Milton Mayer, "From Yahweh to Yalta," *Progressive* 9 (March 5, 1945): 5.

13. A. H. Vandenberg to J. C. Grew, February 19, 1945, in *Private Papers*, pp. 148–51; Thomas, "The Yalta Conference and the Burden of Hate," *Socialist Call* 12 (February 19, 1945): 1; Taft, speech before the American Polish Association, New York, May 20, 1945, *CR*, p. A2412. Darilek notes the size of Vandenberg's Polish constituency, "Loyal Opposition," p. 201.

14. Samuel B. Pettengill, *CR*, May 24, 1945, p. A2470; La Follette, *CR*, May 31, 1945, p. 5324.

15. Beston, "'The Slav Has Won'," *Human Events* 2 (December 26, 1945); Chamberlin, *America: Partner in World Rule* (New York: Vanguard, 1945), p. 13; Wheeler, *New York Times*, June 5, 1945, p. 5, August 4, 1945, p. 4. For examples of similar anxieties at the end of World War I, see Arno J. Mayer, *The Politics and Diplomacy*

*of Peacemaking: Containment and Counterrevolution at Versailles, 1918–1919* (New York: Knopf, 1967), pp. 3–9.

16. Morley, "The Unification of Europe," *Human Events* 2 (February 7, 1945); Hoover, *New York Times*, August 12, 1945, pp. 1, 34.

17. Rubin, "The Time is Now, Mr. Roosevelt," *Progressive* 9 (February 5, 1945); Wheeler, radio address of January 5, 1945, *CR*, p. 85.

18. Morley, "The Unification of Europe"; Wheeler, *CR*, January 15, 1945, p. 252.

19. Taft, p. A2413; Oswald Garrison Villard, "Who Will Win This War?", *Progressive* 9 (February 19, 1945): 12.

20. Vandenberg, *CR*, January 10, 1945, pp. 164–68.

21. For the failure of America's economic diplomacy, see Thomas G. Paterson, *Soviet-American Confrontation: Postwar Reconstruction and the Origins of the Cold War* (Baltimore, Md.: The Johns Hopkins University Press, 1973), chap. 2. For the difficulties lying in abandoning the unconditional-surrender policy, see Raymond G. O'Connor, *Diplomacy for Victory: FDR and Unconditional Surrender* (New York: Norton, 1971), pp. 87–89. For Soviet rejection of a pact with the United States, see Herbert Feis, *From Trust to Terror: The Onset of the Cold War, 1945–1960* (New York: Norton, 1970), p. 130.

22. H. Hoover to W. R. Castle, February 18, 1945, Box 14, the Papers of William R. Castle, Hoover Presidential Library; H. Hoover to A. Landon, February 18, 1945, Box 66, Hoover Papers.

23. Allen Drury, *Senate Journal*, entry of December 30, 1944, p. 324.

24. For biographical material on Frederick J. Libby, see his own *To End War: The Story of the National Council for the Prevention of War* (Nyack, N.Y.: Fellowship Publications, 1969). The description of Libby comes from Charles Chatfield, *For Peace and Justice: Pacifism in America, 1914–1941* (Knoxville: University of Tennessee Press, 1971), p. 148. The Keep America Out of War Congress in which Libby played such a prominent role is described in Justus D. Doenecke, "Non-Interventionism of the Left: The Keep America Out of War Congress, 1938–41," *Journal of Contemporary History* 12 (April 1977): 221–36.

25. F. J. Libby to W. H. Regnery, March 3 and May 19, 1945, F. J. Libby to the Directors of the Foundation for Foreign Affairs, November 3, 1945, NCPW Papers. Among the prominent isolationists consulted were Flynn, Senator Wheeler, and Borchard. Trustees included publisher Henry Regnery, who agreed to be treasurer; Eugene Davidson, editor of the Yale University Press; James Shanley, former Democratic Congressman from New Haven; Flynn; Hanighen; Georgia Harkness, a pacifist professor of applied theology at Garrett Biblical Institute; and Yale professor Harry Rudin, specialist in German history.

26. W. H. Regnery to F. J. Libby, October 12, 1945, NCPW Papers; Borchard and Morrison cited in undated Libby memo to Board of Directors, NCPW Papers.

27. Wheeler, *New York Times*, August 4, 1945, p. 4; La Follette, *CR*, May 31, 1945, p. 5322.

28. Charles W. Tobey, address before America's Town Meeting of the Air, January 18, 1945, *CR*, p. A223; Alexander Wiley, *CR*, November 28, 1945, pp. 11087–88; and April 24, 1945, p. 3702; Hamilton Fish, *The Challenge of World Communism* (Milwaukee, Wis.: Bruce, 1946), p. 111; Joseph P. Kennedy in David E. Koskoff, *Joseph P. Kennedy: A Life and Times* (Englewood Cliffs, N.J.: Prentice-Hall, 1974), p. 348.

29. Johnson, radio interview, July 14, 1945, *CR*, p. 8003; George D. Aiken, statement in *Free World* 9 (January 1945): 35–36; Frances P. Bolton, *CR*, April 25, 1945, p. 3799.

30. For Vandenberg's career, see C. David Tomkins, *Senator Arthur H. Vandenberg: The Evolution of a Modern Republican, 1884–1945* (East Lansing: Michigan State University Press, 1970); *Current Biography, 1940*, pp. 821–23; and *Current Biography, 1948*, pp. 637–41. For a critical portrait, see Richard Rovere, "Arthur Hays Vandenberg: New Man in the Pantheon," in Richard Rovere, ed., *The American Establishment and Other Reports, Opinions, and Speculations* (New York: Harcourt, Brace and World, 1962), pp. 182–91.

31. Vandenberg's defense of prewar isolationism is found in A. Vandenberg to B. E. Hutchinson, October 28, 1944, in *Private Papers*, p. 123; role in MacArthur campaign, *Private Papers*, chap. 5; position on Congressional warmaking in Darilek, "Loyal Opposition," p. 136. His comments on Hull's proposal may be found in diary entry, May 11, 1944, *Private Papers*, pp. 95–96.

32. For Vandenberg's role at San Francisco, see *Private Papers*, pp. 172–219; Walter S. Poole, "The Quest for a Republican Foreign Policy, 1941–1951," Ph.D. diss., University of Pennsylvania, 1968, pp. 76–90. For his comments on Poland and the "iron curtain," see *CR*, March 8, 1945, pp. 1890–91, and November 15, 1945, pp. 10696–97. For a sophisticated treatment of Vandenberg as a conservative nationalist, see Thomas M. Campbell, *Masquerade Peace: America's UN Policy, 1944–1945* (Tallahassee: Florida State University Press, 1973), p. 83.

33. For Vandenberg's vanity, see the sketch in James T. Patterson, *Congressional Conservatism and the New Deal* (Lexington: University of Kentucky Press, 1967), p. 102. For the shift in General Motors, see Cole, *Nye*, p. 71.

34. Unidentified senator in Drury, *Senate Journal*, entry of July 28, 1945, p. 478; O. G. Villard to F. J. Libby, July 24, 1945, NCPW Papers; Charles A. Beard to O. G. Villard, July 18, 1945, Villard Papers. Senator Hiram Johnson opposed Senate approval of the Charter but was too ill to vote on the issue. Wheeler gave a major speech against it, but voted for ratification. See *CR*, July 24, 1945, pp. 7973–86; Drury, *Senate Journal*, entries of July 24 and 28, 1945, pp. 471, 479.

35. Testimony of John T. Flynn before the Senate Foreign Relations Committee, July 13, 1945, *CR*, p. A3663; E. M. Borchard to F. J. Libby, July 17, 1945, NCPW; Langer, *CR*, January 29, 1945, pp. 540–41; Henrik Shipstead, *CR*, July 27, 1945, p. 8121.

36. Address of Cordell Hull, November 18, 1943, *U. S. Department of State Bulletin* 9 (November 20, 1943): 341–45; Roosevelt in *New York Times*, March 2, 1945, pp. 1, 12.

37. Wheeler, *CR*, January 15, 1945, p. 241; Shipstead, *CR*, July 27, 1945, p. 8121; Flynn testimony, *CR*, p. A3661; Morley, "San Francisco—An Interim Analysis," *Human Events* 2 (May 16, 1945).

38. Villard, "War by One Man's Will: The Danger of Dumbarton Oaks," *Progressive* 8 (December 11, 1944): 1; Wheeler, *CR*, December 4, 1945, pp. 11392–96; Edwin M. Borchard, "The Charter and the Constitution," *American Journal of International Law* 39 (October 1945): 770–76; Taft in Patterson, *Mr. Republican*, pp. 296–97. Taft received only six supporting votes.

39. La Follette, *Congressional Record*, May 31, 1945, p. 5324; "They Call It Peace" (editorial), *Chicago Tribune*, December 3, 1945.

40. Wheeler, radio broadcast of January 5, 1945, *CR*, p. 85; Flynn testimony, *CR*, p. A3662; La Follette, *CR*, May 31, 1945, p. 5324; Hugh A. Butler, *CR*, February 26, 1945, p. 1426.

41. Jessie Sumner, *CR*, December 18, 1945, p. 12281; Hart, "America Promotes World Communism," *Economic Council Letter*, #133 (May 1945); Frederick C. Smith, *CR*, December 18, 1945, p. 12284; Shipstead, *CR*, July 27, 1945, p. 8120. Mrs. Waters's

story is cited in Robert A. Divine, *Second Chance: The Triumph of Internationalism in America During World War II* (New York: Atheneum, 1967), p. 306.

42. Rankin, *CR*, November 23, 1945, pp. 10948–50; Hoffman, *CR*, December 13, 1945, p. 12277; McCormick in Waldrop, *McCormick of Chicago*, p. 265.

43. Flynn, "What is the President's Foreign Policy?" (undated memo for Paul Palmer) in Dumbarton Oaks folder, Box 5, Flynn Papers; Borchard, "The Impractability of 'Enforcing' Peace," *Yale Law Journal* 55 (August 1946): 972; Morley, "San Francisco—An Interim Analysis."

44. Wheeler, *CR*, January 15, 1945, p. 251, and radio broadcast of February 27, 1945, *CR*, p. A913; Langer, *CR*, January 29, 1945, pp. 541–42, and Smith, "Senator William Langer," pp. 103–4; Hoover, series for North American Newspaper Alliance, *CR*, March 30, 1945, p. A1613.

45. "Hoover Says Political Rights Must Be Assured in Charter," *CR*, March 27, 1945, p. A1508; Wheeler, *CR*, January 15, 1945, pp. 248–50; La Follette, *CR*, May 31, 1945, p. 5329; Taft, *CR*, June 28, 1945, p. 8153.

46. "Dewey Attacks Four-Power Move to Control World," *New York Times*, August 17, 1944, pp. 1, 11.

47. For the foreign policy implications of the 1944 election, see Darilek, "Loyal Opposition," p. 299; Robert A. Divine, *Foreign Policy and U. S. Presidential Elections*, Vol. I: *1940–1948* (New York: New Viewpoints, 1974), p. 163; and George H. Mayer, *The Republican Party* (2d ed.; New York: Oxford University Press, 1967), p. 464.

# 3

# Fears of Victory, 1945-1946

Old isolationists soon found that Yalta and the United Nations Charter marked the beginning, not the end, of postwar commitments, for other events of 1945 and 1946 increased their sense of anger and frustration. First, the decisions made at Bretton Woods in the middle of 1944, and debated in 1945, seemed to support extravagancy on a global scale. Second, the British loan of 1946 appeared to signify American underwriting of a regime that, since the elections of 1945, embodied the twin perils of the Old World: socialism and imperialism. Third, the Baruch plan, on the surface, had all the earmarks of an abject surrender of the country's most vital weapon into hostile hands. To many isolationists, the new Truman administration, like its predecessor, was surrendering the nation's material bounty and military assets to destructive and predatory rivals.

In July 1955 forty-four countries met at Bretton Woods, New Hampshire, and held the United Nations Monetary and Financial Conference. These countries established an International Monetary Fund that—they hoped—would stabilize national currencies, end discriminatory exchange controls, and foster world trade. Participants agreed to define their money in terms of gold, to keep their money within one percent of its defined value, and to avoid exchange restrictions. The Fund itself was capitalized at $8.8 billion, of which the United States was to contribute $2.75 billion. These same countries also set up an International Bank for Reconstruction and Development (later called the World Bank) and pledged $9.1 billion to get it started. The initial contribution of the United States to the IBRD came to $3.175 billion. The Bank could extend direct loans to countries requiring economic rehabilitation and guarantee similar loans to private investors and public officials. Each of the two agencies would be run by a board of governors, with voting power scaled to capital contributions.

Most defenders of Bretton Woods stressed that the American contribution, totaling close to $13 billion, would foster an export trade essential to the country's prosperity, while enabling foreign countries to restore their factories and farms. Administration spokesmen predicted a bleak outlook in the event of defeat. Will Clayton, Assistant Secretary of State for Economic Affairs, pointed to domestic surpluses and warned, "Most wars originate in economic causes."[1]

The intricacies of Bretton Woods made debate difficult, and few legislators and publicists ventured into the complex world of balances of payments, currency transfers, and capitalization quotas. Allen Drury quipped that only Assistant Secretary of the Treasury Harry Dexter White and Senator Taft understood the ageements, and each denied that the other comprehended them. The proposals received little debate in the House, passing on June 7, 1945, by a vote of 345 to 18. Although Taft presented extensive arguments against both the Bank and the Fund, the Senate, acting on July 18, voted 61 to 16 to accept the agreements.[2]

Only a few extreme rightists, such as Frederick C. Smith, saw Bretton Woods as "a scheme to set up world communism." The arguments advanced by most isolationists were more sober. Bretton Woods, so critics claimed, was sacrificing not only America's sovereignty but its wealth as well. The United States would contribute about seventy percent of the gold holding of the Fund, while possessing only twenty-seven percent of the votes. Taft commented, "I see no reason why we should entrust our money to a board controlled by our debtors." In addition, isolationists believed that Bretton Woods would set dangerous precedents for more extensive American aid. The United States, said Flynn, was on the verge of becoming a "planetary Santa Claus," with such loans ending up supporting large-scale welfare programs, massive armaments, nationalization schemes, and increased trade competition.[3]

Such a scheme, certain isolationists argued, could not possibly stabilize the world's currency. Other countries, they predicted, would fail to honor their obligations, and, as Representative Smith commented, "more and more of our gold and goods" would be poured into a "bottomless pit." As in Gresham's law, bad money would drive out the good, and the United States would face severe depression.[4]

Taft tackled the administration's chief selling point: that Bretton Woods assured an interdependent and prosperous world economy. He noted that no nation was legally obligated to give up trade restrictions. In fact, during a transitional five-year period, they not only could keep such discriminating practices, but could add new ones. The Ohio Senator claimed that Russia could get as much as it pleased from the Fund, using the loans to build steel plants valuable in producing armaments.[5]

Not content with asserting that currency stabilization did not necessarily lead to increased trade, Taft went so far as to deny that modern wars were brought about by economic causes. The prosperity of both Germany and Japan had not depended, he said, upon their going to war. In addition, he found it dangerous for the United States government to guarantee private investments abroad. People overseas were likely to regard foreign investors as absentee landlords, individuals interested only in exploiting their natural resources and cheap labor. To Taft, the value of overseas activity was greatly exaggerated: "No people," he said, "can make over another people."[6]

Several veteran isolationists proposed alternatives. One of the more impractical came from Congressman Smith, who sought to restore a free gold market throughout the world. Wheeler attempted to distinguish between needed aid in the form of food, fuel, and transportation and any possible "give away" of "our country's national resources and our money." Taft suggested that it was far better to use America's contributions for direct bargaining. He hoped that the Senate would postpone consideration of Bretton Woods until after a general economic conference had met. Taft also claimed that five or six billion dollars could be loaned through America's own Export-Import Bank, and that the United States could use two or three billion dollars to remove British trade restrictions. Such sums, said Taft, would restore foreign trade quicker and faster, as well as having the added advantage of necessitating no further commitment.[7]

These suggestions had little chance on the Senate floor. The Senate voted down Taft's motion to postpone the bill fifty-two to thirty-one. It also turned down his amendment to make borrowing from the Fund and the Bank contingent upon removal of trade restrictions, and did so by a vote of fifty-three to twenty-three. Langer introduced an amendment that would have prohibited the use of any loan for the production of armaments, but his proposal was rejected by voice vote.[8]

The critics of Bretton Woods usually failed to make a strong case. There was little likelihood, for example, of a run on dollars. Each participant had to subscribe twenty-five percent of its quota, or a full ten percent of its monetary resources, and to make the subscription in gold. The Fund limited the purchase of foreign exchange, and, since it could stop a member from using its resources at any time, its assets could not easily be dissipated by a flight of capital. There was some justice in Senator Tobey's claim that the International Bank contained stricter provisions than any private bank in the United States.[9]

Fears concerning a raid upon American resources were equally foolish. The influence of the United States extended far beyond the votes it possessed. Both agencies were housed in Washington, and in March 1946 United States Secretary of the Treasury Fred Vinson became chairman of the board of governors of both bodies. The Soviet Union would not even join the institutions in order to secure a loan, and by 1950 the Bank had lent only $750 million. Neither the Bank nor the Fund functioned as international institutions; instead, they served as agencies of American policy and contributed relatively little to reconstruction or monetary cooperation.[10]

Taft's alternatives appear to be more governed by political exigencies than by economic theories. The British would have found it extremely difficult to dissolve their sterling bloc in the midst of postwar hardship. The Ohio Senator himself had often tried to limit the activities of the Export-Import Bank and probably would not have entrusted it with several billion dollars worth of loans. Postponing consideration would, as Tobey claimed, have avoided confronting "a serious international problem until after the problem had somehow solved itself." Taft's comments about the dangers of foreign investment appear prophetic to a later generation. His case, however, would have been strengthened had he protested against the principle of investing overseas, rather than merely stressing the folly of government guarantees.[11]

In retrospect, opposition to Bretton Woods centered upon threats that proved to be unreal. In the debate, however, isolationist opponents had placed the administration on warning: They would continue to fight possible inroads on economic self-sufficiency, a balanced budget, and the sanctity of the dollar. No greedy and ravaging foreigners, least of all the British Empire, were going to plunder the country's resources without being called to account.

The British loan of 1946 greatly added to isolationist suspicions. By the end of the war, the once-mighty empire faced financial ruin. Britain had lost a quarter of its national wealth; it had been forced to liquidate one-half of its foreign investments and to cut exports by one-third. As the European war came to an end, most Britons were quick to realize that economic recovery depended upon outside funding.

In December of 1945 the British negotiated a $3.75 billion loan with the United States. Under its terms, Britain would pay only two percent interest for the next fifty years, and even this sum could be waived in periods of severe hardship. In turn, however, it pledged major concessions: the elimination of its most stringent exchange restrictions by 1947, assuring American exporters of payment in dollars; the abolition of its "dollar pool," a device by which sterling area countries (who conducted one-half of the world's international trade) had restricted their own purchasing power in the United States; the converting of "blocked sterling" into dollars; and an end to restrictions upon American imports. England accepted multilateral trade and nondiscrimination as general goals, although the agreement established no deadline for reducing imperial trade preferences. By the end of January 1946 the treaty had been transmitted to Congress, and during the first half of the year it was hotly debated.

The Truman administration offered several arguments on behalf of the loan. First, it claimed that the loan promoted American prosperity by stimulating employment. Congress was bombarded with statistics indicating that the American economy relied upon British trade.[12]

In addition, the administration asserted that a bankrupt Britain would find itself forced to resume bilateral trading. With the world again composed of great commercial blocs, the United States would face complete regimentation. And, asked Will Clayton, "if we have regimentation in our foreign trade, how long do you think free enterprise can continue in our domestic commerce?" Furthermore, proponents claimed that the loan granted America access to the sterling bloc, thereby opening markets in Egypt and India.[13]

Increasingly during the debate, loan advocates asserted that British power was needed to contain Communism. It was probably no accident, for example, that Secretary of State James F. Byrnes spoke the most ardently on the political implications of the loan two days after Stalin had given a major speech, one in which the Russian dictator proclaimed his eternal hostility to capitalism. All during the spring of 1946, as Congress debated the loan, Iran—long in the British sphere of influence—was seeking the evacuation of Russian troops from its northern areas. Without the loan, warned House majority leader John McCormack (Dem.–Mass.), Russia would take over the world's leadership. Similarly, on the last day of debate, House speaker Sam Rayburn (Dem.–Texas) stepped down from the chair to declare: "I do not want Western Europe, England, and all the rest pushed . . . toward an ideology that I despise."[14]

A few old isolationists were swayed by various economic arguments. Chester Bowles, director of the Office of Economic Stabilization, found such lending "essential to our long-run prosperity and peace." Senator Wiley, noting that Britain was America's best customer, defined "a good samaritan" as one who helps "his brother to help himself." Congresswoman Bolton hoped that America, not Russia, would get Near Eastern markets, and Congressman Charles A. Wolverton (Rep.–N.J.) claimed that his home district of Camden depended upon foreign trade.[15]

To be sure, the Russian issue influenced a few old isolationists. Joseph P. Kennedy, in endorsing an outright gift, claimed that the British formed "the last barrier in Europe against Communism." As the United States had just spent $200 billion "in a war we were told would save civilization," it could well afford another four billion. Both Wiley and Taber found England a bulwark against Communism, Taber commenting that the loan strengthened "a buffer state which would be friendly to us against Russian aggression." Noting the vote of 219 to 155 in the House, and 46 to 34 in the Senate, the *New York Times* stressed that anti-Soviet sentiment assured passage. "Multilateralism," it said, "was not a very exciting issue, and trade and loan statistics were tedious."[16] It remains doubtful, however, whether old isolationists were more swayed by Cold War arguments than by economic ones. For most of them, the British loan was sheer folly.

Isolationist opponents advanced several claims: (a) the loan made the United States dangerously insolvent; (b) Great Britain, the world's first "socialist empire," was an unworthy recipient; (c) America, despite administration promises, could not penetrate the British economic orbit; and (d) warnings of Communist danger were spurious.

The most repeated arguments centered on the need for economy. To many isolationists, America could not afford such spending. Indeed, they argued, it had been the deficits of the New Deal and World War II that had brought the country to the verge of bankruptcy. Current prosperity was little more than a façade, and huge foreign aid and welfare appropriations only made the inevitable doom more certain. Some comments were caustic. Congressman Harold Knutson (Rep.–Minn.) said, "Uncle Sam has become a glorified Santa Claus. I think it is high time we take the old gentleman into a barber shop and give him a shave." Representative Roy O. Woodruff (Rep.–Mich.) asked how "Europe ever passed through over 2,000 years of recorded history without the help of the United States."[17]

The precedent alone was awesome. To the *Washington Times-Herald*, a paper loosely connected to the McCormick chain, the United States was inviting "most of the other nations of the world past our paymaster's window." Administration talk of a possible loan to Russia, an item never formally proposed, had reached congressional ears and, to some, made the British venture all the more embarrassing. Congressman John M. Vorys (Rep–Ohio) remarked, "If we are going in for buying off threats, a Russian loan might be a good one."[18]

A few old isolationists claimed that the loan left domestic needs untended. Senator La Follette said that continued "transfusions" would only jeopardize America's own social and economic programs. The *New York Daily News* hoped that the loan could be replaced by veterans' bonuses. Congressman William H. Stevenson (Rep.–Wis.) suggested that the money be used for cancer and polio research, and Langer facetiously proposed a urine analysis for every American. Knutson, who himself seldom voted for welfare measures, lamented that America's aged were "receiving less than a bare subsistence allowance." To some degree, crocodile tears were being shed, for only La Follette and Langer consistently supported welfare programs.[19]

Attacks on Great Britain, often held in abeyance during the wartime alliance, were resumed with fervor, and the virgin republic was continually compared to an empire both effete and self-indulgent. Congressman Dewey Short (Rep.–Mo.) commented, "So long as I know they have crown jewels of the king and the czar, . . . as long as they wear ermine and emeralds in London and Moscow, . . . I am not going to vote for one dollar to take food out of the mouths of my own people." Congressman Gerald W. Landis (Rep.–Ind.) entered the salaries of the world's ruling houses into the *Congressional Record*. Langer quoted from Andrew Carnegie's *Triumphal Democracy*, written in 1893, in order to prove that the British were still conspiring to dominate the United States. Congressman Fred Bradley (Rep.–Mich.) saw the loan as the product of Rhodes scholars, that elitist group ever conspiring to advance British interests. "I am," the Michigan Republican commented, "getting sick and tired listening to the 'cheerio's,' 'right-ho's,' etc. down here in Washington."[20]

Such attitudes had long been represented among the Democratic isolationists by Senator Edwin C. Johnson. A man of huge frame, with bull shoulders and hands like a boilermaker's, Johnson had begun life as a railroad laborer and homesteader. Elected to the Senate from Colorado in 1936, he soon possessed such a reputation for conservatism that two liberal journalists called him "a Republican who is masquerading as a Democrat." He strongly criticized the draft, once commenting that conscription "substituted sex training and guzzling for spiritual training, and moral stagnation for the development of a healthy, wholesome, self-reliant and energetic morale." In respect to the British loan, Johnson declared,

"Billions for the relief of starving children, but not 1 cent of American taxpayer's money for the relief of empires." Such decadent patterns of government, Johnson continually repeated, were unworthy of support.[21]

Several old isolationists found perpetuation of the British empire even more irritating and gladly revived prewar hatreds of the realm where "the sun never sets." Colonel McCormick drew parallels between the British "massacre" of Fort Dearborn (the site of his native Chicago) in 1812 and British-backed "massacres" of Indonesian nationalists in 1945. Congressman Woodruff accused the British of having employed American lend-lease weapons in order to suppress the Greek rebellion in 1944.[22]

Now, with the new Labor government, certain isolationists saw Great Britain as embodying the twin perils of the decaying Continent—the traditional imperialist plutocracy and a new collectivist despotism. In the election of July 1945, the Labor Party had gained a sweeping victory over the Conservatives. Within a year the nation had launched a major program of socialization and social service. By the end of 1945 the Bank of England was nationalized; public transportation, gas, railroads, road haulage, and steel soon followed. Britons soon had compulsory workmen's compensation and free medical service. Senator Raymond E. Willis (Rep.–Ind.) found no contradiction in saying that "the [loan] money will be used to enrich the monopolists and to bolster a shaky Socialist regime." Hamilton Fish told his former House colleagues that England had "followed after the pattern of the Nazis, national socialism, but [did] not go so far as terror and force." Representative Knutson claimed that Britain was engaged in "Communist experimentation." To these old isolationists, and to others, Britain was neither an object of pity nor a fitting partner. Rather, it stood as a living warning of "the road to serfdom," a nation that, in the words of Congressman Jesse P. Wolcott (Rep.–Mich.), had taken "a very long step toward communism."[23]

The measure, several veteran isolationists maintained, was essential neither to American prosperity nor to the world economy. The health of the United States, they believed, depended upon a high tariff and a thriving internal trade; therefore the British loan could only damage the nation. Broadcaster Close denied that credits alone could force "trade blood through the hardened arteries of this post-war world." Pettengill feared that government-dominated foreign trade would turn "every race for a new oil field" into the mobilization of "a million men with triggers set." Taft turned the administration's argument on its head; the loan, he claimed, produced political blocs far more dangerous to world peace than economic ones.[24]

Some old isolationists flatly denied that England would ever give up imperial preference. Instead, they predicted that British competition would be more acute than ever. Senator C. Wayland ("Curly") Brooks (Rep.–Ill.) noted that the loan by no means ended England's tariff system. American markets, he said, might eventually be flooded with merchandise from nations who "pay from 15 cents to $1 a day to their labor." Fish predicted that America would soon trade with Commonwealth countries in any case; in fact, the United States was already finding its greatest market in

Canada. Vorys called upon his countrymen to show the same resistance to Britain's "economic warfare" that they once did to the Barbary pirates! [25]

And, throughout the debate, several veteran isolationists objected to the subsidizing of American exports. Johnson asked, "Are we going to put up the money for them to buy goods from us? Is that good business?" Why, isolationists argued, engage in such irresponsible diplomacy when the nation was already almost self-sufficient. Wheeler boasted, "The greatest market in the world is right here in the United States."[26]

The British loan compounded the anxieties that isolationists had felt over Bretton Woods. It would, they believed, further erode the solvency needed for America's survival. The fact that Britain was turning Socialist while retaining trappings of empire was even more galling. By 1946 arguments against Socialist regimes had become a major part of the isolationist ideology. Those countries engaged in a planned economy would find themselves particularly anathematized by many old isolationists, and no amount of administration Cold War rhetoric could change this fact.

Even if administration efforts to stress the Russian danger aided the bill's passage, they failed to sway many old isolationists, and Winston Churchill's famous Fulton, Missouri, speech only increased isolationist anxiety. Delivered on March 5, 1946, at Westminster College, Churchill's message centered on a plea for an Anglo-American alliance. The former Prime Minister claimed that the two powers, backed up by atomic weaponry, could create "a unity in Europe from which no nation should be permanently outcast."[27]

A few old isolationists, believing that the West was finally standing up to the Russians, welcomed the address. Rankin claimed that Churchill had "turned the pitiless sunlight of merciless publicity onto the attempts that are now being made to undermine and destroy the free Christian nations of the world." Castle found it "high time that people began to tell the truth about Russia." Kennedy, while not specifically mentioning the speech, asserted that the West should meet Russian expansion in Europe or North Africa, and meet Soviet dominance in atomic energy with threats of war.[28]

Yet, for those already fearful of British designs, Churchill's plea understandably possessed no allure. Only six years after the destroyer-bases deal, the old isolationists saw the English spider again enticing the American fly. And it was Winston Churchill himself—the agent for Roosevelt's "betrayal" of the national interest—who was now attempting to "seduce" Truman and his advisers. Such an individual, who had boasted never to preside "over the liquidation of the British Empire," could never be midwife to a sound and constructive alliance. The *Chicago Tribune* accused Churchill of attempting to tie America to an "old and evil empire" that had imposed "slavery" upon millions, while the more sober Felix Morley feared that even a greater "empire" would arise under joint sponsorship. Congressman Louis Ludlow (Dem.–Ind.), author of the famous war referendum of the late 1930s, was reminded of the warning given by his fellow-Hoosier,

President Benjamin Harrison: "We have no commission from God to police the world." Vorys, claiming that the six countries of the British Commonwealth would outvote the United States, cited Washington's Farewell Address. Senator Langer even attacked the man himself. Churchill had fought alongside the Spaniards in 1898 while a journalist, thereby betraying his desire to "serve in Cuba with the Spanish forces against the Americans."[29]

For a few old isolationists, America was again about to enter a world war. As John O'Donnell, Washington columnist for the *New York Daily News,* saw it, "We're off again, hell-bent for a nice rough and tumble with all the 1938–39 build-up." Economist Frank Chodorov, finding parallels between Churchill's Fulton address and Roosevelt's Quarantine Speech of 1937, wrote: "Soon the propaganda will start. Stalin will replace Hitler as the hobgoblin and the menace of the Mongolian horde will be planted on our doorstep." Fish saw Churchill harkening back to "the prewar days of hysteria," when "people could almost conceive of a panzer division marching up Pennsylvania Avenue and women were ready to believe that there were Nazi storm troopers under their beds."[30]

Several World War II isolationists, in calling for caution, linked the Churchill visit to the emerging crisis in Iran. Russia, in violation of a wartime agreement with Britain, had not only refused to evacuate its forces from Iran; it had attempted to establish puppet governments in Azerbaijan and Kurdistan. Stalin demanded that Russia have access to Iranian oil, a privilege possessed by British and Americans. Both the United Kingdom and the United States promptly registered protests within and outside the UN, and by May the Russians had withdrawn. For the first time, America was directly confronting the Soviet Union.[31]

Some old isolationists were apprehensive. Russia, said Fish, had as much right in Iran as Britain. The *Chicago Tribune* accused the United States of adhering to a double standard: the United States, it claimed, protested against Russian aggression in Iran while remaining silent about British colonialism. Congressman John Marshall Robsion (Rep.–Ky.) feared that Churchill's attempt to draw America into war over Iranian oil would destroy the United Nations. Enforcement of the former Prime Minister's demands upon Russia, asserted Father Gillis, would cost America a million casualties and possessed little prospect of victory.[32]

As the United States was not yet involved in armed confrontation with the Soviet Union, a good many old isolationists still pointed with greater alarm to British "aggression." Only after the crises of 1947 and 1948 would they see a greater threat lying in Soviet expansion. Even then, as it became increasingly obvious that Britain was losing its Empire, they would often deny that Russia directly threatened the United States. Churchill's Fulton speech and the Iranian crisis did not alter their most fundamental argument: the British loan would lead to national bankruptcy. However, if the administration and the ex-Prime Minister wanted to conjure the Russian "bogey," their claims should be met head-on, with some warnings administered in the process.

Even in 1946 at least one old isolationist was willing—to use the phrasing of a later day—to "think about the unthinkable." Lawrence Dennis sought total American withdrawal from Europe. In his extremely varied career, Dennis had been a boy evangelist, Harvard student, State Department chargé d'affaires in varied Latin American countries, and representative of the Seligman banking firm in Peru. As a result of his observations of diplomacy and business, Dennis became a strong critic of overseas economic expansion and laissez-faire. Both the *New Republic* and the *Nation* welcomed his articles assailing finance capitalism, but soon found his advocacy of a centralized corporate state abhorrent. Dennis called his ideal system "Fascism," although it lacked many earmarks of German and Italian totalitarianism. In an anti-British and pro-German bulletin written from 1939–1942, *The Weekly Foreign Letter,* he continually claimed that the Axis possessed the *élan vital* and dynamic leadership to make victory certain. In 1944 Dennis was indicted for sedition, and though never convicted, he was thereafter deemed too unsavory for the commercial press.[33]

After the war Dennis edited a weekly newsletter, *The Appeal to Reason,* in which he continued his crusade against policy-makers who, he said, needed war in order to alleviate unemployment and underconsumption. It was, as Dennis saw it, the dynamics of the American economy—not any Russian "threat"—that made Cold War conflicts inevitable. Although this mimeographed journal, written from his farmhouse in the Berkshires, reached only a few hundred subscribers, it received endorsements from a variety of noninterventionists. In his very first issue Dennis called upon his countrymen to "make it clear that we are not guaranteeing the British Empire, the status quo of every nation's rights as it or we may see fit to define them." Because some Russian expansion was inevitable, America had to "ride it out, not stop it." Given administration obtuseness, however, the British loan might be necessary. It subsidized England's trade deficit, and, he claimed, "We need a contented Britain to help us fight World War III."[34]

If few old isolationists were as cynical as Lawrence Dennis, neither the Churchill speech nor the Iranian crisis changed many minds. Some suggested alternatives to the British loan. Senator Aiken, who voted for the final measure, wanted to limit the loan to a billion dollars until the British opened their currency bloc. General Wood proposed food, clothing, and other assistance. Vorys sought a higher interest rate and enforcement of British tariff pledges. Taft spoke in terms of an outright grant of $1.25 billion, with the stipulation that the British use the money to purchase American goods. Edwin C. Johnson recommended that the Treasury Department float British bonds: the proceeds would go to England, while the interest and principal would be paid to the American investor. The Colorado Senator in fact facetiously called upon the wealthy Will Clayton to invest some of his own money in such securities. Colonel McCormick said that a delegation of energetic Americans should teach English laborers "how to work!"[35]

Isolationists often called for British collateral. Congressman Everett McKinley Dirksen (Rep.–Ill.), in offering an amendment that would have forced the British to put up such backing, pointed to holdings in the Anglo-Iranian Oil Company, the Empire's wool pool, and gold mines in the Rand. Congressman Reed referred to large British investments in such companies as General Motors, the Radio Corporation of America, and Socony-Vacuum. Several veteran isolationists hoped to annex British islands in the Caribbean. Colonel McCormick, recalling that the British had used such islands to attack the United States in 1812, warned that they could now be utilized to launch atom bombs. Fish would have paid $3.7 billion for every British island on the hemisphere's east coast; otherwise, he said, they might end up belonging "to world Communist power, right at our doorstep."[36]

All such proposals were in vain. Congress approved the loan without qualification. The debate, however, shows that many old isolationists were still suspicious of further commitments. Far more than the controversy over the United Nations Charter or Bretton Woods, their reaction to the loan reflected the depth of their feeling. Most isolationists were willing to accept limited and guarded political involvements with the rest of the world; they were far less willing to accept economic commitments, particularly if such obligations involved money going overseas. Familiar themes of 1940—hostility to the British Empire, anti-socialism, domestic priorities, fear of binding alliances, a desire for more bases in the hemisphere— were again revived. Isolationists placed greater weight, to be sure, upon such conservative arguments as national solvency than upon such liberal ones as benefits for depressed groups within America. There was, however, one theme common to both Senator La Follette and the *Chicago Tribune*: the British loan would deplete the country's resources and deplete them dangerously.

It was the "liberal" and interventionist Truman administration, not the predominantly "conservative" isolationists, who first called for confronting the Soviets. To the isolationists, the British, not the Russians, still remained the major threat to American interests. As Upton Close commented, "A Hindu nationalist would not admit any basic difference between a Siberian labor camp and a political prison camp in India or the Andaman Islands." Indeed, when Secretary of Commerce Henry Wallace broke with Truman in September 1946 over America's Cold War policy, a few old isolationists, such as John O'Donnell and Lawrence Dennis, were surprisingly sympathetic to the deposed Secretary of Commerce.[37]

As yet, Arthur Vandenberg's pleas for bipartisanship had made few converts. The small number who followed the Senator usually came from three geographical areas: Vandenberg's own state of Michigan, the Pacific coast, and the Northeast. Never again could the isolationists list among their ranks George D. Aiken from Vermont, Henry Cabot Lodge from Massachusetts, or Charles W. Tobey from New Hampshire. Representatives of the coastal states, with ties to commerce and international finance, undoubtedly backed the loan, at least in part, in the hopes of gaining a thriving export trade. Labor constituencies probably affected the attitudes of Tobey and Aiken. Former isolationists in Michigan were undoubtedly influenced by those market-conscious automobile companies that dominated the state's economy. Vandenberg himself commented as he endorsed the loan, "One out of five workers in my own State of Michigan normally depends upon export orders for his job."[38]

Representatives from the other Great Lakes states and the Central Plains areas often held firmly to their traditional isolationism. The interior regions possessed few manufacturing firms with the kind of oligopolistic organization exhibited by the automobile industry. Understandably, many people from these areas saw the loan as weakening the American economy.

Contrary to the expectations of administration planners, the loan was soon exhausted. England's trade leveled off, its dollar deficit grew, and, in the fall of 1946, it faced an especially severe winter. Occupation costs in Germany and Greece were especially costly, and, once sterling was converted into dollars, Britain faced a disastrous financial drain. And, when England was then forced to suspend the loan's nondiscriminatory provisions, the multilateralist expectations of the administration received a heavy setback.

In 1946 several old isolationists perceived a threat that would make financial drain and the creation of an "Anglo-American Empire" small by comparison. The United States, they feared, might possibly lose its monopoly of the most devastating weapon the world had yet seen. And this time it was the Soviet Union, not "Perfidious Albion," that was branded the source of danger. To do full justice to isolationist reactions to this problem, it is necessary to begin just a bit earlier.

On August 6, 1945, at Hiroshima, and on August 9 at Nagasaki, the United States dropped a weapon unprecedented in the history of warfare: an atomic bomb that possessed an explosive force of some 20,000 tons of TNT. In Hiroshima alone, over four square miles were destroyed and 160,000 people were killed or injured.[39]

When the atomic bomb was first used, most isolationists were undoubtedly as relieved as their fellow countrymen that World War II would probably be ended soon. If President Truman proudly called the explosion "the greatest thing in history," Edwin C. Johnson asserted that "God Almighty in his infinite wisdom dropped the atomic bomb in our laps."[40]

A few isolationists, however, did oppose the use of such a weapon, and a greater proportion of isolationists were more critical of the dropping of the bomb than was the country at large. Father Gillis told readers of the *Catholic World* that America had just struck "the most powerful blow every delivered against Christian civilization and the moral law." Norman

Thomas called Nagasaki "the greatest single atrocity of a very cruel war";
Morley found it an "infamous act of atrocious revenge." Joseph P. Kennedy
considered Hiroshima so senseless that he immediately asked Cardinal
Francis Spellman to seek a prompt Japanese surrender. (The New York
chancery had special links to the White House.) At first the ultra-nationalist
*Chicago Tribune* praised the feat, even boasting that atomic research
performed at the University of Chicago had helped make the Windy City
"the scientific center of the world." Once it had learned to its satisfaction
that atomic bombings did not really shorten the war, however, the *Tribune*
called the bomb a prime example of "the brutal century."[41]

A small minority of old isolationists even began to suspect that the
bombing of Hiroshima had really been intended to frighten the USSR, not
Japan. In 1947 financier Robert Young, a member of the national committee
of America First, claimed that the atomic bomb was dropped in order
to "serve frightful warning upon possible Russian postwar ambitions in
Europe and Asia." Upton Close declared that had Roosevelt lived, "Stalin
would have got the ultimatum: recognize who is boss, or get the bombs."
Indeed, it is not one of the least of ironies that it was an isolationist
businessman and an isolationist commentator who—along with British
scientist P. M. S. Blackett, liberal editor Norman Cousins, and attorney
Thomas Finletter—ranked among the first to propound the thesis of
"atomic diplomacy."[42]

Yet, whether isolationists welcomed the bomb or feared it, they usually
endorsed a United States monopoly and ardently sought to retain American
control. In 1945 such old isolationists as Senators Vandenberg, Capper,
and Willis, as well as Congressman Knutson, demanded that America
retain the secret until Russia's intentions were known. Alexander Wiley
claimed that he would no more reveal atomic secrets than he "would place
a stick of dynamite with a lighted fuse in the hand of a child." Representative Dirksen cabled the North American Newspaper Alliance: "LET'S
KEEP THE SECRETS OF THE ATOMIC BOMB AND INSURE THE
PEACE OF THE WORLD."[43]

A few comments were even more extreme. Congressman Rankin
declared that America's atomic monopoly "could take us into that golden
age of which Tennyson dreamed." Close suggested that Stalin be presented
with an ultimatum: either withdraw to Russia's 1939 boundaries by
November 1 or be on the receiving end of some fifty atomic bombs.[44]

By 1946 proposals for domestic and international control of atomic
power began to take a more concrete form. In June financier Bernard M.
Baruch, American representative to the United Nations Atomic Energy
Commission, presented "the Baruch Plan." His design, vehemently opposed
by Russia and never adopted by the UN, called for an International
Atomic Development Authority that would control the world's resources,
production, and research. Mechanics of the scheme assured that a monopoly of atomic power would remain in the hands of the United States.

Then, in August of 1946, Truman signed a bill establishing the Atomic Energy Commission. The President chose David E. Lilienthal, a former director of the Tennessee Valley Authority, to head the five-man civilian board empowered to administer all research and production.[45]

A few old isolationists endorsed the Baruch Plan. The *Washington Times-Herald* declared that the Wall Street magnate had "figured out a sharing plan which will put our interests first." Morley asserted that Russia's willingness to give up a veto over international control and inspection—a cardinal principle of the proposal—would show "whether we can still speak hopefully of one world."[46]

More old isolationists, however, remained suspicious of Baruch's proposal and of the newly formed AEC as well. Chicago industrialist Sterling Morton, national committeeman of America First, told Albert Einstein that the revolutionary doctrines of Lenin and Stalin made it imperative that the West retain its atomic secrets. Hamilton Fish spoke vaguely of using the "threat of that fearful weapon" to "stop aggression and promote the creation of a United States of Europe." Congressman Woodruff accused the Atomic Energy Commission of stealing "property rights" of "the most valuable new potential industry" from the American people. Merwin K. Hart pointed to Lilienthal's "Eastern European antecedents" and his "life long leftist views" as evidence that the AEC should be abolished. To Hart, United Nations control of atomic energy would even be worse, for it would be "the same as giving the bomb to Stalin."[47]

Some old isolationists, as will be shown, believed that atomic power was so decisive in foreign policy that they often refused to countenance ground forces. Even after the Soviet Union exploded its own nuclear device in September 1949, they adhered to an atomic strategy. During the debates over NATO, and later over the waging of the Korean War, such prominent isolationists as Taft found the weapon a quick and effective solution to possible military threats. The Truman administration was unwilling to rely so heavily upon this weapon, for as policymaker Louis J. Halle commented, "One does not use a hand-grenade to kill mosquitoes in one's living room." Yet it did all it could to retain absolute control, and in November 1950, the President claimed that the administration was actively considering the use of the bomb in Korea.[48] To certain isolationists, however, the bomb remained *the* one device that could stop the erosion of American power. If Russia was still not a direct threat to American security, they were taking no chances. Far better to keep one's powder dry.

Many old isolationists were continuing to engage in shadowboxing. Bretton Woods soon proved no threat to American interests and the Baruch Plan was not accepted by the Soviets. The British loan helped to stave off full-scale economic disaster for one year. Yet, as tensions with Russia increased, more aid and far greater commitments were clearly in the offing. And in 1947 the President would present an appeal that would start the United States on a road to greater, more extensive, and longer-lasting commitments than either the isolationists or the interventionists of World War II had ever dreamed.

## NOTES

1. Will Clayton, "The Foreign Economic Policy of the State Department," address delivered to the Economic Club of Detroit, May 21, 1945, in Frederick J. Dobney, ed., *Selected Papers of Will Clayton* (Baltimore, Md.: The Johns Hopkins Press, 1971), p. 135; Tobey, *CR*, July 18, 1946, p. 7677. For general surveys of Bretton Woods and subsequent measures, see Alfred E. Eckes, Jr., *A Search for Solvency: Bretton Woods and the International Monetary System, 1941–1971* (Austin: University of Texas Press, 1975), and Richard N. Gardner, *Sterling-Dollar Diplomacy: The Origins and Prospects of Our International Economic Order*, new, expanded ed. (New York: McGraw-Hill, 1969).

2. Drury, *Senate Journal*, entry of July 18, 1945, p. 465. For Senate vote on Bretton Woods, see *CR*, July 19, 1945, p. 7780; House vote, *CR*, June 7, 1945, p. 5723. Among the old isolationists in the Senate favoring the proposal were Aiken, La Follette, Tobey, Wiley, Edwin C. Johnson, Raymond E. Willis (Rep.-Ind.), Dennis Chavez (Dem.-N.M.), and David I. Walsh (Dem.-Mass.). Among those opposed were Butler, Hiram Johnson, Reed, Langer, Wheeler, Taft, Arthur Capper (Rep.-Kan.), C. Wayland Brooks (Rep.-Ill.), and Harlan J. Bushfield (Rep.-S.D.).

3. Smith, radio address on CBS network, April 10, 1945, *Congressional Digest* 24 (May 1945): 141; Taft, *CR*, July 12, 1945, p. 7441; Flynn in Frey, "John T. Flynn," pp. 253–54.

4. Smith, address before annual convention of the Colorado State Mining Association, Denver, January 27, 1945, *CR*, p. A426.

5. Taft, *CR*, July 12, 1945, p. 7442, and July 17, 1945, pp. 7622–23.

6. Ibid., July 12, 1945, pp. 7441–42.

7. Smith, *CR*, p. A427; Wheeler, *CR*, July 18, 1945, p. 7674; Taft, *CR*, July 12, 1945, pp. 7439–40, 7445, and July 17, 1945, pp. 7609–10, 7620.

8. For the vote on Taft's motion to postpone, see *CR*, July 18, 1945, pp. 7679–80; for Taft amendment on borrowing and Langer amendment on armaments, *CR*, July 19, 1945, p. 7774.

9. For Tobey's claim, see *CR*, July 12, 1945, p. 7445.

10. For the activities of the Bank and Fund, see Paterson, *Soviet-American Confrontation*, pp. 154–58.

11. For a trenchant comment on Taft's alternatives, see Patterson, *Mr. Republican*, pp. 293–94. For Tobey, see *CR*, July 16, 1945, p. 7567.

12. A general description of the terms of the loan and the administration defense may be found in Paterson, *Soviet-American Confrontation*, pp. 161–64.

13. Clayton, cited in Lloyd C. Gardner, *Architects of Illusion: Men and Ideas in American Foreign Policy, 1941–1949* (Chicago: Quadrangle, 1970), p. 134.

14. The tie between the Stalin and Byrnes speeches, and as well as the events in Iran, are noted in Thomas Philipose, "The 'Loyal Opposition': Republican Leaders and Foreign Policy, 1943–1946," Ph.D. diss., University of Denver, 1972, p. 227. For John McCormack, see Paterson, *Soviet-American Confrontation*, p. 168; for Sam Rayburn, *CR*, July 13, 1946, p. 8915.

15. Bowles, cited in Paterson, *Soviet-American Confrontation*, p. 171; Wiley, *CR*, May 8, 1946, pp. 4617–18; Bolton, *CR*, July 11, 1946, p. 8698; Wolverton, *CR*, July 12, 1946, p. 8860.

16. Kennedy, *New York Times,* March 4, 1946, pp. 1, 3; idem, "The U. S. and the World," *Life* 20 (March 18, 1946): 118; Wiley, *CR,* May 8, 1946, p. 4617; John Taber to K. I. Dougherty, July 13, 1946, Box 77, the Papers of John Taber, Cornell University Library; *New York Times,* July 14, 1946, p. E5. Out of 102 members of the House who had opposed the bulk of Roosevelt's interventionist proposals in 1940 and 1941, seventy-seven (or 75.5%) voted against the loan, sixteen (or 15.7%) voted for it, and nine (8.8%) abstained. A similar examination of 18 Senators shows twelve (66.6%) voting no, four (22.2%) voting yes, and two (11.1%) not voting. For the vote in the Senate, see *CR,* May 10, 1946, p. 4806. For the House, see *CR,* July 13, 1946, p. 8957. One should note the large number of abstentions in both houses.

17. Harold Knutson, *CR,* September 11, 1945, p. 8512; Roy O. Woodruff, *CR,* October 29, 1945, p. A4661.

18. "Does England Want to be Kept?" (editorial), *Washington Times-Herald,* September 30, 1945; Vorys, *CR,* March 19, 1946, p. A1487.

19. Robert La Follette, Jr. to J. P. Frank, April 12, 1946, Box 58, the Papers of Robert La Follette, Jr., Library of Congress; "The British Loan" (editorial), *New York Daily News,* April 2, 1946; Knutson, *CR,* September 11, 1945, p. 8512; William H. Stevenson, *CR,* January 28, 1946, p. A270; Langer in Paterson, *Soviet-American Confrontation,* p. 169.

20. Dewey Short, American Forum of the Air, February 26, 1946, *CR,* p. A4080; Gerald W. Landis, *CR,* December 19, 1945, p. A5674; Langer, *CR,* April 18, 1946, p. 3970; Fred Bradley, radio broadcast of January 6, 1946, *CR,* p. A25.

21. Johnson is described in Robert S. Allen and William V. Shannon, *Truman Merry-Go-Round* (New York: Vantage, 1950), p. 136, and Thor Severson, "Colorado's Senator Johnson," *CR,* May 5, 1950, pp. A3283–84. Johnson's comment on conscription is found in "P.M.," "Army's New Game—The Old Army Game," *New Republic* 117 (December 1, 1947): 9. He attacks the loan in NBC University of the Air, *CR,* February 18, 1946, pp. A797–99.

22. Colonel McCormick, address before the Foreign Policy Association, *CR,* November 27, 1945, pp. A5125–27; Woodruff, *CR,* October 29, 1945, p. A4660.

23. Raymond E. Willis, *CR,* May 2, 1946, p. 4317; Fish, testimony before House Committee on Banking and Currency, June 3, 1946, *Anglo-American Financial Agreement* (Washington, D.C.: U. S. Government Printing Office, 1946), p. 546; Knutson, *CR,* September 11, 1945, p. 8512; Jesse P. Wolcott, June 3, 1946, *Anglo-American Financial Agreement,* p. 547.

24. *Closer-Ups* 1 (March 4, 1946): 4; Pettengill, "A Letter to Laski," *CR,* February 18, 1946, p. A987; Taft, *CR,* April 24, 1946, p. 4108.

25. C. Wayland Brooks, "Shall Congress Approve the Proposed Loan to Britain?", address to Illinois Manufacturers Association, Chicago, January 15, 1946, *CR,* p. A368; Brooks, *CR,* December 17, 1945, p. 12155; Fish testimony, *Anglo-American Financial Agreement,* p. 556; John M. Vorys, *CR,* March 19, 1946, p. 1487.

26. Johnson, American Forum of the Air, February 26, 1946, *CR,* p. A4081; Wheeler, *CR,* May 3, 1946, p. 4378.

27. For the text of Churchill's speech, see *New York Times,* March 6, 1946, p. 4. Truman had seen the speech beforehand and had praised it. See Herbert Feis, *From Trust to Terror,* p. 76.

28. Rankin, *CR,* March 14, 1946, p. 2226; W. R. Castle to H. Hoover, March 6, 1946, Castle Papers; Kennedy, "The U. S. and the World," pp. 106–18.

29. "Mr. Churchill's Plea" (editorial), *Chicago Tribune,* March 7, 1946; Morley, "A Practical Move Toward Unity," *Human Events* 3 (March 20, 1946); Louis Ludlow, *CR,* April 3, 1946, p. 3067; Vorys, *CR,* March 19, 1946, p. A1487; Langer, *CR,* May 9, 1946, p. 4724.

30. John O'Donnell, "Capitol Stuff," *Washington Times-Herald,* March 14, 1946; Frank Chodorov, "Communism is Imperialism," *analysis* 2 (March 1946): 2; Fish testimony, *Anglo-American Financial Agreement,* p. 483.

31. For a summary of the crisis in Iran, see Gary R. Hess, "The Iranian Crisis of 1945-46 and the Cold War," *Political Science Quarterly* 89 (March 1974): 117-46.

32. Fish testimony, *Anglo-American Financial Agreement,* p. 542; "Mr. Byrnes Threatens a New War" (editorial), *Chicago Tribune,* March 2, 1946; John Marshall Robsion, *CR,* March 14, 1946, p. 2287; Gillis, "The Clash of Empire," *Catholic World* 163 (April 1946): 7-8.

33. For biographical sketches of Dennis, see *Current Biography, 1941,* pp. 218-20; transcript of interview with Lawrence Dennis, 1967, Oral History Collection, Butler Library, Columbia University; Justus D. Doenecke, "The Making of a 'Seditionist': The *Realpolitik* of Lawrence Dennis," paper delivered at the Duquesne History Forum, Pittsburgh, November 1, 1973; idem, "Lawrence Dennis: Cold War Revisionist," *Wisconsin Magazine of History* 55 (Summer 1972): 275-86; and Radosh, *Prophets on the Right,* pp. 275-322. A list of subscribers to the *Appeal to Reason* and selected endorsements are in the Papers of Lawrence Dennis in Mr. Dennis's possession.

34.4 *Appeal to Reason,* #1 (March 30, 1946); ibid., #3 (April 13, 1946); ibid., #5 (April 27, 1946).

35. Aiken, *CR,* May 6, 1946, p. 4494; R. E. Wood to A. H. Vandenberg, April 24, 1946, Box 7, Wood Papers; Vorys, *CR,* July 11, 1946, p. 8725; Taft, *CR,* May 9, 1946, pp. 4739-40; Johnson, *CR,* pp. A799, A4080; McCormick, *CR,* p. A5126.

36. Everett McKinley Dirksen, *CR,* July 13, 1946, p. 8919; Reed, *CR,* July 13, 1946, p. 8922; McCormick, *CR,* p. A5127; Fish testimony, *Anglo-American Financial Agreement,* pp. 484-86.

37. *Closer-Ups* 1 (February 4, 1946): 3; O'Donnell cited in Liston Oak, "Wallace, Lerner, O'Donnell, Foster & Co.," *New Leader* 29 (September 21, 1946): 3; Dennis, *Appeal to Reason,* #26 (September 21, 1946).

38. Vandenberg, *CR,* April 22, 1946, p. 4080. One scholar claims that it was really the political objective of the loan, not the economic rationale, that converted Vandenberg. See Philipose, "The 'Loyal Opposition,'" pp. 243-44.

39. For material on the dropping of the atomic bomb, see Herbert Feis, *The Atomic Bomb and the End of World War II* (Princeton, N.J.: Princeton University Press, 1966), and Martin J. Sherwin, *A World Destroyed: The Atomic Bomb and the Grand Alliance* (New York: Knopf, 1975). For a thorough study of public opinion, see Michael J. Yavendetti, "American Reactions to the Use of Atomic Bombs on Japan, 1945-47," Ph.D. diss., University of California at Berkeley, 1970.

40. Truman quoted in Lawrence S. Wittner, *Rebels Against War: The American Peace Movement, 1941-1960* (New York: Columbia University Press, 1969), p. 125; Johnson quoted in *New Republic* 113 (December 17, 1945): 839.

41. Gillis, "The Atomic Bomb," *Catholic World* 161 (September 1945): 449; Morley, "The Return to Nothingness," *Human Events* 2 (August 29, 1945); Thomas, "When Killing Becomes Pleasurable," *Human Events* 2 (September 26, 1945); Richard J. Whalen, *The Founding Father: The Story of Joseph P. Kennedy* (New York: New American Library, 1964), p. 387; "Chicago: Scientific Center of the World," *Chicago Tribune,* August 13, 1945; "The Brutal Century" (editorial), *Chicago Tribune,* December 31, 1945.

Roosevelt's aide Admiral William D. Leahy supposedly told *Tribune* staff columnist Walter Trohan that in January 1945 Hirohito had sent MacArthur a forty-page document. In this document the Japanese emperor offered the surrender of his country in exchange for preserving his title. MacArthur in turn had supposedly transmitted these Japanese peace proposals to Roosevelt, but the dying President ignored them. The

*Socialist Call,* drawing upon Trohan's account, ran the story in September 1945, "Japanese Peace Offer Made 7 Months Ago." See Trohan, *Chicago Tribune,* August 19, 1945; *Socialist Call* 12 (August 20, 1945): 8. Brigadier General Bonner Fellers, who headed the psychological warfare section of MacArthur's staff, said that once Manila fell, Hirohito tried to end the conflict. See "Hirohito's Struggle to Surrender," *Reader's Digest* 51 (July 1947): 90–95. The story may well be apocryphal. MacArthur does not mention the incident in his *Reminiscences* (New York: McGraw-Hill, 1964), and in the spring of 1945 sought Russian participation in the Pacific war.

42. Robert Young, "Notes of an International Meddler," *Saturday Review of Literature* 30 (March 8, 1947): 38; *Closer-Ups* 3 (February 16, 1948): 2; P. M. S. Blackett, *Fear, War, and the Bomb: Military and Political Consequences of Atomic Energy* (New York: Whittlesey House, 1949); Norman Cousins and Thomas Finletter, "A Beginning for Sanity," *Saturday Review of Literature* 29 (June 15, 1946): 5–9, 38–40. For the most articulate presentation of this highly contested thesis, see Gar Alperovitz, *Atomic Diplomacy: Hiroshima and Potsdam; The Use of the Atomic Bomb and the American Confrontation with Soviet Power* (New York: Simon and Schuster, 1965).

43. For the legislators listed, see Gaddis, *The United States,* p. 255; Dirksen cable, September 26, 1945, *CR,* p. 9041.

44. Rankin, *CR,* December 18, 1945, p. 12283; *Closer Ups* 1 (October 8, 1945): 4.

45. For analyses of the Baruch Plan, see Gaddis, *The United States,* pp. 332–35; Gardner, *Architects,* pp. 191–201; Barton J. Bernstein, "The Quest for Security: American Foreign Policy and International Control of Atomic Energy, 1942–1946," *Journal of American History* 60 (March 1974): 1032–44.

46. "No Secret Bomb Deals" (editorial), *Washington Times-Herald,* July 8, 1946; Morley, "Mr. Baruch Poses the Issue," *Human Events* 3 (June 19, 1946).

47. Sterling Morton to A. Einstein, October 21, 1946, the Papers of Sterling Morton, Chicago Historical Society; Fish, *Red Plotters,* p. 84; Woodruff, *CR,* October 13, 1949, p. A6262; Hart, "Again—Put None But Americans on Guard," *Economic Council Letter,* #161 (February 15, 1947).

48. The policymaker is Louis J. Halle, *The Cold War as History* (New York: Harper and Row, 1967), p. 173. For Truman's threat of the atomic bomb, see John W. Spanier, *The Truman-MacArthur Controversy and the Korean War* (Cambridge, Mass.: Belknap Press, 1959), p. 166.

# 4

# The Truman Doctrine:
# Point of No Return

Such demands were not long in coming. In February 1947 President Truman used a crisis in the Mediterranean to issue a full-scale manifesto pledging containment of Russian power. The Soviet threat, he said, was imminent, the need to respond pressing. Many veteran isolationists remained unconvinced, fearing that once such undertakings were begun, the country could never turn back. The results of the President's program could only be fatal.

Even as the British loan and the Baruch Plan were being debated, the United States was watching the eastern Mediterranean with apprehension. During 1946 the nation had protested against the Yugoslavian shooting of two American transport planes, pressed the Soviets to evacuate northern Iran, pledged support to the Greek royalist regime, and backed Turkish resistance to Russian demands for fortification rights in the Straits. Then, at the beginning of 1947, England experienced such a severe fuel crisis that it was forced to abandon many "imperial" obligations, including the financing of the Greek and Turkish governments.

Truman, wasting little time, told the Congress on March 12, 1947, that $400 million was needed, and needed immediately, to save Greece and Turkey from Communism. If the two countries became Communist, "confusion and disorder" might well permeate the entire Middle East, an event bound to "have a profound effect" upon Europe itself. Truman admitted that the corrupt Greek rightist regime was "not perfect" and had "made mistakes"; he made no effort to claim that Turkey even approached the status of a democracy. Yet, finding Britain bankrupt and the United Nations unequal to the task, the President asserted that only the United States could supply the necessary resources.[1]

Rather than limiting the venture to specific political and strategic action,

Truman placed the issue on an ideological level. With his March 12 address, a form of what was later called the "domino theory" became official administration policy, and the President's name, like that of James Monroe, became affixed to a "doctrine." "I believe," Truman said, "that it must be the policy of the United States to support free peoples who are resisting attempted subjugation by armed authorities or by outside pressures." Given such rhetoric, the ensuing debate was bound to be contentious, and the interventionist *Time* magazine was hardly exaggerating when it claimed to have seen nothing so impassioned since the "lurid neutrality fight of 1939."[2]

Embittered controversy over the degree and nature of American intervention could no longer be avoided. If much of the speech (e.g., proposed assistance, a sum of $400 million) was conventional, several aspects made it a radical departure from traditional foreign policy. The President had officially defined the conflict in Manichaean terms, declaring that "nearly every nation must choose between alternative ways of life." He had pledged his nation to a hard line, had announced that the United States would be overtly involved in Balkan and Middle East affairs, and had applied similar action for other areas.[3]

A sense of emergency hung over the proceedings, and the very Arthur Vandenberg who had recently told Truman to "scare hell out of the American people" now suddenly deplored the making of "such important decisions . . . on a crisis basis."[4] Neither Truman nor the State Department had consulted Congress about America's role in the European balance of power or alternative ways of dealing with Russian expansion, and this made the debate all the more bitter.

Most of the new converts to interventionism offered predictable arguments. So convincing, however, did their conversion often appear, and so impassioned were their pleas, that one would never have suspected that less than a decade before they had vehemently opposed such measures as the destroyer-bases deal, lend-lease, conscription, and convoys. For, despite misgivings, Vandenberg and his fellow backers of bipartisanship rallied around the President.

Such converts continually stressed that the threat was worldwide. The Michigan Senator, warning of another Munich, spoke in terms of "a chain reaction" reaching from "the Dardanelles to the China Sea and westward to the rims of the Atlantic." Congressman Vorys, while still pointing proudly to his pleas for a "peace offensive" in 1941, warned that Communism must be stopped, and stopped "before it gets to the borders of our country as a possible military force." Congressman Karl E. Mundt (Rep.–S. D.), once an important adviser to America First, specifically denied any inconsistency between his earlier isolationism and his present endorsement of Truman's efforts. "The Red torrent," he claimed, must be kept from United States shores.[5]

Another argument centered on immediate strategic considerations, with certain geographical areas singled out. Congressman Taber hoped that the bill could stabilize the European continent, while Henry Cabot Lodge, returning to the Senate after an absence of three years, commented: "We refuse to be shut out of the Near East."[6]

In addition, the Truman Doctrine appeared to mark the end of American "appeasement." Frank Gannett, conservative publisher from Rochester, New York, rejoiced that Truman had finally brought the threat of Soviet domination out into the open. Hart found the manifesto the necessary "fork in the road," and Chamberlin saw it as "the right note at last." The Doctrine, said Vandenberg, was the United States' last opportunity "pacifically to impress the next aggressor with any degree of success."[7]

Moreover, supporters stressed the President's international credibility. Taft feared overcommitment and the risk of war, but did not want to tie Truman's hand at coming peace conferences. Congressman Francis H. Case (Rep.–S. D.) claimed to speak for at least seventy-five House colleagues in telling Truman that the bill could have only one genuine justification: to strengthen the administration's position at the bargaining table. Representative Frank B. Keefe (Rep.–Wis.) declared that an America divided over Greece and Turkey simply played into the hands of "reds" and "pinks."[8]

Finally, for a few old isolationists, the nation of Greece symbolized the eternal struggle for freedom. Congresswoman Bolton found Greece's resistance to Soviet threats an echo of its former battles against the Ottoman Empire. Congressman Edwin Arthur Hall (Rep.–N.Y.) declared that throughout "the whole history of humanity Greece has emerged as the only genuine democracy known to the world." Dirksen, pointing to atrocities committed by Greek rebels, was reminded of the plea once heard by St. Paul: "Come over into Macedonia, and help us."[9]

After several weeks of hearings and debates, the bill passed Congress by sizable majorities. The Senate vote, taken on April 22, was 67 to 23; the House vote, tallied on May 8, was 287 to 107.[10]

Two-thirds of the World War II isolationists remaining in the Senate voted against the British loan; only one-third of the old isolationists voted against the President's proposal. Isolationist ranks held firmer in the House. Even there, however, the relative percentages diminished from three-fourths to little more than a half. Noninterventionists not only faced a statistical loss, but experienced a loss of influence as well. Such new Senators as John W. Bricker (Rep.–Ohio), George W. Malone (Rep.–Nev.), and Wherry —all of whom entered during or after the war—could not compensate for the absence of the steadfast Shipstead, the articulate La Follette, and the politic Wheeler.

Isolationism had probably played a role in all three defeats. Shipstead faced the opposition of former Governor Harold E. Stassen, a strong interventionist, who made international cooperation the central issue of the Republican primary. He lost the primary to incumbent Governor Edward J. Thye. La Follette was bitterly attacked by the C.I.O. for his prewar isolationism and for his more recent assaults upon the Soviet Union. This opposition caused him to lose such industrial areas as Kenosha, Racine, and Milwaukee. Labor generally stayed aloof from the crucial Republican primary contest in which La Follette was defeated by a returning Marine veteran named Joseph Raymond McCarthy. (La Follette had led his Progressives back into Republican ranks in 1946.) The Wisconsin Senator was partly to blame for his own defeat, for he had failed to keep in touch with his constituents. Wheeler ascribed his loss of the 1946 Democratic primary to labor defection in western Montana, although he admitted that he too had not done the necessary campaigning.[11]

Several old isolationists saw much to criticize in the new Mediterranean policy. Representative Lawrence H. Smith (Rep.–Wis.) found Truman's bill "smelling" of oil politics. Johnson accused the administration of sponsoring "a political insurance policy for the Standard Oil companies," with the American flag flying "from the highest derrick." Case even went so far as to claim that Middle Eastern oil was not necessary to American survival: the Secretary of the Interior had supposedly assured him that the lignite fields of Montana and the Dakotas contained far more valuable fuel.[12]

Such opponents often found difficulty reconciling any American sense of mission with the oppressive Greek regime. Greece, they said, was a corrupt dictatorship and one unworthy of American support. The *Chicago Tribune* denied that Greece was still the home of scientists, artists, and philosophers. Rather, it was "the center of the world's narcotic trade" (and supplier to British drug houses), a nation "incapable of stable self-government," and one "in which kings and dictators have chased each other in and out like characters in a bedroom farce." Langer called the Greek monarch, Paul I, "a little tin-horn king," while Robsion said that the ruler occupied a "motheaten throne." Johnson found Communism, as compared to Greece's present rule, "a bright and shining star." Truman should back the Greek rebels, said the Colorado Senator, for the regime itself was the real "armed minority."[13]

If anything, Turkey was worse. To some veteran isolationists, all Turks were murderers and tyrants, and had been enemies of civilization almost as long as the concept had had any meaning. And no Congressman was more critical of Turkey than George H. Bender (Rep.–Ohio). An insurance executive from Cleveland, Bender had been in the House since 1938. In domestic matters this abrasive and acerbic man was long an opponent of New and Fair Deal legislation. In foreign policy, he had been strongly critical of Roosevelt's interventionism. In 1940, for example, he claimed that the President deliberately fostered conscription "to get us into this war by the back door."[14]

During the debate on the Truman Doctrine, Bender might have been the nearest thing to an opposition leader that the House possessed. "Every old, worn-out, moth-eaten sheik in the Middle East will be filling his pockets with our tax money," he claimed. In assailing the Greek government, Bender accused it of fostering fixed elections, a black market, and concentration camps. His attacks on Turkey were particularly ferocious, and his rhetoric was so impassioned that one commentator has been tempted to conclude that he "was once scalded in a Turkish bath or had attempted to smoke a Turkish cigarette before breakfast. For in his daily discourses he recited every Turkish atrocity for the past 1000 years." With examples ranging from former Nazis in the Turkish army to Turkish persecution of political dissenters, Bender would speak with all the intensity of a medieval Crusader attacking the Infidel.[15]

Bender and various isolationist colleagues spoke often and spoke vehemently. Johnson noted "the religious persecutions which Christians suffered from the Turks for a thousand years," while Daniel A. Reed recalled "the throat cutting of the Christian Armenians." Nor was the present regime left unscathed. Brooks called the country a "tyrannical dictatorship." Representative Robert F. Rich (Rep.–Pa.) claimed that the Turkish government did Hitler's regime one better: at least the German *Führer* had rigged elections; Turkey's leaders ruled without even the appearance of democracy.[16]

If Turkey's history and form of government afforded little comfort, its international aspirations offered even less. Dennis denied that supplying arms and funds to "expansionist Turks" was genuine containment. Bender went further, warning that Turkey would always sell out to the highest bidder. Veteran progressives Villard and Beard feared that Turkey would be used for an American invasion of Russia.[17] To such isolationists, the Truman Doctrine almost assured that the United States would tangle with the Soviets.

Besides, argued several old isolationists, there was no reason to interfere with Russia's legitimate goals. Johnson declared that the USSR had as much right to the Dardanelles as the United States had to the Panama Canal. America, he said, was "attempting to deny to the great Soviet Union freedom of the seas." Bender, too, endorsed Russian control of the Straits: the Soviets had every reason to fear a power that had assisted the Nazi assault upon Russia.[18]

Such observations concerning oil diplomacy were often perceptive. By 1949 the Middle East would contain forty-one percent of the world's oil reserves, and this percentage would increase with time. Strategically, the Middle East resembled a hugh aircraft carrier, invaluable in launching attacks upon central and Eastern Europe, Africa, and India. Although Presidential aide Clark Clifford discarded a draft of Truman's March 12 address noting that Middle Eastern resources "must be accessible to all nations," there is no doubt that many policymakers agreed with Will Clayton: "If Greece and Turkey succumb the whole Middle East will be lost." *Time* magazine commented, "The loud talk was all of Greece and Turkey, but the whispers behind the talk were of the ocean of oil to the south."[19]

In their comments on the Greek and Turkish regimes, critics also made some telling points. Both governments were autocratic and authoritarian; neither could seriously be considered a democracy. Greece was ruled by a corrupt right-wing oligarchy and was strongly dependent for survival first upon the British, then upon the United States. In waging its guerrilla war against Communists, it had blacklisted hundreds of schoolteachers and minor civil servants, engaged in mass arrests and executions, and detained several thousand political prisoners. Turkey, also governed by a small elite, had played tight and cagey games during World War II. Not only had it stayed neutral, but it had flirted with both the Axis and the Allies when each side appeared to be victorious. Military spending placed a severe drain on the Turkish economy, and it lacked major social services and free elections. Arguments against aid to Greece and Turkey strongly resembled the attacks made upon the Truman Doctrine by Cold War critics of two decades later, and it is hardly surprising that latter-day revisionists often pointed to the Greek and Turkish regimes as evidence that the United States had long been involved in counter-insurgency.[20]

In other ways, the isolationist analysis lacked balance. The wake of World War II had left Greece with problems—inflation, starvation, civil strife—that would sorely try the best of democracies. Its economy made remarkable gains once massive American aid arrived, although its politics remained subject to periodic convulsions. Turkey, contrary to isolationist appraisals, modernized much of its society with American aid. It was a highly reliable member of the anti-Russian coalition, joining the North Atlantic Treaty Organization in 1950 and contributing a brigade of 5,000 men to the United Nations forces in Korea. Repression, however, remained an all-too-familiar part of its political life.

There is another factor. Conservative isolationists would protest loudly when it came to supporting "anti-democratic" regimes in the eastern Mediterranean; they were far less indignant concerning equally despotic puppets of the United States in the Caribbean or South America. They expressed little if any opposition, for example, to the Rio Conference. This meeting, held in the summer of 1947, bound the United States to defend various Latin American regimes, few of whom could accurately be called republics. Nor would many of these conservatives manifest similar anger over such client states as Taiwan and South Korea. For many veteran isolationists, it was fear of embroilment in an area distant from American shores, not the nature of the two regimes, that was at stake. In pointing out the inequities of Greece and Turkey, they may have spoken more truly than they knew.

Some old isolationists found still greater dangers lying within the Doctrine. Truman's alarmism, several declared, was artificial. Steel manufacturer Ernest T. Weir, a heavy contributor to America First, saw the techniques of "the high-powered salesman" at work. Taft pointedly, if privately, asked whether a Communist takeover in Greece would really be duplicated throughout the entire Middle East.[21]

Several isolationists maintained that the President's policy could not possibly prevent World War III; rather, it might well lead to it. Events bore too close a resemblance to the period before Pearl Harbor to be anything but alarming. The *Chicago Tribune* tersely commented, "Here

We Go Again." Finding Truman's message more belligerent than Roosevelt's quarantine speech of 1937, the newspaper predicted armed conflict. Congressman William Lemke (Rep.–N.D.), in recalling the lend-lease bill of 1941, declared, "There was never the arming of other nations that did not end in war."[22]

Parallels to Roosevelt went deeper than presidential "machination," and involved new warnings of destruction and death. Johnson found America again "being sold down the river of blood." Congressman J. Edgar Chenoweth (Rep.–Colo.) hoped that those "trying to get us into World War III would have the decency to wait until we get back the bodies of the 300,000 boys killed in World War II." Father Gillis pointed to the difficult logistics involved in conquering Russia. Dennis wrote with his usual brevity that "Time and the world-wide trend are with Russia, communism and Asiatics. Russia will play firebug; America will play fireman."[23]

And even if Russia would not confront the United States directly, several isolationists feared that the Truman Doctrine made further intervention inevitable. For if the Communist menace, as the administration argued, threatened "free peoples" everywhere, Greece and Turkey could be only the first steps down a very long road. Both Bender and Chenoweth foresaw impending involvements in Korea. Brooks predicted that America would be policing the Adriatic, Aegean, Black, and Mediterranean seas. Fish listed Syria, Iraq, Palestine, India, Korea, and China as possible sites for the outbreak of the coming global conflict. Congressman Rich asked facetiously whether "some of our military experts [were] already contemplating outposts on Mars and the Moon for the conduct of atomic warfare? Where do we propose to stop?"[24]

For a few veteran isolationists, stakes went higher than over-extended commitments and possible wartime casualties: the American Republic itself, they feared, would become an "imperial" power. In other words, the "redeemer nation" would become despotic, and the New World would become all too similar to the Old. Felix Morley commented that the United States Constitution, while "amazingly elastic," could never "stretch far enough to serve a modern Rome." Historian Harry Elmer Barnes asked, "Shall the United States become the new Byzantine Empire?" Senator Brooks accused the administration of taking over "the British program of suppression around the world," while the *Chicago Tribune* called Truman the "spiritual legatee" of the Axis leaders. Hitler too, commented the *Tribune*, had proclaimed himself "the defender of civilization against Russian barbarism."[25]

The arrival of James Burnham's book, *The Struggle for the World* (1947), compounded such anxieties. Burnham, a former Trotskyist and militant anti-Communist, combined geopolitical theories first developed by Sir Halford MacKinder with vague metaphors concerning a pending struggle for "World Empire." The Third World War, asserted Burnham, had already begun. In fact, he made the timely claim that the first shots had been fired in Greece in 1944, when Communist-led elements of the Greek navy had rebelled against the royalists. The United States, Burnham said, needed to accomplish "quick, firm, sufficient intervention" in order to impose a democratic world order upon the Soviets. By brandishing the atomic bomb, America would prove its willingness to "rule the world." *Life* magazine published a condensed version, and Arthur M. Schlesinger, Jr. reviewed Burnham favorably in the *Nation*. The Harvard historian did, however, demur at the thought of Burnham's becoming Secretary of State.[26]

Several veteran isolationists found Burnham's attitudes gaining a dangerous hold upon Americans. Congressman Lawrence H. Smith called the book "a veritable Mein Kampf." If others were not willing to see *Struggle* as an administration manifesto, critics were wary about explicit claims that the United States was already fighting a Third World War. Father Gillis, drawing upon his acquaintance with the Gospel of Mark, accused Burnham of attempting to "cast out Beelzebub by Beelzebub, to rescue democracy by destroying democracy." Barnes called it a more belligerent document than anything that had ever emanated from either the Comintern or the Nazis; Morley found Burnham's book additional evidence that "the American Republic" was becoming an "empire." Norman Thomas, writing in *Human Events*, used Burnham to show that a victorious America could itself turn totalitarian.[27]

Even without Burnham's speculative blueprints, the implications of current policy remained awesome. Bender suspected possible United States pledges to underwrite rightist forces in France and Italy. Case approvingly cited warnings of columnist Walter Lippman: "We are not rich enough to subsidize reaction all over the world." Sterling Morton feared that once "Uncle Sucker" started to deter Communism with cash, "All the spigotty 'republics' will develop active and very threatening Communist parties —even if they have to import them!" Claimed Senator Johnson, "The cry of 'wolf, wolf' will be raised by every royal punk the world over."[28]

Given administration militancy, some veteran isolationists charged that the United States could well become the aggressor nation. Bender called the Truman Doctrine the revival of the *cordon sanitaire* drawn around Russia at Versailles. Libby saw a new "Maginot Line" encircling Russia (and was ruthlessly Red-baited for his pains by Congressman John David Lodge [Rep.–Conn.]). Rubin found the United States' Greek policy orchestrated to a world strategy that ranged from Greenland to the Philippines. Morton said that Russia's open assertion of power in Hungary, manifested in May 1947, was a direct response to Truman's "rather fumbling and muddled" intervention in Greece.[29]

Indeed, a few old isolationists suddenly found themselves adopting the very "balance of power" principle that they had so strongly assailed in the United Nations Charter. If the United States intervened in the Balkans, so they reasoned, the Soviets had an equal right to interfere in Latin America. Joseph P. Kennedy suspected that the "Russian people"—not just the leaders—would resent such American activity, and resent it just as much as "our people would resent Russian aid to a Mexican Pancho Villa or a Communist adventurer in Cuba." To Taft, a nation that assumed a special position in Greece and Turkey could hardly object "to the Russians' continuing their domination in Poland, Yugoslavia, Rumania, and Bulgaria." Robert Young went so far as to deny that the Russians were aggressive;

their every move had been made in response to American initiative.[30]

Invading Russia's sphere of influence was not the least danger for, in the eyes of certain conservative isolationists, the President's policy threatened the very fiber of national life. Rather than protecting the country's domestic institutions, the Truman Doctrine undermined them, endangering in particular the institution of capitalism. Congressman Ben Jensen (Rep.-Ia.) quoted an aphorism ascribed—probably incorrectly—to Lenin: "We will force America to spend herself into bankruptcy, then we will take her over." Lemke accused "Uncle Sam" of having "deserted beautiful Miss Columbia" to become "an international philanderer," one who was "chasing red, pink, green and off-colored skirts all over the world." Johnson declared, "We start out to rid the world of communism and wind up by destroying the last remaining citadel of capitalism."[31]

Veteran isolationists saw other threats to a more traditional America. The Doctrine could transform the country's political structure, with the Executive usurping powers given to other federal branches. Father Gillis feared alteration of the entire government. Johnson found Truman's crisis diplomacy smacking of "dictatorship." Dennis wrote: "Totalitarianism will be conquering us as we scuttle American tradition for a messianic crusade all over the planet." A few isolationists predicted that civil liberties would be scrapped, and at least one strong rightist, fearing that he would personally become victimized, spoke out on this matter. It was Clare Hoffman who commented, "Now we will be accused of aiding the Communists."[32]

Frank Chodorov was one veteran isolationist much concerned with civil freedom. A journalist and economist, Chodorov combined opposition to intervention with philosophical anarchism. Born on New York's East Side, the son of a peddler from Russia, he had headed the Henry George School of New York, an institution promoting the single tax and free-trade doctrines of its namesake. Removed as school director during World War II because of his isolationism, Chodorov began in 1944 to publish *analysis* (the lower case initial itself indicative of the editor's extreme individualism), a small monthly devoted to doctrines of laissez-faire. In 1946 he questioned whether the United States had any mission to halt Russian armies, asking, "Must we go gunning for every dictator the world spawns?" A year later, as the Truman Doctrine was being debated in the halls of Congress, Chodorov feared that the label *red* would be applied to "every person who raises his voice against the going order."[33]

The isolationists' opposition to Mediterranean commitments gave certain of their arguments a more liberal turn. Although these critics had long warned against sustaining British "imperialism," they had never cried out so loudly or so frequently against the creation of an "American Empire." Many isolationists firmly believed that intervention in the Balkans would ruin the country domestically and, despite much conservativism, they opposed bolstering reactionary regimes or containing Russian power. Only in light of such fears do their outcries against "warmongering" and "messianism" make sense. Even as they continued their accusations concerning the "Yalta betrayal," they were tacitly denying that the status quo in Europe had to be maintained. United States activity so close to the borders of the Soviet Union, they believed, would only increase tensions. And, if the administration was confronted with Russian hostility, it had only itself to blame. So far as overseas action was concerned, the Cold War was remaining the war of the liberals.

Isolationist alternatives to the Truman Doctrine ranged from more "internationalist" solutions to those more intensely nationalistic. There was a renewed flurry of interest, for example, in the United Nations. A Gallup poll had revealed that a majority of Americans—some fifty-six percent in fact—regretted that the Greek-Turkish issue had not immediately been placed on the UN agenda, and noninterventionists eagerly seized on this fact. It was only natural for those of pacifist leanings to plead for a strong United Nations role. Libby, for example, wanted the UN's Food and Agriculture Organization to administer all American aid to Greece. Thomas recommended that the smaller countries create a UN police force that would serve in the two ailing nations.[34]

However, several conservative isolationists also regretted that the UN was playing so little a role. Knutson accused the United States of scrapping the peace machinery and of reinstating "the old order" of murder, pillage, and destruction. Langer, who had bitterly opposed ratification of the Charter less than two years before, mourned that the world organization was approaching an untimely death. Morley suggested that all of Greece be put under the UN's control.[35]

Some Doctrine opponents took a different tack, harping on so-called subversion. To certain right-wing isolationists, the real menace lay not with Soviet ships in the Dardanelles, or even insurgents in Macedonia and Thrace, but with dangers lying well within American boundaries. Representative Paul W. Shafer (Rep.–Mich.) preferred "ferreting" domestic Communists out of the civil service and trade unions to bolstering "a dissolute king" overseas. Frank Waldrop asked why Communists were any more dangerous in Greece and Turkey than they were in the nation's capital. Robsion, while boasting that no red flag flew in his ninth Kentucky district, found "more Communists in the United States than there are in Greece, and several times more." Rankin (who voted for the bill) said, "If we are going to fight communism, let us begin . . . in the Library of Congress." Rightist opponents undoubtedly found it both cheaper and safer to attack Communists at home than to contain them abroad.[36]

And, many old isolationists believed, it was not just overt subversion that was weakening the United States. It was a whole series of major upheavals that had taken place during the Roosevelt administration. The *Chicago Tribune* accused Truman of intending to "establish the New Deal variant of American communism in Greece." Commented Frederick C. Smith, "It is not Russian communism we have to fear but New Deal communism."[37] Underlying such reasoning lay one implicit premise: an America "cleansed" of both potential traitors and New Deal "statism" faced no serious dangers abroad. And if the republic ever did face perils overseas, they would best be countered by swift, unilateral action.

Several veteran isolationists claimed that America had to act rapidly and act alone. The *Chicago Tribune* admitted that an ultimatum to the USSR, demanding that it liquidate all puppet governments, "might not work"; it was far preferable, however, to "habit-forming loans." Congressman Frederick L. Crawford (Rep.–Mich.) suggested an atomic showdown with the Russians, while Shafer called for terminating diplomatic relations and imposing a trade embargo. If Communism—asked Sterling Morton—was as dangerous to the world as Truman claimed, why did "he let a few scruples stand in the way of ridding the world of its leaders?"[38] As yet, only a small minority within isolationist ranks expressed such sentiments. But as frustrations increased over the decade, a growing number of old isolationists would seek a diplomacy of confrontation.

Even amid the atmosphere of crisis, a few old isolationists advocated total withdrawal from foreign controversies. Queried Clare E. Hoffman, "What kind of business is it of ours if the people of Russia want to be Communists?" The United States, said John O'Donnell, should be little concerned whether the Greeks had "a Plato's Republic, or Stalin's communism." Professor Borchard cited his mentor, jurist John Bassett Moore, who had once said, "By our interventions in Europe we can always make matters worse, never better."[39]

Borchard touched upon an important isolationist theme—that the United States, in the long run, could do more by doing less. After all, the world of international politics possessed an inherent balance. If a country became over-expansionist, or if a totalitarian ideology attracted many and diverse groups, Americans should not despair. Given "a common-sense" knowledge of human nature, or the economic laws of the free market, or the global balance of power, the international system was bound to right itself. The *Chicago Tribune* denied that Communism, an economic failure in Russia itself, could ever work in the far more complex societies of Europe. And if even if Stalin seized the Continent, he would be no military threat to the United States. Similarly, Chodorov predicted that Communism—which he saw as already the "religion of Europe"—would fall of its own weight. "Slaves," wrote the libertarian economist, "are poor producers." Kennedy predicted that once the smaller countries had tasted Stalinism, they would willingly join the West. Whatever the reason, withdrawal was bound—as Frank Waldrop of the *Washington Times-Herald* expressed it—to do one thing: it could keep the United States "from getting a bloody nose."[40]

In presenting their alternatives, old isolationists did not always make sweeping proposals. Some, such as Hamilton Fish and Edwin Johnson, wanted appropriations limited to food and rehabilitation. Others, such as Norman Thomas and Harold Knutson, suggested that such aid was misplaced, for Germany—not Greece and Turkey—held the key to European containment. Still other veteran isolationists distinguished between the act itself and possible implications. Borchard, for example, claimed not to begrudge the $400 million appropriation, but feared that the precedent could "only lead to war." Castle too approved the funding of Greece and Turkey, while deploring Truman's anti-Soviet rhetoric.[41]

Few isolationists ever came to grips with the strategic role played by Greece and Turkey. Knutson declared vaguely that if American security depended upon Middle Eastern oil, "let us act like men rather than like crawling worms."[42] The Minnesota congressman spoke, however, only for himself. Like the administration it was attacking, the old isolationists usually relied upon ideological arguments and remedies. Their specific solutions were usually no solutions at all. The United Nations could, in itself, no more resolve the Greek crisis than it could clear up the issue of atomic control or a Soviet presence in Iran.

There is also the question of sincerity. Although such a scholar as Morley had given years of thought to problems of international organization, it was obvious that Langer—and perhaps Knutson—were seeking merely to embarrass the administration. Then, if the Truman Doctrine in itself harmed relations with Russia, confrontation diplomacy could ruin any chance of settlement. And, as long as Russian armies stood on the Elbe River, it would be difficult to limit concern with Communism to American domestic life alone. One could side with Chodorov and the *Chicago Tribune,* and acquiesce in abandoning Europe entirely. Such a policy, however, would probably gain little support from a people who had just fought a costly war to keep the Continent out of hostile hands.

Yet, if their alternatives were impractical, the isolationists had made impressive points. They noted the reactionary nature of the Greek and Turkish regimes, the deliberate manufacture of a crisis atmosphere, the implicit and dangerous commitment to contain Communism anywhere in the world, the latent potential for "imperialism" in United States ambitions, and the simplistic and truculent rhetoric used by Truman. On all of these issues the isolationists were on sounder ground than their opponents.

Administration spokesmen attempted to meet, in fact to anticipate, isolationist arguments. Lincoln MacVeagh, United States Ambassador to Greece, assured the Senate Foreign Relations Committee that the Greek rebels were instruments of Moscow. Edwin C. Wilson, Ambassador to Turkey, said that the Turks had been friendly to the Allies—not Germany— during World War II. Assistant Secretary of State Dean Acheson denied that the United States had impartial aims in the eastern Mediterranean; it was simply a matter of preventing Soviet control. Senator Alben Barkley (Dem.–Ky.) claimed to endorse Russia's access to the Dardanelles while opposing fortification plans.[43]

Recent "converts" to interventionism reinforced administration efforts to defend the Doctrine. As the Republican Party had regained control of the Congress in 1946, such GOP leaders as Arthur H. Vandenberg and Henry Cabot Lodge found themselves in the position of defending Fair Deal foreign policy. If the isolationists complained about the introduction of "emergency" legislation, Vandenberg could only agree, while—at the same time—declaring that he saw "no safe alternative but to uphold the President's hands at this dangerous hour." If the isolationists claimed that the

Doctrine broke all diplomatic precedents, Lodge pointed to a landing of American marines at Derna, Libya, in 1805. To those critical of the Greek regime, Vandenberg admitted that Greece was "not a democracy in any such sense as we use the word" while asserting that it had recently experienced an "absolutely free election." Lodge went even further, declaring that until Greece was adequately supplied, it would face a "dog-eat-dog" environment. The appropriations, argued Vandenberg and Lodge, did not automatically commit the Senate to future programs. Vandenberg denied, for example, that any aid to Korea (already appropriated as part of America's military occupation funds) could be derived from the Greek-Turkish aid bill.[44]

However, such Senate interventionists as Vandenberg and Lodge were not simply content to challenge isolationist arguments. They attempted to parry such opposition by offering certain amendments. Lawrence H. Smith and Bender, for example, had proposed resolutions and amendments placing the Greek-Turkish crisis squarely under United Nations jurisdiction; Edwin C. Johnson offered an amendment declaring that the Truman Doctrine did not imply unilateral action in defiance of the UN. In order to counter such proposals and to retain a free hand for the United States, Vandenberg introduced his own amendment. America, according to the Vandenberg provision, would permit the UN to terminate administration aid once the international organization itself assumed responsibility.[45] If Vandenberg's amendment could not placate Bender and Johnson, it allowed the tabling of their embarrassing alternatives.

Johnson's oil amendment met with a somewhat similar ploy. On April 22 Johnson introduced an amendment declaring that the bill should support no agreements between American oil companies and foreign governments. Vandenberg simply accepted the amendment, all the while denying that it was necessary, and it passed without a roll call just before the final vote.[46]

Some amendments proposed by isolationists fared less well, and Vandenberg was able to deter them without substantial opposition. For example, Bender and Johnson made efforts to delete military aid to Turkey from the bill, but these suggestions were eliminated from consideration before the final vote. In the Senate, Vandenberg spoke against such "flank movements," which, he said, were aimed at emasculating the bill, and he received the support necessary to defeat such proposals. The same fate awaited efforts, again made by Bender and Johnson, to insist that Greece abolish royal titles and provide for universal suffrage.[47]

The debate brought out some new and peculiar alignments. Such an isolationist as Congressman Francis H. Case promoted a critique made by the erstwhile interventionist columnist Walter Lippmann. The conservative Johnson lauded his far more liberal Senate colleague Claude Pepper (Dem.–Fla.), a man who had often been at odds with the isolationists. Nor was agreement in one direction, for certain "internationalists" harbored suspicions of the Doctrine similar—in some ways—to those of the isolationists. Diplomat George F. Kennan, for example, expressed skepticism of American messianism; international lawyer John Foster Dulles showed apprehension concerning the possible financial burden.[48]

Yet how does one account for the large percentage of support given the Doctrine by old isolationists? Some, like Taft, were undoubtedly fearful of limiting the President's options and thereby causing the country to lose credibility with the Russians. The Soviet Union, Taft believed, had shown continually that it could not be trusted. It would be sheer folly to strengthen its power in Eastern Europe. Others, like Frank Gannett, believed that the Soviets' hand was finally being forced. Still other isolationists were undoubtedly reassured by the apparent safeguards introduced by Vandenberg.

Surely, however, such analysis merely touches the surface, and even a geographical explanation cannot fully explain the congressional results. True, the great preponderance of opponents, at least among the veteran isolationists in Congress, represented interior and farming areas. But to capture both spirit and ethos of much of the opposition, an ideological framework is necessary. For old isolationists, unequivocally and in no uncertain terms, were stating that the specific proposals for Greece and Turkey, along with the implications of Truman's manifesto for the rest of the world, would ruin their America beyond repair.

The indictment was specific and blunt. Constitutional restraints upon presidential war-making power would be abandoned. The country would bankrupt its economy, risk its security, and—perhaps most important of all—violate its historic mission. The Monroe Doctrine, with its implicit recognition of separate hemispheric spheres of influence, would be negated, and the United States (at least in the eyes of a few old isolationists) would launch itself blindly upon a repressive global crusade.

In some ways the arguments of the old isolationists bear a strong resemblance to the ideology of the anti-imperialists of 1900. Common to both groups was the theme of the "lost republic." From comparisons with ancient Rome to warnings of impending bankruptcy, the anti-imperialists and the isolationists both sought the preservation of a self-sufficient and solvent nation. Truman's pledge to aid "free peoples" everywhere, like McKinley's decision to annex the Philippines, was no fulfillment of the American mission; indeed, it was the greatest of betrayals. And, like such anti-imperialists as E. L. Godkin and Charles Eliot Norton, the isolationists believed that further intervention would so transform the social landscape of an Arcadian America that it could never be restored. Gone forever was "a nation of neat and picturesque farms and clean, attractive, manageable cities where all classes lived together in harmony."[49]

If veteran isolationists did not always share the elitism of the anti-imperialists, both groups often found themselves displaced in an industrialized and "corporatized" society. A program as comprehensive as Truman's, the isolationists believed, would soon take the pristine republic beyond the point of no return.

# NOTES

1. Address of President Truman before a joint session of the Senate and House of Representatives, March 12, 1947, *New York Times,* March 13, 1947, p. 2.

2. *Time* 49 (May 19, 1947): 21.

3. For a brief discussion of these aspects, see Bernard Weiner, "The Truman Doctrine: Background and Presentation," Ph.D. diss., Claremont Graduate School, 1967, pp. 152–63. Weiner offers the most thorough account of the crisis.

4. Vandenberg, *CR,* April 8, 1947, p. 3198.

5. Ibid., pp. 3195–96; Vorys, *CR,* May 6, 1947, pp. 4623–24; Karl E. Mundt, *CR,* May 6, 1947, p. 4636.

6. Taber, statement to the people of his district, May 17, 1947, Box 155, Taber Papers; Henry Cabot Lodge, address to the Clover Club of Boston, March 15, 1947, *CR,* p. 2109.

7. Gannett, *Elmira Advertiser,* March 19, 1947; Hart, "The Last Fork in the Road," *Economic Council Letter,* #164 (April 1, 1947); Chamberlin, "The Right Note at Last," *New Leader* 30 (March 22, 1947): 16; Vandenberg, *CR,* April 16, 1947, p. 3473.

8. Patterson, *Mr. Republican,* pp. 370–72, and Bryniarski, "Against the Tide," p. 113; Francis H. Case to Harry S. Truman, May 10, 1947, Box 1278, Official File, the Papers of Harry S. Truman, Truman Presidential Library, Independence, Missouri; Frank B. Keefe, *CR,* May 9, 1947, p. 4953.

9. Bolton, *CR,* May 7, 1947, p. 4687; Edwin Arthur Hall, *CR,* May 6, 1947, p. 4799; Dirksen, *CR,* May 6, 1947, p. 4632.

10. Vote in Senate, *CR,* April 22, 1947, p. 3793; vote in House, *CR,* May 9, 1947, p. 4975. Out of fifteen former isolationists in the Senate, ten (or 66.6%) voted in favor and only five (or 33.3%) opposed. The ratio was somewhat different in the House. Here out of ninety-two Congressmen, forty (or 43.7%) voted yea, forty-seven (51%) voted nay, and five (or 5.3%) abstained.

11. For Shipstead, see *New York Times,* March 15, 1946, p. 4. For La Follette, see Roger T. Johnson, *Robert M. La Follette, Jr. and the Decline of the Progressive Party in Wisconsin* (Madison: Wisconsin State Historical Society, 1964), pp. 157–58, and Kent, "Portrait in Isolationism," p. 419. For Wheeler, see *Yankee from the West,* pp. 400–410, and John Gunther, *Inside U.S.A.* (New York: Harper, 1947), pp. 178–79.

12. Lawrence H. Smith, *CR,* May 6, 1947, p. 4611; Johnson, *CR,* April 15, 1947, p. 4303; Johnson, statement on Blair Moody Radio Forum, April 13, 1947, *CR,* p. A1822; F. H. Case to H. S. Truman, May 10, 1947, Box 1278, Official File, Truman Papers.

13. "Truman in Search of the Golden Fleece" (editorial), *Chicago Tribune,* March 10, 1947; Langer cited in Bryniarski, "Against the Tide," p. 144; Robinson, *CR,* May 7, 1947, p. 4702; Johnson, *CR,* April 16, 1947, p. 3504, and April 22, 1947, p. 3760.

14. George H. Bender, *CR,* September 3, 1940, p. 11394. For a biographical sketch, see *Current Biography, 1952,* pp. 44–47.

15. Bender on sheiks, *CR,* May 6, 1947, p. 4612; on Greece, *CR,* March 28, 1947, p. 2833; on Turkey and ex-Nazis, *CR,* April 2, 1947, pp. A1504–12; on Turkey and dissent, *CR,* May 6, 1947, p. 4612. For the comment on Bender, see Weiner, "Truman Doctrine," p. 226.

16. Johnson, *CR,* April 10, 1947, p. 3291; Daniel A. Reed, *CR,* April 28, 1947, p. A1951; C. Wayland Brooks, *CR,* April 16, 1947, p. 3467; Robert F. Rich, *CR,* May 6, 1947, p. 4599.

17. Dennis, *Appeal to Reason,* #69 (July 19, 1947); Bender, *CR,* March 28, 1947, pp. 2833–34; O. G. Villard to C. A. Beard, March 6, 1947, and C. A. Beard to O. G. Villard, March 9, 1947, Villard Papers.

18. Johnson, debate over CBS, March 18, 1947, *CR,* p. A1117; Johnson, *CR,* April 10, 1947, p. 3292; Bender, *CR,* April 14, 1947, p. 3373.

19. For the quotations of Clifford and Clayton, see Thomas G. Paterson, "The Economic Cold War: American Business and Economic Policy, 1945–1950," Ph.D. diss., University of California at Berkeley, 1968, pp. 380–82. For *Time,* see 49 (March 24, 1947): 83.

20. For examples of revisionist critiques of United States foreign policy toward Greece and Turkey, see Joyce and Gabriel Kolko, *The Limits of Power: The World and United States Foreign Policy, 1945–1954* (New York: Harper and Row, 1972), pp. 218–45; Todd Gitlin, "Counter-Insurgency: Myth and Reality in Greece," in David Horowitz, ed., *Containment and Revolution* (Boston: Beacon, 1967), pp. 140–81; and Richard J. Barnet, *Intervention and Revolution* (New York: New American Library, 1968), pp. 97–131.

21. Ernest T. Weir to J. M. Robsion, March 20, 1947, *CR,* p. A1196; Taft in Paterson, *Mr. Republican,* p. 370.

22. "Here We Go Again" (editorial), *Chicago Tribune,* March 13, 1947; William Lemke cited in Robert P. Wilkins, "The Non-Ethnic Roots of North Dakota Isolationism," *Nebraska History* 44 (September 1963): 214.

23. Johnson, *CR,* April 22, 1967, p. 3762; J. Edgar Chenoweth in *Time* 49 (May 19, 1947): 21; Gillis, "We Declare War," *Catholic World* 165 (May 1947): 100; Dennis, *Appeal to Reason,* #51 (March 15, 1947).

24. Bender, *CR,* April 2, 1947, p. 3079; Chenoweth, *CR,* May 6, 1947, p. 4615; Brooks, *CR,* April 16, 1947, p. 3467; Fish testimony, House Foreign Affairs Committee, March 31, 1947, *Assistance to Greece and Turkey* (Washington, D.C.: U.S. Government Printing Office, 1947), p. 198; Rich, *CR,* April 1, 1947, p. 2993.

25. Morley, "The Twilight of an Empire," *Human Events* 4 (March 5, 1947); Harry Elmer Barnes, "Shall the United States Become the New Byzantine Empire?" (pamphlet; privately printed, 1947); Brooks, *CR,* April 16, 1947, p. 3467; "Truman Moves Toward Another War" (editorial), *Chicago Tribune,* March 18, 1947.

26. James Burnham, *The Struggle for the World* (New York: John Day, 1947), pp. 177, 216; idem, "Struggle for the World," *Life* 22 (March 31, 1947): 59–80; Schlesinger, Jr. review, *Nation* 164 (April 5, 1947): 398–399. For an able exposition of Burnham's thought and background, see John P. Diggins, *Up From Communism: Conservative Odysseys in American Intellectual History* (New York: Harper and Row, 1975), pp. 303–37.

27. Smith, *CR,* May 9, 1947, p. 4945; Gillis, "Clarity in Political Discussion," *Catholic World* 165 (June 1947): 194; Barnes review, *Annals of the American Academy of Political and Social Science* 252 (September 1947): 106; Morley review, *Human Events* 4 (July 30, 1947); Thomas, "The Illusion of War," *Human Events* 4 (September 17, 1947).

28. Bender, *CR,* May 7, 1947, 4693–94; Lippmann column, "Truman and Monroe," April 8, 1947, *CR,* p. 1769; S. Morton to A. Landon, March 31, 1947, Morton Papers; Johnson, radio program "Open Hearings," March 18, 1947, *CR,* p. A1117.

29. Bender, *CR,* March 28, 1947, pp. 2831–32; Libby testimony and exchange with Lodge, House Foreign Affairs Committee, April 1, 1947, *Assistance to Greece and Turkey,* pp. 249–57; Rubin, "Russia Rules America," *Progressive* 11 (March 17, 1947): 1–2; S. Morton to A. Landon, June 13, 1947, Morton Papers.

30. "Confusion, Insecurity Peril United States, Says Kennedy," *Detroit Sunday Times,* May 25, 1947; Taft in Paterson, *Mr. Republican,* p. 370; Young, "Notes of an International Meddler," p. 9.

31. Ben Jensen, *CR,* May 9, 1947, p. 4950; Lemke, *CR,* May 9, 1947, p. 4924; Johnson, radio speech over MBS, April 9, 1947, *CR,* p. A1821.

32. Gillis, "Truman Speaks Out," *Catholic World* 165 (April 1947): 9–10; Johnson, radio broadcast over ABC, April 12, 1947, *CR,* p. A1821; Dennis, *Appeal to Reason,*

#51 (March 15, 1947); Hoffman, *CR*, March 17, 1947, p. A1050.

33. Chodorov, "Communism is Imperialism," p. 2; "A Byzantine Empire of the West?," *analysis* 3 (April 1947): 3. Chodorov's life can be found in *Out of Step: The Autobiography of an Individualist* (New York: Devin Adair, 1962); Chodorov, "How a Jew Came to God: An Intellectual Experience," *analysis* 4 (March 1948): 1–4; George H. Nash, *The Conservative Intellectual Movement in America Since 1945* (New York: Basic Books, 1976), pp. 16–18, 28–30.

34. Libby testimony, *Assistance to Greece and Turkey*, p. 247; Thomas, "As I See It," *Socialist Call* 13 (March 19, 1947): 5.

35. Knutson, *CR*, May 6, 1947, p. 4640; Langer in Bryniarski, "Against the Tide," p. 144; Morley, "Greece and the Monroe Doctrine," *Human Events* 4 (March 12, 1947).

36. Paul W. Shafer, *CR*, March 17, 1947, p. A1073; Waldrop, "Start at Home," *CR*, March 18, 1947, p. A1101; Robsion, *CR*, May 7, 1947, p. 4701; Rankin, ibid., April 28, 1947, p. 4172. For a linkage of Communism and economy, see Bryniarski, "Against the Tide," p. 126.

37. "Soviet and New Deal Bridgeheads" (editorial), *Chicago Tribune*, March 20, 1947; Smith, *CR*, March 4, 1947, p. 1671.

38. "Habit Forming Loans" (editorial), *Chicago Tribune*, April 14, 1947; testimony of Frederick L. Crawford, House Foreign Affairs Committee, March 31, 1947, *Assistance to Greece and Turkey*, pp. 180–83; Shafer, *CR*, March 17, 1947, p. A1073; S. Morton to A. Landon, March 31, 1947, Morton Papers. Morton might well have been facetious, since he was strongly isolationist on all issues.

39. Hoffman, *CR*, May 9, 1947, p. 4918; O'Donnell, *CR*, March 10, 1947, p. A943; E. M. Borchard to O. G. Villard, March 12, 1947, Villard Papers.

40. "Habit Forming Loans" (editorial), *Chicago Tribune*, April 14, 1947; Chodorov, "A Byzantine Empire of the West?", pp. 1–3; Kennedy in *Time* 49 (March 24, 1947): 19.

41. Fish testimony, *Assistance to Greece and Turkey*, p. 197; Johnson, statement at the University of Chicago Round Table, April 20, 1947, *CR*, p. A1822; Thomas, "As I See It," *Socialist Call* 13 (April 16, 1947): 12; Knutson, *CR*, May 6, 1947, p. 4640; Borchard in *United States News and World Report* 22 (April 4, 1947): 34; W. R. Castle to J. W. Gerard, with covering letter of Gerard to Truman, April 18, 1947, Box 1278, Official File, Truman Papers.

42. Knutson, *CR*, May 6, 1947, p. 4641.

43. Testimony of Lincoln MacVeagh, Senate Foreign Relations Committee, March 28, 1947 (executive session), in *Legislative Origins of the Truman Doctrine*, historical series (Washington, D.C.: U.S. Government Printing Office, 1973), pp. 34–37; testimony of Edwin C. Wilson, March 28, 1947 (executive session), *Legislative Origins*, pp. 57–60; testimony of Dean Acheson, April 1, 1947 (executive session), *Legislative Origins*, p. 84; remarks of Alben Barkley, April 2, 1947 (executive session), *Legislative Origins*, p. 138.

44. Vandenberg on emergency, *CR*, March 18, 1947, p. 2167; Lodge on Libya, *CR*, April 11, 1947, p. 3336; Vandenberg on Greek democracy, *CR*, April 16, 1947, p. 3478; Lodge on Greek chaos, *CR*, April 11, 1947, p. 3337; Vandenberg on Korea, *CR*, April 16, 1947, p. 3482.

45. Smith amendment, *CR*, May 9, 1947, p. 4945; Bender resolution, *CR*, May 2, 1947, p. A2062; Johnson statement, April 1, 1947 (executive session), *Legislative Origins*, pp. 101–3; Vandenberg amendment, *Private Papers*, pp. 345–46.

46. Johnson, *CR*, April 22, 1947, p. 3792.

47. Proposals on Turkey, see Johnson, *Legislative Origins*, April 1, 1947, p. 105; Bender, *CR*, May 2, 1947, p. A2063; Vandenberg, *CR*, April 22, 1947, p. 3772. The vote was almost the same on Johnson's amendment as on the final bill. Of the old isolationists in the Senate, only Pat McCarran (Dem–Nev.) backed the amendment and

still voted for the final bill. *CR*, April 22, 1947, p. 3792. Bender's amendment was rejected without a formal vote. *CR*, May 9, 1947, p. 4973. For amendments on Greek democracy, see Johnson statement, *Legislative Origins*, pp. 103–4; Bender, *CR*, May 2, 1947, p. A2062. In Johnson's amendment, he proposed amnesty for all opponents of the regime.

48. Case, *CR*, April 17, 1947, pp. A1768–69; Johnson, *CR*, April 10, 1947, p. 3292; George F. Kennan, *Memoirs*, Vol. 1: *1925–1950* (Boston: Little Brown, 1967), pp. 313–24; Dulles in Poole, "Quest," p. 149.

49. Robert L. Beisner, *Twelve Against Empire: The Anti-Imperialists, 1898–1900* (New York: McGraw-Hill, 1968), p. 222.

# 5

# The Revisionist Counteroffensive: The Battle of the Books

Among the charges made by veteran isolationists against the Truman Doctrine, few carried greater force than excessive use of presidential power. Fear of the executive, in fact, had long been part of the tradition that had produced isolationism. And even as the debate on the Truman Doctrine was taking place, a new movement was rekindling that ancient feeling.

This movement has since been called "World War II Revisionism." Revisionism itself, as historians use the term, means a challenge to a conventional or generally accepted version of the part. Revisionists ordinarily are critical of "what happened, how it happened, and why it happened." Contemporary opposition, new evidence, unexpected turns of history, plain political animosity—all have been, and will continue to be, reasons for "revising" interpretations of past events.[1]

World War II revisionism had begun even before the war itself and had gained momentum as a result of investigations by the Army and Navy, and then by the Congress. Between 1948 and 1950, as it came to a climax, it attracted increasing numbers of respectable spokesmen. In its mature form, revisionism amounted to no less than a charge that President Roosevelt had deliberately, secretly, and diabolically maneuvered the United States into war by inciting the Japanese to bomb Pearl Harbor.

From the outset, a number of staunch isolationists refused to accept the official story that the Japanese strike was an unprovoked one. Doing so, of course, was dangerous. To speak of domestic blunder, and of possible betrayal, while American troops were stationed from Saipan to Salerno could invite charges of defeatism, perhaps of treason.

Even so, a number of isolationists spoke out, as some had been doing for several months before Pearl Harbor. On August 5, 1941, a group of Republican leaders including Landon, Hoover, Morley, and John L. Lewis had demanded that Congress "put a stop to step-by-step projection of the United States into undeclared war." Isolationists mentioned the possibility of a Pacific conflict with increasing frequency. In September 1941 Hoover found the administration "certainly doing everything to get us into war through the Japanese backdoor." A month later Wheeler called for caution in dealing with Japan.[2]

Once the Japanese attacked, several prominent isolationists blamed Roosevelt. General Wood said, "Well, he got us in through the back door." Lindbergh, who had often warned that the "Asian" powers of Japan and Russia threatened the United States, declared that "we have been prodding them into war for weeks." "Putting pins in rattlesnakes," claimed Hoover, had finally got the country "bitten." On December 8, the day after the Pearl Harbor strike, Vandenberg privately commented that administration rigidity regarding China had needlessly driven Japan into war.[3]

Almost immediately isolationists sought an investigation. Within four days of the Japanese attack, Senator Tobey called for a complete congressional search and demanded the removal of Secretary of the Navy Frank Knox. Before the end of December 1941 Taft asked why news of an American "ultimatum" seeking Japanese withdrawal from China was not forwarded to the Hawaiian commanders. A year after the attack Congresswoman Jeanette Rankin (Rep.–Mont.), a pacifist who had cast the lone vote against declaring war, asked a host of embarrassing questions concerning possible administration foreknowledge. After another year Senator Bennett Champ Clark and Representative Short raised the issue. Ostensibly they sought to insure that the commanders most directly involved—Admiral Husband E. Kimmel, Commander-in-Chief of the Pacific Fleet, and his Army counterpart, Lieutenant General Walter C. Short, Commanding General of the Hawaiian Department—received a proper court-martial. But they had another motive as well: such a trial, they believed, would cast a far wider net, perhaps absolving the Hawaiian commanders and implicating important officials in Washington. When the administration balked at the proposed inquiry, Hamilton Fish asked, "What is the Administration trying to cover up? Who is the Administration attempting to cover up?" Even Congresswoman Clare Boothe Luce (Rep.–Conn.), an ardent interventionist in 1941, accused Roosevelt of lying "us into a war because he did not have the political courage to lead us into it." And, in an effort to document her case, she entered a critique by historian Charles A. Beard, written for the *Progressive,* into the *Congressional Record.*[4]

Administration activity did little to smooth ruffled sensibilities. Supreme Court Justice Owen J. Roberts, in preparing a report requested by the President, placed primary responsibility upon the Hawaiian commanders. Kimmel and Short, said Roberts's five-man board, should be court-martialed.[5] When the isolationists themselves, led by Short, secured a bill providing for a public court-martial, Roosevelt approved it only with the understanding that such proceedings would not "interrupt or interfere with the war effort." The administration, speculated Vandenberg, realized that exposure would harm the party in the forthcoming presidential elections. Almost as if to prove Vandenberg's point, Congressman Emanuel Celler

(Dem.–N.Y.), a strong party partisan, claimed that a public court-martial would only add "grist to Goebbels' mill and would give aid and comfort to Emperor Hirohito."[6]

During the 1944 presidential campaign Republican candidate Dewey learned that, back in the spring of 1941, American naval intelligence had broken the Japanese diplomatic codes. Such information implied that Washington had enough foreknowledge to be prepared; it could obviously embarrass the administration. The armed forces had relied heavily upon this discovery in fighting the war, and Chief of Staff George C. Marshall told Dewey that disclosure would have a "calamitous" effect upon the military effort. Dewey kept silent, perhaps partly out of patriotism, perhaps partially out of the fear that revealing a closely guarded secret during wartime would injure his party. One historian, however, had noted that such a disclosure would aid the Republicans. "A dramatic revelation that Roosevelt was reading secret Japanese messages and still was unprepared for the attack on Pearl Harbor," writes Robert A. Divine, "might have had a devastating impact on the election."[7]

It was only in a series of pamphlets that the Roosevelt leadership was first publicly accused of irresponsible diplomacy, then of conspiracy. John T. Flynn, in a campaign tract entitled "The Truth about Pearl Harbor," leveled the first broadside. Born in Bladenburg, Maryland, in 1882, and educated at the law school of Georgetown University, Flynn had worked for several newspapers before becoming an editor of the *New York Globe*. He became well-known among intellectuals in the 1920s and 1930s for his attacks on Wall Street manipulation, and contributed a weekly column, "Other People's Money," to the *New Republic*. He backed Roosevelt in 1932, and helped staff Judge Ferdinand Pecora's investigation of Wall Street finance. He soon broke with the New Deal, claiming that such agencies as the National Recovery Administration were simply way stations on the road to Fascism.

Flynn's isolationism grew out of his general economic perspective. As one of a three-man advisory council to the Nye Committee, the journalist proposed severe and rigorous limitations on war profits. In 1939 Flynn suspected that Roosevelt would attempt to bolster the nation's impoverished economy by seeking martial adventures abroad, and in 1940 he headed the New York Chapter of the America First Committee. In this capacity he took a more militant posture than the national organization, opposing draft extension and blaming the President for the breakdown of relations with Japan. It was Flynn's belief in Roosevelt's mendacity that led him to investigate Pearl Harbor.[8]

His pamphlet was a bombshell. After tracing Roosevelt's warlike moves in the Atlantic, Flynn indicted the President for provoking the Japanese attack. Rather than allowing Japan to live with "a few shreds of her tattered garments of honor and prestige," Roosevelt, Flynn charged, had demanded Japanese evacuation of China proper. The overburdened Japanese had sincerely wanted to withdraw from China but needed enough garrisons there to suppress Communism. General Short, Flynn concluded, may have been "crucified in order to shield the guilt of the United

States." The *Chicago Tribune,* seeing in Flynn's arguments another chance to indict the Roosevelt regime, compared Flynn's brief tract to Zola's *J'Accuse.*[9]

Two other pamphlets soon followed. In April 1945 the Pacifist Research Bureau released William L. Neumann's "Genesis of Pearl Harbor." Neumann was a young pacifist serving in conscientious objector camps during the war. The holder of a master's degree in history from the University of Michigan (where he later earned a doctorate), he had been converted to an absolute anti-war position by reading revisionist accounts of World War I. Over the decades, Neumann maintained, intelligent American conciliation could have avoided war with Japan. Like Flynn, Neumann stressed United States intransigence over China and Indochina. Japan had been weary from long years of fighting, Neumann asserted, but was determined to make no peace without retaining economic or military privileges in China.[10]

In the meantime Flynn was learning what Thomas E. Dewey had discovered. Walter Trohan, Washington bureau chief of the *Chicago Tribune,* told Flynn that the United States was aware of every move the Japanese were making. The President and his Secretaries of State, War, and Navy knew, and knew on the evening before the Pearl Harbor attack, that the Japanese were about to break off diplomatic relations with the United States. Yet, according to Flynn, they deliberately concealed this vital information from Kimmel and Short.[11] With Flynn's second pamphlet, "The Final Secret of Pearl Harbor," World War II revisionism combined its attack on America's Pacific statecraft with charges of a conspiracy designed to obstruct adequate preparation. To Flynn and his followers the issue was no longer limited to "impossible" diplomatic demands upon the Japanese. Rather it involved a deliberate "back door to war," and the President himself, acting as a silent partner in the Japanese strike, could well be accused of murdering American servicemen.

Neumann and Flynn were both scathingly attacked and staunchly defended. Broadcaster William L. Shirer claimed that Neumann's pamphlet read as if it were written "by the clever little men in Tokyo"; revisionist historians Charles A. Beard and Harry Elmer Barnes warmly endorsed the work. Barnes told Neumann to show how the present conflict has been rooted in the teachings of Admiral Alfred T. Mahan, "John Hay's Anglo-mania," and a British-dictated Open Door policy that "only meant open season for all big powers in China." *New Republic* columnist "T. R. B." mused: "Good old Flynn has Roosevelt doing everything except swimming under water with the bombs in his teeth."[12]

The isolationists found even more ammunition with the release of special Army and Navy reports. These reports were prepared by high-ranking service personnel (in the Navy's case, retired admirals) and were published in 1945. The results of a congressional resolution adopted a year earlier, they both placed some responsibility with Washington. The Army Pearl

Harbor Board put blame upon Secretary Hull, Army Chief of Staff Marshall, and Major General Leonard T. Gerow, Chief of the War Plans Division. General Short, however, did not escape responsibility. The Naval Court of Inquiry absolved Kimmel and found much responsibility lying with Admiral Harold R. Stark, Chief of Naval Operations.[13]

Once the Army and Navy reports were released, Senator Homer Ferguson (Rep.–Mich.), author of the resolution that authorized the inquiry, capitalized upon the resulting furor by introducing a resolution calling for a full-fledged congressional investigation. In a *Life* magazine article, journalist John Chamberlain praised Ferguson for discovering that the administration had been decoding Japanese messages months before the attack.[14]

In an effort to seize the initiative from the Republicans, and undoubtedly to steer any such inquiry into safer channels, Senator Alben Barkley, a Democratic stalwart, introduced his own resolution to investigate Pearl Harbor. Although Republicans were wary, Barkley's resolution was adopted without dissent. Since his Joint Committee was lined up six to four in favor of the Democrats, an entire battery of House GOP isolationists fought unsuccessfully to obtain equal representation from both parties.[15]

The Joint Committee began hearings in the middle of November 1945, and from the time Barkley rapped for order, sessions were stormy. The chief actors of the Pearl Harbor drama paraded across the witness stand: the aged, ill Cordell Hull; the bald and fumbling General Sherman Miles, chief of army intelligence; the erect George C. Marshall (a man freer than most to admit personal failings); the twangy, caustic Admiral Richmond Kelly Turner, Chief of the Naval War Plans Division; the stoop-shouldered, pneumonia-stricken General Short; the gray, heavy-jowled Admiral Kimmel. Each had his turn under the klieg lights, and sometimes more than once.

More issues were raised than settled. Captain L. F. Safford, for example, chief of radio intelligence in Washington, had supposedly read decoded Japanese messages warning embassies that relations with America were in danger. The naval cryptographer claimed to have received a "winds execute" message, called "East Wind Rain," indicating the imminence of war. When Senators Ferguson and Owen Brewster (Rep.–Me.) asserted that the Winds Execute messages were missing from official files, Senator Scott Lucas (Dem.–Ill.) accused his GOP colleagues of engaging in a "childlike debate about useless papers."[16]

The Winds controversy grew even more intense, for the Navy was accused of badgering Commander Alwin D. Kramer, who had been in charge of handling translations of the Japanese codes. Kramer had told the Naval Court of Inquiry that he had seen the "Winds Execute" message, but later told the joint committee that he had not. Congressman Short, referring to Kramer's internment in a Washington psychopathic ward, said, "I am surprised they have locked him up; I am surprised he has not been liquidated." Committee member Bertrand W. Gearhart (Rep.–Calif.), who was isolationist enough to oppose lend-lease in 1941, took advantage of the Winds controversy to assail Hull's diplomacy before the House: the Secretary's "ultimatum" of November 26, 1941, would have forced Japan to "humiliate herself" by withdrawing from China proper and Manchuria, and by breaking its alliance with Hitler.[17]

The controversy over the Winds Execute message soon led to wider charges of conspiracy. The *Chicago Tribune* accused the administration of deliberately sacrificing the lives of three thousand Americans (inadvertently adding over 600 to the number dead). "The defendants," it declared, "are no longer Kimmel and Short; they are Mr. Roosevelt; his Secretary of State, Cordell Hull; his Secretary of War, Henry L. Stimson; and his Secretary of the Navy, Frank Knox." Congress's only task, said the *Tribune*, was to impeach all still living "who may have played a guilty part" and bring them "to the bar of justice." A few extreme isolationists were so exercised by Safford's testimony that, like Upton Close, they talked wildly about the "mass murder of American G. I.'s"; the nation's top leadership, said Close, were "war criminals."[18]

The total committee record involved some ten million words and seventy days. The hearings ended late in May 1946, and a month later the Majority and Minority reports were released. The Majority Report accused the Japanese of unprovoked aggression, asserted that Roosevelt and Hull had made "every possible effort" to avert war, and found Kimmel and Short erroneous in judgment but not derelict in duty. Yet, while declaring that the Hawaiian commanders had failed to use the information given them, the Majority Report also criticized Washington commanders Stark and Turner for not ensuring that Kimmel received the decoded Japanese messages. It was signed by all Democratic members as well as by Gearhart and, in part, by Congressman Frank B. Keefe (Rep.–Wis.). Adding his own "Additional Remarks," Keefe, an isolationist before Pearl Harbor, accused the Majority of applying a double standard to Washington and Hawaii. The administration, charged Keefe, had hoped for an "incident" to "unify public opinion behind an all-out war-effort" and had therefore failed to inform Americans of their peril.[19]

The Minority Report, signed only by Brewster and Ferguson, placed part of the responsibility squarely upon the Roosevelt administration. Stimson, Knox, Marshall, and Stark were all singled out for blame, and Hull, as the nation's leading diplomat, bore especially "grave responsibility for the events leading to the attack." In other ways, however, there was more agreement between the Minority and Majority reports than one would first suspect. The Minority, like the Majority, found that military commanders in Washington had not thoroughly informed the officers in Hawaii and had issued unclear messages. Kimmel and Short, in turn, had failed to have achieved an "effective state of readiness consistent with the warnings being sent them."[20]

For many anti-interventionists, the Minority Report told what had "really" happened at Pearl Harbor. Norman Thomas denied that America had sought peace in the Pacific. Libby accused Roosevelt of waging "provocative economic warfare," and thereby prompting the Japanese to attack. Borchard maintained that Cordell Hull and Stanley K. Hornbeck, Director of the Far Eastern Division of the State Department, desired to punish an overpopulated Japan for spilling over to the Asian continent.

Japan, said the Yale professor, had made every effort to maintain peace. Even Wall Street attorney John Foster Dulles, not rigidly isolationist in 1940 and 1941, found Ferguson's case "unanswerable."[21]

The hearings, far from settling the issue as Democrats had hoped, widened the controversy, and it soon focused on Europe as well as Asia. A wide variety of writers began to strike at Roosevelt's prewar policies and to strike hard: journalists Flynn, George Morgenstern, and William Henry Chamberlin, international lawyer Frederic Sanborn, Rear Admiral Robert A. Theobald, and an assortment of historians, including Charles A. Beard, Charles C. Tansill, and Harry Elmer Barnes.

The journalists began the attack. Early in 1947 George Morgenstern, a *Chicago Tribune* editor who had opposed intervention before America entered the conflict, published *Pearl Harbor: The Story of the Secret War.* In this, the first extended revisionist account, Morgenstern went beyond the Minority Report. The administration, he said, needed war to divert public attention from New Deal failures, and hence it deliberately withheld its knowledge of impending attack from Kimmel and Short. Morgenstern attempted to place the Pearl Harbor controversy in a wider context, one shared by isolationists before the Japanese strike. "There was not a major power," he said, "involved in the mess in Europe or Asia that could come to the United States with clean hands, or represent itself as either a democracy or an exemplar of justice." If the Fascist "slave states" were "abhorrent to decent people," the British Empire "rested upon the exploitation of hundreds of millions of natives," Stalin led a dictatorship "no more exemplary" than Hitler's, and China was "afflicted with a corrupt, devious, and scheming central administration."[22]

In its advertisements, the publisher made a special pitch to servicemen. A reader could learn "why you wound up in a jungle or found yourself unexpectedly on an atoll." Morgenstern's house, Devin-Adair, had specialized for many years in Catholic and Irish topics. Its owner, Devin Adair Garrity, had himself been a strong isolationist before Pearl Harbor. An alumnus of Princeton, Garrity had personally edited several volumes of Irish poetry, and was as much devoted to such causes as natural foods and ecology as he was to revisionism. The book, with its *Chicago Tribune* imprimatur, was praised by isolationists and attacked by interventionists. Beard, Borchard, and the *Christian Century* welcomed the volume. Chodorov concurred with Morgenstern's indictment of American policymakers, using Albert Jay Nock's label *the professional criminal class.* Professor Samuel Flagg Bemis of Yale, however, accused Morgenstern of ignoring the world balance of power and the need for prompt United States action.[23]

Another journalist broadside came with John T. Flynn's *The Roosevelt Myth* (1948). Polemical as only Flynn could be polemical, he accused Roosevelt of finding war a "glorious, magnificent escape from all the insoluble problems of America." The results of the conflict were as sordid as its causes: "Our government," he declared, "put into Stalin's hands the means of seizing a great slab of the continent of Europe, then stood aside while he took it and finally acquiesced in his conquests." Flynn's charges were so incendiary that all major publishers turned the manuscript down, whereupon Flynn allowed Devin-Adair to publish it. To the surprise of all concerned, the book soon occupied the number two slot on the *New York Times* best-seller list.[24]

Of all the revisionist books, Flynn's elicited the stormiest reaction. The liberal journalist Karl Schriftgiesser claimed that Flynn made Hitler look like more of a saint than FDR; columnist Robert S. Allen saw the book as reflecting the "weird gyrations of Flynn's malice." Alf Landon, however, told Flynn that the book made him so angry at Roosevelt that he had to pace the floor awhile, and Colonel McCormick wrote, "We are finally catching up with the conspirators against our country.'[25]

The next major onslaught by a journalist came two years later with William Henry Chamberlin's *America's Second Crusade*. Though condemning Nazi brutality, Chamberlin blamed the British and French for failing to "canalize Hitler's expansion in an eastward direction." He denied that "the conquest of western Europe, much less of overseas territory, was an essential part of Hitler's design." The Nazi war machine, he declared, could well "have bogged down indefinitely in Russia." Continuing his indictment, Chamberlin asserted that the Germans had no plan for invading the hemisphere, criticized America's insistence upon an Open Door in the Pacific, and reiterated the accusation that United States leaders had manipulated the Japanese into war. In the final part of the book, Chamberlin struck at unconditional surrender, the Morgenthau Plan, and the Yalta and Potsdam agreements. "The scenes that took place in Berlin, Vienna, Budapest, and other cities captured by the Red Army," he said, "were probably never equalled in European warfare as orgies of lust and pillage." The author concluded by calling for a worldwide anti-Communist alliance.[26]

As usual, genuine dialogue and debate were lacking, and opinions were confirmed, not challenged. Frank Hanighen and General Wood declared that Chamberlin had justified the stances taken by America Firsters, and Herbert Hoover and Charles A. Lindbergh quietly encouraged the book's sale. The journalist J. M. Minifie, writing in the *Saturday Review of Literature*, charged Chamberlin with "ladling out the same dish" as the Axis propagandists Virgilio Gayda and Joseph Goebbels. The more friendly William L. Neumann, attempting to separate Chamberlin's diagnosis from his remedy, asked, "*Why* in attacking the First and Second Crusades must he himself begin the ballyhoos for the Third Crusade?"[27]

As in the case of Morgenstern and Flynn, old isolationists had a hand in the publication as well as the text. Chamberlin's book was published by the firm of Henry Regnery, a man who probably came to his revisionism by way of his father. He was the son of William H. Regnery, a prominent Chicago manufacturer of window shades and the greatest individual contributor to the America First Committee and later the National Council for the Prevention of War. Henry was educated at the Massachusetts Institute of Technology, the University of Bonn, and Harvard. Sympathetic to America First in 1941, Regnery soon voiced the fear that the country's spirit of liberty was being sacrificed for "the American Empire, or the American Century." He was a particularly outspoken critic of the United States occupation of Germany and began his publishing career with a pamphlet by an exiled German economist, Karl Brandt, entitled "Germany is Our Problem." The seal of the company, the Roman gate at Porta Nigra in the family's ancestral city of Trier, symbolized the firm's mission: to withstand the advent of new collectivist "barbarians" and thereby assure the survival of the West.[28]

The next popular revisionist account, Frederic R. Sanborn's *Design for War: A Study of Secret Power Politics, 1937–1941* (1951), was almost redundant, for it contained little not covered by earlier revisionists. A New York attorney with a Columbia doctorate in international law and diplomacy, Sanborn covered familiar ground, ending his work with a plea for open diplomacy. With expected reactions taking place, it would take more thorough arguments to refine the debate.[29]

Such sophisticated challenges were, in fact, already in the mill, and professional historians were offering a far more scholarly revisionism. Critics could easily ignore an editorial writer from an ultra-conservative newspaper; it was far more difficult to dismiss one of the intellectual godfathers of American liberalism. This, of course, was Charles Austin Beard, whose two revisionist volumes virtually amounted to a lawyer's brief against the Roosevelt administration. A strong supporter of the early New Deal, with its stress upon centralized planning, Beard had long advocated economic self-sufficiency. The alternative, he believed, spelled ruin. Once the United States began to supply belligerents with major war materials, it so tied its economy to warring states that it would evenually be forced into conflict itself. Roosevelt's drift away from centralized planning worried Beard. Rather than take such radical and necessary measures as nationalizing the banks, Roosevelt—predicted Beard in 1935—would seek to escape from continued depression by plunging the country into war in the Pacific. The advent of World War II in Europe found Beard a staunch isolationist: in 1940 he endorsed America First; in 1941 he testified before the Senate Foreign Relations Committee against lend-lease.[30]

After the United States entered the war, Beard attempted to prove his forecast of 1935. In 1944 George H. E. Smith, a researcher for the Republican National Committee, told Beard that the Japanese code had been broken. Smith had learned this fact from Admiral Kimmel and Senator Taft. Beard hoped to write this material for *Life* magazine, and preliminary arrangements were made, but at the last minute editor Henry R. Luce decided against the story. Edwin M. Borchard then told Eugene Davidson, editor of Yale University Press, about Beard's plans to write a comprehensive revisionist account of America's entry into World War II. Davidson, who had headed an informal isolationist group among the Yale faculty before Pearl Harbor, was able to clear the project with Yale president Charles Seymour and the press's board of directors within twenty-four hours.[31]

The first volume, entitled *American Foreign Policy in the Making* and published in 1946, disputed claims that the American people and the Senate were fundamentally to blame for the nation's isolationism. The President, said Beard, had hewed closely to the anti-interventionist line throughout the 1930s, and had led the public to believe as late as 1940 that he strongly opposed direct involvement. Reviews of the book were mixed, with some administration defenders finding the book's purposes "confusing."[32]

The second of Beard's books, *President Roosevelt and the Coming of the War* (1948), left no room for doubt. Accusing the President of calculated duplicity, the work examined such issues as the *Greer* incident, the debate over convoys, and the abortive negotiations with Japan. The high cost went beyond the lives of the personnel stationed at Pearl Harbor; the whole principle of an American Republic had been placed in jeopardy. Taking on commentators who defended Rooseveltian duplicity on grounds of national interest, Beard found the war leaving the country more endangered than ever. The Four Freedoms and the Atlantic Charter had been betrayed; Russia—among the most ruthless of military empires—possessed more power than Germany; and the United States was converted into "a kind of armed camp for defense."[33]

The book ended on a pessimistic note, for Beard was clearly apprehensive about the future. Contrary to the manifesto of the Truman Doctrine, America, said the historian, could not support a host of "poverty-stricken, feeble, and instable governments" surrounding the Soviet sphere. The more the United States attempted to influence events beyond its borders, the more it faced "terrible defeat" in Europe or Asia. Beard again stressed an old theme: United States attempts to secure foreign markets would invariably collide with "the controlled or semicontrolled economies of foreign nations," thereby sowing the "seeds of discord at home and abroad." Most dangerous of all, the President's new authority would give him "limitless authority publicly to misrepresent and secretly to control foreign policy, foreign affairs, and the war power."[34]

Beginning in 1947 Harry Elmer Barnes formally entered the fray, adding a capacity for invective and vitriol unmatched in scholarly writing. Half Savanarola and half Diderot, the Columbia-trained Barnes had written prolifically in the areas of history, social thought, and criminology. In his many works he showed himself to be "ye compleat reformer." Barnes opposed prohibition and censorship, assailed capital punishment, and demanded prison and court reform, more liberalized divorce laws, abolition of sexual taboos, and far greater equality for women and blacks. Never a partisan of free-market economic theories, Barnes maintained a lifetime allegiance to Sweden's "Middle Way," an economy that had modified its capitalism with large doses of state ownership and cooperatives. Like Beard's, his isolationism was rooted in his liberalism: an America fighting to preserve the empires of Britain and France would sacrifice all opportunities to construct an egalitarian democracy at home. Unlike many isolationists, Barnes was not vehemently anti-Soviet. In 1945, for example, he claimed that Soviet domination of Eastern Europe was far preferable to continued chaos in the Balkans.[35]

The author of a widely acclaimed revisionist work, *The Genesis of the World War* (1926), Barnes firmly believed that World War II, like its predecessor, was the product of Allied machinations. He had tried for several years to secure financial backing for a revisionist history of World War II. In 1947 he finally obtained it from a conservative lumber merchant and America First backer, John W. Blodgett, Jr., and soon Barnes was serving as a virtual clearing-house for subsequent revisionist projects.[36]

In a pamphlet entitled "The Struggle against Historical Blackout," Barnes attempted to rebut Walter Millis's pro-Administration account *This is Pearl!* (1947). He accused Millis, a staff writer for the interventionist *New York Herald-Tribune*, of having endorsed Nazi unification of central Europe in 1937 and of failing to recognize legitimate Japanese needs in Asia. By 1952 "The Struggle" had undergone nine printings, with each edition containing much new material. Critics of revisionism, said Barnes, foreshadowed the thought-control patterns described in George Orwell's futuristic novel *1984*. These intellectuals, unable to confront the logic of a Beard or comprehend the indignation of a Flynn, ignored unwelcome facts, offered *ad hominem* arguments by branding revisionists as unreconstructed isolationists, and rationalized whatever Rooseveltian duplicity they discovered.[37]

In 1952 perhaps the most extreme revisionist account of all was published. This was Charles Callan Tansill's *Back Door to War*. A native of Texas and a descendant of a Confederate general, Tansill had written voluminously in the field of American diplomatic history and served on the faculty of Georgetown University. While technical adviser to the Senate Foreign Relations Committee during the League controversy of 1919, Tansill prepared a study that became the seed of *America Goes to War* (1938), a revisionist work of World War I.[38]

Tansill was never one to shun controversy. In 1947 he told a group of Confederate Dames—gathered in Statuary Hall in the Capitol to celebrate the 193rd birthday of Jefferson Davis—that Lincoln was a "do-nothing" soldier, "invincible in peace and invisible in war." The Civil War President was "the Sphinx of Springfield," a man who played "fast and loose" with the South by tricking it into bombarding Fort Sumter, and hence triggering the War Between the States. Even Congressman Rankin, who hailed from Tupelo, Mississippi, claimed that the professor had gone "too far." An ardent conservative and segregationist, Tansill frequently combined his attacks on New Deal foreign and domestic policy. To Tansill, Benedict Arnold was more patriotic than the Roosevelt administration. In 1941 Tansill served as a national sponsor of the No Foreign War Committee.[39]

Certainly no previous revisionist work was so ambitious in scope, and given the author's idiosyncrasies, Tansill's book began provocatively. The first sentence read, "The main objective in American foreign policy since 1900 has been the preservation of the British Empire." The Open Door notes—the product of English machinations—were only the first example of American blundering, for the United States erred many times over by continuing to resist Japanese expansion. From William Howard Taft's fostering of American investments in North China to the drafting of the Stimson Doctrine, the United States was continually blocking the only Far Eastern power that could contain Asian Communism.

Equally outspoken in his treatment of Europe, Tansill asserted that American intervention in World War I had helped shatter "the old balance of power and sowed the seeds of inevitable future conflict." Roosevelt's torpedoing of the London Economic Conference of 1933 simply served as the capstone of American irresponsibility. While no defender of Nazism, Tansill denied that Hitler wanted war with the Poles and claimed that the *Führer* had offered Poland "the role of chief satellite in the Nazi orbit." The Georgetown historian said that Britain's irresponsible guarantee to Poland, an event that triggered the war, had originated with American policymakers. "Nowadays," wrote Tansill, "it seems evident that the real Mad Hatter was Franklin D. Roosevelt who pressed Chamberlain to give promises to the Poles when there was no possibility of fulfilling them." The final section of the book recapitulated the theme, by now driven home by the revisionists, that Roosevelt had resisted accommodation with the Japanese in order to have his "back door to war."[40]

The most ambitious effort of all came with Barnes's anthology, *Perpetual War for Perpetual Peace* (1953), a project that—like the Tansill book—was financed by Blodgett. The title came from a phrase coined by Beard, who had once told Barnes that the term offered the best description of American policy. As in the case of Devin-Adair and Regnery, the publishing house, the Caxton Press of Caldwell, Idaho, was owned by an isolationist. James H. Gipson, a onetime Bull-Mooser who later fought New Deal "bureaucracy," had openly called for a negotiated peace in 1941. Even after the United States had entered World War II, Gipson claimed that the conflict would destroy all civilization.[41]

There was little doubt as to the book's purpose. In his preface, Barnes expressed the hope that the volume would convert Americans to "a sane foreign policy, based on continentalism, national interest, ideological coexistence, international urbanity, and rational co-operation in world affairs." The only isolationism the contributors advocated, he said, was "isolationism from global meddling." In a postscript, Barnes warned against "a system which transforms every border war into a potential world war" and that makes "war scares and armament hysteria the basis of domestic political strategy and economic 'prosperity.' "[42]

The arguments of the authors were familiar, and so was the drama: Barnes on the "historical blackout," Tansill on United States relations in Europe and Asia, Sanborn on Roosevelt's Atlantic policy from 1937 to 1941, Neumann on America's policy in the Pacific, Morgenstern on events leading to Pearl Harbor, and Chamberlin on the fatal consequences of World War II. There were two new contributors: Percy L. Greaves, Jr., chief researcher for the Republican members of the joint investigating committee of 1945, who offered an account of the varied Pearl Harbor investigations; and George A. Lundberg, past president of the American

Sociological Society, who supported diplomat George F. Kennan and political scientist Hans J. Morgenthau on the need to develop a realistic concept of "national interest."

Some scholars and publicists endorsed revisionist historians with the same fervor as they had the journalists. John Chamberlain, noting Beard's conclusions with approval, commented that "under the Rooseveltian theory of statecraft, the Republic must soon become a thing of the past." Political scientist Denna F. Fleming of Vanderbilt, a bit more cautious, accused Barnes's anthology of overlooking threats from the Axis, but asserted that "the revisionist case deserves to be heard, and we can learn something from this statement of it."[43]

The great majority of reviewers, however, remained unreservedly hostile, and a fierce counterattack was soon forthcoming. Professor Samuel Eliot Morison, who still used such wartime slang as *Jap*, accused Beard of remaining culturally isolated in his Connecticut farm. "You get more back talk even from freshmen than from milch cows," Morison wrote. He found Beard tacitly presenting a pro-Axis picture; reading such revisionism, Morison said, would lead one to think that "a dim figure named Hitler was engaged in a limited sort of war to redress the lost balance of Versailles," and that Japan was "a virtuous nation pursuing its legitimate interests in Asia." The atmosphere of 1940, the Harvard historian continued, compelled Roosevelt "to do good by stealth." Historian Mason Wade opposed granting Beard access to official papers. "A polemicist," said Wade, "should not enjoy the privileges of a historian." Arthur M. Schlesinger, Jr., claimed that Beard had done a useful job in bringing to light Roosevelt's contradictions, but criticized him for failing to suggest viable alternatives. The reproach from fellow reformers was unusually severe: writer Louis Mumford resigned from the National Institute of Arts and Letters when that body awarded a gold medal to the "isolationist" Beard.[44]

Surprisingly, Tansill's book elicited some professional reactions that were a bit more friendly. Julius Pratt of the University of Buffalo, while dissenting from most of Tansill's conclusions, found *Back Door to War* "a work of great learning." In fact, said Pratt, America's adherence to the Open Door policy in 1941 "may not have been wise." Historian C. C. Griffin, though critical of Tansill's invective and innuendo, commented that the United States had long underestimated Russia's role in the Far East. Some Tansill defenders were similarly qualified in their endorsements. Neumann regretted that "too many Tansillisms" would prevent a fair hearing. Richard N. Current of the University of Illinois found most of Tansill's "detailed and fully documented study . . . pretty well justified by the facts," but insisted that Pearl Harbor had resulted from "bungling and blundering." The attack, claimed Current, was not produced by the "deliberate calculation" that Tansill implied.[45]

Interventionists were not simply content to review revisionists; they wrote their own defense of Roosevelt's diplomacy. The memoirs of Cordell Hull and Henry Stimson were soon published, as was Robert E. Sherwood's *Roosevelt and Hopkins* (1948). Retired diplomat Herbert Feis wrote *The Road to Pearl Harbor* (1950), an endorsement of the President's Pacific policy. Here the former State Department adviser denied that the administration had lost any real chance for peace. The United States, Feis claimed, did not threaten Japan's independence; it only insisted that Japan disgorge its ill-gotten gains.[46]

Although such partisans made a spirited defense, Basil Rauch of Barnard College contributed an account possessing less restraint. The study, entitled *Roosevelt from Munich to Pearl Harbor* (1950), attempted to refute Beard's claims point by point. Yet, because of its polemical overkill, it remained unconvincing to all but the converted. Rauch, for example, claimed that the Newfoundland Conference of August 1941 was held primarily to draft the Atlantic Charter, not to discuss the nature of American participation in the Allied struggle. He denied that Roosevelt had deceived the American people and accused isolationists of ignoring economic and political ties with the rest of the world. "If [the President's vision] is ever realized," Rauch concluded, "wherever men gather to honor the architect of their happiness, they will gratefully remember the work of Franklin Delano Roosevelt."[47]

The interventionists soon found more able defenders. The Council on Foreign Relations received funds from the Rockefeller and Sloan Foundations to sponsor a two-volume study of Roosevelt's diplomacy. William L. Langer, a Harvard diplomatic historian, and S. Everett Gleason, executive secretary of the National Security Council, offered *The Challenge to Isolation, 1937–1940* (1952) and *The Undeclared War, 1940–1941* (1953). Presenting an impressive array of sources, the volumes thoroughly presented the administration's position. The authors did admit that the President had been less than candid with the public, but claimed that, if anything, his leadership was not forceful enough. Although the authors, both of whom had held prestigious government posts during World War II, received private access to materials, they denied that the volumes were "court history." "In no sense," they declared, were they "an official or even a semi-official account."[48]

The revisionists were not so sure. Neumann noted that the Rockefeller Foundation's Annual Report for 1946 clearly specified that "the debunking journalistic campaign following World War I should not be repeated." Because of Langer's wartime intelligence service, his history resembled that of a Civil War scholar of the Gilded Age who had either served with Lincoln or been an active Copperhead. Barnes personally told Langer that he considered Roosevelt's foreign policy "the greatest public crime in human history" (an area that he admitted covered "a lot of ground") and accused the Harvard historian of betraying the tradition of Von Ranke; Langer, he said, was following "in the footsteps of Sallust, Thuanus and Vandal."[49]

The revisionists were far more diverse than is generally realized. For example, Beard, Barnes, and Neumann saw an increasing need to socialize large segments of the economy, whereas Tansill, Morgenstern, Flynn, and (to a lesser degree) Chamberlin believed that the New Deal had gone too far on "the road ahead" to collectivization. When Neumann claimed that some printed views of Gipson made the Idaho publisher sound "like a wild man," Barnes responded that "those of us who have some sanity on domestic matters (and on Korea and China) have a heavy cross to bear in those with whom we must work on this war guilt matter. But beggars cannot be choosers."[50]

Even in foreign policy—although all but Sanborn had actively fought Roosevelt's interventionism in 1941—there were major differences. While the revisionists certainly differed among themselves as to the degree of support that they would give the military, only Neumann was a pacifist. There was the matter of focus as well. Neumann and Tansill insisted upon tracing the Pacific crisis to McKinley and the Open Door notes; other revisionists were content to take a much shorter view. (Beard, of course, had devoted much of his past writing to the Open Door policy.) Beard, Neumann, and Barnes, men who were by no means pro-Soviet, harbored far greater suspicions of Cold War rhetoric than did Chamberlin or Tansill. In fact, both Barnes and Neumann saw the United States as bearing heavy responsibility for the Cold War. Neumann wrote in 1952 that "the whole Communist bogey, on which much of the Truman program is based, is at least 50% a creation of our government." Barnes believed that "Truman began his cold war as an act of the most desperate and momentary political expediency at a low ebb of his political popularity." Chamberlin, however, sought "world-wide cooperation of anti-Communist nations" in order to contain Soviet power.[51]

The World War II revisionists also differed in their attitudes toward Nazi Germany. Barnes was more conciliatory toward some of Hitler's activity than was either Tansill or Chamberlin. Though he called Hitler "an unbalanced neurotic," he went on to comment that all of his moves (except the Spanish Civil War) down to the occupation of Czechoslovakia "had some justification as rectifying Versailles." Hitler's demands in 1939, he said, were "the most reasonable of all." Tansill, on the other hand, had little use for the leaders of Poland and Czechoslovakia, but even less for Hitler. The German leader, claimed the Georgetown historian, was thoroughly dishonest, had the ethos of a bully, and operated from aggressive designs.[52]

Revisionists placed different emphases upon Roosevelt's role in the Pearl Harbor attack. Neumann held the administration guilty only of irresponsible diplomacy and blundering. But had Roosevelt and Stimson never been born, "other eastern, power-hungry Anglophiles would have risen in their stead to take us into World War II."[53] Most revisionists, however, perceived more sinister and personal schemes at work. As in the case of much writing about World War I, the revisionism of the Second World War often centered on hidden and conspiratorial forces. World War I revisionism stressed predatory munition makers, pro-British diplomats, and an American capitalist system dependent upon war prosperity for survival. That of World War II indicted the leaders of the Roosevelt government and the economic failings of the New Deal. In the opinion of the latter group, Roosevelt was far more responsible in 1941 than Wilson had been in 1917.

The drawbacks of World War II revisionism were obvious. Only by the most tortured reasoning could one "prove" that Roosevelt, or any of his associates, had direct foreknowledge of the Pearl Harbor attack or had deliberately permitted over two thousand men to die. Revisionists made little allowance for human frailties, usually preferring to trace an unfolding "plot." Morgenstern, for example, accused the administration of intentionally withholding vital information from the Pearl Harbor commanders. Some revisionists argued by innuendo. Tansill, for instance, contrasted a horseback ride taken by General Marshall on the morning of Pearl Harbor to Paul Revere's "famous ride to warn his countrymen of the enemy's approach and thus save American lives." Revisionists seldom commented on possible Axis threats to the balance of power in Europe and Asia, a point needing rigorous analysis, and stressed instead the fact that captured Axis archives contained no plans to invade the hemisphere. They occasionally cited unreliable witnesses, such as Commander Kramer, and could also, as in the case of Stimson's supposed desire to "maneuver" the Japanese into "firing the first shot," fail to interpret a document correctly.[54]

A deeper critique may be in order. In a desire to expose the personal guilt of Roosevelt and his advisers, the revisionists were forced to focus upon the activities of the historical actors. The obsession with motives often led to a neglect of the social context within which those actors were forced to operate. Both revisionists and "court historians" had their favorite villains and heroes: neither group investigated the economic and ideological background of decision-making.

Given their obvious limitations, many of the hard questions raised by revisionists went unanswered. Most professors of American history paid little attention to their arguments or their assumptions. Revisionist works would find their way into graduate seminars stressing historiography and into "problem" anthologies giving undergraduates a variety of interpretations on a given topic. Revisionist claims were not, however, usually found in textbooks or other vehicles of the "conventional wisdom." Only the old isolationists gave such doctrines an intellectual home. The fact that so many historians were extremely anxious to defend all of Roosevelt's activities made it even harder for revisionists to receive a fair hearing.

Amid the attacks made upon the revisionist "devil theory," legitimate and telling points were often neglected. Revisionists correctly stressed the constitutional limits of presidential war-making power, and they pointed out conscious and calculated deception by the nation's highest leadership. Revisionists were not afraid to say the obvious: the Roberts Report had involved an obvious "cover-up" and the Majority Congressional Report did not apply the same criteria to Washington leaders that it did to Hawaiian commanders. They assailed with accuracy the abdication on the part of some historians of professional responsibilities in order to defend major prewar actions of their "Commander-in-Chief." The precedent of administration duplicity, they argued, was bound to backfire on interventionist liberals when they least expected it. Furthermore, revisionists pointed to dangerous illusions concerning the Open Door and the viability of Nationalist China. No self-respecting state, revisionists argued, could accede to such American demands as Japanese evacuation of the Asian mainland.

Only with the advent of a newer generation of historians did such significant points begin to find appreciation. Beginning with the reception given to books by Rear Admiral Robert A. Theobald and Professor Richard N. Current, commentators began to be more dispassionate. In 1958 the American Historical Association bestowed its coveted Albert J. Beveridge Award on a work offering trenchant criticism of Hull's Pacific diplomacy, and by 1973 a prominent historian could write (with possible exaggeration) that the majority of his colleagues probably viewed the war with Japan as one that could have been avoided.[55]

For the time being, revisionists had to rest content with supplying needed ammunition to the isolationist arsenal. They believed that Truman's crusades, like Roosevelt's, were rooted in secret and veiled decisions. If executed, such policies would most certainly result in further betrayal of the national interest. Frank Chodorov used the advent of Morgenstern's book to warn that Truman might well be planning a new Pearl Harbor. Beard, at the end of his second volume, warned against expending the nation's "blood and treasure" to contain "the gigantic and aggressive Slavic Empire."[56] Among the revisionists, only Chamberlin became an ardent and consistent interventionist. Of all the veteran isolationists, the revisionists, as a group, probably remained the most true to the old faith.

## NOTES

1. For a good definition of revisionism, see Raymond G. O'Connor, *Diplomacy for Victory*, p. 130.

2. Petition noted in McCoy, *Landon of Kansas*, p. 472; H. Hoover to W. R. Castle, September 4, 1941, Box 14, Castle Papers; Wheeler, *New York Times*, October 19, 1941, p. 10.

3. For both Wood and Lindbergh, see entry of December 8, 1941, in *Lindbergh Journals*, pp. 560–61; H. Hoover to W. R. Castle, December 8, 1941, Box 14, Castle Papers; Vandenberg, diary, December 8, 1941, *Private Papers*, pp. 17–18. An example of Lindbergh's warning concerning Asian powers may be found in C. A. Lindbergh to J. T. Flynn, January 6, 1942, Box 18, Flynn Papers.

4. Tobey, *CR*, December 11, 1941, pp. 9656–60; Taft, address to the Executive Club of Chicago, "The United States at War," December 26, 1941, *CR*, p. A5710–11; Jeanette Rankin, *CR*, December 8, 1942, pp. A4439–41; Clark, *CR*, December 7, 1943, pp. 10347–50; Short, *CR*, December 6, 1943, pp. 10319–21; Fish, *CR*, June 5, 1944, p. 5342. For Clare Boothe Luce, see *Time* 44 (November 20, 1944): 23 and *CR*, September 5, 1945, pp. A3759–60.

5. The committee was composed by Major General Frank R. McCoy, Brigadier General Joseph T. McNarney, Admiral J. M. Reeves, and Admiral W. H. Standley. Standley later claimed that "from the beginning of our investigation, I held firm belief that the real responsibility for the disaster at Pearl Harbor was lodged thousands

of miles from the Territory of Hawaii." See Standley's comment on Roberts Commission in Husband E. Kimmel, *Admiral Kimmel's Story* (Chicago: Regnery, 1955), pp. 136–37. If so, he must have been conspicuously silent, for Roosevelt seen appointed him Ambassador to Russia.

6. Vandenberg in Darilek, "Loyal Opposition," pp. 208–9; Emanuel Celler, *CR*, June 5, 1944, p. 5348.

7. Robert A. Divine, *Presidential Elections*, 1:147.

8. The ablest and most thorough exposition of Flynn's general ideology is found in the dissertation by Richard C. Frey, Jr. For his activities immediately before Pearl Harbor, see Michele Flynn Stenehjem, *An American First: John T. Flynn and the America First Committee* (New Rochelle, N.Y.: Arlington House, 1976). His Cold War activities are covered in Radosh, *Prophets on the Right*, pp. 231–73.

9. John T. Flynn, "The Truth about Pearl Harbor," pamphlet (New York: published by the author, 1944); "J'Accuse, 1944" (editorial) *Chicago Tribune*, October 23, 1944.

10. Interview with William L. Neumann, July 19, 1971; William L. Neumann, "The Genesis of Pearl Harbor," pamphlet (Philadelphia: Pacifist Research Bureau, 1945). For the sources from which Neumann drew his study, see Joseph C. Grew, *Ten Years in Japan* (New York: Simon and Schuster, 1944); Department of State, *Peace and War: United States Foreign Policy, 1931–1941* (Washington, D.C.: U.S. Government Printing Office, 1943).

11. John T. Flynn, "The Final Secret of Pearl Harbor," pamphlet (New York: published by the author, 1945); Trohan, *Political Animals*, pp. 167–68.

12. For attacks on Neumann, see Arthur Ekirch, Jr., "William L. Neumann: A Personal Recollection and Appreciation," paper delivered at the joint session of the Conference on Peace Research in History and the Organization of American Historians, Washington, D.C., April 6, 1972, p. 1. For endorsements of Neumann, see H. E. Barnes to W. L. Neumann, April 28, 1945, and August 31, 1945, and C. A. Beard to W. L. Neumann, September 15, 1945, the Papers of William L. Neumann, University of Wyoming. For Barnes on the Open Door, see H. E. Barnes to W. L. Neumann, September 12, 1946, Neumann Papers. For "T.R.B.," see *New Republic* 113 (September 24, 1945): 373.

13. The conclusions of the Army Pearl Harbor Board and the Navy Court of Inquiry are found in Joint Committee on the Investigation of the Pearl Harbor Attack, Part 39, *Pearl Harbor Attack* (Washington, D.C.: U.S. Government Printing Office, 1946), pp. 1–386.

14. Homer Ferguson, *CR*, November 21, 1944, p. 8224; John Chamberlain, "The Man Who Pushed Pearl Harbor," *Life* 20 (April 1, 1946): 84–97. A prewar isolationist, Forrest Harness (Rep.-Ind.), had introduced a similar resolution in the House. See *CR*, September 18, 1944, p. 7881.

15. For the House debate, see *CR*, September 11, 1945, pp. 8495–510; September 6, 1945, pp. 8389–90; October 25, 1945, pp. 10046–50. Committee membership included Ferguson as well as such fellow-Republicans as Congressman Bertrand W. Gearhart of California and Frank B. Keefe of Wisconsin, and Senator Owen Brewster of Maine. Democrats included Senators Barkley, Walter George of Georgia, and Scott Lucas of Illinois, as well as Congressmen J. Bayard Clark of North Carolina and John W. Murphy of Pennsylvania.

16. For the Senate debate, see *CR*, November 6, 1945, pp. 10431–39; Lucas quotation, *CR*, p. 10432.

17. For the House debate, see *CR*, November 6, 1945, pp. 10444–50, and November 14, 1945, pp. 10684–88. For Short quotation, see *CR*, p. 10446.

18. "The Truth at Last" (editorial), *Chicago Tribune*, November 9, 1945; *Closer-Ups* 1 (February 11, 1946): 3.

Thomas D. Parrish, "How Henry Regnery Got That Way," *Reporter* 12 (April 7, 1955): 41–44; "Fifteen Years of Publishing: Henry Regnery Company," *Human Events* 20 (February 23, 1963): 151; and "Henry Regnery: A Conservative Publisher in a Liberal World," leaflet (LaSalle, Ill.: Open Court, 1972).

19. For the Majority Report, see *The Report of the Joint Committee on the Investigation of the Pearl Harbor Attack* (Washington, D.C.: U.S. Government Printing Office, 1946), pp. 253–56; additional remarks of Mr. Keefe, *Report of the Joint Committee,* pp. 266 A-W.

20. For the Minority Report, see *Report of the Joint Committee,* pp. 495–573.

21. Thomas, "Pearl Harbor Reports," *Socialist Call* 13 (August 5, 1946): 8; Libby, *Peace Action* 12 (March 1946): 2; E. M. Borchard to G. H. E. Smith, November 24, 1945, copy in Taft Papers, Box 657.

22. George Morgenstern, *Pearl Harbor: The Story of the Secret War* (New York: Devin-Adair, 1947), pp. 4, 7. Morgenstern's comment on domestic policy is derived from Albert Jay Nock, *Memoirs of a Superfluous Man* (New York: Harper, 1943). See Morgenstern, p. 283. In 1941 Morgenstern had attacked the "Wall Street chaps" who were "leading the war march." *Washington Times-Herald,* November 6, 1941.

23. Such advertising was noted by Walter Millis in *New York Herald-Tribune Book Review,* February 9, 1947, p. 4. For a sketch of Devin Adair Garrity, see Cleveland Amory, "Trade Winds," *Saturday Review of Literature,* 37 (September 29, 1954): 6–8. Garrity had been a member of the College Committee for Defense First, a group that later united with the America First Committee. CCDF release, August 11, 1941, Box 1, AFC Papers. For praise, see C. A. Beard to H. E. Barnes, January 16, 1948, the Papers of Harry Elmer Barnes, University of Wyoming; Borchard, *American Journal of International Law* 41 (April 1947): 500–501; *Christian Century* 64 (April 23, 1947): 528; Chodorov, "The Professional Criminal Class," *analysis* 3 (February 1947): 3. For criticism, see Samuel Flagg Bemis, "First Gun of a Revisionist Historiography for the Second World War," *Journal of Modern History* 19 (March 1947): 55–59.

24. Quotations may be found in John T. Flynn, *The Roosevelt Myth* (New York: Devin-Adair, 1948), pp. 293, 395. For the story of the book's publication, see Frey, "John T. Flynn," pp. 292–93.

25. Karl Schriftgiesser, *New York Times Book Review,* September 5, 1948, p. 3; Robert S. Allen, "Hymn of Hate," *Saturday Review of Literature* 31 (September 4, 1948): 13; A. Landon to J. T. Flynn, October 28, 1948, R. R. McCormick to J. T. Flynn, August 31, 1948, Box 8, Flynn Papers.

26. Chamberlin on the European War, *America's Second Crusade* (Chicago: Regnery, 1950), pp. 49–51; on United States diplomacy before Pearl Harbor, pp. 136, 157–58, 168–75; on Soviet looting, p. 323; on an anti-Soviet alliance, p. 354.

27. R. E. Wood to C. A. Lindbergh, October 30, 1950, Box 3, Wood Papers; Hanighen, "Not Merely Gossip," *Human Events* 7 (October 11, 1950); Hoover noted in H. Regnery to J. T. Flynn, May 2, 1950, Box 19, Flynn Papers; C. A. Lindbergh to R. E. Wood, November 2, 1950, Box 3, Wood Papers; review by J. M. Minifie, *Saturday Review of Literature* 33 (November 18, 1950): 20; W. L. Neumann to H. E. Barnes, May 29, 1950, Neumann Papers (emphasis Neumann's).

28. For sympathy to America First, see Henry Regnery to the author, February 9, 1970. For references to an American empire, see Henry Regnery, "The Dangers of Victory," *Progressive* 8 (October 16, 1944): 3. The firm was incorporated in March 1948. In 1953 most of the stock remained in the hands of the Regnery company, although the family of William F. Buckley, Jr. owned slightly less than a fifth of the shares. Investors included such isolationist veterans as General Robert E. Wood and Edwin Webster, senior partner of Kidder Peabody investment house and a member of the national committee of America First. Brief accounts of Regnery are found in

29. Frederic R. Sanborn, *Design for War: A Study of Secret Power Politics, 1937–1941* (New York: Devin-Adair, 1951). Tribute was offered by William Henry Chamberlin, *Chicago Tribune Book Review*, February 18, 1951, and Walter Trohan, *Human Events* 8 (February 28, 1951). Bemis dissented from Sanborn's argument, reaffirming that America went reluctantly into war in order to defend itself from Axis conquest. *New York Times Book Review*, February 18, 1951, p. 3.

30. For Beard's belief in a planned economy, see Richard Hofstadter, *The Progressive Historians: Turner, Beard, Parrington* (New York: Knopf, 1968), pp. 322–34. For his endorsement of America First and opposition to lend-lease, see *New York Times*, September 9, 1940, p. 7, February 5, 1941, p. 10. A fresh defense of Beard's position is found in Radosh, *Prophets on the Right*, pp. 17–65, and a fresh analysis in Thomas C. Kennedy, *Charles A. Beard and American Foreign Policy* (Gainsville: University of Florida, 1975), pp. 78–167.

31. For Luce's initial interest, see C. A. Beard to O. G. Villard, October 20, 1944, Villard Papers; letter to author from Mrs. Alfred Vagts, September 28, 1974. For publication by Yale University Press, see interview with Eugene Davidson, Chicago, June 29, 1974.

32. Charles A. Beard, *American Foreign Policy in the Making, 1932–1940: A Study in Responsibilities* (New Haven, Conn.: Yale University Press, 1946). For the arguments that Beard was attacking, see Claude Pepper, *CR*, January 15, 1945, pp. 256–57; Forrest Davis and Ernest K. Lindley, *How War Came: An American White Paper* (New York: Macmillan, 1942), pp. 316–17; and Walter Johnson, *The Battle Against Isolation* (Chicago: University of Chicago Press, 1944), pp. 10–30. Examples of friendly reviews include Louis Martin Sears, *American Historical Review* 52 (April 1947): 532–33; Frank Chodorov, *analysis* 3 (February 1947): 3; and the *New Yorker* 22 (August 24, 1946): 64. Hostile reviews include Thomas K. Finletter, *Saturday Review of Literature* 29 (August 17, 1946): 9; Denna Fleming, *Annals of the American Academy of Political and Social Science* 249 (January 1947): 186–87. For a contemporary defense of Roosevelt's duplicity, see Thomas A. Bailey, *Man on the Street*, pp. 12–13. Here Bailey declared that "because the masses are notoriously shortsighted, and generally cannot see danger until it is at their throats, our statesmen are forced to deceive them into an awareness of their long-run interests."

33. Charles A. Beard, *President Roosevelt and the Coming of the War, 1941: A Study in Appearances and Realities* (New Haven, Conn.: Yale University Press, 1948), pp. 576–78.

34. Ibid., pp. 580, 590–98.

35. Justus D. Doenecke, "Harry Elmer Barnes," *Wisconsin Magazine of History* 56 (Summer 1973): 311–23; Barnes, "The Wreck of the Atlantic Charter," *Progressive* 9 (June 11, 1945): 5, 11.

36. Barnes's initial efforts are noted in C. A. Lindbergh to R. E. Wood, June 4, 1946, Box 3, Wood Papers; Charles Callan Tansill to H. E. Barnes, April 20, 1943, Barnes Papers. Barnes as clearing-house is noted in Henry M. Adams, "World War II Revisionist," in Arthur Goddard, ed., *Harry Elmer Barnes: Learned Crusader* (Colorado Springs, Colo.: Ralph Myles, 1968), pp. 299–300.

37. For Barnes and Millis, see Harry Elmer Barnes, "The Struggle against Historical Blackout," pamphlet (n.p.: privately printed, 1947); Walter Millis, *This is Pearl!: The United States and Japan—1941* (New York: Morrow, 1947). The Millis reference concerning central Europe is found in his *Viewed Without Alarm: Europe Today* (Boston: Houghton Mifflin, 1937), p. 53.

38. For Tansill's life, see Honhart, "Charles Callan Tansill," and Louis Martin Sears, "Historical Revisionism Following the Two World Wars," in George L. Anderson, ed., *Issues and Conflicts: Studies in Twentieth Century American Diplomacy* (Lawrence: University of Kansas Press, 1959), pp. 127–46.

39. For Tansill's Statuary Hall speech, see *Time* 49 (June 16, 1947): 29. For Tansill on New Dealers, see C. C. Tansill to H. E. Barnes, April 4, 1947, Barnes Papers. For Tansill's role in the No Foreign War Committee, see listing of national sponsors, April 10, 1941, the Papers of Verne Marshall, Box 7, Hoover Presidential Library. The NCPW, more strident than America First, is described in Justus D. Doenecke, "Verne Marshall's Leadership of the No Foreign War Committee," *Annals of Iowa* 41 (Winter 1973): 1153–72.

40. On preserving the British Empire and the Open Door notes, see Charles Callan Tansill, *Back Door to War: The Roosevelt Foreign Policy, 1933–1941* (Chicago: Regnery, 1952), p. 3; on American entry into World War I, p. 9; on the London Economic Conference, pp. 43–44; on Hitler and Poland, p. 510; on Roosevelt and Poland, pp. 554–55.

41. James H. Gipson in *CR*, February 10, 1941, p. A582; J. H. Gipson to O. G. Villard, April 6, 1942, Villard Papers. For a summary of Gipson's career, see Lawrence Henry Gipson, "James Herrick Gipson, RIP," *National Review* 17 (June 15, 1965): 508; obituary, *Caldwell Tribune*, February 20, 1965; Paul E. Johnston, "Caxton Printers, Ltd., Regional Publishers," *Pacific Northwest Quarterly* 48 (1957): 100–105.

42. Harry Elmer Barnes, ed., *Perpetual War for Perpetual Peace: A Critical Examination of the Foreign Policy of Franklin Delano Roosevelt and its Aftermath* (Caldwell, Idaho: Caxton, 1953), pp. viii, x, 659.

43. Chamberlain review, *Human Events* 5 (May 12, 1948); Fleming, *Nation* 222 (December 19, 1953): 552–53. Of course much of the reception remained hostile. See, for example, Frank M. Russell on Barnes, ed., *Perpetual War*, in *Annals of the American Academy of Political and Social Science* 292 (March 1954): 157–58.

44. Samuel Eliot Morison, "Did Roosevelt Start the War?: History Through a Beard," *Atlantic* 182 (August 1948): 91–97; review by Mason Wade, *Commonweal* 48 (May 21, 1948): 143; review by Schlesinger, Jr., *New York Times Book Review*, April 11, 1948, pp. 4, 24; Mumford incident, *New York Times*, February 7, 1948, pp. 1, 13.

45. Review by Julius Pratt, *American Historical Review* 58 (October 1952): 150–52; review by C. C. Griffin, *Nation* 175 (October 4, 1952): 305–6; W. L. Neumann to M. R. Beard, January 1, 1952, Neumann Papers; review by Richard N. Current, *Progressive* 16 (October 1952): 37.

46. *The Memoirs of Cordell Hull*, 2 vols. (New York: Macmillan, 1948); Henry L. Stimson and McGeorge Bundy, *On Active Service in Peace and War* (New York: Harper, 1948); Robert E. Sherwood, *Roosevelt and Hopkins: An Intimate History* (New York: Harper, 1948); Herbert Feis, *The Road to Pearl Harbor: The Coming of War between the United States and Japan* (Princeton, N.J.: Princeton University Press, 1950).

47. Basil Rauch, *Roosevelt from Munich to Pearl Harbor: A Study in the Creation of a Foreign Policy* (New York: Creative Age, 1950), p. 496.

48. William L. Langer and S. Everett Gleason, *The Challenge to Isolation: The World Crisis of 1937–1940 and American Foreign Policy* (New York: Harper, 1952); *The Undeclared War, 1940–1941: The World Crisis and American Foreign Policy* (New York: Harper, 1953). For the denial of official history, see p. xii of the first volume.

49. Review by Neumann, *Progressive* 16 (August 1952): 26–27; H. E. Barnes to W. L. Langer, February 14, 1952, copy in Neumann Papers.

50. W. L. Neumann to H. E. Barnes, no date, Neumann Papers; H. E. Barnes to W. L. Neumann, February 8, 1952, Neumann Papers.

51. W. L. Neumann to H. E. Barnes, October 3, 1952, H. E. Barnes to W. L. Neumann, September 20, 1952, Neumann Papers; Chamberlin, *America's Second Crusade*, pp. 354–55.

52. H. E. Barnes to C. C. Tansill, November 7, 1950, Barnes Papers; C. C. Tansill to H. E. Barnes, November 10, 1950, Barnes Papers.

53. W. L. Neumann to H. E. Barnes, February 12, 1951, Neumann Papers.

54. Morgenstern on conspiracy, *Pearl Harbor*, p. 328; Tansill innuendo, *Back Door to War*, p. 651; lack of Axis war plans, Chamberlin, *America's Second Crusade*, p. 136, and Barnes, *Perpetual War*, p. 9; testimony of Alwin D. Kramer in Morgenstern, *Pearl Harbor*, pp. 213–15. For an essay showing proper and improper uses of the Stimson Diary, see Richard N. Current, "How Stimson Meant to 'Maneuver' the Japanese," *Mississippi Valley Historical Review* 40 (June 1953): 67–74.

55. Robert A. Theobald, *The Final Secret of Pearl Harbor* (New York: Devin-Adair, 1954); Richard N. Current, *Secretary Stimson: A Study in Statecraft* (New Brunswick, N.J.: Rutgers University Press, 1954); Paul W. Schroeder, *The Axis Alliance and Japanese-American Relations, 1941* (Ithaca, N.Y.: Cornell University Press, 1958); introduction to Warren F. Kimball, ed., *Franklin D. Roosevelt and the World Crisis, 1937–1945* (Lexington, Mass.: Heath, 1973), p. xviii.

56. Chodorov, review of Morgenstern in *analysis* 3 (February 1947): 3; Beard, *President Roosevelt*, p. 580.

# 6

# Dollars, Ratholes, and Elections:
# The Challenges of 1948

Despite such sustained efforts to discredit Roosevelt's prewar diplomacy, isolationists could not afford to live in the past. Revisionism was necessary, but not sufficient. Too much danger lay ahead. In March 1947 the administration had committed the United States to the principle of containment —at least in Europe—and, within a year, Truman had asked Americans to underwrite the recovery of Western Europe with massive resources and funds. No less threatening was Truman's possible reelection in 1948, or the election of a Republican who shared the President's commitment to global involvements. If such obligations became permanent, the future looked dark indeed.

At the beginning of 1947, Western Europe stood on the brink of collapse: it was short of food and fuel, prices were rising dangerously, factories were running at a small fraction of capacity. By late April the administration began to speak about the condition of the Continent with urgency. Reporting to the country on April 28 after a meeting of foreign ministers, Secretary of State George C. Marshall warned: "The patient is sinking while the doctors deliberate."[1]

Administration leaders, believing that industrial inefficiency was at the root of Europe's plight, stressed the need for transnational planning. Hence the Secretary, speaking at Harvard's commencement on June 5, 1947, outlined his proposed "Marshall Plan," in which he promised that integrated European recovery efforts would receive major American support. Such economic coordination would obviously pay an added dividend, since it would permit safe use of West Germany's indispensable resources.[2]

Autumn brought further crises, when Communists in both France and Italy launched a series of general strikes. In late October Truman issued a warning: unless Congress voted emergency relief funds, food, and fuel, and voted them soon, the two countries would face collapse. On November 17, as France was reducing bread rations, the President pleaded for the passage of an Interim Aid Bill, under which some $597 million would be appropriated for France, Italy, Austria, and Nationalist China. The *New York Times,* commenting on Truman's speech, compared the situation to the fall of 1940 and the desperate winter of Pearl Harbor. Press reports soon indicated that the themes of relief and of anti-Communism struck a ready chord among Americans, and the House passed emergency aid by voice vote. In the Senate, Langer was the only veteran isolationist to vote against the bill.[3]

On December 19 Truman presented the Marshall Plan to Congress. "No economy," said the President, "not even one as strong as our own, can remain healthy and prosperous in a world of poverty and want." He suggested that rejection of his proposal would be dangerous: a garrison America might not only be compelled to modify its economic system, but forgo "the enjoyment of many of our freedoms and privileges." Truman asked for $6.8 billion for the first fifteen months, a total of $17 billion over four years. After long wrangling ("the most critical debate since the end of the war," declared the interventionist *Time* magazine), Congress authorized $4.3 billion, plus an increase of a billion in Export-Import lending authority, over the next twelve months.[4]

Despite administration fears, several factors helped assure the bill's passage. These included an independent European Cooperation Administration divorced from the State Department, a $465 million appropriation for Nationalist China, and the paring down of Truman's request to $5.3 billion over the next calendar year. Even more important, as far as the bill's ultimate reception was concerned, was the Czech crisis. In late February 1948 a Communist coup d'état insured direct Soviet control of Czechoslovakia. The death of Foreign Minister Jan Masaryk, an apparent suicide, had overtones of foul play that shocked Americans. A Russian defense treaty with Finland merely added to the nation's anxieties.[5]

The crises in Czechoslovakia and Finland helped create a war scare. Diplomat W. Averell Harriman declared publicly that Stalin was an even greater menace to the world than Hitler; Premier Smuts saw the West as facing its most critical moment in a thousand years. General Lucius Clay, American commander in Germany, cabled Washington on March 5 that war appeared imminent, although the Central Intelligence Agency gave the nation at least sixty days of grace. Truman, in addressing the Congress on March 17, combined his strong plea for the European Recovery Program with proposals for universal military training and resumption of the draft. *Time* magazine commented in mid-March, "All last week in the halls of Congress, on the street corners, U.S. citizens had begun to talk about the possibility of war between the U.S. and the U.S.S.R."[6]

By arguing the negative side of the debate, isolationists found themselves, as in 1941, with the unenviable task of opposing measures that the administration claimed were promoting "freedom," defending the country's "security," and halting "aggression." Both the United States Chamber of Commerce and the National Association of Manufacturers, which had refused to take a direct position on the debate of 1940–41, supported the Marshall Plan, and a new business organization founded in 1942, the Committee for Economic Development, pushed even harder for ECA.[7]

Under such conditions, the bill passed the Senate 69 to 17, the House 329 to 74. (The House bill authorized $4.3 billion.) In the House, half of the old isolationists voted for the authorization; in the Senate two-thirds supported it. Although on April 2 a conference report passed both houses, the Marshall Plan suddenly ran into trouble. Congressman Taber, chairman of the House Appropriation Committee, attempted to chop off two billion dollars—over a quarter of the authorized amount—and to stretch the remaining sum over fifteen months.[8]

Taber, a tall, brusque man, had long and vociferously opposed federal spending. Reporters relished referring to him as "The Knight of the Shining Meat Axe" or "Generous John." Born in 1880 in Auburn, New York, Taber —a Yale alumnus and lawyer—had represented his home area in Congress since 1923. During the 1930s he consistently opposed New Deal measures and was once accused of being the most reactionary member of Congress. "That's not true," he snapped back. "I'm not as reactionary as [Congressman] Jim Wadsworth [Rep.–N.Y.]. He's still fighting women's suffrage." The upstate Congressman was a strong isolationist until March 1941, when Congress passed lend-lease. Taber then asserted that the United States, for all practical purposes, was already in the war and voted for draft extension and shipments to belligerent zones. Retaining his fervent belief in economy as the conflict ended, Taber believed that ECA pampered peoples who were continually revealing their unworthiness. After traveling to Europe in the fall of 1947, Taber went so far as to call the British lazy, denied that the Germans were starving, and asserted that neither the French nor the Italians were experiencing great need.[9]

Congressman Dirksen proposed an amendment to restore the full sum, warning that "this cut may be the gentle little shove that may throw the government of France into the ashcan." Yet, on June 5 the House confirmed all of Taber's alterations. Only pressure by Vandenberg and Taft (who was most suspicious of the Marshall Plan) enabled ECA to end up with $4.3 billion, plus the increase of $1 billion in Export-Import loans, for the calendar year.[10]

Again, as in the case of aid to Greece and Turkey, isolationist converts to bipartisanship made quite predictable arguments. (Since their claims —both pro and con—often applied equally to the Interim Aid bill of November 1947 and to the Marshall Plan of March 1948, they are grouped together in this chapter.)[11] They stressed Europe's precarious condition, with Vandenberg speaking of "elemental human survival in a free society" and Lodge pointing to a possible Communist "world continent" composed of Europe, Asia, and Africa. They maintained that aid bolstered America's own defenses: Vandenberg referred to a "self-interest which knows that any world revolution would rate America as a top-prize scalp"; Dirksen warned against "this red tide . . . like some vile creeping thing which is spreading its web westward and westward." They claimed that the world economy needed such strengthening: "We cannot," said Vandenberg, "indefinitely prosper in a broken world."[12]

A few supporters among the old isolationists felt compelled to explain their apparent "apostasy." Dirksen denied that he would vote on international measures as he had a decade before. "Open confession," he remarked, was "good for the soul." Congressman Edwin Arthur Hall claimed that circumstances were different: in 1940 Europe's efforts at self-preservation were ineffective; in 1948 the threatened Continent was making substantial efforts to protect itself and hence deserved American support. Of course, not all admitted such overt conversion, and at least two backers combined grudging support of the plan with attacks upon the administration. Representative Charles A. Halleck (Rep.–Ind.) blamed Europe's cold and hunger upon "New Deal" mismanagement. Congressman Walter C. Ploeser (Rep.–Mo.) declared that the sheer formulation of the Plan involved a tacit acknowledgment of past government errors.[13]


Administration pleas for Interim Aid and the Marshall Plan by no means converted all of the old isolationists. For many, particularly those from the Middle West, the Marshall Plan reinforced insular sentiments, and these critics attempted to answer interventionist claims point by point.

Old isolationists advanced a whole series of arguments relating to America's condition. Massive aid, some argued, would help ruin the United States. Taft warned against underwriting "the food supply of the world," and Keefe claimed that Marshall Plan fuel was desperately needed at home. Such predictions even extended to small items, with Short warning that the passing of the ECA meant no nylons for American mothers.[14]

Critics found the financial cost severe. Senator Butler commented, "This is not our first attempt to fill up a leaking barrel by pouring more water into it." The United States could only drain itself, and if it went bankrupt in order to bolster another continent, there would be no one to come to its rescue. Although most opponents expressed their views in moderate terms, a few extreme conservatives spoke more stridently. Congressman Shafer commented, "The body of Harry Hopkins is dead, but his spirit lingers on." Pettengill suspected that Stalin, a man "skilled in oriental cunning," might secretly be promoting ECA in order to bankrupt the United States.[15]

And even if the country as a whole was not squandering its bounty or filing for bankruptcy, it could—so several isolationists feared—face such autarchy that traditional freedoms would be jeopardized. No Marshall Plan benefits, said Taft, were worth the return of price controls. Chodorov asserted that America's war preparations were already leading it "into that very totalitarianism which destroyed the civilization of Europe." Claiming that both private property and civil liberties were threatened, he mentioned that "the only war which will do us any good is a war with Washington."[16]

Several old isolationists questioned whether the United States needed to increase exports markedly. Taft asked how an export reduction could injure a country lacking sufficient steel, grain, and oil for its own people. Beard repeated the challenge made first in his book *The Open Door at Home* (1934): full employment and prosperity lay in more equitable distribution of domestic wealth, not in the manipulation of overseas trade and credit.[17]

Aggressive commercial policies might, said Taft, bolster Soviet accusations of economic imperialism: "We give the Russians a basis for the charge that we are trying to dominate the countries of Western Europe." America would be justified in going to war "for freedom's sake," Congressman Thomas A. Jenkins (Rep.–Ohio) commented, but it had no business fighting "for the sake of world trade."[18]

It was, various veteran isolationists maintained, "Wall Street" and "the farm bloc," not the majority of Americans, who were the most apprehensive about possible gluts on the domestic market. They often mentioned "international bankers," "the steel trust," "big oil interests," and "munitions millionaires." Congressman Ross Rizley (Rep.–Okla.) blamed the nation's farmers, asking if the United States was "going to feed the hungry people of Europe tobacco and clothe the naked with corn husks?" If economic pressure groups received hidden subsidies, the rest of the country was only growing poorer. Then, once Europe recovered, its manufactured goods would flood the world market, creating—in the words of Senator Johnson—"idle smokestacks and devastating unemployment here at home."[19]

Another series of arguments related to Europe's predicament. Old isolationists maintained that some governments on the Continent were notoriously unreliable. Foreign bureaucrats and despots would build up personal political machines, not aid the poor and needy or promote economic integration. And if American aid did happen to reach "the people," Europe's socialistic experiments assured continental stagnation and stultified the faith of Americans in their own system of "free enterprise." Pettengill asked, "Are we to fill rat holes in Europe, and go socialist at home?"[20]

A few old isolationists believed with Merwin K. Hart that socialism and Communism were "to a large extent blood brothers." Lobbyist Catherine Curtis, for example, delighted to quote George Bernard Shaw to the effect that "Socialism is nothing but communism with better English." Congressman Frederick C. Smith, throwing caution to the winds, claimed that "all of Western civilization" had "become immured in communism." Flynn took a slightly different tack, declaring that "Fascism masquerading as Socialism is creeping over the fields and factories of the once great, free England of Pitt and Fox and Gladstone."[21]

Besides, sheer "bribery"—so a few old isolationists argued—could never work. "If the people of Europe want Communism," wrote Chodorov, "a few loaves of bread will not dissuade them from their purpose." Indeed, there was no necessary relationship between poverty and radicalism. Harold Knutson mused, "If communism could be halted with money, there would not be any communism in Hollywood."[22]

As part of their campaign to insure national solvency and to avoid subsidizing socialist regimes, isolationists challenged other administration claims. They denied, for example, that Europe was in crisis. Instead, they asserted that the Truman leadership was deliberately manufacturing hysteria in order to gain appropriations. In November 1947, for example, Bender denounced the Truman government for dividing Europe into hostile camps, while John Taber blamed "some of the sob-sisters" for attempting to lead the country into a world war. In March 1948 in his new monthly journal, *Today's World,* Hamilton Fish entitled an editorial "War it NOT inevitable." Because Russia possessed no atomic bombs and already feared American strength, it was the administration, not the Soviet Union, that might instigate "incidents that may result in war." Soon after the Czech coup, Dewey Short warned against talk of "Bulgarian hordes ranging over the plains of Texas" or of "Russian submarines off the coast of California." The *Chicago Tribune* found the 1948 emergency just as rigged as the Pearl Harbor one, with the administration "trying to order the world to our design through the use of force at ruinous moral and material expense."[23]

To a small number of old isolationists, the Czech crisis offered no basis for alarm. Taft found the fallen republic lying well within the sphere of influence that the Allies had assigned Russia at the end of the war. The Soviet Union, the Ohio Senator argued, had committed no new aggression. A few old isolationists refused to cast the Czech nation in the role of a martyred state. Frank Chodorov, for example, compared the Communist coup to "the brutal expulsion from their homes of three million Sudetan Germans [*sic*] by the Czechoslovakian government." Father Gillis called the polyglot country, composed of several nationalities, "something artificial, synthetic, unnatural, . . . a nation . . . held together by a coefficient of hatreds."[24]

Such artificially created war scares, isolationists often declared, had little to do with genuine American security. Rather they were, as Robert Young suspected, a ploy to reelect the Truman leadership, or as Villard feared, an effort to militarize the country. No matter what the motive, the results could be dangerous. Morley, who endorsed the economic aspects of the Marshall Plan, commented that "the lives of our youth are not the property of the State," and hence should not be thrown on "a rubbish heap in Korea or Yugoslavia as some brass hat may ordain."[25]

A few old isolationists, such as Ernest T. Weir, denied that Europeans were really starving, or that their continent was about to turn Communist. The *Chicago Tribune* found Europe quite capable of producing enough food for its own needs. Taft tersely commented in December 1947, "People don't completely collapse. They go on living anyway."[26]

And if Europe did face hardship, its salvation—so several veteran isolationists maintained—lay not in receiving more American dollars but in large-scale emigration. The Continent simply had too many mouths to feed, too many families to sustain. General Wood, asserting that the larger part of Europe was "finished," claimed that Englishmen, Germans, and Belgians should all leave en masse. Edwin C. Johnson saw Africa as "the only way out," for its minerals and foodstuffs could accommodate "a wholesale migration."[27]

Several isolationists went so far as to deny, and deny explicitly, that Europe was essential to America's defense. The Continent could well be expendable. The western hemisphere had existed independently of Europe in the past and it could in the future. If Europe had to go through another Dark Age before it recovered, so be it. Chodorov deemed it wise to "write off that continent until such time as its political structure collapses entirely and a breed of sensible people restore it to decency." The *Washington Times-Herald* was equally blunt: America, it said, must withdraw immediately from Europe, even allowing it "to go Communist if the Europeans haven't the guts to resist the Reds."[28]

Some isolationist observations were  most astute. The artificial nature of the Czech crisis has been confirmed by a later generation of historians. Despite administration alarms, the Soviet Union was probably too weak to launch, much less support, a major attack. Czechoslovakia, as Taft pointed out, was a Russian effort to consolidate its sphere of influence, not to expand its empire. Hence it is doubtful whether the Marshall Plan saved Europe from a Soviet invasion. The isolationist analysis of economic roots was also perceptive: the administration fully realized that such aid subsidized certain types of manufacturing and farming. Beard, for example, mused that "Providence" had worked in wondrous ways "for Methodist & Baptist tobacco growers."[29]

Other isolationist arguments were far less thoughtful. Even had European countries so desired, they would have found it difficult to abandon centralized economic planning and a welfare state. Conservative isolationists were often so blinded by their hatred of all "statism" that they could not comprehend how social democracy and mixed economies might actually retard the spread of Communism.

Isolationists also underestimated Europe's poverty. When industrialist Weir claimed to have seen no starvation while visiting Europe in the fall of 1947, Congressman John David Lodge caustically reminded him that people died in heatless rooms, not on the streets. Some isolationist attacks on American export subsidies were inconsistent. Taft, by insisting that ECA recipients purchase United States products, encouraged the very trade practices he claimed to deplore.[30]

Most important of all, the country as a whole refused to see Europe as expendable, and only a handful of isolationists seriously spoke of letting the Continent go. And to those who believed that the Soviet Union must not be allowed to dominate all of Europe, isolationist alternatives were not always reassuring.


This is not to say that they did not try. As with their response to other administration proposals, old isolationists offered a variety of options.

One group of suggestions involved a return to "Fortress America." Although continentalism did not draw many advocates, it bore the closest relationship to classic isolationism. Clare E. Hoffman tersely remarked, "Let those fellows fight it out over there." The virgin hemisphere, not the decaying Old World, contained the country's real future. Joseph P. Kennedy sought "a Marshall plan for the Americas," one that included strong transportation. General Wood, then in the process of building Sears stores south of the border, claimed that Latin America—unlike Europe—possessed abundant natural resources and financial solvency.[31]

An equally small minority of isolationists demanded a continental defense. Colonel McCormick, flying over the Rockies, found the mountain chain ideal for anti-aircraft installations: "With air shelters for our people, mountain top . . . artillery and a superior air force, we can, as always, defy the world." John Rankin called for "an ample supply" of atomic bombs, capable of delivery by "the strongest air force on earth."[32]

A few old isolationists used the aid debate to stress the domestic nature of the Communist "menace." Representative Hoffman put the issue crudely: "Let us clean the vermin out of our own home first." The more urbane Taft found it incongruous "to pour out dollars to prevent communism abroad," while "criticizing a congressional committee for trying to find out who the influential Communists are in the United States."[33]

Occasionally, but not often, isolationists suggested that sums for foreign aid should be spent on relief at home. Dewey Short, noting the poverty in his own Ozark region, said that he could personally "throw a rock and hit half a dozen families who need help and relief." (Because Short seldom voted for welfare measures, his sincerity might be open to question.) Liberal isolationists could stress such themes with more conviction. Lemke, for example, noted starvation among America's Navahos. Langer called for an "American Recovery Plan," one that would allocate equally large sums for farm supports, education, reclamation, and pension projects.[34]

Another spasmodic group of proposals concerned different ways of taking the relief initiative. General Wood called for "more in the nature of charity." Frank Gannett commented, "We must feed Europe, not finance it." Such altruism would have immediate visible results, for people would once again be fed and clothed. At the same time, his proposal pleased conservatives by avoiding long-range financial commitments. Far better, said Hoffman, to have the Red Cross and religious organizations administer needed aid than to establish a major agency with the power and scope of ECA.[35]

While a few World War II isolationists spoke in terms of greater charity, a few others sought more coercion. Fish vaguely referred to an anti-Communist "International," supposedly possessing power to carry on the struggle within the Soviet bloc. Hart called for backing Franco's Spain. Sterling Morton suggested that America hire "some Hessians—to say nothing of Prussians, Pomeranians, Nurtembergers [sic] and Bavarians." In proposing a foreign legion recruited from Germans and Japanese, the Chicago manufacturer wrote, "We know from experience they are good fighters." Representative Shafer recommended that the United States withdraw diplomatic recognition from Russia, "a regime that has blood not only on its hands but splattered over the clothes of every man who is a part of it."[36]

Several isolationists hoped to sever all trade with Communist countries. The United States had drastically cut exports to Russia since V-J day, but in 1947 still sent $149 million worth of goods. If the Soviets, they claimed, really intended to invade Western Europe, it was foolish to send them valuable goods. Hoffman pointed to shipments of American motors to Russia. John Taber claimed personally to have seen "the sale of a large quantity of trucks, automobiles, and other supplies out of army surplus, at a low cost, to a communist controlled company in Italy." If aid must go to France and Italy, it should, said the New York Congressman, be administered by firm anti-Communists—people who would "not trifle with the communists nor attempt to traffic with them."[37]

Still another group of options, and one receiving more support from old isolationists, would have kept much of the Marshall Plan. At the same time, it would have modified many of its provisions. Some isolationists demanded far more stringent conditions and often spoke of the need for "businesslike terms." Morton suggested that Europe draw upon the Reconstruction Finance Corporation, an agency that could make loans to private producers on easy terms and thereby help "those who are willing to help themselves." Congressman Bartel Jonkman (Rep.–Mich.), harking back to Bretton Woods, advised Europe to seek credit from the World Bank. America, said Merwin K. Hart, should demand that the Europeans terminate all nationalization projects before it allocated Marshall Plan funds. Several old isolationists, including General Wood, George H. Bender, and Francis H. Case, recommended that Europe spend its assets in the United States before seeking aid overseas. Congressman Smith of Wisconsin wanted European farmers paid with dollars, with which they would buy American-made consumer goods: "A Sears Roebuck catalog would stimulate agricultural produce to a great extent."[38]

Old isolationists kept returning to the principle of loans. Catherine Curtis sought a multibillion-dollar investment trust that would sell bonds to the taxpayers. Robert Young suggested that emergency aid be repaid in kind. After Europe got through another difficult winter, a business committee—"completely dissociated from either politics or the New York international bankers"—could unfreeze the world's raw materials and markets. Bender called for commercial credits by which recipients could purchase American goods. He also suggested that all aid programs be handled through the United Nations. Trade, said the Ohio Congressman, should be conducted on "business principles," not ideological ones.[39]

Both Senator Taft and ex-President Hoover were particularly outspoken in proposing alternatives. Taft endorsed the administration goals of preventing starvation and Communism, but claimed that food and machinery should be supplied on credit. He also introduced an amendment cutting the first year's ECA appropriation from $5.3 billion to $4 billion. Hoover had a whole series of objections, including the folly of a four-year commitment; neglect of such countries as China, Japan, Korea, and Germany; and the high cost to the American taxpayer. Among the highly publicized proposals of the ex-President were: restricting all appropriations to fifteen months; confining gifts to surpluses in food, coal, fertilizer, and cotton; demanding European repayment for grants of steel and other capital goods; concentrating upon German production; abandoning foreign exchange for all transactions; and levying a ceiling of three billion dollars. Both men ended up supporting the original House bill, Hoover in fact calling it "a major dam against Russian aggression."[40]

Taft and Hoover were not the only old isolationists who attempted directly to modify or cripple varied aid proposals. Some Congressmen demanded substantial reductions in interim aid allocations and occasionally tried to slash Marshall Plan appropriations. For example, Harold Knutson, chairman of the House Ways and Means Committee, called for a billion dollar limit on ECA spending.[41]

At times old isolationists tried to change the nature of the Marshall Plan. Langer backed an amendment proposed by Senator Glen Taylor to channel all aid through the United Nations. Brooks introduced an amendment to convert all the President's ECA representatives into mere agents of the ECA administrator. Senator Homer E. Capehart (Rep.–Ind.), a former backer of America First and president of Packard Manufacturing Company, submitted an amendment to replace the ECA with an international division of the RFC. The domestic RFC would purchase stock in its new international division, the participating countries would match American dollars, and hopefully the United States taxpayer would receive dividends from a profitable enterprise.[42]

Not all modifications of the plan were proposed by conservative businessmen and Congressmen, and not all were on the side of greater stringency. Liberals and socialists among the old isolationists had quite different anxieties. Chester Bowles endorsed the principal of long-term foreign aid to check Soviet aggression, but feared that the United States was neglecting the far more serious poverty of Asia and Africa. America, Bowles continued, was foolish in seeking to impose "free enterprise" upon such countries as Italy; it was equally unwise to involve the Defense Department in such aid programs. Similarly, Norman Thomas favored much of the Marshall Plan, but feared that it would be used to inflict capitalism upon the Ruhr and to denationalize British steel. Morris Rubin of the *Progressive* found the ERP the most constructive step taken since the war, but he warned against turning it into an anti-Russian device.[43]

Liberals and conservatives among the old isolationists could share mutual hostility to the Truman Doctrine, with both groups stressing the strategic risk involved. Once it came to the Marshall Plan, however, the two camps parted company. Conservatives might agree with Bowles and Rubin that such aid increased the danger of war. Other fears, however, differed markedly. Whereas the conservatives believed that ECA would foster European socialism, liberals—whose ranks were infinitesimally smaller—thought that the plan might hinder needed socialization; they were also far more acquiescent concerning the sums involved. Even before debate on such issues as China, liberals were breaking from the mainstream of veteran anti-interventionist activity.

Few old isolationist remedies were practical. Americans, believing that the balance of power was at stake in Europe, probably would not have stood for traditional isolation and a stress on continental defense. Proposals limited to mere relief could well have left the Continent's deep-rooted production problems intact; so would policies concentrating upon withdrawal and the severance of diplomatic relations. Efforts to substitute elaborate trust and investment schemes could defeat the whole purpose of the project —to get money and goods to Europe rapidly enough to assure political and economic stability. It remains doubtful whether Europe would have averted depression so easily, or have seen its production rise far above prewar levels by 1952, without the Marshall Plan intact.

Such converts to interventionism as Henry Cabot Lodge frequently responded to the isolationist critics. When opponents declared that the Congress had no power to authorize payments spanning several years, Lodge pointed to precedents in naval, harbor, and road appropriations. When foes wanted to replace relief measures with defense spending, the Massachusetts Senator stressed that fifth columns could not always be stopped by military means. And when antagonists declared that the Marshall Plan could not have saved Czechoslovakia, he answered that it was still not too late to salvage other nations.[44]

Lodge was not the only World War II isolationist who responded to former kinsmen. Critics who claimed that the administration had manufactured the March crisis were met by Vorys's projection: there was, the Ohio Congressman said, a "Communist timetable . . . working in Italy, in the Near East, and the Far East." Old isolationists who harped upon domestic subversion faced the claim of Congressman John Jennings, Jr. (Rep.–Tenn.), who asserted that American Communists—unlike the Russians—could not "bring enemy submarines within gunshot of our great cities." If opponents of ECA blamed Europe's poverty upon the laziness of its people, Dirksen reported that he had personally seen Europeans so starved that they could not work. If, on the other hand, some isolationists feared that the plan would feed Communists, the Illinois Congressman retorted that the West could only benefit from healthy Communist laborers in the Ruhr.[45]

Vandenberg, in particular, would claim to agree with much of the isolationist critique, but then go on to say the ERP was still worth the gamble. For example, he endorsed increased defense appropriations but called the Marshall Plan "one of the best ways to stop World War III before it started." While supporting the principle of long-term aid, he denied that the authorization of one Congress could actually bind another. The plan, he said, did not bleed the country white; rather, it was designed to stop further emergency appropriations. Occasionally sounding like the most militant isolationist, Vandenberg told an audience at the University of Michigan in November 1947, "We cannot indefinitely underwrite the world."[46] The Michigan Senator had again played his hand skillfully, and hence was able to secure major appropriations. Long-term foreign aid remained a staple of American foreign policy.

After the financial commitments made by the Marshall Plan, the defeat of potential standard-bearers in the 1948 election was, to some degree, anticlimatic. This is not to say that many old isolationists did not fervently seek to capture the post of Chief Executive. Since the Democrats would either nominate Truman or choose a candidate (such as General Dwight Eisenhower) who might be more interventionist, the battle would have to be fought within Republican ranks.

The more militant among the veteran isolationists put their hopes in General Douglas MacArthur. During the 1940s, no American was more idolized among this particular group of nationalists than the embattled "Hero of Bataan." The fact that MacArthur himself had been a moderate interventionist before Pearl Harbor made little difference. The last issue of the virulently isolationist *Scribner's Commentator*, appearing in January 1942, featured him on the cover. Senator La Follette secured a congressional resolution proclaiming June 13, 1942, as "Douglas MacArthur Day" and, in February 1944, Vandenberg wrote an article for *Collier's* entitled "Why I Am For MacArthur." (The General, said Vandenberg, possessed "a great mind, a great heart, a great capacity and a great devotion.") In 1948 as in 1944, a group of isolationist leaders, including General Wood, General Hanford MacNider, Hamilton Fish, Colonel McCormick, and Philip La Follette, rallied to his support. The initial strategy was a simple one: to win the Wisconsin primary of April 6, 1948, and thereby secure the visibility and the momentum needed to make a strong showing at the Philadelphia convention. Then, in the event of deadlock, the party could turn to the charismatic General.[47]

Such old isolationists stressed several themes in promoting MacArthur. They found the General a strong vote-getter, possessing the magnetism that Taft obviously lacked. They claimed that MacArthur had a far greater grasp of the country's defense needs than did the administration. Attorney Lansing Hoyt, who had headed the MacArthur movement in 1944, commented—without conscious irony—that only MacArthur had a sufficient knowledge of army practice to rid the country of "military despotism"! They asserted that the General's leadership was indispensable in the wider arena of Cold War leadership. With MacArthur as President, said Philip La Follette, "no hotheads, no blunderers, no redbaiters would get us into war with Russia"; at the same time, the General would supply a missing firmness to American diplomacy.[48]

Perhaps most in the General's favor was the fact that he could be all things to all men. If some rightists saw MacArthur as the most conservative of all the Republican candidates, the more liberal La Follette could claim that the General was basically a reformer, a man who would "work for that delicate balance between individual liberty and the general welfare which is the goal of our American way of life." His record in Japan, said Wisconsin's former Governor, was ample evidence that he favored both civil liberties and economic benefits for the masses.[49]

Yet, for many more old isolationists, Taft was the man without equal. When Randolph Churchill objected to a Congressman who linked the Ohio Senator with his own father as one of the world's two greatest men, journalist Freda Utley snapped back, "I think the Member of Congress paid your father a very fine compliment by bracketing his name with that of Senator Taft." Veteran isolationists made continual references to his courage and intelligence. Felix Morley, writing a campaign profile for *Life*, found in Taft the revival of Madison's philosophy that we "rest all our political experiments on the capacity of mankind for self-government." Wheeler, still a Democrat with close personal ties to Truman, saw him as the best of the Republican candidates. The Ohioan, he stated, was "intelligent, hard working, and an honest conservative who would not be pushed around by Wall Street or the unintelligent reactionaries." Like MacArthur, Taft received generous contributions from many businessmen who had given to the America First Committee and was backed by prominent old isolationists at the Philadelphia convention.[50]

Several Cold War converts to internationalism wanted Vandenberg as their standard-bearer. Obviously conscious of his new role as "elder states-man," Vandenberg did not seek delegates but awaited a draft and carried an acceptance speech in his pocket at the convention. If, as claimed, the bipartisan leader "was as pompous and windy as ever," he could still hope to trade upon his involvement with wider "affairs of state." In 1948 Lodge and Tobey were among Vandenberg's backstage supporters, and even Taft, a rival for the nomination, told Vandenberg that if he became President, he would make the Michigan Senator his Secretary of State.[51]

Interventionist Vandenberg, however, was no more able than isolationist Taft to combat the highly organized forces of Thomas E. Dewey. Taft was handicapped by a negative personal image and poor results in the polls. MacArthur lost the Wisconsin primary and soon dropped out of sight. Vandenberg, by making such a strong issue out of Marshall Plan cuts just before the convention, could draw little support from Republican isolation-ists.[52] The New York Governor received the nomination on the third ballot.

During the campaign Dewey, who in 1940 had occasionally spoken like an isolationist, made all-too-obvious efforts to escape association with anti-interventionists in the GOP. He passed over House Majority Leader Charles A. Halleck of Indiana, a pro-Dewey partisan who had long possessed strong isolationist sentiments, to choose the interventionist Governor Earl Warren of California as his running mate. Similarly, his choice for national chair-man, Congressman Hugh D. Scott, Jr. (Rep.–Pa.), had sided with the interventionists, if only since the Pearl Harbor attack. With Truman scoring the record of the Eightieth Congress so heavily, Dewey avoided such Senators as "Curly" Brooks and froze Taft out of campaign councils. He chose unity as his theme and dropped attacks made earlier on administra-tion China policy and the Truman Doctrine. Fearful that such partisan rhetoric would undermine national morale at a time the Russians were blockading Berlin, Dewey followed Vandenberg's advice and avoided serious challenges.[53]

Dewey's weak campaign and subsequent defeat infuriated many old isolationists. Flynn described the debacle as "stupid beyond the dreams of imbecility"; he feared that both parties might foster "a war to recapture Berlin, or a war to save Israel." General Wood, never fond of Dewey, said that the New York Governor was "a man without a program except the program of winning the election." The very fact that the candidates did not debate foreign policy infuriated the isolationists. George Morgenstern saw only future wars and welfare state measures ahead. Dennis wrote, "The dumb Republicans thought they could go along on foreign policy and win by putting labor in its place through the Taft-Hartley act. What ninnies."[54]

Dewey's loss was compounded by the defeat of such staunch congressional isolationists as Brooks, Bender, and Knutson. Yet, if old isolationists claimed that Dewey's mild campaign had cost him the election, they failed to realize that the more partisan Taft might well have done worse. Taft's major weakness at the Philadelphia convention—the heavily sectional nature of his support—would have been still more compounded in a wider electorate. Taft would have been less likely than Dewey to capture the millions of ethnic, black, urban, and unionist voters who contributed so strongly to Truman's coalition. Although the campaign might well have stayed on domestic issues, Taft's long-standing isolationism would undoubtedly have harmed him in coastal states.[55]

For the old isolationists, 1948 was another bad year. The country had pledged itself to underwrite the recovery of unsound governments and a shattered Continent. In addition, it had elected leadership committed to supporting the regimes of Western Europe. Even the Republican presidential nominee made no indication that he would change the direction of American foreign policy. There was only one region where the isolationists approved the course the administration was taking, although even here they continually prodded the government. This region was Germany.

## NOTES

1. George C. Marshall, speech in *New York Times*, April 29, 1947, p. 4.

2. For the text of Marshall's speech, see ibid., June 6, 1947, p. 2. For the philosophy and events leading to the Marshall Plan, see Joseph Marion Jones, *The Fifteen Weeks* (New York: Viking, 1955); Kennan, *Memoirs*, 1: 325–53; Richard M. Freeland, *The Truman Doctrine and the Origins of McCarthyism: Foreign Policy, Domestic Politics, and Internal Security, 1946–1948* (New York: Schocken, 1971), pp. 151–56.

3. Harry S. Truman, *New York Times*, October 25, 1947, p. 2; idem, message to Congress, ibid., November 18, 1947, p. 1; "Winter of Decision" (editorial), ibid., November 23, 1947, Sec. E, p. 8. For the voting on Interim Aid, see for House, *CR*, December 11, 1947, p. 11307; for Senate, *CR*, December 1, 1947, p. 10980. Only six senators voted against Interim Aid. Of the old isolationists, only Langer voted in opposition. Taft, Henry P. Dworshak (Rep.–Idaho), and McCarran did not vote, although all three favored the bill.

4. Truman, message to Congress, *CR*, December 19, 1947, pp. 11749–54; *Time* 50 (December 29, 1947); 11. An authorization is simply a statement of congressional intent. The money still must be appropriated, and in this step too Congress must vote.

5. For factors aiding passage, see Freeland, *Truman Doctrine*, pp. 247–92.

6. W. Averell Harriman, *New York Times*, February 28, 1948, p. 3; Jan Christian Smuts cited in Denna Fleming, *The Cold War and Its Origins*, Vol. 1: *1917–1950* (Garden City, N.Y.; Doubleday, 1961), pp. 496–97; telegram of Lucius Clay in Walter

Millis, ed., *The Forrestal Diaries* (New York: Viking, 1951), p. 387; Truman, address to Congress, *New York Times*, March 18, 1948, p. 4; *Time* 51 (March 22, 1948): 19.

7. For general business reaction to the Marshall Plan, see Robert J. Chasteen, "American Foreign Aid and Public Opinion," Ph.D. diss., University of North Carolina, 1958, pp. 239–45.

8. The ECA passed the Senate on March 13, the House on March 31. Out of eighty-six World War II isolationists in the House, fifty (or 58.1%) did not vote. In authorization, thirty-five (or 40.6%) voted against it, and one (1.16%) did not vote. In the Senate, ten of fifteen old isolationists (or 66.6%) voted for the bill, three (or 20%) voted against it, and two (or 13.3%) did not vote. For Senate, see *CR*, p. 2793; House, ibid., pp. 3874–75.

9. For Taber's career, see Cary S. Henderson, "Congressman John Taber of Auburn: Politics and Federal Appropriations, 1923–1962," Ph.D. diss., Duke University, 1964; *Current Biography, 1948*, pp. 608—10; H. H. Harris, "Crustiest Crusader: John Taber, Knight of the Shining Meat Ax," *Reporter* 8 (May 26, 1953): 27–28. Taber explained why he shifted to interventionism in 1941 in his letter to Mr. and Mrs. H. D. Brown, November 7, 1941, Box 87, Taber Papers. For the anecdote concerning James Wadsworth, see Bulkley, "Daniel A. Reed," p. 128.

10. Dirksen in *Time* 56 (June 14, 1948): 13. On June 19, the House restored the full amount by a vote of 318–62. See *CR*, June 19, 1948, p. 9299.

11. Of course, the administration, in calling for passage of the Interim Aid bill, stressed the need for emergency relief and, in defending ECA, emphasized long-term recovery.

12. Vandenberg on survival and competition, *CR*, November 24, 1947, pp. 10702–3; Lodge, address to Annual Midcontinent Meeting of the Mississippi Valley World Trade Conference, April 17, 1948, *CR*, p. A2441; Vandenberg on defense in Freeland, *Truman Doctrine*, p. 195; Dirksen, *CR*, p. 196.

13. Dirksen, *CR*, March 30, 1948, p. 3724; Hall, *CR*, March 30, 1948, p. 3723; Charles A. Halleck, *CR*, December 11, 1947, p. 11283; Walter C. Ploeser, *CR*, March 31, 1948, p. 3856.

14. Taft, address to Ohio Society of New York, November 10, 1947, *CR*, p. A4253; Keefe, *CR*, December 16, 1947, p. 11479; Short, *CR*, March 30, 1948, p. 3720.

15. Butler, *CR*, March 13, 1948, p. 2763; Shafer, *CR*, December 10, 1947, p. 11264; Pettengill, "Is Stalin Promoting the Marshall Plan?," *CR*, March 24, 1948, p. A1892.

16. Taft, Ohio Society address, *CR*, p. A4252; Chodorov, *analysis* 4 (March 1948): 4.

17. Taft, Ohio Society address, *CR*, p. A4252; Charles A. Beard, "Neglected Aspects of Political Science," presidential address to the American Political Science Association, Washington, D.C., December 29, 1947, *American Political Science Review* 42 (April 1948): 220.

18. Taft, Ohio Society address, *CR*, p. A4252; Thomas A. Jenkins, *CR*, May 9, 1947, p. 4925.

19. Ross Rizley, *CR*, March 31, 1948, p. 3815; Johnson, address to North Park College Forum, March 2, 1948, *CR*, p. 2132. For attacks on international bankers, see William Clark, "Marshall Plan Group Includes Many Bankers," *Chicago Tribune*, February 25, 1948; on exporters, General Robert E. Wood, "Look Away from Europe," *American Affairs* 10 (October 1947): 206; on manufacturers, Lemke, *CR*, July 24, 1947, p. A4088; on steel and oil, Rankin, *CR*, March 29, 1948, p. 3635; on munitions millionaires, Short, *CR*, March 30, 1948, p. 3720.

20. Pettengill, "The Rat Hole of Elin," *CR*, December 14, 1947, p. A4926. For an accusation of European mismanagement, see S. Morton to A. Landon, February 12, 1948, Morton Papers. For an attack on a planned economy, see speech by C. Wayland Brooks, *American Affairs* 10 (January 1948): 58.

21. Short, *CR*, December 9, 1947, p. 11267; Hart, testimony before the Senate

Foreign Relations Committee, January 24, 1948, *Congressional Digest* 27 (March 1948): 91; Catherine Curtis, "Analysis and Historical Review Relative to the Marshall Plan," Women's Investors Research Institute, March 24, 1948, *CR*, p. A4441; Smith, *CR*, March 5, 1948, p. 2274; Flynn in Frey, "John T. Flynn," p. 304.

22. Chodorov, "Trailing the Trend," *analysis* 4 (November 1947): 7; Knutson, *CR*, December 8, 1947, p. 11151.

23. Statement by George Bender, November 17, 1947, Box 16, the Papers of Daniel Reed, Cornell University Library; J. Taber to Bruce Barton, November 21, 1947, Box 42, Taber Papers; H. Fish, "War is NOT Inevitable," *Today's World* 2 (March 1948): 16; Short, *CR*, March 30, 1948, p. 3720; "Later Than You Think" (editorial), *Chicago Tribune*, March 31, 1948.

24. Taft, *CR*, March 12, 1948, pp. 2643–44; Chodorov, "Trailing the Trend," *analysis* 4 (April 1948): 2; Gillis, "The Lesson of Czechoslovakia," *Catholic World* 167 (April 1948): 10.

25. Young, address before the Annual Governor's Luncheon Conference of the New England Council, Boston, November 20, 1947, *CR*, p. A4514; Morley, "Here Let Us Stop," *Human Events* 5 (March 24, 1948).

26. Weir, testimony before the House Foreign Affairs Committee, February 25, 1948, *United States Foreign Policy for a Post-War Recovery Program* (Washington, D.C.: U.S. Government Printing Office, 1948), pp. 1705–9; "Lazy Europe" (editorial), *Chicago Tribune*, February 4, 1948; Taft cited in *Time* 50 (December 29, 1947): 11. Taft did endorse interim aid on the grounds that it relieved suffering and discouraged the spread of Communism. *CR*, November 28, 1947, p. 10928.

27. Wood, *New York Times*, July 16, 1947, p. 1; Wood, "Look Away from Europe," p. 206; Johnson, North Park College speech, *CR*, p. 2134.

28. Chodorov, *analysis* 4 (March 1948): 4; "Marshall Pins It On Stalin" (editorial), *Washington Times-Herald*, April 29, 1947.

29. C. A. Beard to O. G. Villard, February 10, 1948, Villard Papers. For Russia's weakness, see Freeland, *Truman Doctrine*, pp. 276–77.

30. Lodge-Weir exchange, February 25, 1948, in *United States Foreign Policy for a Post-War Recovery Program*, p. 1719. For Taft on exports, see Patterson, *Mr. Republican*, p. 386.

31. Hoffman, *CR*, March 25, 1948, p. 3513; "Kennedy Says ERP Can't Save All Europe's Ills," *New York Journal-American*, June 13, 1948; Wood, *New York Times*, July 16, 1947, p. 1, and "Look Away from Europe," p. 206. Wood had long pushed the expansion of Sears in Latin America. In 1941 he started a store in Havana. After World War II, Wood built stores in Mexico City, Sao Paulo, and Rio de Janeiro. See *Newsweek* 33 (March 28, 1949): 70; *Business Week*, no. 1031 (June 4, 1949), pp. 105–6.

32. McCormick cited in *Time* 50 (November 17, 1947): 81; Rankin, *CR*, November 25, 1947, p. 10871.

33. Hoffman, *CR*, December 5, 1947, p. 11095; Taft, Ohio Society speech, *CR*, p. A4253.

34. Short, *CR*, November 25, 1947, p. 10870; Lemke, *CR*, December 4, 1947, p. 11052; Langer in Smith, "Senator William Langer," pp. 190–91.

35. Wood, "Look Away from Europe," p. 206; Gannett, address to the New York State Federation of Women's Clubs, Rochester, November 11, 1947, Box 13, Gannett Papers; Hoffman, *CR*, December 5, 1947, p. 11095.

36. Fish, *Red Plotters*, p. 86; Hart, "The Last Fork in the Road"; S. Morton to E. Dirksen, November 19, 1947, S. Morton to C. W. Brooks, March 23, 1948, Morton Papers; Shafer, *CR*, March 25, 1949, p. 3520.

37. Hoffman, *CR*, March 25, 1948, p. 3514; Taber, speech to Auburn Rotary Club, October 28, 1947, Taber Papers. For Soviet-American trade in 1947, see Paterson, *Soviet-American Confrontation*, p. 71.

38. Morton, speech to the directors of the Illinois Manufacturers Association, October 10, 1947, Morton Papers; Bartel Jonkman, *CR*, December 10, 1947, p. 11264; Hart, "Let's Not Subsidize European Socialism," radio broadcast, February 23, 1948, *CR*, p. A1275; R. E. Wood to R. M. La Follette, Jr., July 21, 1947, Box 624, Robert M. La Follette, Jr. Papers; Case, *CR*, December 16, 1947, p. 11479; Smith, *CR*, January 22, 1948, p. 454.

39. Curtis, "Analysis and Historical Review," *CR*, p. A4442; Young, Governor's luncheon address, *CR*, p. A4514; Bender, letter to John Taber, September 21, 1947, *CR*, p. 10876; G. H. Bender to R. A. Taft, July 14, 1947, Box 548, Taft Papers.

40. Taft, *CR*, November 28, 1947, p. 10930; Patterson, *Mr. Republican*, p. 388; Hoover, letter to Arthur Vandenberg, January 18, 1948, *United States Foreign Policy for a Post-War Recovery Program*, pp. 797–802. Taft's measure lost fifty-six to thirty-one. Backing him were such old isolationists as Aiken, Brooks, Dworshak, Edwin Johnson, and Langer. Taft had also tried to lower the December interim aid bill from $597 to $400 million. However, he ended up voting for the entire amount. Patterson, *Mr. Republican*, p. 385.

41. Jonkman, Robert Chiperfield (Rep.–Ill.), Lawrence H. Smith were among those who signed the minority report of the House Committee on Foreign Affairs dated April 5, 1947. They wanted the $350 million appropriation of May reduced to $200 million. See *Foreign Relief Aid: 1947*, executive session (Washington, D.C.: U.S. Government Printing Office, 1973), pp. 268–72. Jonkman also wanted the $597 appropriation of December reduced to $300 million. See *CR*, December 10, 1947, p. 11263. Lawrence H. Smith wanted a reduction of $90 million. See *CR*, p. 11264. For Knutson, see *Time* 50 (November 3, 1947): 19.

42. Glen Taylor was supported by only one other senator, Claude Pepper. See *CR*, March 10, 1948, p. 2460. For the Brooks amendment and defense, *CR*, March 11, 1948, pp. 2536–37. Although the measure was defeated fifty-two to twenty-five, it won support from such old isolationists as Aiken, Butler, Langer, Taft, and Henry C. Dworshak (Rep.–Idaho), March 11, 1948, p. 2541. For Capehart, see speech at Peoria, "American Principle Applied to a Joint European Recovery Program," February 7, 1948, *CR*, p. A890–92; March 9, 1948, *CR*, p. 2364. For Homer E. Capehart's role in America First, E. Jeffries to P. Hufty, October 6, 1941, Box 2, Charles L. Smith File, AFC Papers.

43. C. Bowles, "We Need a Program *For* as Well as *Against*," *New York Times Magazine*, April 18, 1948, pt. VI, pp. 7, 61–67; Thomas, "Marshall Plan Worthy of Support, But Some Changes Must Be Made," *Socialist Call* 13 (October 1, 1947): 2; Rubin, Pathways to Peace," *Progressive* 12 (May 1948): 5–9.

44. Lodge, *CR*, March 2, 1948, p. 1966; *CR*, March 3, 1948, p. 2025.

45. Vorys, *CR*, March 23, 1948, p. 3324; Jennings, *CR*, March 30, 1948, p. 3710; Dirksen, *CR*, March 30, 1948, pp. 3725–26.

46. Vandenberg, on stopping World War III, *CR*, March 2, 1948, p. 1983; on binding successive Congresses, *CR*, March 2, 1948, p. 1966; University of Michigan address, *CR*, p. A4176.

47. MacArthur's mild interventionism in D. Clayton James, *The Years of MacArthur*, Vol. 1: *1880–1941* (Boston: Houghton Mifflin, 1970), pp. 552, 695 n. 39; cover, *Scribner's Commentator* 11 (January 1942); La Follette in Kent, "Portrait in Isolationism," p. 346; Arthur H. Vandenberg, "Why I Am for MacArthur," *Collier's* 113 (February 12, 1944): 14, 48–49. For a detailed discussion of the MacArthur movement, see Howard B. Schonberger, "The General and the Presidency: Douglas MacArthur and the Election of 1948," *Wisconsin Magazine of History* 57 (Spring 1974): 201–19. For the abortive efforts of 1944, see the second volume of James's biography, *1941–1945* (Boston: Houghton Mifflin, 1975), chap. 10.

48. For comparisons of Taft and MacArthur, see R. E. Wood to D. MacArthur,

June 16, 1947, the Papers of General Douglas MacArthur, Douglas MacArthur Memorial Library, Norfolk, Virginia; and Lemke in Patterson, *Mr. Republican*, p. 700 n. 26. For Lansing Hoyt on defense, see *New Republic* 118 (February 16, 1948): 38. For MacArthur as strategic and political leader, see comments of Philip La Follette, unidentified clipping dated January 25, 1948, Philip La Follette Papers. Other endorsements can be found in Lemke, *Today's World* 2 (February 1948): 21; F. Gannett to R. E. Wood, December 10, 1947, copy in Philip La Follette Papers.

49. Philip La Follette in Kent, "Portrait in Isolationism," p. 424; unidentified clipping dated January 25, 1948, Philip La Follette Papers.

50. Utley quoted in Hanighen, "Not Merely Gossip," *Human Events* 5 (February 4, 1948); Morley, "The Case for Taft," *Life* 24 (February 9, 1948): 64; B. K. Wheeler to R. E. Wood, April 12, 1948, Box 7, Wood Papers. For the large number of veteran isolationists giving to the Taft campaign, see Box 296, Taft Papers.

51. Vandenberg's pomposity in Mayer, *Republican Party*, p. 470; and Trohan, *Political Animals*, p. 234; role of Lodge, Tobey, and Taft in Vandenberg, *Private Papers*, pp. 437–38.

52. Taft in Patterson, *Mr. Republican*, pp. 416–17; MacArthur in Schonberger, pp. 217–19; Vandenberg in Divine, *Presidential Elections*, 1: 211.

53. For Dewey's early isolationism, see Divine, *Presidential Elections*, 1: 14–15. For the tone of the campaign, see Mayer, *Republican Party*, p. 472; Patterson, *Mr. Republican*, pp. 419–24; Robert A. Divine, "The Cold War and the Election of 1948," *Journal of American History* 59 (June 1972): 100–110. Vandenberg was so confident of victory that he thought that a muted campaign would lead to post-election Democratic backing for President Dewey! Divine, "The Cold War," p. 104.

54. J. T. Flynn to C. Brown, November 4, 1948, Box 20, Flynn Papers; J. T. Flynn to W. Trohan, June 6, 1948, Trohan Papers; R. E. Wood to R. M. La Follette, Jr., November 11, 1948, Box 624, Robert La Follette, Jr. Papers; G. Morgenstern to O. G. Villard, November 27, 1948, Villard Papers; Dennis, *Appeal to Reason*, #137 (November 6, 1948).

55. Patterson, *Mr. Republican*, pp. 416–17, 425–26.

# 7

# Germany: The Key to Europe

Hostility to the Marshall Plan by no means implied that the old isolationists were indifferent to the fate of all Europe. During the debates of the late forties, veteran isolationists, almost to a man, were making one claim: a revived Germany could save Western Europe, and save it without the necessity of America's underwriting half the Continent.

At first, such an argument had little appeal. German atrocities and wanton destruction had become hauntingly familiar to Americans who remained apprehensive that the Reich's military machine, successful enough to dominate Europe from the Atlantic to the Urals, could possible emerge again. And even if some people in the United States could bring themselves to forgive and forget, such wartime allies as France, the Netherlands, and Great Britain would be far more reluctant to grant Germany full equality among the nations.

In promoting the cause of German rehabilitation, isolationists worked on several fronts. They stressed the harshness of the Potsdam agreement, sought immediate food and relief shipments, assailed the occupation, and called for an end to plant dismantling and production restrictions. In addition they attempted to redeem the image of the German "people"—as contrasted to their "leaders"—by minimizing the impact of atrocity accounts, emphasizing the resistance to Hitler, and underscoring the "inhumanity" of both denazification programs and war crimes trials.

For two years before World War II ended, American policymakers had debated the question of Germany's future. In 1944 much publicity was given to the so-called Morgenthau Plan, proposed by Secretary of the Treasury Henry Morgenthau, Jr. Under its stipulations, Germany would be partitioned, prohibited to engage in basic industry, and forced to serve primarily as a producer of food and raw materials. (Although the Morgenthau scheme was never implemented, the views of the Treasury Secretary were reflected in JCS/1067, a directive issued in April 1945 by the

Joint Chiefs of Staff. The orders forbade fraternization, demanded thorough denazification, and opposed any "steps looking toward the economic rehabilitation of Germany or designed to maintain or strengthen the German economy.")[1]

Almost immediately several old isolationists attacked Morgenthau's proposal. Colonel McCormick told his Washington bureau chief to put "some sense" into "these crazy people in the White House and State Department." Columnist Frank C. Waldrop claimed it would turn Germany into "a medieval goat pasture," hence playing into the hands of Stalin, a "dirty old oriental who sleeps in his underwear and doesn't care who knows it." Henry Regnery published a pamphlet bearing the same title as Morgenthau's book on German policy. Written by Karl Brandt, an economist teaching at Stanford, "Germany is Our Problem" found similarities between the Treasury proposal and Nazi plans to starve millions of Jews.[2]

As the remnants of the German army surrendered in Rheims courthouse, some old isolationists continued to warn the administration against imposing a severe settlement. A few of them may have sided with Dewey Short, who, after having personally seen liberated concentration camps, called for the "complete extermination" of all Gestapo members. "I would not care, he said, "if there were 1,000,000 or 10,000,000." But far more veteran isolationists agreed with Edwin C. Johnson, who sought merciless treatment for war criminals while opposing "destruction" of Germany's masses. Morris Rubin, finding Nazism the inevitable outcome of the Versailles Treaty, wanted no peace "based on vengeance, dismemberment, and enslavement." Robert Maynard Hutchins, president of the University of Chicago and a strong opponent of intervention in 1941, gave a V-E Day speech in which he accused the United States of holding racist attitudes toward Germany and Japan.[3]

From July 17 to August 7, 1945, Truman, Stalin, and Churchill (replaced at midpoint by Britain's newly elected Prime Minister, Clement Attlee) met at Potsdam. There at the Berlin suburb, the Big Three confirmed a decision, made at Yalta, to divide Germany into British, French, Russian, and United States occupation zones. They pledged to treat Germany as a single economic unit, while allowing each of the four occupying commanders to veto any decision. Germany was slated for total disarmament, demilitarization, and denazification. Other provisions included reparations (with the final sum unspecified), the forced return of large masses of Germans from Poland, Czechoslovakia, and Hungary, and the temporary retention of the Oder-Neisse boundary. A demolished and partitioned nation, it appeared, was going to have to get along on the scantiest of resources.[4]

Few old isolationists found the Potsdam meeting their criteria of a just peace. Villard called the conference "Vansittartism and Morgenthauism almost to the limit, only stopping short—and not very far short—of complete enslavement and extermination." Economist Samuel Crowther claimed that Truman's unfortunate pilgrimage merely confirmed "Russian sovereignty of Europe." The *Chicago Tribune* expressed indignation over Potsdam's economic provisions but still demanded that American troops leave Europe as quickly as possible. Although it asserted that a crippled Germany was bound to become Communist, it found the United States in no position to resist.[5]

From the moment that the diplomats signed the agreement, isolationists stressed one theme and stressed it continually: Germany held the key to the stability of Europe. William Henry Chamberlin, adopting the terms of geopolitics popularized in wartime, quoted Sir Halford MacKinder: "Who rules East Europe commands the Heartland. Who rules the Heartland commands the World-Island. Who rules the World-Island commands the world." Congressman Short agreed. In the very speech in which he demanded the execution of every member of the Gestapo, he called for "a pretty strong stabilized state in central Europe." *Human Events* cited the warning of Charles Zimmerman, an official of the Jewish Labor Committee, who claimed that an "industrial vacuum" in Germany would result in disaster for the Continent as a whole. As late as 1949 Senator Langer, whose rhetoric was seldom restrained, found that "the whole cause of human freedom . . . in Europe, as well as in Asia" depended upon Germany.[6]

Several old isolationists stressed that only the Communists could gain from a severe occupation. Senator Henry C. Dworshak (Rep.–Idaho) attacked the Treasury Department for giving the Soviets engraving plates used to create rampant inflation. Congressman George A. Dondero (Rep.–Mich.), an arch-conservative, cited an anarchist magazine, *Politics*, in order to prove that the American occupation favored Communists at the expense of democratic socialists.[7]

A few veteran anti-interventionists feared that the Russians would gain the loyalties of the conquered nation. When in July 1946 Molotov publicly opposed limitations on Germany's production or further cession of its land, Libby asserted that it could "fall into the lap of Soviet Russia by default." America, surmised Lawrence Dennis, could not match Stalin's promises of lost territories and an alliance aimed at grabbing the spoils of the British Empire.[8]

Old isolationists also expressed concern over possible German starvation. In the Western occupation zones, many people received well below 1,500 calories per day; at times allocations fell to 600, with some laborers not receiving enough nourishment to do a day's work. When pacifists and religious leaders sought to alleviate this condition, veteran isolationists often rallied to their support. At least ten old isolationists signed a petition drafted by Albion P. Beverage, former Congregationalist clergyman in charge of congressional liaison for Frederick J. Libby's National Council for the Prevention of War. Seeking immediate aid to Germany and Austria, thirty-four Senators informed the President that "the people of these countries are today facing starvation on a scale never before experienced in Western Civilization."[9]

The petition was not the only effort. Wheeler inserted a *Christian*

*Century* editorial calling for prompt aid to Germany into the *Congressional Record*, while both the *Progressive* and *Human Events* noted that Leo Baeck, Chief Rabbi of Berlin, sought sufficient food for the Germans. *Human Events* printed an essay by Alexander Boeker, a German-born Rhodes scholar and anti-Nazi emigré (and later West Germany's ambassador of the Vatican), who pointed to the mass starvation existing east of the Elbe.[10]

At first Truman appeared indifferent. In September 1945 he was quoted as saying, although the source was a biased one, that the peoples of Europe must "do things for themselves," not just sit around and wait "like birds to be fed." By December, however, the President—obviously on the defensive—was claiming that he was doing all that was possible to alleviate European starvation. Truman told the Senate petitioners that substantial relief could not yet go to Germany because its postal and communications systems had totally collapsed. He could not resist commenting that, although he had no desire to be "unduly cruel," he felt little "sympathy for those who caused the death of so many human beings by starvation, disease, and outright murder." (Villard reacted by asking what constituted "duly cruel?") When Senator Kenneth S. Wherry continued to prod the administration, Truman privately commented that the Nebraska Republican was making "a political inquiry for embarrassing purposes." The President, meeting with Senators La Follette, Wherry, and James A. Eastland (Dem.–Miss.) on January 8, 1946, again stressed transportation inadequacies.[11]

The senatorial protests must have had some effect. On February 19, 1946, Truman lifted the ban on private relief shipments, and eleven agencies started sending over 2,000 tons of medicine and food to Germany. Within two weeks, General Mark Clark, commander-in-chief of American occupation forces in Austria, acknowledged that relief missions were welcome in his military area.[12]

Despite such initial steps, a few of the more extreme old isolationists accused the administration of deliberately starving the Germans. The *Chicago Tribune* referred to "the famine Truman helped make." Langer went so far as to speak of "a savage and fanatical plot" to destroy fifteen million women and children. Even the Black Hole of Calcutta, said the North Dakota Senator, did not involve "a more vicious, more savage plan of mass murder."[13]

Libby and Beverage pressed for further aid, initiating an investigation headed by Senator Patrick A. McCarran (Dem.–Nev.), an old isolationist and chairman of the Judiciary Committee. On April 22 McCarran appointed a special subcommittee, consisting of himself, Eastland, Langer, Wheeler, and Wherry. Meeting in closed session, the group heard a variety of witnesses, ranging from Major General O. P. Echols, an army administrator in Germany, to Professor Boeker, whose mother was starving in Munich. The subcommittee unanimously reported an amendment designed to expedite food shipments, which within a week was approved by both houses of Congress and signed by the President.[14]

Even as late as 1948, however, some old isolationists still pressed the issue of starvation. Beverage's successor with Libby's NCPW, journalist James Finucane, petitioned Premier Robert Schuman of France to raise the food level in the French occupation zone, and nineteen Senators endorsed his effort. Henry Regnery printed another pamphlet by Karl Brandt claiming that occupation restrictions kept West Germany from producing enough to pay for its own food. The *Progressive* accused the United States of maintaining the "original Morgenthau madness" by keeping the official ration at 1,450 calories a day. "Sick and starving men," wrote editor Rubin, "cannot mine coal or labor in factories."[15]

Although many isolationists were sympathetic to the plight of all of Europe's needy, they spoke far more often about food to Germany than to other areas of Europe. In part, this is because Allied restrictions on Germany were more severe. In part, this is because some of the most ardent petitioners—Langer, Villard, Regnery—were either German-Americans or represented German-American constituencies. The old isolationists, or at least a few of them, could now point to one instance where the administration appeared to be the malicious power, Germany the victimized one.

If many veteran isolationists saw starvation as the most pressing issue, they did not find it the only one. Isolationists assailed mass deportation of Germans from Czechoslovakia and Poland. The Potsdam agreement had called for evacuation in "an orderly and humane manner," but the refugees faced much hardship. The expellees, unable to bring much clothing or goods with them, often lived in abysmal conditions. Out of sixty-six million people living in all of occupied Germany, some twelve million had been displaced. Langer declared that between twenty and twenty-five percent of the refugees had perished en route. "I doubt whether the Mongolian invasion was as bad as what we are witnessing at the present time," he said.[16]

The stormy Dakotan was not alone. To correspondent Freda Utley, forced removals from the Sudetenland and Silesia equaled those "crimes against humanity" (a phrase of the Nuremberg indictment) committed by the Nazis. Indeed, for the women and children who perished on the forced march, "a quick death in a gas chamber would have been comparatively merciful." If Langer and Mrs. Utley could be discounted as polemical partisans, the more sober Villard asserted that he preferred methods of the seventeenth century. "In the Thirty Years War," he wrote, "you knew what would take place when the invading army captured a city."[17]

Such old isolationists occasionally commented on the fate of German prisoners of war. The Yalta agreement had specifically provided for the use of forced labor, and at least 1.6 million captives were kept in Russia alone. Attacking the Crimean decision, Villard declared that "we have turned over 500,000 people to Stalin to be murdered or exiled." Langer, in claiming that at least five million were being held by the Russians, asked an Illinois audience what Abraham Lincoln would have thought about such exploitation! The *Chicago Tribune* accused the French of keeping over 600,000 Germans, and hence of violating the Geneva Convention. To the *Tribune*, France was aping Simon Legree, for it denied its new "slaves" sufficient food to work adequately and had them beaten by "Moroccan savages."[18]

Some old isolationists did not limit their attacks to issues of food, refugees, and prisoners; they assailed the entire occupation. William Henry Chamberlin accused the Allies of matching Nazi practices of looting, rape, deportation, and slave labor. Only the "maniacal attempt" to exterminate Europe's Jews distinguished the Germans from their recent foes. Rankin and Wheeler claimed that Senegalese troops, dressed in American uniform, raped between two to five thousand girls in Stuttgart.[19]

For all their patriotism, isolationists did not permit United States forces—who occupied Bavaria, Hesse, and Würtemberg—to go unscathed. Villard, with some justice, accused American troops of looting German houses. Restrictions prohibiting Germans from receiving money or foreign journals, hospital equipment, or drugs revealed a "sadistic policy." Similarly, the *Chicago Tribune* accused the American forces of engaging in "brutality, exploitation, refined larceny, and starvation." The arbitrary arrest of some 80,000 occupants of southwestern Germany, it commented, betrayed the spirit of the United States Constitution; such deeds could only create "another war more bitter and bloody than the last one."[20]

Other occupation practices met with opposition. O. K. Armstrong, a publicist active in organizing isolationist groups in 1940 and 1941, noted with irony that "WACS, wearing their uniforms and fruit salad, make talks to German youth on 'demilitarization.'" The *Progressive* published an attack by John Haynes Holmes, in which the pacifist clergyman strongly criticized Allied authorities who had burned works by Oswald Spengler and Heinrich von Treitschke. Chamberlin, observing the bans on intermarriage of German nationals and American troops, recalled Nazi restrictions: America's new "master race" psychology, in fact, extended to prohibiting German use of the washrooms at Berlin's Tempelhof airport. Dennis claimed that the Americans were supporting "slavery for five million people, an infant mortality rate of nearly 50%, etc."[21]

A few isolationists worked closely with pacifists in order to alleviate Germany's plight. Henry Regnery published two books by Victor Gollancz, prominent London publisher, as well as a small volume of letters smuggled out of Germany and edited by Villard. Both the National Council for the Prevention of War and the Foundation for Foreign Affairs were particularly active: Beverage went to Germany in November 1946, and spent several weeks in the western zone; Boeker, temporarily with the NCPW, drafted a bill to release all German prisoners. (The legislation became attached to a wider ECA provision.) *Peace Action* carried dispatches from the American press noting "the drunken, teen-age GIs reeling and clutching at their slovenly frauleins." The Foundation for Foreign Affairs helped finance Freda Utley's fact-finding trip to Germany in 1948, and James Finucane warned that bitter and frustrated German youth "might rise some day to plague their oppressors, and fight another war."[22]

Once the immediate threat of starvation passed, and the occupation forces began to act a bit less like conquerors, old isolationists concentrated on two other issues: ending limitations on German production and terminating the dismantling of German plants. In March 1946 the four occupying powers had announced a plan designed to reduce Germany's productive capacity to well below prewar levels. Germany was forbidden to manufacture implements of war, aircraft, or ships, or the machinery essential to such production. Enforcement led to prohibitions on ball-bearings, aluminium, heavy tractors, and machine tools. The Allies also placed severe limitations—called "levels-of-industry" agreements—upon certain basic industries. Metallurgical and chemical industries, for example, were limited to about forty percent of 1936 capacity and electroengineering to about fifty percent of 1938 production. The March conference, while setting no specific figures, agreed to a general policy of dismantling German factories and hauling them off as reparations. Ball-bearing, steel, and tractor plants went to the victor nations, with the Russians receiving the greatest number.[23]

Various veteran isolationists found such strictures self-defeating. Arguing that Western Europe's livelihood depended upon Germany's prosperity, they demanded that the United States foster, not reduce, its production. Otherwise, said Libby, "France will shiver, Britain will lack a vital market, and the United States will foot the bills." Langer claimed that Germany lacked sufficient funds to buy food from Hungary and Rumania, a handicap that could only retard the recovery of Eastern Europe. The Allied passion to prevent production, Chodorov commented, reflected an obtuse effort to "starve the patient into rationality."[24]

Herbert Hoover's highly publicized trip to Germany, made in February 1947, did much to focus public attention on the need for German economic recovery. An isolationist before Pearl Harbor, Hoover had been sympathetic to the work of the America First Committee and had occasionally advised its leadership. In 1941 he denied that the United States could ever conquer Germany, predicting instead that internal pressures would eventually destroy Nazism.[25]

Truman, fully aware of Hoover's desire for Germany's recovery, realized that the publicity given the trip could help ease occupation restrictions, and he may have encouraged Hoover to write his own orders. In reporting back to Truman, the former President claimed that standards of food and shelter had sunk to "the lowest level in a hundred years of Western history." Hoover, noting the traditional economic ties between Germany and the rest of the Continent, warned that holding "Germany in economic chains" would "keep Europe in rags," and thereby destroy "any hope of peace in the world."[26]

Hoover soon advanced more specific proposals, calling for a unified federal state, an end to dismantling and production restrictions, and a separate peace with Bizonia, the recently merged American and British zones. Claiming that Russia and France had violated Potsdam pledges to unify Germany, he denied that the United States was bound any longer to honor Big Three stipulations. Hoover also pleaded with the frugal John

Taber for $725 million in emergency aid, declaring that only the preservation of Germany and Japan could save Europe and the Far East. The New York Congressman, who greatly admired the ex-President, saw to it that emergency funds soon materialized.[27]

Several old isolationists noted that Hoover's findings confirmed their own sentiments. A petition of some forty-eight prominent citizens endorsed his recommendations, with Villard, Thomas, and Morley joining such World War II interventionists as Nicholas Murray Butler, former president of Columbia University, and James T. Shotwell, prominent Columbia historian. Langer arranged for a delegation of the German-American Steuben Society to tell Truman that Hoover's suggestions were valid. A. S. Barrows, former president of Sears and contributor to America First, said the nation must choose between Hoover's proposals and the continuation of an occupation that was "a disgrace to our flag."[28]

The Hoover visit was only one indication that the administration was becoming more lenient. In May 1946 General Clay had suspended reparations from the American zone until, he said, France and Russia agreed to abide by Potsdam pledges and treat Germany as a single economic unit. Secretary of State Byrnes, speaking at Stuttgart in September 1946, endorsed merging the western zones and establishing a provisional government. In what was obviously an attempt to counter Molotov's bid of July, Byrnes called for raising levels of industry and pledged sustained interest in Germany's recovery. Acheson's Delta Council address of May 1947 stressed that the United States must reconstruct both Germany and Japan, "those two great workshops of Europe and Asia." In July 1947 JCS/1067 was replaced by the far more liberal JCS/1779, a directive based upon the premise that Germany's revival was essential to Europe's recovery. Truman obviously was not merely responding to the isolationists' arguments; he had soon realized that German recovery was necessary to implement containment in Europe.[29]

Of course such easing of restrictions received strong support from veteran isolationists. Chamberlin expressed delight that the administration was finally repudiating Yalta and Potsdam. By 1948 Libby's *Peace Action* was featuring such articles as "Brightened Outlook for Germany." Villard, while still complaining of mail and food restrictions, began harboring a new anxiety: efforts to integrate Germany into a Western defense structure could result in the whitewash of former Nazis, with Americans cheering a German regiment marching down Fifth Avenue.[30]

Germany also played a significant role in the debate over the Marshall Plan. Old isolationists had long argued that funds appropriated for general rehabilitation of Europe would be better spent on Germany, a nation that, they claimed, possessed far greater resources, occupied the most strategic of locations, and housed an industrious population. Lawrence H. Smith believed that "ten Marshall Plans" would "not do the job so long as industrial Germany is crucified." The original draft of Marshall's proposal had excluded Germany, but in September 1947 the sixteen ECA nations reported that a successful program depended upon German economic integration. By December Germany was included, eventually receiving

$3.2 billion. Such Marshall Plan backers as Congressman Dirksen used ECA allocations for Germany to help stimulate other appropriations. The defeated nation, said the Illinois Republican, was "the key to recovery and peace over in the Old World at the present time."[31]

As general Western policy shifted, far fewer German plants faced dismantling. In 1946 the number of plants scheduled for dismantling in all four zones ran from 1,500 to 2,000; a year later the total for the western zones had been reduced to 859. As early as April 1947 Marshall had pressed the Council of Foreign Ministers to raise the quota on German steel production. Within several months Bizonia unilaterally raised its limits, and by the summer of 1947 even the intransigent French were beginning to favor an easing of restrictions.[32]

For many old isolationists, such welcome measures did not go far enough and, throughout 1948 and 1949, they continued protesting against production ceilings and the breakup of factories. O. K. Armstrong made a survey for the Council of Relief Agencies, in which he charged that German schools and hospitals were being taken apart. Upon his return to the United States, he organized a Conference Against Dismantling in Washington.. The NCPW, using Boeker's skill, drafted a measure requiring the Secretary of State to negotiate an end to such reparations, and a watered-down version appeared as an amendment to an ECA bill. Hoover too continued to press for the abolition of plant removals.[33]

Some old isolationists still used impassioned rhetoric. Even Great Britain, a nation that—like the United States—favored easing restrictions, faced their criticism. Langer accused both the United Kingdom and France of engaging in a "criminal deforestation program," thereby "making a mockery of the claims that Germany can become a self-supporting agrarian people." The *Chicago Tribune* charged the British with trying to prohibit German production of synthetic rubber in order to protect their Malayan holdings. Mrs. Utley pointed out that *The British Jewel and Metal Worker*, an English trade journal, had praised the "level-of-industry" edicts for allowing its particular industry a "breathing space."[34]

Those old isolationists who sought bipartisanship attempted to play down the dismantling issue. Vandenberg, in fact, went so far as to endorse temporary dismantling, finding it preferable to granting reparations out of current German production. In February 1948 the Michigan Senator's Foreign Relations Committee reported that the Soviet Union was then receiving only three plants, and that deliveries to other nations had much speeded their recovery. Henry Cabot Lodge noted that Secretary of the Army Kenneth C. Royall had claimed that the plants slated for dismantling could be removed without affecting Germany's recovery. The administration, however, continued to make efforts to stop all dismantling, and by 1952, the process had been completely halted. In the three western zones, some 668 German plants had been taken apart.[35]

The isolationists were fully aware of continued administration moves toward economic leniency. However, by seeking to accelerate German recovery even further, they might be able to limit major financial and military commitments on the European continent. Truman's pleas for economic aid, and later for arms and troops, could be made to appear useless as long as the one nation essential to Europe's stability remained crippled.

The struggle to gain equal economic and political status for Germany necessarily involved efforts to restore *Deutschland* with some image of moral worth. Few Americans would want to aid a people continually presented as cruel, if not genocidal. Veteran anti-interventionists sought to portray a "different Germany," and hence to take the sting out of Western indictments. By such attempts they might end the continual stress upon German guilt and create more sympathy for Germany's predicament as well.

Even news of concentration-camp atrocities, a few isolationists maintained, provided no justification for Allied inhumanity. Lindbergh, who personally visited the German camp at Dora, demanded punishment for those guilty of such crimes, but opposed applying the principle of "an eye for an eye." Frank Gannett, who also saw the result of Nazi rule firsthand, maintained that this was no time for "revenge." Hutchins insisted that "the wildest atrocity stories" could not alter the "simple truth" that "no men are beasts." Libby remarked that "no nation has a monopoly on atrocities. War itself is the supreme atrocity." The first victims of Nazi brutalities, said Philip La Follette, were the Germans themselves. The *Progressive* featured an article by William B. Hesseltine, historian at the University of Wisconsin, who implicitly compared mythical atrocity stories popular immediately after the American Civil War to those currently in circulation.[36]

Several old isolationists criticized the denazification proceedings. In the United States zone, the process centered on a lengthy questionnaire (*Fragebogen*) designed to identify and isolate genuine National Socialists. However, the whole process had become so tedious, and so subject to inequity, that even Germans who had been ardent anti-Nazis sought its abolition. Important collaborators evaded punishment, while nominal party members were treated at outcasts. Armstrong noted that the operation subjected whole masses to a "cloud of guilt," with certain categories of people subject to automatic arrest. Hoover privately claimed that many Germans had been forced to join the Nazi party in order to participate in national affairs. Taber declared that even a grocer compelled to pay a monetary tribute to the Nazis was subject to trial. Langer asserted that arbitrary political classifications made every German guilty "until he or she can prove himself innocent."[37]

In an effort to show that many Germans did not support Nazism, a few old isolationists stressed the role played by the resistance. Early in 1946 *Human Events* featured two articles by former intelligence officers lauding rebellious generals. Henry Regnery published Hans Rothfels's *German Resistance to Hitler* (1948), a careful study of those who participated in the July 1944 putsch. The implication was obvious: United States support for a strong German underground could have deposed Hitler, thereby ending World War II years earlier. Hanighen, in endorsing Allen Dulles's

*Germany's Underground* (1947), emphasized that unconditional surrender and area bombing made opposition more difficult. Chodorov claimed that American cooperation with dissident Germans might have saved "thousands of lives and billions of dollars."[38]

To many veteran isolationists, the Nuremberg trials epitomized occupation injustice. The tribunal had been established by an agreement made at London in August 1945 and was composed of jurists from each of the four major occupying powers. The proceedings, comprising over forty-two bulky volumes of testimony, lasted from November 1945 to October 1946. Of the twenty-one persons tried, thirteen were sentenced to hang. The chief American prosecutor, Associate Justice Robert Jackson of the Supreme Court, denied that the trials were merely engaging in prosecuting vanquished soldiers; rather, he said, they were punishing those selected German leaders who had waged a war of aggression, and who had persecuted, exterminated, enslaved, and deported countless individuals in the process. Truman approved of the tribunal, defending the court's effort to define atrocities as "crimes against humanity" and declaring that "aggressive war" was indeed criminal activity.[39]

Many old isolationists were far less sure. Taft's claim that the proceedings were colored by "the spirit of vengeance" received widespread publicity. The Nuremberg hangings, he said in October 1946, would "be a blot on the American record which we shall long regret."[40] Protests by old isolationists, however, were far more extensive, both in the numbers who objected and in the range of their arguments.

One argument centered on violations of Anglo-Saxon law. Norman Thomas denied that the offenders had violated any codified law. Borchard commented that the framers of the Kellogg-Briand Anti-War Pact, an agreement that the Germans had supposedly transgressed, never intended to apply it to individuals. Furthermore, at the time of ratification in 1929, the signatories had supplied enough reservations to make the treaty innocuous. Neumann declared that the court had pronounced culpable all members of certain organizations, hence institutionalizing "guilt by association."[41]

Another claim concerned Allied hypocrisy. Neumann declared that Allied atrocities had matched those of the Nazis point by point. Chodorov wrote, "At Nuremberg an international tribunal sentenced a number of scoundrels to death for the crime of dropping an atomic bomb on a defenseless city, killing half the population, maiming many others—or do we have our dates mixed?" Members of the anti-Hitler coalition, said Libby, had themselves committed major acts of war: Stalin invaded Poland in 1939, England and France declared war against Germany that year, and the United States was involved in "acts of aggression" against Germany long before Pearl Harbor. Villard wondered why Justice Jackson did not establish a posthumous court of honor to try such warlike American leaders as Polk and Lincoln.[42]

There were other points as well. The *Chicago Tribune* claimed that Russia's presence made the tribunal a "kangaroo court." Beard recalled the Hitler-Stalin Pact; Thomas noted Russia's invasion of Finland; Pettengill cited Russia's more recent confrontations with Turkey and Iran. Several old isolationists found the precedent ominous. The *New York Daily News* commented, "Everybody knows these men's real crime was that they did not win." Dennis concurred, declaring that Nuremberg had only assured that future wars would be more savage. "You can bet," asserted Lawrence Smith, "that Stalin and the Politburo has prepared its list of American war criminals."[43]

A few veteran isolationists denied that soldiers following orders were culpable. Borchard claimed that a military directive left the soldier with no moral choice. The precedent of indicting soldiers for obeying instructions, said Dondero, would invariably weaken America's defenses against Communism. Some anti-interventionists doubted whether such trials would deter aggression. Neumann, writing at the outset of the Cold War, saw little evidence that Nuremberg was relieving international tensions. The *Progressive* featured an article by pacifist Milton Mayer, who asked, "What good will it do us to shoot these atrocity gazeebos, anyway? Their evil work is all done." In 1950 Langer commented acidly, "The Nuremberg trials have not deterred the Reds in Korea."[44]

Not all arguments against Nuremberg were limited to issues of justice and equity; a few assertions were a bit more extreme. The *Chicago Tribune*, noting the suicide of two imprisoned German generals, said that the United States was "likely to wind up convincing the German people that all the defendants are innocent." Its publisher, Colonel McCormick, refused to lunch with Francis Biddle, Roosevelt's Attorney General and a member of the tribunal, on the grounds that he would not dine with a "murderer." Dondero claimed that the trials had been inspired by Communists, while Langer asserted that "practically the entire prosecution staff" was composed of "leftists" and Communist sympathizers.[45]

Within three years after the trials were over, revisionist presses began publishing attacks on Nuremberg. The firm of Henry Regnery took the lead, publishing Montgomery Belgion's *Victor's Justice* in 1949. In this work a British journalist claimed that the tribunal degraded the established law of nations. During the same year, Regnery came out with Freda Utley's *High Cost of Vengeance*, a book that combined an indictment of varied war crimes trials with a general condemnation of the occupation. More strident than Belgion, Mrs. Utley accused Brigadier General Telford Taylor, Chief American Counsel for War Crimes, of harboring pro-Soviet sympathies. She went so far as to deny that Germany had possessed any military tradition until "centuries of French aggression."[46]

Other revisionist publishers began offering their own critiques. In 1953 Devin-Adair published *Unconditional Hatred: German War Guilt and the Future of Europe*, in which Captain Russell Grenfell, a British naval officer, argued that the bombing of Hiroshima had turned the West into "moral humbugs of Olympic standard." A small Wisconsin firm, C. C. Nelson of Appleton, released *Advance to Barbarism* (1953), an account by an English lawyer, Frederick John Partington Veale. Although the book focused upon Allied bombing of civilians, Veale found Nuremberg reminding him of the Red Queen in Lewis Carroll's *Alice in Wonderland*: "Sentence first—verdict afterwards." A host of isolationists and pacifists were particularly enthusiastic about the Veale volume. Mary Ritter Beard, the widow of Charles A. Beard and herself a noted historian, claimed that if she were dictator, she would make the book required reading.[47]

Protests against Nuremberg did not imply that most old isolationists condoned Nazi activities or failed to present alternatives. Taft preferred to see an Allied court-martial sentence the guilty. Thomas claimed that recognized laws already existed for those who had committed atrocities. The *Washington Times-Herald* suggested that the chief justices of such neutral nations as Ireland, Sweden, Switzerland, Spain, and Portugal conduct a truly impartial tribunal. Felix Morley would have preferred to have shot such men as Goering and Streicher; that, at least, would have been an "honest and forthright action."[48]

Some old isolationists, although far fewer in number than those who protested against Nuremberg, opposed the so-called Malmédy trials. Like Nuremberg, these trials were rooted in German atrocities. In December 1944, during the Battle of the Bulge, an SS panzer division captured some 101 American soldiers, marched them through wheatfields near Malmédy, Belgium, and machine-gunned them down. A hundred Belgian civilians were similarly slaughtered.[49]

After the war, American troops interned the offenders at Schwäbisch Hall, a small town near Stuttgart, and questioned them under conditions of solitary confinement. In July 1946, after trial at Dachau, the army sentenced forty-three of these prisoners to death. The Chief Defense Counsel, Colonel Willis M. Everett, claimed that several of those sentenced had given their confessions under duress. The prosecution, he declared, had used such illegal means as mock trials, stool pigeons, faked hangings, impersonation of priests, starvation, and beatings. An investigation ordered by the Judge Advocate found little substance to Everett's charges.

The case, however, would not die. Everett continued his fight, the Secretary of the Army made a series of pardons and, late in 1948, several new Army inquiries reopened the issue. The major efforts to save twelve unpardoned Malmédy defendants, plus seventeen other prisoners, were made by Libby's NCPW and Senator Langer. Edward Leroy Van Roden, a judge in the children's court of Media, Pennsylvania, and a participant in the Army investigations, revealed that one Army report had condemned the Malmédy trials. Libby and Finucane, with strong backing from Henry Regnery, got in touch with both Van Roden and Senator Langer, and soon gave the judge's account to the press. Finucane, who first had learned of the incident while being stationed with the American army near Malmédy, was particularly active in seeking redress. He wrote an article for the *Progressive* under Van Roden's name entitled "American Atrocities in Germany" and drafted a letter to Secretary Royall, this time over Langer's signature, claiming that the trial was "certainly no credit to American justice."[50]

Soon Congress took up the issue. In January 1949 Langer introduced a resolution drafted by Finucane calling for an investigation of military trials, with special attention to be focused on Malmédy. Speaking on the

Senate floor, the Dakotan accused the United States of acting like a "hate-happy hangman." He had hoped that the Senate Judiciary Committee, of which he was a ranking member, would hold hearings. However, the investigation fell to a subcommittee of the Senate Armed Services Committee and was chaired by Senator Raymond Baldwin (Rep.–Wis.). Senator Joseph R. McCarthy (Rep.–Wis.), a strong partisan of the prisoners, was permitted to sit on the hearings.[51]

During the subcomittee investigation Libby continued his pleas for amnesty, even praising the "masterly job" performed by the volatile and truculent McCarthy. Chamberlin and Mrs. Utley both give the Malmédy case strong play, as did *Human Events* and the *Christian Century*. On the other hand, a sensationalistic interventionist group, the Friends of Democracy, accused Van Roden of having endorsed a pro-Nazi book.[52]

By and large, the subcommittee, which had a proprietary interest in maintaining the Army's good name, exonerated the American occupation. Baldwin himself admitted that the Army might have beaten the prisoners, but denied that such practices were condoned or used to gain confessions. Arguing *ad hominum,* the subcommittee accused the NCPW of playing into the hands of neo-Nazi elements, who in turn had sought to discredit the American presence and work in alliance with the Soviet Union. Only later did historians claim that the case made by Langer and Libby, and by McCarthy as well, did not lack merit.[53]

Libby continued his amnesty pleas, even writing John McCloy, United States High Commissioner to Germany. In June 1950 McCloy replied that no new evidence had established the innocence of the condemned prisoners. While noting that he had set up a War Crimes Clemency Committee, he denied that he could commute the sentences of "men found guilty of serious crime." McCloy's clemency board soon reduced the number of condemned to twenty-one. Eventually only seven faced the executioner, none of whom had participated in the Malmédy incident. One defendant had been a lieutenant general in the SS and director of a concentration camp. Another, an SS major general, led an *Einsatzgruppe* that had liquidated over a million Russian Jews.[54]

The NCPW continued its efforts to keep the remaining seven alive, and Armstrong, elected to the House in 1950 (Rep.–Mo.), introduced a bill to postpone the executions. All, however, was in vain. When the seven were hanged at Landsberg prison in June 1951, Libby could only write William H. Regnery that "we did everything we could." The prisoners, he maintained, had been killed because they obeyed superiors in wartime. The case of Malmédy, and of other military executions, was closed.[55]

In no area of the world were old isolationists less "isolationist." Far from being indifferent to Germany's future, most of them continually worked to foster its recovery. Only a few, such as Senator Guy Gillette (Dem.–Iowa), warned against a lenient peace. German-Americans, of course, stood in the forefront of efforts to restore the land of their ancestors.

Oswald Garrison Villard, for example, was descended from "forty-eighters," his own father, Henry Villard, possessing banking ties to Frankfurt and Hamburg. The Regnery family came from Alsace, and Henry Regnery had once attended the University of Bonn. Although Frederick J. Libby was not of German ancestry, he had studied theology in Heidelberg and Berlin. Among the heavy contributors to the NCPW were such German-American families as the Regnerys and the Speidels.[56]

Others among the veteran isolationists combined ancestry with more direct political interest. Senator Langer would go as far as to inform audiences that Americans of German stock had designed the Capitol and the Library of Congress building. German-Americans were one of the two dominant ethnic groups in Langer's North Dakota, and areas of German concentration backed Langer heavily at the polls. If ethnic loyalties were not always the dominant factor in American isolationism, the German issue shows that they were undoubtedly a significant one.[57]

West Germany's staunch and vocal allegiance to a "free enterprise" system undoubtedly delighted many conservatives among the old isolationists. In July 1948 the Allied administrators of Bizonia gave economist Ludwig Erhard permission to abolish price controls. Prices rose, but production more than kept pace. By the early 1950s, Erhard, as Economic Minister of the German Federal Republic, was continually preaching the gospel of the free market and initiating a policy of incentives and competition. For conservatives, Germany not only embodied the "Protestant ethic," but appeared as the major outpost of a competitive economy in Europe.[58]

One must, however, beware of oversimplification, for other factors were also at work. Isolationists in 1940 and 1941 had not let genuine abhorrence of Nazism dim their belief that a strong Germany, in some form, was needed to prevent both Communism and ruin in Europe. Hitler's defeat, declared General Wood in December 1940, would result in victor and vanquished alike facing "some form of Communism or National Socialism." America First Committee leaders, including the liberal Democrat Chester Bowles, had urged a negotiated peace, a move that would surely have retained a powerful Germany on the Continent.[59]

By 1945 postwar Europe was experiencing some of the very chaos that isolationists had often feared. Hence, it is hardly surprising that so many found German recovery essential. In 1947 Felix Morley put the issue well: aid to Greece and Turkey merely massaged "the pedal extremities"; the European patient was "striken with coronary thrombosis," and therefore needing work at the German "heart."[60]

In addition to partisan motives, as seen in the case of Langer, or geopolitical considerations, as typified by the argument of Morley, old isolationists were often prompted by humanitarianism and a sense of justice. The inflammatory rhetoric and obvious exaggerations made by Langer, Dondero, and the *Chicago Tribune* did not adequately represent the depth of genuine concern. It was by no means accidental that Germany was the one issue in which both conservative and liberal isolationists, not to mention certain pacifists, were able to work together. Only later, during the debate over rearming Germany, would left and right isolationists part company.[61]

Isolationist anger should not obscure the tacit agreement of the administration. Admittedly, occupation policy—particularly in its earliest stages— was harsh and confused. But as early as 1946 the government realized the need to restore Germany as a self-sustaining nation and acted accordingly. Complaints from veteran isolationists became focused less and less on the nature of the occupation, more and more on the pace permitted German recovery. Critics could embarrass the administration by harping on dismantling; they could create American sympathy for the Germans by stressing unjust aspects of the occupation; they could side with Germany's own political leaders in declaring that the Basic Law of the Federal Republic, propounded in September 1949, did not give Germany sufficient freedom.[62] But, unlike so many clashes between the old isolationists and the interventionists, no fundamental conflict existed. Interests were surprisingly similar.

## NOTES

1. Gaddis, The United States, pp. 117–23; Harold Zink, The United States in Germany, 1944–1955 (New York: Macmillan, 1957), p. 94. The final draft of JCS/1067 ordered the shutdown of such industries as iron, steel, chemicals, and machine tools. All such facilities were to be converted to the production of consumer goods. Paterson, Soviet-American Confrontation, p. 239.

2. Trohan, Political Animals, p. 199; Frank Waldrop, "Joe's Big Moment," Washington Times-Herald, December 27, 1944; Karl Brandt, "Germany Is Our Problem," pamphlet (Hinsdale, Ill.: Human Affairs, Inc., 1946).

3. Short, CR, May 16, 1945, p. 4674; Johnson, "Let's Talk Turkey," Progressive 9 (January 8, 1945): 1; Rubin, "The Time Is Now, Mr. President," Progressive, 9 (February 5, 1945); 1, 8; Robert Maynard Hutchins, "The New Realism," commencement address, University of Chicago, June 15, 1945, Vital Speeches 11 (July 15, 1945): 601–3. Hutchins had been an important adviser to America First. See Cole, America First, p. 23.

4. Reparations for the Western nations were to come from the Western-occupied zones, those for Russia from the Soviet-occupied zone. Russia would also receive ten percent of the disposable plants in the West. The West would exchange another fifteen percent for commodities more plentiful in the Russian zone. Gaddis, The United States, p. 241.

5. Villard, "The Potsdam Pact: Disaster for Europe," Progressive 9 (August 13, 1945): 1; Samuel Crowther, "Stop, Look and Listen," Economic Council Papers 4 (October 1945); "The Red Star Rises" (editorial), Chicago Tribune, March 4, 1945.

6. Chamberlin, "Our Failure in Germany," Human Events 4 (April 16, 1947); Short, CR, May 16, 1945, p. 4673; Hanighen, "Not Merely Gossip," Human Events 3 (January 9, 1946); Langer, CR, February 8, 1949, p. 957.

7. Henry C. Dworshak, CR, December 19, 1947, p. 11685; George A. Dondero, CR, February 28, 1949, pp. A1123–25.

8. F. J. Libby to W. H. Regnery, November 21, 1946, NCPW Papers; Dennis, Appeal to Reason, #26 (September 21, 1946). For Molotov's overtures, see Feis, From Trust to Terror, pp. 133–34. For an example of isolationist reasoning, see Morley, "Russia Fills the Vacuum," Human Events 3 (July 24. 1946).

9. For editorial opinion that includes a plea coming from a joint committee representing Protestants, Catholics, and Jews, see "Are We Murderers?," *Christian Century* 62 (November 14, 1945): 1247–49. For letters from congressmen and church groups advocating aid to Germany, see Boxes 1274–75, Official File, Truman Papers, and "Conditions in Germany," Box 63, Robert La Follette, Jr. Papers. For the petition drafted by Albion P. Beverage, December 7, 1945, see Box 1272, Official File, Truman Papers. Among the signers were such old isolationists as Capper, Edwin Johnson, La Follette, Langer, Shipstead, Walsh, Tobey, Wheeler, Wiley, and Willis. For Beverage's role in the petition, see F. J. Libby to W. H. Regnery, January 5, 1946, NCPW Papers.

10. For Wheeler, see *CR*, December 13, 1945, p. A5709–5711. For references to Leo Baeck, see *Progressive* 10 (January 14, 1946): 12; Hanighen, "Not Merely Gossip," *Human Events* 3 (January 9, 1946). For Alexander Boeker, see "The Nativity," *Human Events* 2 (December 19, 1945), and Morley, "Early Days," p. 28.

11. Truman cited by Kenneth S. Wherry, *CR*, December 9, 1946, p. 515 (Wherry's source was the magazine *Politics*); H. S. Truman to Senator J. C. O'Mahoney (Dem.–Wyo.), December 17, 1945, Box 1272, Official File, Truman Papers; H. S. Truman to Senator A. W. Hawkes (Rep.–N.J.), December 21, 1945, *CR*, January 29, 1946, p. 512; O. G. Villard to P. Hutchinson, January 2, 1946, Villard Papers; Truman handwritten comment on the letter sent to him by Wherry, January 4, 1946, Official File, Box 1272, Truman Papers; meeting of January 8 in Harl A. Dalstrom, "Kenneth S. Wherry," Ph.D. diss., University of Nebraska, 1966, p. 523. La Follette, commenting on his meeting with Truman, declared that the President offered little encouragement concerning either postal services or relief work. R. M. La Follette, Jr. to E. Stinnes, January 15, 1946, Box 61, Robert La Follette, Jr. Papers.

12. Truman press release, February 19, 1946, Box 1274, Official File, Truman Papers; Mark Clark to A. Wiley, March 2, 1946, *CR*, pp. 2399–400.

13. "The Famine Truman Helped Make" (editorial), *Chicago Tribune*, April 20, 1946; Langer, *CR*, March 29, 1946, p. 2801, and April 18, 1946, p. 3962.

14. Libby, *To End War*, pp. 178–80.

15. Finucane petition noted in F. J. Libby to Mrs. L. C. Schaffey, September 30, 1948, NCPW Papers; Brandt, "Is There Still a Chance for Germany?", pamphlet (Hinsdale, Ill.: Regnery, 1948), p. 14; Rubin, "Fading Peace," *Progressive* 12 (February 1948): 4.

16. Langer, *CR*, March 8, 1948, p. 3222–23.

17. Freda Utley, *The High Cost of Vengeance* (Chicago: Regnery, 1949), 13–14; Villard, "Our Lunatic Policy in Germany," *Progressive* 9 (November 12, 1945): 4.

18. O. G. Villard to P. Hutchinson, March 5, 1946, Villard Papers; Langer, speech to the Civic Committee to Welcome Senator Langer, Chicago, May 5, 1947, *CR*, p. A3471; "Slaveholders Always Defend Slavery" (editorial), *Chicago Tribune*, December 10, 1946.

19. Chamberlin, "Shifting American Alignments," *Human Events* 3 (May 22, 1946); Rankin and Wheeler, *CR*, July 18, 1945, pp. 7738–39.

20. Villard, "Our Lunatic Policy in Germany," p. 4; Villard, "No Humanity for Germans," *Human Events* 5 (January 21, 1948); "Never Had It so Good" (editorial), *Chicago Tribune*, February 25, 1947; "Excesses in Germany" (editorial), *Chicago Tribune*, July 25, 1945.

21. O. K. Armstrong, testimony before House Foreign Affairs Committee, February 3, 1947, *United States Foreign Policy for a Post-War Recovery Program*, p. 816; John Haynes Holmes, "Burning the Books Again!", *Progressive* 9 (November 5, 1945): 4; Chamberlin, "We Play Master Race," *Progressive* 10 (October 6, 1946): 9; Dennis, *Appeal to Reason*, #21 (August 17, 1946).

22. Victor Gollancz, *Our Threatened Values* (Chicago: Regnery, 1946); Gollancz, *In Darkest Germany* (Chicago: Regnery, 1947); Villard, ed., "Letters from Germany," pamphlet (Hinsdale, Ill.: Human Affairs Publishers, 1946). On Beverage's mission, see undated sketch of Beverage's life in the NCPW Papers. On Boeker, see Libby to Mrs. L. C. Schaffey, September 30, 1948, NCPW Papers. On occupation immaturity, see *Peace Action* 13 (February 1947): 3. On Utley trip, see A. I. Gamber to F. J. Libby, October 14, 1948, NCPW Papers. On the views of James Finucane, see "Thaws Toward Humbled Germany," *Peace Action* 14 (March 1948): 3.

23. Feis, *From Trust to Terror*, pp. 60–61; Paterson, *Soviet-American Confrontation*, p. 242.

24. Libby, *Peace Action* 12 (October 1946): 6; Langer, *CR*, March 29, 1946, p. 2803; Chodorov, "Why Europe Starves," *analysis* 2 (May 1946): 4.

25. For his closeness to America First, see R. Douglas Stuart, Jr. to H. Hoover, December 17, 1941, Box 132, Hoover Papers. For a summary of Hoover's thought before Pearl Harbor, see Joan Hoff Wilson, *Herbert Hoover: Forgotten Progressive* (Boston: Little, Brown, 1975), pp. 241–49, and Harold Wolfe, *Herbert Hoover: Public Servant and Leader of the Loyal Opposition* (New York: Exposition Press, 1956), pp. 379–401.

26. Rumor in Hanighen, "Not Merely Gossip," *Human Events* 4 (February 5, 1947). For accounts of Hoover's trip, see Louis P. Lochner, *Herbert Hoover and Germany* (New York: Macmillan, 1960), pp. 178–201, and Wolfe, pp. 425–26. Hoover's two reports were entitled "German Agriculture and Food Requirements," February 28, 1947, and "Necessary Steps for Promotion of German Exports, so as to Relieve American Taxpayers of the Burden of Relief, and for the Economic Recovery of Europe," March 18, 1947, Box 129, Hoover Papers.

27. H. Hoover to J. Taber, May 26, 1947, mimeographed copy in Taber Papers, Box 166; Lochner, pp. 189–93.

28. Petition in Lochner, *Herbert Hoover and Germany*, p. 187; Langer action in *Prevent World War III*, #22 (October-November 1947), p. 22; A. S. Barrows to R. E. Wood, May 19, 1947, copy in Robert La Follette, Jr., Papers, Box 624. For Barrows and America First, see Large Contributors File, AFC Papers.

29. Clay in Gaddis, *The United States*, p. 329; Speech of James F. Byrnes at Stuttgart, *New York Times*, September 7, 1946, p. 5; Acheson speech in Jones, *The Fifteen Weeks*, p. 280; change in German occupation in Paterson, *Soviet-American Confrontation*, p. 245.

30. Chamberlin, "Germany: The Race against Time," *Progressive* 11 (April 14, 1947): 2; "Brightened Outlook for Germany," *Peace Action* 14 (July 1948): 4; O. G. Villard to P. Hutchinson, March 31, 1948, Villard Papers.

31. Lawrence H. Smith, "Republican Responsibility," *Human Events* 5 (December 29, 1948); Dirksen, *CR*, June 4, 1948, p. 7191.

32. Feis, *From Trust to Terror*, pp. 216–17, 271–72; Paterson, *Soviet-American Confrontation*, p. 246.

33. For Armstrong's arguments and activities in the United States, *Kansas City Times*, October 12, 1949; memo in NCPW Papers; and O. K. Armstrong, "German Destruction at *Our* Expense," *Reader's Digest* 53 (July 1948), 132–36. For Boeker petition, see Libby to Mrs. L. C. Schaffey, September 30, 1948, NCPW Papers. For Hoover position, see H. Hoover to J. Martin, March 24, 1948, *CR*, p. 3436. For examples of protest against dismantling, see Taft, Ohio Society address, *CR*, p. 2133; "Marshall the Wrecker" (editorial), *Chicago Tribune*, February 12, 1948; Hart, "Stop Those Dismantlings—Now!," *Economic Council Letter*, #223 (September 15, 1949).

34. Langer, *CR*, February 28, 1949, p. 1605; "Wrecking German Plants" (editorial), *Chicago Tribune*, June 20, 1948; Utley, *High Cost of Vengeance*, p. 94.

35. Vandenberg, *CR*, December 19, 1947, pp. 11680–81; Vandenberg in Senate Committee on Foreign Relations, February 26, 1948, *Report on European Recovery Program* (Washington, D.C.: U.S. Government Printing Office, 1948), pp. 39–40; Lodge, *CR*, March 8, 1948, p. 2314; Paterson, *Soviet-American Confrontation*, p. 248.

36. Lindbergh, *Chicago Tribune*, July 26, 1945; Gannett, CBS broadcast, July 4, 1946, Box 13, Gannett Papers; Hutchins quoted in *Prevent World War III*, #10 (July-August 1945), p. 10; Libby, *Peace Action* 9 (July 1945): 3–4; P. La Follette to I. La Follette, May 5, 1945, Philip La Follette Papers; Hesseltine, "Atrocities Then and Now," *Progressive* 9 (May 9, 1945): 4.

37. Testimony of O. K. Armstrong, House Committee on Foreign Affairs, February 3, 1947, *United States Foreign Policy for a Postwar Recovery Program*, p. 818; Hoover conversation discussed in S. Morton to R. Herbst, July 24, 1947, Morton Papers; Taber, press release, June 4, 1948, Box 154, Taber Papers; Langer, *CR*, June 27, 1947, p. 7814. For a description of the breakdown of denazification, see Koppel S. Pinson, *Modern Germany: Its History and Civilization*, 2d ed. (New York: Macmillan, 1966), pp. 544–46.

38. Alexander B. Maley, "The Epic of the German Underground," *Human Events* 3 (February 27, 1946); E. A. Bayne, "Resistance in the German Foreign Office," *Human Events* 3 (April 3, 1946): Hans Rothfels, *The German Opposition to Hitler* (Hinsdale, Ill.: Regnery, 1948); Hanighen, "Not Merely Gossip," *Human Events*, 4 (April 16, 1947); Chodorov, "Trailing the Trend," *analysis* 4 (July 1948): 3.

39. Robert H. Jackson to H. S. Truman, October 7, 1946, and H. S. Truman to F. Biddle, November 23, 1946, Box 1008, Official File, Truman Papers.

40. Taft, "The Heritage of the English-Speaking Peoples and Their Responsibility," October 5, 1946, in *Vital Speeches* 13 (November 1, 1946): 17; Patterson, *Mr. Republican*, pp. 328–29.

41. Thomas in Bernard K. Johnpoll, *Pacifist's Progress: Norman Thomas and the Decline of American Socialism* (Chicago: Quadrangle, 1970), p. 252; E. M. Borchard to R. A. Taft, October 7, 1946, Box 561, Taft Papers; W. L. Neumann, undated and unpublished memorandum on the Nuremberg trials, p. 2, Neumann Papers.

42. W. L. Neumann to H. E. Barnes, January 30, 1946, Barnes Papers; Chodorov, "Trailing the Trend," *analysis* 2 (October 1946): 2; Libby, *Peace Action* 11 (October 1945): 6; O. G. Villard to M. Rubin, October 1, 1946, Villard Papers.

43. "The Nazi Trials" (editorial), *Chicago Tribune*, July 24, 1945; C. A. Beard to O. G. Villard, November 8, 1946, Villard Papers; Thomas, "America's Drift," *Socialist Call* 13 (October 7, 1946): 8; Pettengill, "Inside Your Congress," #814 (October 10, 1946); *New York Daily News*, October 6, 1945; Dennis, *Appeal to Reason*, #21 (August 17, 1946); Smith, *CR*, January 27, 1949, p. A460.

44. Borchard, "International Law and International Organization," *American Journal of International Law* 41 (January 1947): 107; Dondero, *CR*, April 20, 1948, p. 2369; Neumann memo, Neumann Papers, p. 3; Mayer, "The Hanging of the Tiger," *Progressive* 9 (December 17, 1945): 5; Langer, *CR*, December 18, 1950, p. 16708.

45. "The War Crimes Backlash" (editorial), *Chicago Tribune*, February 11, 1948; McCormick in Waldrop, *McCormick of Chicago*, p. 263; Dondero, *CR*, December 19, 1947, pp. 11745–46; Langer, *CR*, December 18, 1950, p. 16709.

46. Montgomery Belgion, *Victor's Justice* (Chicago: Regnery, 1949). Utley on Taylor, *High Cost of Vengeance*, pp. 177–78; on military tradition, p. 3. In 1950 Regnery came out with still another work, Lord Maurice Hankey's *Politics: Trials and Errors*, in which a retired British diplomat stressed the hypocrisy of Russia's presence on the tribunal.

47. Russell Grenfell, *Unconditional Hatred: German War Guilt and the Future of Europe* (New York: Devin-Adair, 1953); F. J. P. Veale, *Advance to Barbarism* (Apple-

ton, Wis.: C. C. Nelson, 1953); Mary Ritter Beard to H. E. Barnes, May 17, 1953, Barnes Papers. For favorable comments on Veale, see *New Yorker* 3 (May 22, 1954): 123–24; George A. Lundberg, *Social Forces* 32 (March 1954): 303; Harry Elmer Barnes, *Chicago Sunday Tribune Book Section*, May 31, 1953, p. 2; Merwin K. Hart, "Let Us Assess the Future," *Economic Council Letter*, #320 (October 1, 1953); endorsements by John Haynes Holmes and Frederick J. Libby in memorandum, NCPW Papers.

48. Taft in Patterson, *Mr Republican*, p. 328; Thomas, *Appeal to the Nations* (New York: Holt, 1947), pp. 68–69; "Justice Versus Vengeance" (editorial), *Washington Times-Herald*, June 1, 1945; Morley; "Travesty of Justice," *Human Events* 2 (November 21, 1945).

49. For an account of the Malmédy incident, see Charles Whiting, *Massacre at Malmédy* (New York: Stein and Day, 1971).

50. For the NCPW role, see Finucane memo, December 3, 1948; F. J. Libby to H. Regnery, November 23, 1948, J. Finucane to H. Regnery, December 10, 1948 and April 6, 1949, NCPW Papers; Edward LeRoy Van Roden, "American Atrocities in Germany," *Progressive* 13 (February 1949): 21–22; W. Langer to K. C. Royall, December 3, 1948, NCPW Papers. Finucane acknowledged authorship of Langer's letter in his December 3 memo. Finucane's authorship of the Van Roden essay is acknowledged in a letter from F. J. Libby to W. H. Regnery, November 25, 1949, NCPW Papers. Van Roden retracted some of his charges under cross-examination by the Senate subcommittee. However, he accepted payment for the article from the *Progressive* and thereby acknowledged responsibility for it. Interview with James Finucane, Washington, D.C., June 17, 1973.

51. Langer resolution, *CR*, January 27, 1949, pp. 599–600; Langer on "hate-happy hangman," *CR*, February 8, 1949, p. 957. Penciled above the draft of Langer's resolution and speech of January 27 were the words "Remarks for Langer by Jim," NCPW Papers.

52. F. J. Libby to J. R. McCarthy, March 18 and May 20, 1949, F. J. Libby to W. L. Neumann, April 20, 1949, NCPW Papers; Chamberlin, "A Scandal Exposed," *New Leader* 32 (January 15, 1949): 16; Utley, *High Cost of Vengeance*, pp. 185–91; Hanighen, "Not Merely Gossip," *Human Events* 6 (April 27, 1949); "German Bishops on War Crimes Trials" (editorial), *Christian Century* 66 (June 15, 1949): 725–26; "Van Roden Takes Sides," Friends of Democracy, *Battle* 7 (June 15, 1949): 1; C. Montieth Gilpen to *New York Herald-Tribune*, May 29, 1949, pt. 2, p. 7; Gilpen to *Progressive* 13 (August 1949): 13. Van Roden was attacked for having endorsed Ludwig Adolphus Fritsch, *The Crime of Our Age*. The author, a former Lutheran pastor, said that his book intended to show how "the Jews and the Anglo-Saxons succeeded in uniting the nations of the world into an unholy alliance in order to destroy Germandom."

53. Raymond Baldwin, *CR*, October 14, 1949, pp. 14512–34. For comments on the performance of the Baldwin committee, see Robert Griffiths, *The Politics of Fear: Joseph R. McCarthy and the Senate* (Lexington: University of Kentucky Press, 1970), p. 22, and the introduction to Allen J. Matusow, ed., *Joseph R. McCarthy* (Englewood Cliffs, N.J.: Prentice-Hall, 1970), p. 15. For an analytical treatment of American courts in Germany that admitted to unjust practices in early stages of the occupation, see Eli E. Nobleman, "American Military Government Courts in Germany," *The Annals* 267 (January 1950): 87–97.

54. John R. McCloy to F. J. Libby, June 29, 1950, NCPW Papers; Morris Amcham, Deputy Chief Counsel for War Crimes, to *New York Times*, February 20, 1950, pt. IV, p. 8.

55. "New Light on War Crimes Trials," *Peace Action* 16 (July 1950): 3; Armstrong, *Congressional Record*, February 22, 1951, p. 1495; Libby to W. H. Regnery, June 31, 1951, NCPW Papers; Libby, "Seven Germans Hanged at Landsberg," *Peace Action* 17 (July 1951): 4. For an account of NCPW efforts, see Justus D. Doenecke, "Protest Over Malmédy: A Case of Clemency," *Peace and Change* 4 (Spring 1977): 28–33.

56. Interview with Gladys Mackenzie, former staff worker, NCPW, Swarthmore, Pa., July 30, 1971.

57. Langer, address to Chicago civic rally, pp. A3469–70; Smith, "Langer," p. 167. For an exaggerated treatment of ethnic loyalties, see Samuel Lubell, *Future of American Politics,* chap. 7.

58. For manifestations of one conservative's enthusiasm, see Chamberlin, "Germany's Year of Decision," *Human Events* 9 (January 30, 1952); Chamberlin, *The German Phoenix* (New York: Duell, Sloan and Pearce, 1963), chap. 4.

59. Cole, *America First,* pp. 38, 213 n. 13; General Wood cited in *Peace Action* 7 (December 1940): 1.

60. Morley, "Europe's Coronary Thrombosis," *Human Events* 4 (May 21, 1947).

61. For example of support for German rearmament, see Lawrence H. Smith, *CR,* July 27, 1951, p. 9040; "Denationalizing America," (editorial), *Chicago Tribune,* July 26, 1951. For opposition, see Langer, *CR,* December 18, 1950, pp. 16705–7; Rubin, "The Man Who Stayed Too Long," *Progressive* 15 (March 1951): 3.

62. The Basic Law of 1949 gave the occupying powers authority to veto German actions affecting disarmament, demilitarization, foreign trade, control over the Ruhr, reparations, and foreign policy. Feis, *From Trust to Terror,* p. 373.

# 8

# The Atlantic Pact:
# "An Entangling Alliance"

If many old isolationists endorsed the rehabilitation of Germany, they remained far less enthusiastic about other aspects of administration policy. And had they known what was in store within a year of Truman's victory at the polls, they would have been even more skeptical, for the election of 1948 permitted policymakers to plan the most far-reaching commitment the country had ever seen. The Atlantic Pact pledged the United States to consider any attack on some eleven different nations, ranging from Canada to Norway, as an attack upon its own soil. The *New York Times* asserted without exaggeration that the treaty contained "promises not even dreamed of by Woodrow Wilson." As noted over two decades later, the agreement engaged America in "guaranteeing the maintenance of foreign social structures and governments for the next twenty years," and administration demands for a $1.5 billion Military Assistance Program soon drove home the fact that the alliance was not to be a paper one.[1]

By 1948 nations in Western Europe had begun to establish their own security system. In March Britain, France, the Netherlands, Belgium, and Luxembourg pledged themselves to a common defense policy and formed a Western Union. On the very day that the Brussels Pact was signed, and amid the crises over Berlin and Czechoslovakia, Truman endorsed the European plans and called for immediate conscription and universal military training. On March 23, the Policy Planning Staff of the State Department recommended that the United States support the embryonic alliance.[2]

In order to secure senatorial backing, Under-Secretary of State Robert A. Lovett paid homage daily to Senator Vandenberg. The diplomat's effort soon bore fruit, for by May 11 what was soon called "the Vandenberg Resolution" was drafted. The resolution asserted that "regional and other collective arrangements," if based on "continuous and effective self-help and mutual aid," could be bolstered by "association" with the United States.[3]

The language was vague, the specific implications unclear. The resolution did not spell out the nature of this nebulous "association," and endorsers had no way of knowing whether the term *mutual aid* referred to munitions, loans, or men. The State Department stressed the limited nature of the commitment; Lovett denied that the administration envisaged either a binding pact or open-ended military assistance. The United States, he said, was simply trying to keep the Western Union firmly determined to resist aggression. Vandenberg emphasized that his resolution carried no specific obligation, telling an executive session of the Senate Foreign Relations Committee that the United States retained "complete freedom of action."[4]

The resolution passed the Senate almost unanimously, the vote being 64–4. Just one day, June 11, was given over for debate. Of the dozen or so old isolationists remaining in Congress, only Langer, who did not comment during the proceedings, cast a negative vote.[5]

During the summer and fall of 1948, as public attention was focused upon the Russian blockade of Berlin and the national elections, Lovett started a series of conversations with various North Atlantic powers. The countries of the Western Union had soon become dissatisfied with a nebulous "association" and sought a full-scale United States commitment to defend Europe. The Europeans claimed that only a binding alliance could protect economic recovery and integrate a restored Germany. In December 1948 seven European nations began negotiations for a North Atlantic alliance, and on April 4, 1949, twelve countries signed the Atlantic Pact. In addition to the Brussels Pact powers, Canada, Italy, Iceland, Norway, Denmark, Portugal, and the United States subscribed to the new agreement. The signers pledged themselves to mutual assistance, agreeing that they would consider "an armed attack against one or more of them in Europe or North America an attack against them all." A response by armed force might not always be necessary; at the same time, it could not be overlooked.[6]

Beginning in the middle of February 1949, the Senate Foreign Relations Committee conducted hearings. Acheson maintained that the pact would not necessarily commit the United States to outright war, for signatories, he said, retained all constitutional procedures. In addition, the agreement permitted a member nation to meet any threat with a whole range of responses. Of course, said the Secretary of State, if "something happens which any man, woman, or child knows is an armed attack," the United States could have "no doubt about what is necessary." Senator Bourke Hickenlooper (Rep.–Iowa) asked Acheson if the United States would send "substantial numbers" of soldiers to the Continent. A "clear and absolute 'No,'" the Secretary replied. The treaty, it appeared, would limit American participation to arms shipment alone.[7]

In many ways, however, the committee was taking no chances. The two major Republican converts to bipartisanship, Lodge and Vandenberg, joined with Committee chairman Tom Connally (Dem.–Texas) in modifying Article 5. The original agreement had pledged each signatory to meet aggression by an automatic resort to hostilities; the Committee changed the wording to read "such action as it deems necessary, including the use of armed force." Mindful of congressional prerogative in declaring war, Lodge and Vandenberg also added the provision, borrowed from the text of the Vandenberg Resolution, that all signers must use their respective "constitutional processes" both in ratifying and enforcing the treaty. After full debate, the Senate, on July 21, approved the Atlantic Pact eighty-two to thirteen. Only three of nine old isolationists, Taft, Langer, and Edwin C. Johnson, voted against the treaty.[8]

Several World War II isolationists were among the pact's strongest defenders. Vandenberg suggested that the treaty could have prevented both world wars. Wiley asserted that the agreement would not only prevent Western Europe from falling "into Russia's lap," but, because of the economic cooperation promised in Article 2, could possibly reduce American surpluses and end unemployment.[9]

Converts to interventionism continually stressed the pact's deterrent value. Senator Lodge admitted that no West European army could hold the Rhine for more than three weeks, but claimed that the alliance could build up European resistance to fifth-column activity. Hamilton Fish, who had not sided with the interventionists before, asserted that the pact might temporarily hold back a Russian attack.[10]

Such pact supporters found no violation of the Marshall Plan; indeed they reasoned that economic aid without military aid was insufficient. Vandenberg maintained that a mutual Western alliance spread defense responsibilities and hence actually bolstered United States security. Lodge, finding American manpower limited, deemed it imperative to have the burden shared.[11]

Furthermore, defenders claimed that the treaty was well within the scope of the United Nations Charter. With all the pride of a doting parent, Vandenberg continually pointed to those articles which he had promoted at the San Francisco Conference and which, in his mind, sanctioned such regional agreements. In addition, so an occasional convert to interventionism argued, the pact was clearly in the American diplomatic tradition. Vandenberg reinterpreted the most sacred "isolationist" pronouncements of the past: the Monroe Doctrine had been drafted to warn potential aggressors; Washington's Farewell Address had recommended temporary alliances in order to meet an extraordinary emergency.[12]

It soon became obvious that the pact was only the first step. On July 25, the same day that Truman signed the agreement, the President requested $1.5 billion for what was variously called the Mutual Defense Assistance

Program of 1949, the Military Aid or Assistance Program, or, more simply, "MAP." Slated for American money and arms were not only the new treaty signatories, but such countries as Greece, Turkey, Iran, the Philippines, and South Korea as well. MAP united all military projects into a single program, specified the President as director, and gave him emergency powers in determining how the resources would be allocated.

The request, so the administration maintained, could finance the "mobile defensive forces" needed to protect an increasingly prosperous Europe. The Continent would no longer be as tempting a prize to an invader, for it would receive enough equipment to furnish twelve divisions. Acheson pointed to Finland's performance in 1940 as evidence that a small well-equipped force, "backed by a nation with a will to resist," could be surprisingly effective. MAP defenders also stressed counter-subversion. Assistant Secretary of State Ernest A. Gross claimed that a relatively small military establishment could deter "Communist-inspired rioting, political strikes, and all the rest."[13]

Congress, however, was furious with the amount sought, and even major proponents of bipartisanship expressed indignation. Vandenberg, noting that the bill gave the President discretionary authority to ship American military equipment overseas, feared that it would virtually make him "the number one war lord of the earth." Furthermore, he claimed that an agreement intended to stress mutual participation and responsibility was now reverting to "the climate and atmosphere of arms lend-lease." The United States, said Lodge, should not be soliciting requests from the Atlantic powers: "We ought to tell them, 'Here is what it is going to be.'"[14]

For Vandenberg and Lodge, the administration proposal could never do. "I gave 'em an ultimatum—," Vandenberg later wrote. "Write a new and reasonable bill or you will get no bill and it will be your fault!" The new Senate bill authorized $90 million less, a relatively small reduction, but permitted the Department of Defense to veto any shipments and impose greater coordination among pact signers.[15]

Then the House suddenly balked. Acting in mid-August, it voted to cut the Senate appropriation in half. Veteran isolationist John Vorys co-sponsored the cut. Only on September 23, when Truman announced that Russia had tested an atomic bomb, did the House allocate one billion dollars for Atlantic Pact nations. Although Congressman Lawrence H. Smith said that the Russian exploit made such legislation "all the more nonsensical," the House voted 224 to 109 for passage. The day before, the Senate had authorized the full amount by a tally of fifty-five to twenty-four. Acheson, later noting the causal relationship between the Soviet explosion and the MAP vote in the House, wrote "An Ill Wind Blows Some Good."[16]

Much support for both the Atlantic Pact and MAP had come from the industrialized and urban sectors of America. Big business and labor often found the country's prosperity as well as its security dependent upon European military and commercial ties. Urban regions contained large numbers of Roman Catholics, who, if isolationist before Pearl Harbor, soon demanded that the United States stand firm against Soviet expansion. If a few Roman Catholics in Congress, such as Representative Joseph P.

O'Hara (Rep.–Minn.), continued to vote isolationist, far more took an interventionist stance. For example, Congressmen from Irish and Polish area in Detroit and Providence backed Truman foreign policy, as did such western Senators as McCarran and Dennis Chavez (Dem.–N.M.).[17]

Dissenters, both in and out of Congress, felt isolated. When Taft was listed among the Senate opponents of the Atlantic Pact, a *New Republic* columnist gloated that the Ohio Senator had received a "pat on the shoulder" from the *Daily Worker*. Neumann lamented that opposition to the treaty was "becoming a state sin." Because of several radio speeches opposing ratification, the revisionist historian suspected that the Federal Bureau of Investigation was searching into his background. Frederick J. Libby wrote John T. Flynn, "I wish to heaven there was an America First Committee in existence to lead the fight."[18]

Other backers gave their endorsements most reluctantly. Senator Butler, who had supported every restrictive amendment, finally claimed that "bull headed" opposition was futile. Guy Gillette, returning to the Senate after four years' absence, accused the administration of having committed the country in advance, with Congress merely given the "dubious prerogative of nodding its head." George D. Aiken felt presented with a "most unwelcome choice": either support a pact that "is but little better than a military alliance" or "run the risk of further encouraging aggression." Catastrophe, said the Vermont Republican, would be postponed, not avoided. Morley found the agreement "the only immediately practical way of saving something out of the wreck." Yet, for one who sought a genuine Atlantic federation, the treaty remained "at best an undesirable, unsatisfactory, and uninspiring stopgap."[19]

Some arguments against both the Atlantic Pact and MAP possessed a familiar ring. Old isolationists were again reminded of events immediately preceding Pearl Harbor. Walter Trohan, echoing Wheeler's indictment of lend-lease, asserted that MAP could resist in "plowing under a generation of American boys." Similarly, veteran isolationists accused the State Department of manufacturing war scares in order to avert economic depression. Hart, for instance, declared that MAP was rooted in an artificially created crisis, one that the administration was exploiting to help "maintain what is essentially a war-economy." And, as in past emergencies, an occasional old isolationist cited Lenin's "prediction" that the United States would "spend itself into destruction." Lawrence Dennis suspected that the roots of administration policy lay in efforts to dump the nation's surplus upon Western Europe: "It is no mere coincidence that the theatrical smash-hit of the year in New York is the DEATH OF A SALESMAN."[20]

Certain other isolationist critiques, while just as familiar, took on a new tone of urgency. First and foremost, a good many old isolationists stressed that the Atlantic Pact and MAP both overextended American resources. The absolute containment of world Communism, they claimed, was physically impossible and even the most powerful of nations had its obvious limitations. By committing itself to all danger points from Greece to China, the United States would surely be drained of its domestic assets. Francis H. Case found "no surer way to die than to bleed to death." Langer pointed to the prohibitive costs of such burdens: "We are being used to finance our own suicide as a free people." Bruce Barton, advertising executive and former isolationist Congressman (Rep.–N.Y.), asked "Are We Biting Off More Than We Can Chew?" and responded with a resounding "yes."[21]

Some of the more extreme among the old isolationists, such as Clare E. Hoffman, accused the administration of seeking "world-domination." As Lemke saw the issue, the fate of conquerors from Caesar to Hitler revealed that "the very idea of one world government by force means corruption and war."[22]

Several old isolationists believed that Russia itself was overcommitted. Soviet efforts to take over Europe and Asia would inevitably result in revolt, for such an expansive empire could only be weakened by further conquest. Moscow's trouble with Belgrade, said Barton, revealed the inherent limits of worldwide empire. Close declared that if the United States "set up [its] lines on this side of the Atlantic, . . . Russian military and economic power would soon wear itself out in Europe." The National Economic Council claimed that inevitable uprisings of Communist-dominated peoples would face far greater success if the Continent was spared a "bitter, atomic war."[23]

Some anti-interventionists found the binding nature of the Atlantic alliance particularly objectionable, maintaining that such a commitment, of necessity, placed America's fate in the hands of others. Taft claimed that the pact obligated the United States to fight, and fight even if the signers had not consulted with each other. A signatory could receive a negative ruling from an international court, or itself commit an aggressive act, and still find the United States obliged to come to its defense. Libby recalled the British blank check to Polish leader Colonel Josef Beck in 1939, a move that—he claimed—kept Poland from entering into necessary negotiations with Hitler. Borchard, writing his valedictory editorial for the *American Journal of International Law,* warned that the President had become powerful enough to enter alliances at will.[24]

It was ludicrous, old isolationists asserted, to expect that the Atlantic Pact meant less danger, not more. The *Washington Times-Herald* predicted that once Russia secured the atomic bomb, it would attack the United States. Even the dropping of such a weapon upon Russia, warned Flynn, would not prevent Soviet troops from marching across the European continent. Frederick J. Libby, pointing to the prominence of such Communists as Palmiro Togliatti in Italy and Frederic Joliot-Curie in France, saw widespread Communist penetration of Western Europe. Daniel A. Reed, in speaking against MAP, recalled how American munitions shipped to Japan before Pearl Harbor had been "paid for by the blood of our boys in the Pacific." Karl E. Mundt, now a Senator, entered some 272 pacts into the *Congressional Record* as evidence that all alliances were both tenuous and risky. (He reluctantly voted for the treaty on the grounds that the

United States should not "pull the rug out" from under the other signers.)[25]

Several old isolationists, challenging administration disclaimers, warned that European powers would use American supplies, arms, and possibly troops to repress colonial peoples. Langer denied that the alliance insured a peace among equals; instead, it foolishly attempted to enforce repression "upon nearly half of the world's population" and economic slavery in three continents. Morley feared that the United States would help smash the new Indonesian republic. Aiken (who reluctantly voted for the treaty) hoped that American arms shipments would not permit European colonial expeditions below the Tropic of Cancer. The United States, said Dennis, was forcing the Russians into permanent and dangerous partnership with the "colored races." Had America simply allowed Communists "a free hand" in both Europe and Asia, it could watch local resistance and domestic disintegration sap Russian energies.[26]

In addition, a few old isolationists claimed that the Atlantic Pact turned the West, not the USSR, into aggressors. Harry Elmer Barnes denied that the United States faced danger from a Russian attack. The *Progressive* found the pact "about as helpful in halting aggressive Communism as a colonial musket would be in warding off an attack by jet-propelled atomic bombs." To the contrary, it could only provoke the Russians.[27]

Veteran isolationists of a more conservative bent spoke with equal fervor. The United States, said the *New York Daily News*, had entered a military alliance pointed at Russia itself. Morley wrote, "This treaty means war unless Soviet Russia decides to knuckle under." Former Congressman Stephen Day (Rep.–Ill.), an extreme rightist and counsel for a nationalist group entitled "We, the People," called the agreement "a betrayal of the birthright of every American citizen by an underhanded and sneaking approach." Chodorov remarked with his usual wryness, "Every peace treaty is an agreement to make war." The *Chicago Tribune* claimed that the Atlantic alliance was almost identical to the anti-Comintern pact initiated by Hitler in 1936, the only exception being that the latter was "more frank" in stating its intent. Dennis, approving of the *Tribune*'s analogy, wrote, "We fought Hitler, now to ape him."[28]

The obvious tie between the Atlantic Pact and MAP compounded such fears. The United States was not merely guaranteeing the security of Western Europe; it was providing the Continent with an abundance of arms. For Senators Taft and Edwin C. Johnson, it was the administration's linking of the treaty to the arms program that convinced them both to vote against the alliance. Taft exclaimed, "This whole program . . . is not a peace program; it is a war program." By starting an arms race, America was forcing the Russians to respond in kind. To Johnson, MAP assured that the United States would "meddle in world war III," indeed enter "at the first shot." Congressman O'Hara asked how the country would react if Russia took "this same action" regarding either Mexico or Canada.[29]

A handful of old isolationists, exhibiting a concern for Europe rarely manifested, claimed that the pact exploited the Continent in the most ruthless manner possible. Close saw the Europeans as newly recruited mercenaries hired to enforce United States concepts of Atlantic security. Lemke was even more adamant, accusing his native land of hiring "Hessians" to fight its battles. MAP, he said, was the child of the Roman war gods, Mars and Minerva: "If we pass this illegitimate offspring it means world war III." "We are today," said Congressman Robert F. Rich, "one of the greatest warmongering nations in the world." Lawrence H. Smith asserted that the spending of a single cent to arm North Atlantic nations would justify one Russian accusation: that American capitalism in truth sought to dominate the entire globe.[30]

Various old isolationists claimed that the Atlantic Pact weakened the United Nations. Challenging Vandenberg, they denied that vague references in the UN Charter to "collective self-defense" and "regional arrangements" could be stretched sufficiently enough to sanction a military alliance. Morley said that the administration's verbal fealty to the world organization exemplified Hitler's tactic of the "big lie." The National Economic Council, usually a biting critic of the UN, commented: "All the pious talk about the pact being within the charter is eyewash, and every informed person knows it." Taft declared that Article 51, often cited by Vandenberg, did not sanction the arming of one half of the world against the other.[31]

Such old isolationists as Taft and Langer also found the pact violating the United States Constitution. Taft feared that the agreement might entice the country into war without legislative consent. Langer accused the Senate of betraying its long-held trust.[32]

Fear of losing autonomy in foreign policy—the so-called "free hand"— lay at the core of resistance to both the Atlantic Pact and MAP. Both conservatives and liberals, who had often differed on the Marshall Plan, came together on this point, and Senator Taft and the *Chicago Tribune* made even stronger attacks than the *Progressive* or Harry Elmer Barnes. Never again, in fact, would left and right among veteran anti-interventionists be so allied.

The soundness of old isolationist arguments varied. Retired diplomat George F. Kennan and historian Adam Ulam have claimed that in 1949 Russia posed no military threat to Western Europe. They asserted that the Soviets, too weak to advance their troops, were probably waiting for Western Europe to face inevitable depression and collapse. The Atlantic Pact and MAP in all likelihood caused the USSR to react more belligerently and to mobilize more rapidly. At this time, when containment had obviously worked and when Western Europe was on the road to recovery, the United States might well have begun negotiations with the Soviet Union. Because Europe was locked in stalemate, such talks might possibly have alleviated tensions over Germany and the atomic bomb.[33]

Old isolationists made other telling points: administration "allegiance" to the United Nations Charter smacked of duplicity; the United States, despite the pact's formal limitations, became more closely tied to European colonialism; the pact and MAP failed to create a solid deterrent; and the new obligations undoubtedly made congressional participation in war-making more difficult.

The arguments presented by old isolationists, however, were not without a degree of ambiguity. Many old isolationists, particularly those of conservative leanings, had been neither consistent supporters of the UN Charter nor defenders of European "sovereignty." Much of their rhetoric, particularly involving "warnings" of imminent war, was as shrill as that of the administration that it so strongly attacked.

Some old isolationists presented options to the European alliance. Foremost was air power. Here the major spokesman was General Bonner Fellers, soon recognized as the leading strategist of the militant isolationists. A West Point graduate, Fellers had served during the 1930s as adviser to MacArthur in the Philippines. In 1941 he was one of the few active military personnel openly sympathetic to the America First Committee. In World War II Fellers held various posts in the Pacific Theater, including that of MacArthur's military secretary and combat observer. In December 1947 he joined the Republican National Committee as head of its veterans' division.[34]

Unlike some old isolationists, Fellers did not condemn the Atlantic Pact out of hand. Indeed, he claimed that the treaty had "enormous" psychological value. MAP, however, he found foolish. Since the Rhine frontier could not be held by ground forces, American dollars would be wasted. The General saw Europe equally weak economically: "socialist leadership" was "dragging Great Britain into oblivion"; Italy was more impotent than it had been under Mussolini. And even if battles were won, the war itself would be lost, for Communism invariably spreads during armed conflict. "Bayonets and bombs," he told the House Foreign Affairs Committee, "cannot destroy ideologies."

Only air supremacy, the General claimed, could turn the pact into a genuinely viable alliance. Besides being the only strategy that the United States could afford, it could save Europe from the "devastation which inevitably follows in the wake of tanks and guns and bombs." Let the West utilize long-range bombers capable of delivering atomic bombs to Russia itself. Then an invading Red army, dependent upon the Soviet homeland for both "bread and bullets," would find itself cut off and unable to survive.[35]

Walter Trohan, specifically endorsing Feller's military tactics, saw little potential in foot soldiers. One could not, said the columnist for the *Chicago Tribune*, try to "stop an express train with a butterfly net." Air defense, on the other hand, resembled a football game: if rushing or blocking would not win the victory, forward passes were necessary.[36]

For both Fellers and Trohan, however, "psychological warfare" was equally necessary. Trohan spoke of releasing propaganda discrediting "the Kremlin gang," encouraging desertion among Russian occupation forces, and helping anti-Communists escape from Iron Curtain nations. Such "bloodless war" would lead to counterrevolution inside the Soviet Union, after which a combination of a strong air force and the atomic bomb could bring it to its knees. Fellers, even more specific, sought the organization of international brigades composed of anti-Communist refugees.

According to the General, "Discontent is widespread in Stalin's empire, not only among the masses but in the new ruling classes."[37]

Such emphasis coincided well with Taft's alternative to NATO: an American military umbrella. Under this policy, the United States would make a unilateral commitment to Western Europe: if the Continent faced attack by the Soviet Union, America would immediately come to its rescue. Far better, said the Senator, to extend the Monroe Doctrine to Europe than to ship huge quantities of arms as part of a potentially offensive alliance. Claiming that "many experts" believed that United States participation should be confined to the air, Taft said that such a strategy would secure victory. (One isolationist, Lawrence Dennis, was sharply critical, asserting that both Taft and Truman were foolish to believe that putting Stalin on notice would make him less belligerent. Neither Taft nor the administration, Dennis continued, comprehended Stalin's strategy of exploiting economic troubles in the West and encouraging colonial revolts.)[38]

A few old isolationists were even more militant. The *Washington Times-Herald* would meet the "dirty-dog performance of the Reds in Berlin and in China" by a vague warning: the United States would "destroy their trade, corrupt their money, end their meddling in domestic affairs, and kick their commissars in the face whenever they show up abroad." Mundt, a bit more responsible, suggested an international police force that would not be subject to Security Council veto.[39]

Some critics demanded that greater attention be given to Asia. As the larger and more populous continent, it was, they asserted, far more vital than Europe to United States survival. Mundt, for example, noted that Asia enveloped over half the world, whereas Europe possessed less than a sixth of the earth's surface. Vorys found the MAP appropriation "too much, too soon for Europe, too little, too late for Asia." Keefe predicted that Europe was almost certain to be overrun by Communists, but implied that Bolshevism could be halted in the Far East.[40]

A few conservatives tacitly tempered their isolationism by envisioning Spain as the linchpin of an Atlantic alliance. Because the country had been supported by Hitler and Mussolini before the war and was neutral during the conflict, in 1945 the United Nations barred it from membership. For many Americans, even in the late 1940s, the Spanish dictatorship of Generalissimo Francisco Franco represented clericalism, reaction, even Fascism. Certain isolationists, however, perceived Spain as an economically and socially stable power, one fervently anti-Communist and dominating the entrance to the Mediterranean. Such a staunch defender of Spain as Merwin K. Hart might be embarrassed by lack of religious freedom for Protestants, but he continually stressed Spain's economic recovery and strategic importance. Dewey Short put the pro-Franco case succinctly: "Regardless of our opinion of Franco and his Government, it must be admitted that Franco has brought order out of chaos and that Spain is our friend."[41]

If most alternatives were in the direction of greater militancy, a few centered on more conciliatory approaches. Norman Thomas maintained that only a well-organized force could check Stalin's aggression, but desired a last-minute appeal for universal disarmament. The Socialist leader hoped that the pact could evolve into a United States of Europe, for the world had no need for a "whole network of national military machines." The *Progressive* wanted the United States to negotiate directly with the Soviet Union, as did Congressman Rich. To Representative Usher Burdick (Rep.–N.D.) land reform was crucial: from China to Italy, private land and home ownership—not MAP appropriations—were needed.[42]

During the debates over the Atlantic Pact, such Senators as Taft attempted to weaken the agreement. The Ohioan joined two Senate colleagues, Wherry and Arthur Watkins (Rep.–Utah), in proposing that the treaty commit no signer to supply arms to another. Acheson strongly opposed the resolution, declaring that it would cast doubt upon America's determination to aid its Atlantic allies, and the provision was voted down seventy-four to twenty-one.[43]

Taft also united with Senator Ralph Flanders (Rep.–Vt.) in cosponsoring another resolution, one that would replace the treaty with a unilateral extension of the Monroe Doctrine. The measure was not reported out of the Senate Foreign Relations Committee. The two men also favored replacing the new alliance with a "little UN" free of the veto power. Watkins received the support of a few old isolationists when he offered two other resolutions: one denied that the United States had any obligation to maintain North Atlantic security unless Congress so legislated; the other stated that Congress had no moral obligation to declare war if any signer was attacked. Eleven Senators supported the first resolution, only eight the second. Butler and Langer backed both of Watkins's proposals, but Taft, who favored strong warnings to potential aggressors, did not support the latter.[44]

Whenever possible, interventionists challenged such alternatives. Lodge claimed that the more militant proponents of air power would lose more than they would gain, for if United States forces needed help, allies were necessary. Senators Pepper and Lucas thought Taft foolish to speak of unilateral guarantees without demanding reciprocal obligations. America might find itself, argued Pepper, defending a country such as Norway unaided by any other European power. Taft's scheme, the Florida Senator continued, could also deprive the United States of materiel, bases, and technical knowledge vital to defense.[45]

Interventionists denied that such areas as Greece, Turkey, West Germany, and Korea would be neglected, but strongly defended immediate concentration upon Western Europe. Its high productivity, said Lodge, made it the greatest military and cultural asset on earth. China, by contrast, lacked the technology to support its incalculable number of people. Moreover, Lodge went on, Europe had been far more receptive to American aid.[46]

If a few old isolationists sought peace talks with the Russians, many advanced alternatives even more risky than the Atlantic Pact. Air defense, with its tacit reliance upon atomic bombs, was every bit as provocative as arms shipments and, later, the handful of American divisions envisioned by pact advocates. By limiting the options available, an air strategy could quickly turn a localized conflict into an all-out one. The Soviets might well find themselves more provoked than they would be under the treaty; Europeans would simply witness their land being used as a battleground for atomic weapons. It remains doubtful whether Western Europe would have accepted a "Monroe Doctrine" that left all choice for war or peace in the hands of the United States.[47]

Talk of psychological warfare and encouragement of domestic rebellion, as shown by the abortive Hungarian uprising of 1956, involved the riskiest kind of brinkmanship. The cause of China was rapidly becoming a lost one and offered little possibility of regaining the Cold War "offensive." In addition it could involve far greater risks than the most ardent interventionist ever conceived. As for Spain, the American navy and air force were already eying the Iberian peninsula, and Acheson told the Senate Foreign Relations Committee that he hoped that Spain could eventually join the alliance.[48] In general, isolationist prescriptions seldom matched the astuteness that characterized much of their diagnosis.


The fact that only a handful of veteran isolationists in the Senate voted against the Atlantic Pact would well be misleading. Of far greater importance is the large group of old isolationists in the House who voted against the Military Assistance Program. In fact, the percentage of old isolationist opposition to MAP was greater than to either the Truman Doctrine or the Marshall Plan. Even before the China issue had come to the fore, the MAP debate showed that bipartisanship was in serious trouble. Already in 1949 a newer, more strident form of isolationism was being articulated. In addition Vandenberg and Lodge, finding much of the real value of the pact psychological, balked at the scope of the MAP proposals.

Much congressional opposition to major commitments continued to come from interior states and regions. Such areas, which concentrated upon local rather than international trade, could see the new alliance as producing nothing but increased taxes and obligations. If, however, many inland regions still remained vocal in their suspicions of international commitments, their economic base—the midwestern farmer—was losing strength. All during the 1940s, the number of family farms in the country declined, and by 1950 only twelve percent of the population lived on the soil.[49] During the same period, suburbs made continual inroads upon small towns, thereby causing them to lose much of their rural character. If anything, rural areas were greatly overrepresented in Congress and would remain so until 1962, when the Supreme Court ruled differently.

The isolationists might renew their strength in the debate over the MAP appropriations. Yet, if isolationism was, among other things, one means of waging war against urban society, the crucial battles had long been lost. A society based upon international commerce, finance, and labor had already triumphed, and so had its foreign policy projections.

The agrarian and small-town bases of Cold War isolationism, and the increasingly marginal economic base, harmed its appeal to other areas and groups. Disillusionment with the New Deal had made many isolationists, particularly those from strong Republican areas, increasingly conservative. For example, virtually all the leaders and financial backers of the America First Committee opposed centralized economic planning.[50] Such domestic conservatism often increased during the Cold War, putting the overwhelming majority of old congressional isolationists in a bind: the very program that appealed to their rural constituents—little federal spending (with the possible exception of farm price supports), high tariffs, and curbs on trade-union power—was seldom attractive to the urban masses.

At the very time when their political base was steadily weakening, efforts to challenge Atlantic diplomacy placed many isolationists in a strategic and ideological antinomy. On one level they were prisoners of their own attacks upon the administration. Isolationists who claimed that past diplomacy had been marred by continual appeasement were hard put to challenge efforts to strengthen Europe's military forces. On another level they were beginning to share certain government premises concerning the nature and threat of "world Communism," and share them with a vengeance. If, for example, the Communist threat was indivisible (as the administration had often claimed), then the United States needed to extend containment to Asia as well as to Europe. And if the Communist threat had its roots in the councils of Moscow (as the administration argued), then the strategies of air supremacy and a nuclear umbrella were quite logical ones.

In some ways, in fact, there was more "isolationist" military strategy in administration planning than has even been conceded. The Truman government, while sending equipment and, later, troops to Europe, increasingly relied upon a Strategic Air Command armed with atomic bombs and operating from European bases. Two days after the Atlantic Pact was signed, Chief of Staff Omar Bradley said that American military power was, of necessity, borne "on the wings of our bombers." In 1949 and 1950 the North Atlantic Treaty Organization—as the member states soon called themselves—remained designed to bolster European morale.[51]

The crises of 1948 and 1949—Czechoslovakia, Berlin, China, the Russian explosion of the atomic bomb—had put many old isolationists in an unenviable position. Individuals who in 1941 could point to both oceans as American "moats" found it increasingly difficult to alleviate fears over nuclear weapons, transcontinental bombers, and, later, guided missiles. To gain the favor of a public increasingly apprehensive over Communist expansion, and to show their own determination in light of Communist gains, they were forced to present some militant, even reckless, alternatives.

*Isolationism*, for a large number of "old isolationists," was becoming transformed into something a bit different. Some liberals among them would join their conservative brethren in opposing the Atlantic Pact. They could, however, find little comfort in most of the alternatives proposed. Their own pleas for immediate negotiation with the Soviets lacked support from most conservatives, much less a Secretary of State ever seeking "situations of strength." The Socialist Party, a mainstay of the isolationist movement before World War II, had become a small and ineffective band, and its leader, Norman Thomas, was less absolute in his anti-interventionism than he had been during the debates over FDR's policies. As early as 1947 Flynn had declared that pacifists could not supply the "sound reasons" needed to end an armament boom, and the Atlantic Pact was almost the last issue on which Libby would side with many old isolationists.[52] Unlike the handful of liberals, however, most veteran anti-interventionists were by 1949 not content to tolerate continual Communist advances. Even before then they had found little room for retreat, and events were taking place in China that would give them still less.

# NOTES

1. "Full Cycle" (editorial), *New York Times,* March 22, 1949, p. 24; Stephen E. Ambrose, *Rise To Globalism: American Foreign Policy, 1938–1970* (Baltimore, Md.: Penguin, 1971), pp. 178–79.

2. Text of Brussels Treaty, *New York Times,* March 18, 1948, p. 5; Harry S. Truman, *Memoirs,* Vol. 2: *Years of Trial and Hope* (Garden City, N.Y.: Doubleday, 1956), pp. 244–45.

3. Lovett role in Poole, "Quest," p. 319; *Forrestal Diaries,* entry of May 18, 1948, p. 434; Vandenberg, *Private Papers,* p. 406. For text of the Vandenberg resolution, see *CR,* May 19, 1948, pp. 6053–54.

4. Testimony of Robert A. Lovett, Senate Foreign Relations Committee, May 11, 1948, *The Vandenberg Resolution and the North Atlantic Treaty,* executive session (Washington, D.C.: U.S. Government Printing Office, 1973), pp. 7, 9 (herafter cited as *SFRC Executive Hearings*) and May 19, 1948, p. 40; Vandenberg, May 11, 1948, *SFRC Executive Hearings,* p. 2.

5. *CR,* June 11, 1948, p. 7846.

6. For the text of the Atlantic Pact, see ibid., July 20, 1949, pp. 9816–17. The background to the treaty can be found in Lawrence S. Kaplan, "The United States and the Atlantic Alliance: The First Generation," in John Braeman, Robert H. Bremner, and David Brody, eds., *Twentieth-Century American Foreign Policy* (Columbus: Ohio State University Press, 1971), pp. 294–309.

7. Acheson on constitutional processes, February 18, 1949, *SFRC Executive Hearings,* p. 90, on options, April 21, 1949, p. 214, and on armed attack, February 18, 1949, p. 114. For the exchange with Senator Bourke Hickenlooper, see Dean Acheson, *Present at the Creation: My Years in the State Department* (New York: Norton, 1969), p. 285.

8. Acheson, *Present at the Creation,* pp. 280–81; William J. Miller, *Henry Cabot Lodge: A Biography* (New York: James H. Heineman, 1967), p. 204. For a good legislative history of the Atlantic Pact, see Bryniarski, "Against the Tide," chap. 9. For the voting on the Pact, see *CR,* July 13, 1949, p. 9916.

9. Vandenberg, *SFRC Executive Hearings,* February 18, 1949, p. 110; Wiley, *CR,* March 30, 1949, p. 3443, and July 7, 1949, p. 9021.

10. Lodge, April 19, 1949, *SFRC Executive Hearings,* pp. 208–9; Fish testimony, Senate Foreign Relations Committee, May 13, 1949, *North Atlantic Treaty* (Washington, D.C.: Government Printing Office, 1949), p. 950.

11. Vandenberg, *CR,* July 6, 1949, p. 8891; Lodge, *CR,* March 25, 1949, pp. 3168–69.

12. Vandenberg on UN and Monroe Doctrine, *CR,* July 6, 1949, p. 8892, and on Washington's address, p. 8894.

13. For focus on mobile defensive forces, see State Department document, "Foreign Affairs Outlines: Building the Peace," July 8, 1949, *CR*, p. 9109; Truman, *Memoirs*, 2: 251; Acheson testimony, April 21, 1949, *SFRC Executive Hearings*, pp. 215–16. For stress on countersubversion, see Gross testimony, April 12, 1949, *SFRC Executive Hearings*, pp. 188–89.

14. A. Vandenberg to Mrs. A. H. Vandenberg, July 25, 1949, in *Private Papers*, pp. 503–4; Vandenberg, April 12, 1949, *SFRC Executive Hearings*, p. 183; Lodge, *SFRC Executive Hearings*, April 12, 1949, p. 186.

15. A. Vandenberg to Mrs. A. H. Vandenberg, August 2, 1949, in *Private Papers*, p. 508; Acheson, *Present at the Creation*, p. 310.

16. For the House action, see *CR*, September 28, 1949, pp. 13476–77. For the Senate action, see *CR*, September 22, 1949, p. 13168. For L. H. Smith, *CR*, September 28, 1949, p. 13471. For the "ill wind," see Acheson, *Present at the Creation*, p. 312. Of seventy-six isolationists remaining in the House, some thirty-nine (55%) opposed it, and only seventeen (or some 24%) wanted to go on record as favoring the bill.

17. Alfred O. Hero, Jr., *American Religious Groups View Foreign Policy: Trends in Rank-and-file Opinion, 1937–1969* (Durham, N.C.: Duke University Press, 1973), pp. 12–13, 40–43. Among the urban Catholic Congressmen who became Cold War interventionists were John E. Fogarty (Dem.–R.I.), George D. O'Brien (Dem.–Mich.), and Louis Rabaut (Dem.–Mich.). For general Catholic patterns, see Leroy N. Rieselbach, *The Roots of Isolationism: Congressional Voting and Presidential Leadership in Foreign Policy* (Indianapolis, Ind.: Bobbs-Merrill, 1966), pp. 62–67.

18. "T.R.B.," *New Republic* 121 (July 25, 1949): 3; W. L. Neumann to F. J. Libby, July 14, 1949; F. J. Libby to J. T. Flynn, April 5, 1949, NCPW Papers. Some of the other revisionist historians had similar sentiments. Beard promised to write a strong critique of the pact in a forthcoming exposé of American foreign policy. See Neumann's account of conversation with Mary Ritter Beard and William Beard in W. L. Neumann to H. E. Barnes, March 2, 1949, Neumann Papers.

19. Butler in Justus F. Paul, "The Political Career of Senator Hugh Butler, 1940–1954," Ph.D. diss., University of Nebraska, 1966, p. 275; Gillette, *CR*, July 11, 1949, p. 9199; Aiken, *CR*, July 21, 1949, pp. 9913–14; Morley, "What Follows the United Nations?", *Human Events* 6 (March 23, 1949).

20. Trohan, radio broadcast of August 19, 1949, *CR*, p. A5491; Hart, "The Gravest Decision You Will Ever Make—An Open Letter to the 81st Congress," *Economic Council Letter*, #211 (August 15, 1949); Trohan on Lenin, radio broadcast of August 11, 1949, *CR*, p. A5363; Dennis, *Appeal to Reason*, #172 (July 9, 1949).

21. Case, *CR*, February 21, 1949, p. A959; Langer, *CR*, April 26, 1949, p. 5034; Bruce Barton, "Are We Biting Off More Than We Can Chew?," *Reader's Digest* 53 (December 1948): 45–48. Lawrence Dennis helped to write the article. L. Dennis to F. J. Libby, May 15, 1949, NCPW Papers.

22. Hoffman, *CR*, April 11, 1949, p. 4300; Lemke, *CR*, August 17, 1949, p. 11662.

23. Barton, "Are We Biting", p. 47; *Closer-Ups* 4 (March 28, 1949): 3; NEC resolution, submitted to Senate Foreign Relations Committee, *North Atlantic Treaty* May 12, 1949, p. 861.

24. Taft, *CR*, July 11, 1949, p. 9206; testimony of Frederick J. Libby, Senate Foreign Relations Committee, May 12, 1949, *North Atlantic Treaty*, p. 898; Borchard, "United States Foreign Policy," *American Journal of International Law* 43 (April 1949): 333–35.

25. "The Reward of Being Meddlesome" (editorial), *Washington Times-Herald*, September 26, 1949; Flynn, radio broadcast #15 (August 14, 1949); Libby testimony, *North Atlantic Treaty*, p. 897; D. Reed to A. L. Lenhardt, July 28, 1949, Box 20, Reed Papers; Mundt, *CR*, July 14, 1949, pp. 9447–57.

26. Langer, *CR*, July 14, 1949, p. 9445; Morley, "That North Atlantic Treaty," *Human Events* 6 (February 16, 1949); Aiken, *CR*, March 25, 1949, p. 3164; Dennis, *Appeal to Reason*, #156 (March 19, 1949).

27. Unidentified clipping, January 1949, in Neumann Papers; "Pacts or Pax?" (editorial), *Progressive* 13 (April 1949): 3.

28. *New York Daily News*, April 4, 1949; Morley, "What Follows the United Nations?", *Human Events* 6 (March 23, 1949); Day, statement submitted to Senate Foreign Affairs Committee, May 11, 1949, *North Atlantic Treaty*, p. 814; Chodorov, "Trailing the Trend," *analysis* 5 (April 1949): 3; "Invitation to the Hangman" (editorial), *Chicago Tribune*, April 6, 1949; Dennis, *Appeal to Reason*, #159 (April 9, 1949).

29. Taft, *CR*, July 21, 1949, p. 9887; Johnson, *CR*, September 20, 1949, p. 13055; Joseph P. O'Hara, *CR*, August 18, 1949, p. 11755.

30. *Closer-Ups* 4 (March 28, 1949): 1; Lemke, *CR*, August 18, 1949, p. 11761; Rich, *CR*, September 28, 1949, p. 13470.

31. Morley, "What Follows the United Nations?"; NEC resolution, p. 857; Taft, *CR*, July 21, 1949, p. 9909.

32. Taft radio speech of March 30, 1949, *CR*, p. A1907; Langer, *CR*, July 14, 1949, p. 9430.

33. For the lack of Russian military threat, see Kennan, *Memoirs*, 1: 407–13; Adam B. Ulam, *The Rivals: America and Russia Since World War II* (New York: Viking, 1971), p. 151. For possibilities of negotiation in 1949, see John Lewis Gaddis, "Harry S. Truman and the Origins of Containment," and Robert H. Ferrell and David McLellan, "Dean Acheson: Architect of a Manageable World Order," in Frank J. Merli and Theodore A. Wilson, eds., *Makers of American Diplomacy: From Benjamin Franklin to Henry Kissinger* (New York: Scribner's, 1971), pp. 515, 537.

34. See biographical sketch in Bonner Fellers, "'Thought War' against the Kremlin," pamphlet #46 (Chicago: Regnerv, 1949), pp. 1–2; obituary, October 10, 1973, *New York Times*, p. 50. For Fellers's early connections to isolationists, see R. D. Stuart, Jr. to B. Fellers, September 15, 1940, Box 19, AFC Papers; Bonner Fellers to H. Hoover, June 20, 1940, Box 31A, Hoover Papers; interview with General Fellers, Washington, D.C., June 12, 1973.

35. Material in the previous two paragraphs came from Fellers, "The Military Assistance Program," *Human Events* 6 (July 27, 1949), and his testimony before the House Committee on Foreign Affairs, August 8, 1949, *CR*, pp. A5167–69.

36. Trohan, radio broadcast, August 10 and 15, 1949, *CR*, pp. A5303–A5414. Trohan was substituting for the Mutual network commentator Fulton Lewis, Jr.

37. Trohan, radio broadcast, August 17, 1949, *CR*, p. A5415; Trohan, radio broadcast, August 19, 1949, *CR*, p. A5492; Fellers, "'Thought War' against the Kremlin," p. 14.

38. Taft, radio broadcast of March 30, 1949, *CR*, p. A1908, and July 21, 1949, p. 9887; Dennis, *Appeal to Reason*, #174 (July 23, 1949).

39. "Making Stalin Sweat" (editorial), *Washington Times-Herald*, July 13, 1949; Mundt, *CR*, July 14, 1949, p. 9462.

40. Mundt, "Our American Destiny—1949," speech before the annual congress of the Daughters of the American Revolution, April 18, 1949, *CR*, p. A4249; Vorys, *CR*, August 17, 1949, p. 11666; Keefe, *CR*, August 18, 1949, p. 11795.

41. Hart memorandum of his trips to Europe in the summers of 1947 and 1949, the Papers of Merwin K. Hart, University of Oregon Library.

42. Thomas, *New York Times*, May 12, 1949, pp. 1–2; Thomas testimony, Senate Foreign Relations Committee, May 11, 1949, *North Atlantic Treaty*, pp. 730–53; "The Basic Question," *Progressive* 13 (May 1949): 3–4; Rich, *CR*, May 26, 1949, p. 6896; Burdick, *CR*, August 17, 1949, p. 11691.

43. Bryniarski, "Against the Tide," p. 277; D. G. Acheson to T. Connally, July 15,

1949, *CR*, pp. 9914–15. For the substance and fate of the Wherry-Watkins-Taft resolution, see *CR*, July 21, 1949, p. 9915.

44. For the text of the Flanders-Taft resolution, see *CR*, July 14, 1949, p. 9422; Taft and Flanders on "little UN," *New York Times*, April 21, 1949, p. 71, and Bryniarski, "Against the Tide," pp. 283–84; text of the Watkins resolutions, *CR*, July 20, 1949, p. 9806.

45. Lodge, *CR*, March 31, 1949, p. 3571; Pepper and Lucas, *CR*, July 15, 1949, pp. 9594–95.

46. Vandenberg, *CR*, July 6, 1949, p. 8897; Lodge, *CR*, April 1, 1949, p. 3695.

47. For an excellent analysis of these points, see Patterson, *Mr. Republican*, p. 438.

48. Acheson, March 8, 1949, *SFRC Executive Hearings*, p. 167.

49. Joseph Bensman and Arthur J. Vidich, *The New American Society: The Revolution of the Middle Class* (Chicago: Quadrangle, 1971), p. 17.

50. Cole, *America First*, p. 82.

51. Ambrose, *Rise to Globalism*, pp. 180–81; Omar Bradley in Kaplan, "The United States," p. 311.

52. J. T. Flynn to P. Morrison, February 11, 1947, Box 17, Flynn Papers.

# 9

# The Fall of China

By 1949 many old isolationists were becoming increasingly strident in their approach to the Cold War, and the emerging controversy over China greatly intensified this new militancy. Soon much of their traditional isolationism would be distorted beyond recognition. A large number of veteran isolationists were beginning to perceive the Orient as the area where dangers of Communist rule could be the greatest: the Atlantic Pact might be folly, but the survival of a "free Asia" was a most serious matter. And given this perspective, the fall of Chiang Kai-shek's Nationalist regime was not merely the demise of another Chinese warlord; it could well be one of the greatest catastrophes in the history of the entire West.

Such a reaction was not totally predictable. From 1946 to 1948, most veteran isolationists, like their fellow Americans, were indifferent toward the outcome of the Chinese civil war. To them China represented as foolish an international "entanglement" as any in Europe. Even in 1949 a handful of old isolationists remained suspicious of Asian commitments, believing that the official government of the Republic of China was corrupt enough to deserve defeat. The far greater proportion, however, were soon maintaining that the Communist revolution had resulted from conscious and deliberate policies of the Truman administration. They accused the State Department in particular of seeking to transfer China's wealth and power from Chiang's pro-Western forces to the Communist legions of Mao Tse-tung. And, in advancing the argument, the critics of America's China diplomacy found, for once, that they were receiving support from some colleagues who had usually backed Truman's foreign policy.

When the Pacific War ended in August 1945, the regime of Generalissimo Chiang and his Kuomintang party faced severe economic problems, including a rampant inflation and a strong indigenous Communist movement. As Japanese troops surrendered, Nationalist armies in North China raced Communist forces to control strategic bastions. United States forces stationed in China aided the Nationalists, transporting their armies to such major cities as Tientsin and Peking. In Tientsin, in fact, American marines occupied the city until the Nationalist troops arrived.

For two years the Communists made steady gains and, beginning in June 1947, Mao's troops crossed the Yellow River. American assistance to the Nationalists remained limited: from April to September 1947, the United States ordered its marines out of North China, although in May it lifted its arms embargo. During the summer a confused administration, increasingly skeptical of Chiang's chances, sent General Albert C. Wedemeyer to China, there to examine American options. Wedemeyer's confidential report criticized Kuomintang corruption but found Chinese air and naval bases vital to United States security. He called for massive economic and military assistance, suggesting some 10,000 American military advisers. Washington realized that Chiang's forces were fighting a losing battle and refused to redeploy resources already slated for Europe.

Because of congressional protests, particularly from Congressmen Walter Judd (Rep.–Minn.) and John M. Vorys, in December 1947 the administration added Nationalist China to the Interim Aid Bill and gave it $18 million in aid. Then, early in 1948, Truman asked Congress to pass a China Aid Act. As a result, the Chiang regime received some $275 million in economic aid as well as $125 million for military purposes.[1]

Such meager efforts could not stop Communist forces from penetrating deep into Manchuria. By January 1949 much of North China, including Peking, was in Mao's hands, and for many months the Nationalists continued their long retreat. As the year 1950 began, virtually the entire mainland was under Communist control, and the armies of Generalissimo Chiang had retreated to the island of Taiwan (Formosa).

With the Nationalist cause becoming ever more hopeless, the administration was finding itself more and more on the defensive. When in February 1949 fifty-one House Republicans claimed in unison that Mao's victory signified a monumental American setback, Acheson replied that he could not foresee the eventual outcome "until the dust settled." Congress tried in vain to bolster Chiang's retreating forces by voting modest emergency funds. Such aid availed little and, after the surrender of Peking, Truman gradually cut off aid to the Nationalists.[2]

As Chiang's defeat became apparent, the administration felt compelled to defend its China policy. In a White Paper released by the State Department on August 5, Acheson claimed that "the ominous result" of the Chinese civil war caused by "internal Chinese forces," and was therefore beyond American control. The United States had no choice, for it refused to risk "full-scale intervention in behalf of a Government which has lost the confidence of its own troops and its own people."[3]

"Letting the dust settle," as Acheson had phrased it in February, was not quite so easy as it sounded. United States policy toward the Chiang regime on Taiwan and the new Communist government still needed to be defined. In a news conference held on October 12, 1949, Acheson strongly implied that the administration had no immediate plans to recognize Mao's new government. The Russian boycott of the Security Council, made in protest of the continued presence of the Nationalists, led the United States to oppose seating Communist China at the UN. On January 5, 1950, Truman announced that the American government would give no military aid or advice to the Chinese forces on Formosa, and Acheson, in an address to the National Press Club on January 12, intimated that the western perimeters of America's defenses excluded both Taiwan and Korea.[4] Despite such efforts to conceal what was obviously a major defeat for American policy, both Acheson and his critics would learn, and learn quickly, that the nation's Asian troubles were just beginning.

In 1945 and early 1946 few old isolationists spoke out on the China issue. Of those who did, more were anxious to bring United States troops back from the Orient than to offer massive support to the Kuomintang. Upon learning that American pilots were flying supplies to the Nationalist forces, several veteran noninterventionists protested. The conservative Senator Willis asked, "What possible stake has the average American in the outcome of China's civil war?" The liberal Villard claimed that thousands of American marines were bolstering "the crooked and bloody regime of Chiang Kai-shek," and thereby risking a new world conflict. Other old isolationists, such as Mundt, Fish, and Case, argued that the United States could hardly protest against the presence of Russian troops in Manchuria or Iran as long as it was keeping its own forces in China. Father James Gillis commented sardonically, "But why complain? Didn't we promise to police the world?"[5]

Most Americans were silent when in December 1945 Truman announced that General Marshall would attempt to mediate the conflict; the old isolationists were no exception. Similarly, when Marshall reported to the Senate Foreign Relations Committee in March 1946, no committee member voiced criticism of his mission. The rightist Hamilton Fish went as far as to endorse Marshall's efforts, although he did warn that "we are bound by our traditional policy not to interfere in China's internal affairs."[6]

In 1946 Fish's caution typified the reaction of many old isolationists of both the right and the left. Sterling Morton even expressed relief when the Marshall mission was terminated, for it indicated that Truman favored "drawing in a bit from global interference—usually just plain meddling!" His fellow Princetonian Norman Thomas believed that the Communists would act tyranically, but found aid to Chiang most unwise. America, he said, should keep out of the Chinese civil war.[7]

At least two old isolationists, writing in 1946, predicted that a Communist triumph would eventually result in a Sino-Soviet split. Frank Hanighen speculated that the Russians preferred "a permanently divided and weak China" to a full-scale revolutionary regime that might rival "the Communist Motherland." In the past, so the editor maintained, Mao had occasionally been independent of Moscow's policies, and chances were likely that he would be so again. Dennis declared that any Chinese Communist government was "bound to be anti-Moscow"; the Marshall mission, a prime example of "meddling," had invited Russian interference.[8]

In 1947, as accounts of Nationalist corruption and ineptitude reached the general American public, several conservative isolationists denounced the Chiang regime. The *Chicago Tribune* referred to the "oligarchy that runs China as a private racket." Edwin C. Johnson accused Kuomintang leader Chen Yi of brutally murdering some 5,000 Taiwanese; he listed Nationalist China among the countries that had officially denounced the capitalist system. To Fish, the Communists were "actually Agrarian Socialists" who believed in a certain amount of free enterprise and private property.[9]

The Chiang government, such old isolationists claimed, would merely waste American aid and loans. William Henry Chamberlin, who expressed much alarm over the coming "Soviet pattern for China," saw valid objections to large-scale United States commitments. Ernest T. Weir found past aid to China complete folly; Wedemeyer's public demand for Kuomintang reform, he said, proved that China was still experiencing "bad government, graft, starvation, and a growing strength of communism."[10]

Attacks on Chiang's government were occasionally coupled with broadsides against administration "appeasement." Hanighen pointed to Wedemeyer's criticisms of Kuomintang lethargy and defeatism, but had previously feared that Marshall would betray the Chiang cause. Similarly, Congressman Bender, who referred to "the present Fascist Chinese government" in May 1947, by November was accusing the General of unnecessarily mollifying the Chinese Communists.[11]

In 1948 several old isolationists opposed Truman's China Aid Act. Langer claimed to be more concerned with the underprivileged children of St. Louis and Kansas City than with those living in Shanghai, Hong Kong, and Canton. John E. Rankin predicted that goods shipped to either Asia or Europe would fall into Communist hands. In opposing the bill, he cited a returning army captain who had told him that the Chinese simply left the bodies of their dead countrymen on the roadside.[12]

Throughout 1948 and 1949 a small group of old anti-interventionists continued to be suspicious of United States aid to Chiang's forces. Barnes noted the irony in American efforts to rescue the conquered nation from Japan, merely to see it go Communist: "The events in China do not break my heart." William L. Neumann feared that efforts to dominate the vast Asian country would lead to World War III. Norman Thomas, while favoring economic aid, opposed military appropriations: "We Americans are not gods in wisdom and power to put the whole world to rights." The *Progressive* accused the Nationalist regime of "temporizing with the internal problems which keep China weak." Borchard claimed that the United States was violating its own principles of neutrality, and in the process backing "the wrong horse" and wasting huge sums of the taxpayers' money.[13]

Several old isolationists of a more "maverick" or conservative bent possessed similar sentiments. Dennis claimed to welcome the Communist capture of Manchuria, asserting that it might force the United States to reexamine all ruinous commitments. Chodorov used the opportunity of Madame Chiang's visit to the United States in December 1948 to oppose further aid. Colonel McCormick, reporting on a visit to Shanghai, noted that American supplies reached neither the Chinese people nor the Kuomintang army. In demanding direct United States administration of all military assistance, the publisher wrote, "We have got all too many thieves in the American army but that is about all they have in the Chinese army." His *Chicago Tribune* soon attacked the Open Door policy, calling it a product of British designs. The United States, it said, was foolishly attempting to impose its own commerce and culture upon a recalcitrant nation.[14]

Already in 1945, however, an occasional veteran isolationist pointed with alarm to the Chinese situation. At first most attention centered on possible subversion within the State Department. Patrick Hurley, the American ambassador to China, told the Senate Foreign Relations Committee in December that a "pro-Communist, pro-imperialist" faction dominated State Department policy. Once Hurley made his charges, Congressman Carl Curtis (Rep.–Neb.) asked that the FBI examine the careers of such State Department officials as John Stuart Service, Alger Hiss, and John Carter Vincent. Representative Dondero accused Service in particular of engineering Hurley's departure.[15]

Other old isolationists accused the administration of apathy toward Communist gains. For example, several isolationists and pacifists, including Chamberlin, Villard, and Thomas, signed the so-called Manchurian Manifesto, a petition released on May 17, 1946, by John B. Powell, a veteran newspaper editor in China. Although the declaration did not directly attack the Marshall mission, it sought to end Soviet removal of Manchurian industrial equipment and Russia's arming of the Chinese Communists. It also asked for revision of Yalta provisions giving the USSR commercial rights in Manchuria, an area that, it said, held "the key to the future of China and the future peace of the Far East." In addition, a few veteran anti-interventionists, such as Morley, Thomas, and Freda Utley, endorsed an open letter to Secretary of State Byrnes. Dated July 24, 1946, the petition called for unification of China by the Nationalists, full Chinese sovereignty in Manchuria, and no further compromises with the Communists. American efforts to foster a coalition government, it warned, would only make China a Russian satellite, with the United States exchanging "the open door for an iron curtain."[16]

Even in 1945 and 1946 an extremely small number of veteran isolationists wanted deeper American intervention. United States aid, they claimed, could save the Chiang government. Upton Close demanded "U.S. gold, tanks, and men." Although the broadcaster vaguely referred to the regime's "faults," he claimed that the Kuomintang was supported by the majority of the Chinese people. Congressman Raymond S. Springer (Rep.–Ind.), while demanding that the wealthy Soong and Kung families leave the United States, said that only America could prevent the Russians from seizing all Asia.[17]

In 1947 and 1948, as it became obvious that the Marshall mission had failed, many old isolationists, particularly those of Republican and conservative leanings, increased their criticism of Truman's China policy. Taft accused the administration of inconsistency: Europe received much United States aid whereas China was almost completely neglected. The Ohio Senator admitted that appropriating large sums might be unwise but, sensing a Communist threat to Japan, he hoped that the Nationalists would be sent sufficient arms to retain Manchuria. The Far East, he said, was ultimately more important to America's future than was Europe, although he gave no reason for his position. Hoover added his voice, declaring that the front against Communism lay "not alone in Europe," but in Asia (and Latin America) as well. "We have," said Merwin K. Hart, "betrayed our friends and encouraged our enemies."[18]

The new tone was set by Freda Utley, who had long called for strong American backing of the Chiang government. The London-born Mrs. Utley grew up a believer in Manchester socialism, her father, a journalist, having been a friend of both William Morris and George Bernard Shaw. Educated at the London School of Economics, she went to Russia in 1928, there to receive her doctorate from Moscow's Academy of Sciences and to work for the Comintern. The disappearance of her husband, a native of Russia and a Bolshevik, created such bitterness that by 1940 she could find more redemption in Nazi Germany than in Soviet Russia. In 1941 she wrote a series of articles urging the United States to remain aloof from the European conflict.[19]

In a book entitled *Last Chance in China* (1948), Mrs. Utley called upon the United States to equip the Nationalist armies. While hoping that America would foster reform in the Chiang regime, she stressed the need to back "loyal Chinese against foreign-aided rebels seeking to bring the Chinese under Soviet hegemony." Chiang's government, she said, should receive two or three billion dollars. Although the Kuomintang would have to borrow part of the money from the United States, it could pay for the rest by exporting to Japan's former markets in Asia.[20]

Her support of the Chiang regime strongly reflected her impassioned anti-Communism. When she first visited China in 1938, she claimed that Mao's Communists were seeking a democratic and capitalistic regime. Two years later, however, she was asserting that they were instruments of the Stalinist bureaucracy. By 1949 Mrs. Utley was so concerned with the China issue, and with the related question of domestic subversion, that she falsely accused revisionist historian William L. Neumann of harboring Communist sympathies. Although she was unable to get the Foundation for Foreign Affairs, for which Neumann was working, to fire him, she would continue to make accusations with some recklessness.[21]

Several other old isolationists made specific proposals of their own. William Henry Chamberlin hoped that an Asian Marshall Plan could administer aid for China and the Philippines. Former senator D. Worth Clark (Dem.–Idaho), who was sent to China at the request of the pro-Chiang Senator Styles Bridges (Rep.–N.H.), recommended that the United States contribute combat advisers to the Kuomintang forces. The Nationalist Chinese used the services of two isolationists protégés of Father Charles E.

Coughlin, William J. Goodwin and Robert M. Harriss, in an attempt to convert both legislators and the public to Chiang's cause. Congressman Lawrence Smith cited General MacArthur and General Claire Chennault, wartime leader of the Flying Tigers and head of the Nationalist airline, on the need for increased assistance.[22]

If in 1948 outrage over China remained concentrated among foes of bipartisanship, it was reaching some World War II isolationists who had defended much of Truman's foreign policy. Arthur Vandenberg (who privately claimed that China's future was "the greatest speculation of the ages") had said in January 1947 that the time had come to sustain the Chiang government. In seeking its inclusion in the Interim Aid Bill of December 1947, the Michigan Senator declared that Far Eastern stability was indispensable to a sound world economy. And, in defending the China Aid bill four months later, he noted that the Kuomintang government had called for free elections, pointed with pride to "the first constitution in the history of China," and warned that "the iron curtain of Communism" would prevent freedom of choice for the Chinese people.[23]

There were always limits to Vandenberg's enthusiasm. He opposed the use of American combat troops or any underwriting of the China campaign. Late in 1948 he confessed that the Nationalists had not reformed themselves "in a fashion calculated to deserve continued popular confidence over there or over here." During 1949 Vandenberg remained a master of equivocation. He sought continued arms shipments; although finding China's fall inevitable, he said, "This blood must not be on *our* hands." And when the State Department released the White Paper, Vandenberg could not help commenting privately that "F.D.R. sold Chiang Kai-shek down the river in order to get Joe Stalin into the Jap war."[24]

The impact of the China issue among bipartisan supporters can be seen more clearly by considering John W. Vorys, a senior member of the House Foreign Affairs Committee. After graduating from Yale and becoming an attorney in Columbus, Ohio, Vorys held several state posts before being elected to the House in 1938. He was a firm isolationist in regard to Europe, writing a constituent in May 1940 that "We ought to stay at peace, because this is not our war." In April 1941 and again in June, Vorys urged the United States to negotiate the European conflict. Nonetheless he supported an embargo against Japan, declaring that America was tacitly abetting its invasion of China. Although he usually followed Vandenberg's lead on Cold War policy, he often tried to cut appropriations for Europe while increasing them for Asia.[25]

Vorys had gained his impressions of China while teaching in 1919 in the Yale-in-China program at Changsha, and he never lost his fervor for the Chinese cause. Even in 1949, as the Chiang forces were crumbling, he hoped that the United States would step into the breach. In August, as the Communists were capturing Nanking, Vorys claimed that $200 million of military aid could supply General Chennault with enough planes to stop their advance. This power, he said, could be used "with devastating effect," for the Communist forces lacked air support.[26]

Such overtures to Chiang obviously had political as well as ideological roots, with several supporters of bipartisanship undoubtedly realizing that their own political prospects could rise as the Kuomintang's fell. Such converts to interventionism as Hugh D. Scott, Jr., Frances P. Bolton, and Bartel K. Jonkman all pressed for increased aid to the Nationalists. Even Governor Dewey, a favorite of the interventionists, promised during the 1948 campaign to end "the tragic neglect of our ancient friend and ally China." Vandenberg would frequently and fervently deny that the administration had ever consulted him on its Asian policy. He obviously realized that if Truman failed, the Republicans would not only be absolved of blame; they could raise the issue with vigor. In addition, Vandenberg could benefit personally, for he was being boosted for the Presidency by publisher Henry R. Luce, a strong Chiang partisan. Many old isolationists had never been so unified since 1941. Only when the loss of China led to further involvement did concord again turn to discord.[27]


Once it became obvious that the Communists would conquer China, the great preponderance of old isolationists became embittered. The fall of China supplied additional proof that the United States had been mistaken in fighting World War II; American lives and resources had been expended not only to insure the rule of Soviet regimes in Eastern Europe, but to install Communist control in much of the Asian mainland as well. Sterling Morton, in commenting on the results of the conflict, found Mao's domination of China far more ruthless than Japanese rule. The *Chicago Tribune* pointedly asked why the United States entered the war, since its primary goal in Asia, the rescue of China, appeared bound to fail from the beginning. Hart wrote, "Every man who died in our Pacific campaign died in vain."[28]

Such old isolationists often ignored their own criticisms of the Chiang regime in order to denounce the findings of the White Paper, and to accuse the Democrats of "sell-out" and "appeasement." The *Chicago Tribune,* for example, called the State Department document "a salmon concealed in aspic." Frank Chodorov, referring to the White Paper as a "whitewash," reminded readers: "The only foreign policy for which no apology was ever forthcoming or needed was that of George Washington." Morley declared that the White Paper overlooked the destructive role of Yalta.[29]

Other conservatives among the old isolationists were equally intent upon pinning responsibility on "That Man." Congressman Daniel A. Reed remarked, "The New Deal coddled communism in China from the start." Roosevelt, said John T. Flynn, had agreed to Russian rule in Manchuria in order to get votes from the Communist-dominated American Labor Party. Referring to the 1944 presidential election, Flynn commented, "We sold out 400 million Chinese for 400,000 American Communist votes."[30]

During the following years, revisionist presses printed several books attacking the administration. In 1951 Henry Regnery published Freda Utley's *China Story*, in which the author strongly implied that a small clique of Communist sympathizers in America had fomented Chiang's defeat. Its writing and distribution had been subsidized by General Wood, who gave $2,000 for those purposes. Reviews were mixed: Richard L. Walker, a Yale historian, found it a needed corrective to accounts sympathetic to the Chinese Communists; Benjamin Schwartz of the Russian Research Center at Harvard observed that she had barely touched on Kuomintang corruption, had overlooked the heavy stocks of munitions sent to the Nationalists, and had failed to consider the disillusionment of the Chinese masses.[31]

In the same year, Devin-Adair came out with John T. Flynn's *While You Slept*. Flynn used Jesus' parable of the sower to illustrate how the American government had supposedly abandoned the Nationalist armies. Although he admitted at one point that the Kuomintang possessed "selfish . . . and extremely reactionary interests," he accused such prominent writers as Edgar Snow and Owen Lattimore of making Americans receptive to Communist control. In 1953 he wrote a sequel, *The Lattimore Story*, in which he found China's fall rooted in "an alien web of intrigue" more appropriate to a Dumas novel about the court of Louis XV than to twentieth-century statecraft. Flynn accused Owen Lattimore, a scholar who occasionally advised the State Department, of "promoting the policies of Stalin in the United States and against the United States throughout the world."[32]

By 1949 several old isolationists were stressing even more strongly that the Orient was just as vital as Europe. To use the metaphor of Karl Mundt, one could not build a firm dike in Europe while allowing "red waters to rush unchecked through the flood plain of Asia." Remarked Hugh Butler on apparent administration apathy, "The strongest language used by Christ while on earth was used by Him in denouncing hypocrites." Morley cited an aphorism once ascribed to Lenin: "Communism will conquer Europe by a detour over Asia." The Washington journalist warned of "active red movements" in Indochina and Indonesia and feared that Japan would be severed from markets and sources of supply. A Communist Asia, he continued, could threaten the United States from either Alaska or the Pacific as well as making it too costly to sustain independent outposts in Western Europe.[33]

Such sentiments led invariably to what was later called "domino" thinking. With the Communists now in control of China, conservatives saw the entire Asian continent in danger. Hart declared, "We have thrown away all Asia, including Japan and the Philippines." Lawrence Smith warned that "fires of red insurrection" reached from India to Indonesia. Fish, abandoning talk of "agrarian reformers," predicted that within ten years four million Chinese soldiers would "march to Armageddon and the Suez Canal." Taft warned against Communist domination of Indochina, an area whose raw materials he found of vital interest to the United States.

(In December 1949 he did admit privately that he had no real solution to the rapid changes in Asia.)[34]

As soon as the Communists gained control of China, such senators as Taft, Butler, Mundt, and Clyde Reed denied that official recognition of Mao's rule would be consistent with the Truman Doctrine. Similarly, other old isolationists insisted upon some form of commitment to the remnants of Chiang's authority. Congressman Crawford, for example, warned that abandoning Taiwan would lead to Japan's domination by "the Russian bear."[35]

Hoover took the lead in advocating that the United States protect the Kuomintang regime. On the last day of 1949 the former President sent a public letter to Senator William F. Knowland (Rep.–Calif.), who, like Vorys, had combined support for administration policy in Europe with demands for extensive aid to the Chinese Nationalists. Hoover's letter opposed recognizing the Communist state and sought continuous support of Chiang's government. If necessary, the United States should give naval protection to Formosa, the Pescadores, and possibly the Hainan Islands. Such a policy, he said, would not only defend the Philippines and Japan; it might guarantee the "salvation of southeastern Asia."[36]

Taft immediately endorsed Hoover's proposal. Although the Ohio Senator soon opposed occupation of Taiwan by an American army, he called upon the United States Navy—already located in the Formosa Strait—to repulse ships carrying Communist invaders. Taft could not find "the slightest evidence" that Russia would risk war over the matter: "The chance we are taking is 1 to 10 compared to that we are taking in Europe today." He predicted that once the peace treaty with Japan was signed, the people of Taiwan would probably vote to establish an independent republic. Then, when such a government was set up, the United States could force the Nationalists to step down. Recognition of Mao's government could be considered later.[37]

Even while China was succumbing to the Communists, a handful of veteran isolationists refused to forsake their traditional position. This small minority neither regretted Truman's relative aloofness from the Kuomintang nor sought additional commitments to the Nationalist government. The United States, they believed, had been wise to avoid extensive participation in China's struggle.

This group blamed the government of Chiang Kai-shek, not that of Harry Truman, for Nationalist China's demise. Congressman Burdick accused Chiang, whom he suspected was "the richest potentate on the face of the globe," of presiding over the starvation of more millions than anyone else in history. John O'Donnell referred to the "thieving Chinese we dealt with." Chamberlin, although a much firmer believer in Asian containment, admitted that the Nationalists were "not a strong, effective or reliable ally."[38]

Frank Chodorov was particularly acid. Noting that Chiang had supposedly "sent home a few trunks containing bars of gold and other negotiable trinkets," he declared, "These should keep him in eats, now that the taxing power has passed on to other hands." Even if the Russians had temporarily conquered China—a popular myth of the time—they would soon intermarry with its women and become assimilated into its traditional life. Yet the libertarian commentator was afraid: any Communist confiscation of American investments might cause a United States expeditionary force to attempt an invasion. Better to "leave it to the girls" than to send "another shipload of uniformed morons." "Who will be next?", Chodorov asked. "Finally, do you really give a damn about the Chinese question? Is not the outcome of the baseball pennant race of far greater importance to you?"[39]

A small number of old isolationists also dissented over the American diplomatic aloofness and the fate of Formosa. Legal recognition, such people argued, did not necessitate approval of either a nation's ideology or its economic system. *Human Events* featured an article by Henry P. Fletcher—diplomat, former Rough Rider, and World War II isolationist—who called for recognizing the Communist regime. "We are," he said, "confronted in China with a condition as well as a theory." Congressman Rich declared that the United States should stop telling the Chinese "what government they should have." Lawrence Dennis claimed that continued nonrecognition could only play into the hands of Mao's government, for it would permit China to build up its strength in total isolation from the Western world. Dennis was equally unenthusiastic over the Hoover-Taft proposals to protect Taiwan; "Quaker Republican statesmen, over military age," he asserted, were foolishly attempting to whip up a "war fever." The *Chicago Tribune,* noting that Acheson had recently spoken of eventual conflict between the Communist regimes of Russia and China, suggested that the Secretary's analysis should be applied universally: "If enough rope will ensure Stalin's downfall in China, it will ensure his downfall everywhere."[40]

Historians and commentators have long claimed that the isolationists were supposedly "soft" in Europe and "hard" in Asia, and that if the Atlantic Ocean was "the lake" of the interventionists, the Pacific belonged to the isolationists. Evidence includes anxieties over Asia revealed in Lindbergh's speeches of 1940 and 1941; isolationist support for General MacArthur's presidential candidacy in 1944 and 1948; and the stress that several isolationists gave to the Pacific theater during World War II. Philip La Follette, serving as a wartime aide to MacArthur, predicted that Asia, with its undeveloped markets and unexplored territories, could absorb American energies for five hundred years.[41]

Such an interpretation deserves modification. Most isolationists favored China's cause against Japan, but opposed direct United States entry into the conflict. It should be noted, if only in passing, that the America First Committee paid relatively little attention to the Sino-Japanese conflict, that those isolationists who commented on the Asian war in 1941 usually opposed risking war with Japan, and that only a minority of isolationists—in and out of Congress—sought a strident pro-Chiang policy. Even Lindbergh, for all his talk of "Asiatic hordes," blamed Pearl Harbor upon the United States. It was not necessarily in the nature of American isolationism to seek intervention in the Orient.[42]

Most isolationist outrage concerning the fate of China was not rooted in any mythical proclivity toward Pacific involvements. Rather, it was grounded in the peculiar circumstances in which these isolationists—and the nation at large—found themselves at the end of World War II. The year 1949 has, with good reason, been labeled "the year of shocks." The Communist seizure of China occurred at the same time as the sensational espionage trial of Alger Hiss and the Russian explosion of the atomic bomb. To the majority of old isolationists, the United States appeared to be losing the Cold War and losing it rapidly. America, according to popular mythology, had formerly been able to protect China from predatory and exploitative foreign powers; hence its failure to do so in the late 1940s could only have been rooted in domestic conspiracy. Given China's supposed tradition of friendship, a strong and purposeful United States could have halted what Flynn saw as "the Communist Plan to turn China and Korea over to the Soviet."[43] It might at first seem far-fetched to argue that a handful of State Department advisers determined the fate of some 450 million Chinese. However, the "precedents" of the Pearl Harbor and Yalta "conspiracies" were far from reassuring.

There was, of course, much inconsistency in the new concern with China. Many arguments of the old isolationists against economic and military support of Europe could have applied with greater force to China: the Chiang regime was as corrupt as Greece, reactionary as Turkey, and far more unstable than either France or Italy. Although the Kuomintang had not yet engaged in the widespread socialization of Great Britain, Chiang's ideological manifesto, China's Destiny (1947), offered little comfort to adherents of laissez-faire capitalism. Chiang went as far as to call for equalization of land rights and the eventual transformation of all "capital into state capital." Conservative isolationists were fond of quoting Lenin's supposed boast that Russia would force the United States to spend itself into bankruptcy. They did not, however, see how their own demands for aid to China might relate to such a scheme. Isolationists attacked the administration for manipulating crises in the Balkans and Czechoslovakia, but themselves risked confrontation by truculence over Formosa. To add to the irony, certain interventionists of World War II—particularly Roosevelt, Willkie, and Henry R. Luce—were among the first to promote Chiang's reputation in the United States. Roosevelt, in fact, envisioned Nationalist China as one of the world's "four policemen."[44]

Most old isolationists were untroubled about such incongruity. Even in 1947 and 1948, their criticism of American policy in Asia was far more muted than that regarding Europe. Only in 1949 were many starting to join with a more chauvinist right, and the positions of Hoover and Taft could no longer be distinguished from the views of Senator Knowland. Yet, even when the bulk of isolationists were becoming militantly pro-Chiang, their arguments centered far more on internal betrayal than on the geopolitics of the Orient. (Freda Utley and John Vorys were among the few "true believers" in the Nationalist cause; the seasoned anti-Communist William Henry Chamberlin opposed large-scale military assistance.) Cries of "treason" possessed an added convenience: the Communist seizure could be explained without confronting the enormous expenditure that would have been required to keep the Kuomintang in power.[45]

Administration rhetoric inadvertently gave credence to the "conspiracy thesis." The Truman Doctrine had implied that radical revolutions were foreign exports, not domestic products. Because such movements supposedly lacked the support of the people, effective application of United States resources could sustain any "democratic" regime. The President's opponents, therefore, could logically argue that had America's will been as strong as its power, Communism would not have come to China.[46]

Pro-Chiang critics could gleefully take the administration position to its logical conclusion. If the Soviet Union was the comprehensive global threat that the Truman government claimed, and if the Chinese Communists were either tools or enthusiastic allies of the Russians, should not Communism be opposed just as vigorously on the Yangtse as on the Elbe? To act otherwise toward Asia than toward Europe could be presented as more than hypocrisy; it should be turned into a betrayal of the President's own manifesto.[47]

Partisanship, while never absent from issues of foreign policy, played an exceptionally important role during the debates over China. In 1949 it was manifested at almost every turn: in the collective indictment made by the fifty-one Republican congressmen; in the efforts of House Republicans to defeat the Korean Aid Bill; and in the opposition of Vandenberg to confirming a leading administration policymaker, Walton Butterworth, as Assistant Secretary of State for Far Eastern Affairs. The Republican Party as a party realized that it had a popular issue, and it was determined to make the most of it. Truman's election victory a year earlier had already shown that bipartisanship was paying few dividends, and the congressional elections of 1950 were not far away. Vandenberg said that the United Nations should keep Taiwan out of Communist hands and refuse to seat Mao's government. In addition, he opposed immediate recognition of Communist China and its seating in the UN. Unlike Hoover and Taft, he opposed active American military preparations for the defense of Formosa.[48]

Partisanship also explains why so many more old isolationists in Congress were likely to condemn the administration than were those outside. Such veteran isolationist liberals as Barnes, Rubin, and Neumann had no vested interest in the fortunes of the Republican Party. Nor did such "mavericks" as Dennis and Chodorov. They could oppose the Truman Doctrine and the Atlantic Pact with the same fervor as Taft or Lawrence Smith, but still balk at attempts to rescue the Kuomintang.

To this small minority, globalism in Asia was no wiser than globalism in Europe, and the Chiang regime deserved no more support than did the governments of Greece and Turkey. If the majority of old isolationists found new occasions teaching new duties, the remnant saw virtue in consistency. Morris Rubin, in comparing his own noninterventionism on China with such waverers as Taft and Hoover, commented, "We of *The Progressive* are never quite sure whom we're going to find in our bed of a morning, because while we tend to stay put and sleep in the same place, the others have a habit of wandering around like sleepwalkers." Chiang defenders, said Dennis in 1951, did not really believe in neutrality; they just wanted to replace one pattern of intervention with another. Writing in the midst of the Korean War, the commentator would find examples of his indictment at almost every turn.[49]

# NOTES

1. H. Bradford Westerfield, *Foreign Policy and Party Politics: Pearl Harbor to Korea* (New Haven, Conn.: Yale University Press, 1955), pp. 262–64; Tang Tsou, *America's Failure in China, 1941–1950* (Chicago: University of Chicago Press, 1963), p. 472; Ross T. Koen, *The China Lobby in American Politics* (New York: Harper and Row, 1975), pp. 74–75.

2. Petitions, dated February 7 and addressed to the President, *CR*, March 7, 1947, pp. 1950–51; Acheson reply in Westerfield, *Foreign Policy*, p. 347. In April, just before the Communist forces swept across the Yangtse, Congress appropriated $54 million for unoccupied areas of China, and in September, at Vandenberg's suggestion, allocated $75 million for use in the "general area" of China. Westerfield, *Foreign Policy*, pp. 348–58.

3. "Text of Secretary Acheson's Letter Transmitting White Paper on China," *New York Times*, August 6, 1949, p. 4.

4. Acheson, interview, *New York Times*, October 13, 1949, p. 19; "Truman Bars Military Help for Defense of Formosa," *New York Times*, January 6, 1950, pp. 1, 3; Acheson, *New York Times*, January 13, 1950, pp. 1–2.

5. Willis, *CR*, November 30, 1945, p. 11236; Villard, "Gamble Lost," *Progressive* 10 (June 26, 1946): 1; Case, *CR*, November 27, 1945, p. 11061; Mundt, *CR*, December 3, 1945, pp. 11361–65; Fish, *Challenge of World Communism*, p. 122; Gillis, "Intervention Begins to Pay Off," *Catholic World* 142 (January 1946): 294.

6. Fish, *Challenge of World Communism*, p. 121. Several scholars claim that most Congressmen either approved or reserved judgment on Truman's China policy. See Virginia M. Kemp, "Congress and China, 1945–1949," Ph.D. diss., University of Pittsburgh, 1966, pp. 17–22; John R. Skettering, "Republican Attitudes Towards the Administration's China Policy, 1945–1949," Ph.D. diss., Iowa State University, 1952, pp. 33–34.

7. S. Morton to H. G. Wade, March 4, 1947, Morton Papers; Thomas, "Prices and Starvation," *Socialist Call* 13 (July 29, 1946): 8.

8. Hanighen, "Not Merely Gossip," *Human Events* 3 (January 30, 1946); Dennis, *Appeal to Reason*, #8 (May 18, 1946), and #17 (July 20, 1946).

9. "A Work for Knaves and Fools" (editorial), *Chicago Tribune*, January 7, 1947; Johnson on Formosa, radio address over Mutual Broadcasting System, April 9, 1947, *CR*, p. A1821, and on capitalism, radio debate, February 18, 1946, p. A797; Fish, *Red Plotters*, p. 60.

10. Chamberlin, "The Soviet Pattern for China," *Human Events* 4 (November 12, 1947); Weir, testimony before House Foreign Affairs Committee, *CR*, November 25, 1947, p. 10875.

11. Hanighen on Wedemeyer, "Not Merely Gossip," *Human Events* 4 (August 27, 1947), and on Marshall, ibid., 3 (May 15, 1946; May 22, 1946); Bender, *CR*, May 7, 1947, p. 4694, and November 25, 1947, p. 10875.

12. Langer, *CR*, March 30, 1948, p. 3680; Rankin, *CR*, March 29, 1948, p. 3635.

13. H. E. Barnes to W. L. Neumann, December 16, 1948, Neumann Papers; W. L. Neumann to H. E. Barnes, July 9, 1948, Neumann Papers; Thomas, speech at Cleveland, *New York Times*, October 24, 1948, p. 65; "Fading Peace" (editorial), *Progressive* 12 (February 1948): 2; Borchard, "United States Foreign Policy," p. 335.

14. Dennis, *Appeal to Reason*, #140 (November 27, 1948); Chodorov, "Trailing the Trend," *analysis* 4 (December 1948): 3; McCormick, "A Trip to China," *Chicago Tribune*, March 21, 1948.

15. Carl Curtis, *CR*, November 28, 1945, p. A5159; Dondero, *CR*, December 10, 1945, p. A5403. For Hurley's accusations, see Russell D. Buhite, *Patrick J. Hurley and American Foreign Policy* (Ithaca, N.Y.: Cornell University Press, 1973), p. 273.

16. Petition of John B. Powell, *CR*, May 17, 1946, p. A2763–64; open letter, July 24, 1946, *CR*, pp. A4495–96. The Powell document was sponsored by the American China Policy Association, whose president was Powell and whose board chairman was Alfred Kohlberg, a New York exporter and supposed leader of the "China Lobby." See Joseph Keeley, *The China Lobby Man: The Story of Alfred Kohlberg* (New Rochelle, N.Y.: Arlington House, 1969), pp. 236. Villard, a signer of the Manchurian Manifesto, soon resigned from the association on the grounds that it was too pro-Chiang. See O. G. Villard to America China Policy Association, February 20, 1947, Villard Papers.

17. *Closer-Ups* 1 (November 5, 1945): 2; Raymond S. Springer, *CR*, August 1, 1946, p. A4726.

18. Taft, address to Economic Club of Detroit, February 23, 1948, *CR*, p. A1074; H. Hoover to A. H. Vandenberg, January 18, 1948, *Foreign Policy for a Post-War Recovery Program*, p. 799; Hart, "Our Two Foreign Policies," *Economic Council Letter*, #168 (June 1, 1947).

19. For Mrs. Utley's comparison of Nazism and Communism, see *The Dream We Lost*, pp. 259–61. Her writings, which called for American isolation in regard to Europe, were recommended by the America First Committee, and she spoke before such groups as the isolationist Women United. See AFS National Bulletin #629, October 4, 1941. For a sample of her isolationist writing, see "Can Democracy Survive Total War?," *Annals of the American Academy of Political and Social Science* 216 (July 1941): 9–15. For Mrs. Utley's early career, see the first volume of her projected memoirs, *The Odyssey of a Liberal* (Washington, D.C.: Washington National Press, 1970); *Current Biography, 1958*, pp. 448–50; Harvey Breit, "Talk with Freda Utley," *New York Times Book Review*, May 27, 1951, p. 21.

20. Freda Utley, *Last Chance in China* (Indianapolis, Ind.: Bobbs-Merrill, 1948), p. 394.

21. W. L. Neumann to H. E. Barnes, August 24, 1949, Neumann Papers; W. L. Neumann to W. H. Regnery, May 18, 1950, F. Utley to W. H. Regnery, May 25, 1950, copies in NCPW Papers. For the changes in her attitudes toward China, see Kenneth E. Shewmaker, *Americans and Chinese Communists, 1937–1945: A Persuading Encounter* (Ithaca, N.Y.: Cornell University Press, 1971), pp. 241–43, 252–53, 272–75, 330–31.

22. Chamberlin, "Wanted: A Marshall Plan for Asia," *New Leader* 31 (January 3, 1948): 16. For William J. Goodwin, Robert M. Harriss, and D. Worth Clark, see Koen, pp. 39–40, 46–47, 94–95; Malcolm Hobbs, "Washington Front," *Nation* 169 (December 24, 1949): 620; "Bill Goodwin—Chinese Press Agent," Friends of Democracy, *Battle* 7 (October 15, 1949): 3–4; Drew Pearson, "China Lobby Aims at United States Policy," *Washington Post*, June 18, 1951; Senator Wayne Morse (Rep.-Ore.), *CR*, June 11, 1951, pp. A3456–57.

23. Vandenberg, speech of January 11, 1947, and letter to W. Loeb, February 10,

1947, in *Private Papers,* pp. 522–23; Vandenberg, *CR,* November 24, 1947, p. 10704, and March 30, 1948, pp. 3670–71.

24. Vandenberg, letter of November 22, 1948, in *Private Papers,* p. 526; idem, letter of January 18, 1949, ibid., p. 529; Vandenberg diary, February 5, 1949, ibid., pp. 530–31; A. H. Vandenberg to Mrs. A. H. Vandenberg, August 7, 1949, ibid., p. 535.

25. For a biographical sketch of Vorys, see *Current Biography, 1950,* pp. 588–90. For Vorys's isolationism, see J. M. Vorys to J. S. Power, May 22, 1940, the Papers of John M. Vorys, Box 3, Ohio State Historical Society, Columbus, Ohio; *New York Times,* April 27, 1941, p. 25, and June 9, 1941, p. 8. For Vorys on China, see Vorys to H. B. Allison, Box 3, February 7, 1940, Vorys Papers.

26. Vorys, *CR,* August 17, 1949, p. 11668, and August 18, 1948, p. 11789.

27. See, for example, Hugh D. Scott, Jr., *CR,* December 4, 1947, pp. 11053–54; Vandenberg, *CR,* April 26, 1947, p. 3474. For an observation on Vandenberg's political shrewdness, see Westerfield, *Foreign Policy,* p. 247–49. For Luce's backing of Vandenberg, see Robert T. Elson, *The World of Time Inc.: The Intimate History of a Publishing Enterprise,* vol. 2: *1941–1960* (New York: Atheneum, 1973), p. 230; Swanberg, *Luce and His Empire,* pp. 266–69. For Bolton, *CR,* February 7, 1949, pp. 872–73; Jonkman, *CR,* March 24, 1948, p. 3422; Dewey in Divine, *Presidential Elections,* 1: 245.

28. S. Morton to C. W. Vursell, November 8, 1948, Morton Papers; "Confessions of Failure" (editorial), *Chicago Tribune,* August 8, 1949; Hart, "The American Politburo," *Economic Council Letter,* # 214 (May 1, 1949).

29. "Confessions of Failure" (editorial), *Chicago Tribune,* August 8, 1949; Chodorov, "Trailing the Trend," *analysis* 5 (September 1949): 2; Morley, "White Paper on Black Background," *Human Events* 6 (August 17, 1949).

30. D. Reed to A. S. Glose, December 9, 1949, Box 20, Reed Papers; Flynn, "China," radio broadcast #1 (May 8, 1949), in Flynn Papers.

31. Freda Utley, *The China Story* (Chicago: Regnery, 1951); R. E. Wood to F. Utley, September 12, 1950, Box 6, Wood papers; review by Richard L. Walker, *New York Times Book Review,* May 13, 1951, pp. 6, 15; review by Benjamin Schwartz, *Progressive* 15 (August 1951): 27–28.

32. Flynn on Jesus' parable, *While You Slept: Our Tragedy in Asia and Who Made It* (New York: Devin-Adair, 1951); p. 3, and on Chiang corruption, p. 160; idem, *The Lattimore Story* (New York: Devin-Adair, 1953), inside cover, pp. 1–2.

33. Mundt, DAR address, April 18, 1949, *CR,* p. A4249; release of Hugh Butler, June 25, 1949, *CR,* p. 8328; Morley, "State of the Nation," *Nation's Business* 37 (June 1949): p. 17.

34. Hart, "The American Politburo"; Lawrence Smith, *CR,* April 9, 1949, p. 4207; H. Fish to D. Acheson, August 9, 1949, *CR,* January 31, 1950, p. A679; Taft, *CR,* June 24, 1949, p. 8293; Patterson, *Mr. Republican,* p. 705 n. 40.

35. Petition, June 24, 1949, *CR,* p. 13266; Crawford, *CR,* June 22, 1950, p. 9091.

36. H. Hoover to W. F. Knowland, December 31, 1949, *CR,* January 1950, p. 83.

37. Taft, *New York Times,* December 31, 1949, p. 2; idem, *CR,* January 11, 1950, pp. 298–99.

38. Burdick, *CR,* January 24, 1949, p. 528; O'Donnell, "Capitol Stuff," *New York Daily News,* April 1, 1949; Chamberlin, "Asia: Debacle and Drift," *New Leader* 32 (May 28, 1949): 16.

39. Chodorov, "Trailing the Trend," *analysis* 5 (February 1949): 3, and "The Chinese Questions," ibid. (May 1949): 3.

40. Henry P. Fletcher, "China and Bipartisanship," *Human Events* 6 (December 14, 1949); Fletcher on World War II, "15 Republicans Score War 'Steps,'" *New York Times,* August 6, 1941, p. 6; Rich, *CR,* March 30, 1950, p. 4411; Dennis, *Appeal to Reason,* #170 (June 25, 1949) and #198 (January 7, 1950); "Enough Rope" (editorial),

*Chicago Tribune,* January 15, 1950. The *Tribune* was referring to Acheson's speech of January 12.

41. P. La Follette to I. La Follette, April 29, 1944, Philip La Follette Papers. Among the works that present this interpretation are Henry P. Graff, "Isolationism Again, with a Difference," *New York Times Magazine,* May 16, 1965, p. 99; Bernard Fensterwald, Jr., "The Anatomy of American 'Isolationism' and Expansionism, Part I," p. 112; Eric F. Goldman, *The Crucial Decade—and After* (New York: Vintage, 1960), p. 127.

42. For the isolationists and China, see Manfred Jonas, "Pro-Axis Sentiment and American Isolationism," *Historian* 20 (February 1967): 223–25. For the apathy of America First, see Cole, *America First,* pp. 189–90. For Lindbergh, see *Wartime Journals,* entry of December 8, 1941, pp. 560–61. For the record of congressional isolationists, see Justin H. Libby, "The Irresolute Years: American Congressional Opinion Towards Japan, 1947–1941," Ph.D. diss., Michigan State University, 1971.

43. The term *year of shocks* is used in Goldman, chap. 5. For *the Communist Plan,* see book jacket of Flynn, *While You Slept.*

44. For Chiang's ideology, see his *China's Destiny* (New York: Macmillan, 1947). For interventionists, see Swanberg, pp. 183–86, 226–29, and Elson, *World of Time Inc.,* 2: 116–26; Burns, pp. 404, 409, 544; Wendell L. Willkie, *One World* (New York: Simon and Schuster, 1943), pp. 133–34.

45. For the convenience of the conspiracy theory, see Norman A. Graebner, *The New Isolationism: A Study in Politics and Foreign Policy Since 1950* (New York: Ronald Press, 1956), pp. 27–28.

46. Athan Theoharis, *Seeds of Repression: Harry S. Truman and the Origins of McCarthyism* (Chicago: Quadrangle, 1971), pp. 50–51.

47. Freeland, *Truman Doctrine,* pp. 336–37.

48. Vandenberg on Butterworth, see Westerfield, *Foreign Policy,* p. 352; on recognizing Communist China, see *Private Papers,* pp. 537–38; on Formosa defense, see Westerfield, *Foreign Policy,* p. 365.

49. "The Lesser Risk" (editorial), *Progressive* 14 (February 1950): 4; L. Dennis to H. E. Barnes, December 10, 1951, Barnes Papers.

# 10

# Korea and Europe:
# The Great Debate of 1950-1951

In 1949 the majority of old isolationists had strongly demanded United States support for Chiang's regime on Taiwan; a year later an even greater proportion endorsed Truman's decision to repel the North Korean invasion of its southern neighbor. Believing that China was merely the last country to experience American betrayal, they were grateful that their homeland had finally "stood up" to "world Communism." Their approval was mixed with warnings, sometimes with new vilification. It was, however, only when the legions of Mao Tse-tung entered the war that they began to express fundamental misgivings about the conflict and considered anew a return to nonintervention. And when Truman announced "substantial increases" of American forces in Western Europe, a Great Debate—almost as comprehensive as that of 1940–41—was in the offing.

Early in 1950, before the Korean War broke out, congressional isolationists sharply contested a $60 million grant to the Republic of South Korea. Even Vorys, who had been so vocal in pushing massive aid to Nationalist China, was opposed; the appropriation, he declared, was "rathole money." Such large-scale economic appropriations, requested at the very moment that American troops were being withdrawn from the peninsula, would simply make South Korea a richer prize for the Communists. Only when the Far Eastern bill included Formosa as well as Korea did it get Vorys's support.[1]

In opposing the Korean bill, old isolationists cited the administration's own statements. If, as Acheson maintained, the island of Taiwan could not be defended, the far more vulnerable peninsula of Korea faced even more difficulty. Congressman Robert Chiperfield (Rep.–Ill.) compared such aid to "treating a hangnail on one's finger when the arm was swollen with poison from the wrist to the shoulder." John Taber said that localized allocations, if unattached to a comprehensive Asian policy, merely put "the cart before the horse." The minority report of the House Foreign Affairs Committee, signed by both Chiperfield and Vorys, claimed that Korea could no more withstand the "surrounding climate of rampant communism" than could Luxembourg have repelled "the ideology and the tactics of a Hitlerized Europe." It would be far cheaper, commented Congressman Rich, to send American missionaries![2]

On June 24 the army of North Korea crossed the thirty-eighth parallel and attacked South Korea. Acting under the auspices (but without the prior permission) of the United Nations, Truman ordered United States air and naval forces stationed in Japan to repel the attack, and within a week American ground units were fighting on the peninsula. To the President, Korea was "the Greece of the Far East." Without American resistance, the Russians would continue to "swallow up one piece of Asia after another." Then, if Asia were let go, "the Near East would collapse and no telling what would happen in Europe."[3]

Here the President revealed the administration position: the war in Korea did not involve just a peninsula in northern Asia; it was fought over Europe and the Middle East as well. Had the United States failed to respond in Korea—so the government reasoned—Europe would turn neutralist, the Russians would gain a foothold in the Middle East, and the frightened nations of Southeast Asia would fall prey to Communism. As the world balance of power tipped beyond repair, World War III would be inevitable. By 1950 Mr. Truman's set of dominoes had extended around the entire globe.

At the outset an extremely small group of old isolationists opposed American entry. Lawrence Dennis predicted that the war would exhaust the United States, leading to socialism at home and the spread of Communism overseas. Such corrupt and incompetent regimes as the Korea of President Syngman Rhee and the China of Generalissimo Chiang Kai-shek, he continued, would never be anything but liabilities. To the contrary, Russia had already a victory "by getting Americans to fight pitched battles against Asiatics." The *Chicago Tribune* said that not "one Korean in a thousand is worth the life of a husband, a son, or a brother." If China was not important enough for a war, it asked, how could Korea be? Similarly, John O'Donnell doubted whether South Korea was "worth a black eye on the face of one American soldier." The attack was merely a "putsch," arranged "to give the boys in Moscow . . . a big (and deserved) horse laugh." Professor Tansill, fearing that Stalin already controlled the Far East, warned against any further contest with him.[4]

The overwhelming majority of veteran isolationists, however, endorsed United States participation. Like eighty-one percent of their fellow countrymen, they foresaw an intense but short conflict. In their eyes, the administration policy of "drift" and "appeasement" had finally ended, and the "march of world Communism" was finally being checked. Congressman Crawford undoubtedly spoke for most old isolationists when he expressed gratitude that "the show-down" had come; the government, he said, could no longer keep "bleeding our people to death" by "shipping our substance all over the earth."[5]

On the surface all was consensus. Lawrence Smith set the tone when he said, "We must now close ranks, and the command is 'Forward,' together." "The only thing left for us to do," commented Paul W. Shafer, "is to roll up our sleeves and go to work." (As part of such "sleeves-rolling," he suggested that all "fellow-travelers" be detained in concentration camps until "the war against communism is ended.") Dewey Short warned against "losing face" in the Orient. Rich endorsed Truman's call for troops on the grounds that the United Nations needed strengthening.[6]

Both conservatives and liberals among the old isolationists approved the President's initiative. Robert E. Wood told MacArthur that he hoped that the General could "clean up this matter" rapidly. The Chicago merchandiser also wrote Secretary of Defense Louis Johnson, volunteering his services for either supply or liaison. Vorys found himself so moved by the sight of white and black American troops fighting together—part, he said, of "the international posse that is gathering to stop aggression in Korea"—that he recited the first stanzas of the "Battle Hymn of the Republic" to House colleagues. Such conservatives were not alone. Norman Thomas saw no alternative; any other course, believed the Socialist leader, would convince Stalin that the West would yield indefinitely to his demands. The *Progressive,* while acknowledging that Syngman Rhee had avoided basic economic reforms, found the United Nations action "the only meaningful reply" to "Red aggression."[7]

The nature of old isolationist "enthusiasm," however, needs closer examination, for it was often coupled with extreme reluctance. And here it was the reaction articulated by Taft, as revealed in a speech before Congress on June 28, that set so much of the tone for veteran isolationists.

Taft first denied that Korea itself was of vital importance to the United States, then blamed the establishment of the thirty-eighth parallel—an artificial boundary—upon Yalta and Potsdam. Accusing the administration of inviting attack by excluding Korea from America's defense perimeter, he called for Acheson's resignation. Not only was the war the result of disastrous mistakes; its very legality was in question. Authorization by the United Nations, said Taft, could never replace the action of Congress: "If the President can intervene in Korea without congressional approval, he can go to war in Malaya or Indonesia or Iran or South America." Yet he said that Truman had little choice. The line against Communist expansion, he declared, had to be drawn somewhere. The Ohio Senator called upon his countrymen to support the American commitment "wholeheartedly and with every available resource." In the final analysis, he had endorsed the President's action, and in so doing had created such surprise that Truman's press secretary exclaimed, "My God! Bob Taft has joined the UN and the U.S."[8]

A careful reading of Taft's speech would reveal the Ohio Senator as hedging his bets. He questioned both the President's timing and the locale in which he chose to fight, cautiously commenting that these points could "be discussed in the future." Within a month he was privately complaining that the United States was "in real danger of becoming an imperialistic nation." For Robert A. Taft, and for those for whom he spoke, any new bipartisanship was strictly on the surface.[9]

First, there was the point—raised by Taft—that Truman had failed to ask Congress for a declaration of war. The *Chicago Tribune* claimed that Truman needed the consent of Congress before he committed troops, and therefore found the President "a lawbreaker in his own land." Hoffman called Truman's act "impulsive and unconstitutional." Even some who endorsed the President's initial call, or who had backed early military appropriations, opposed the way the United States was entering the conflict. Shafer accused Truman of having "pitchforked this Nation into an undeclared war," while Rich was reminded of "that golden voice" which had promised "again and again and again."[10]

Second, several old isolationists feared that Stalin was deliberately trying to overcommit the United States. Hoffman predicted that Russia would soon start instigating attacks upon such places as Indochina, Iran, Yugoslavia, Turkey, Greece, and West Germany. "It is just like the measles," declared Dewey Short. "You do not know whether they are going to break out around your ankles or your neck."[11]

Third, a few old isolationists saw victory itself as containing the seeds of external and internal defeat. George Morgenstern feared that American occupation of South Korea would lead to "a ravaged country on our hands, a discredited Korean government, and a Korean army impotent to fight its own battles." In the process, the United States would scrap its own constitutional liberties and continue on the path of "world power, aggrandizement, and exploitation of everyone else, Russians included." Flynn demanded that the war be won with "unmistakable force," but predicted that Asia would always be under dictatorial rule. Even more important, the United States was "definitely and permanently launched on a career of militarism" as "an economic institution." Yet at least one old isolationist, Samuel B. Pettengill, denied that one could protest against the conflict. Recalling the vilification faced by the American First Committee, he said, "As we were charged with aiding Hitler before Pearl Harbor, so we would now be smeared as Stalin lovers."[12]

Fourth, rightists among the old isolationists kept maintaining that the administration's record had been little short of treasonous. Dondero, declaring that the State Department had sabotaged miliary aid to South Korea, claimed that such actions could breed revolution. Acheson in particular became a target, with Congressman Noah M. Mason (Rep.–Ill.) calling the Korean conflict "the Acheson War" and Daniel A. Reed accusing the Secretary of State of having long harbored pro-Communist sentiments.[13]

Fifth, those old isolationists already skeptical of the United Nations found in the Korean conflict even more reason to be suspicious. A war under UN auspices, so they argued, could only hinder American action, and the fact that the Joint Chiefs and General MacArthur directed all strategy offered little comfort. Congressman Reed claimed that Soviet participation on the Security Council (which the Soviets had actually been boycotting when the war broke out) had led to the "murder" of American troops. Carl Curtis compared Russia's presence on the Council to "having Satan as a member of the church board." Frederick C. Smith maintained that Secretary General Trygve Lie was Stalin's choice for the post.[14]

United Nations activity, so the more extreme old isolationists maintained, could only insult the nation. UN efforts, said Usher Burdick, had produced no deterrent to war; its only contribution was to supply the flag used by the American command. Only Dennis in fact denied possessing any aversion to the new banner, declaring that he did not want to have United States forces carrying the Stars and Stripes as "they rain death and destruction on Asia."[15]

A few old isolationists found any participation by Russian-dominated nations sheer folly. Hoover continued his pleas, first made two months before, for expelling the Soviet bloc. Flynn combined his tacit endorsement of Truman's mobilization with a request that the United States totally abandon the UN. Langer branded the "Korean mess" as a United Nations war; he continually reminded constituents that he had voted against American entry in 1945.[16]

Sixth, several conservatives feared that the administration would use the crisis to impose "socialistic" controls upon the economy. It was absurd to think, claimed the *Chicago Tribune,* that defeating the North Koreans required full mobilization. Taft, while claiming to see the necessity for some wartime regulations, warned against a "dictated economy." Wrote Representative Reed to a friend, "The Democratic Party is dedicated to wars, elections, deficits, class hatred and socialism."[17]

Seventh, some old isolationists called for United States commitment to the Chiang regime. MacArthur's claim that Taiwan served as the fulcrum of an American island chain reaching "from Vladivostok to Singapore" clearly expressed their views. William Henry Chamberlin warned that Communist occupation of Formosa would strengthen Philippine insurgents and imperil a major source of Japan's food supply. The *Chicago Tribune* accused Truman of deliberately sacrificing security needs in order to appease the UN and the British. Lawrence Dennis alone opposed MacArthur's comments, finding the General's dreams of returning Chiang to the mainland dangerous indeed.[18]

Eighth, a few old isolationists accused the United States of fighting a brutal and racist war. Pettengill, while claiming that Truman's intervention was necessary, foresaw hatreds emerging between Americans and the colonial peoples of the East: "American white men are now killing Asiatic and yellow men." Similarly, Sterling Morton admired Truman's courage in "drawing the line somewhere," but found it "perfectly natural" for the Koreans to want their nation united. *Human Events* printed an article by Henry Beston, who noted that American air force pilots would speak of a bombing raid as "a perfect peach of a big fire." "It is," Beston wrote, "the talk of a culture which has lost its natural humanity."[19]

Undoubtedly many veteran isolationists saw fighting in Korea in 1950 as far more necessary than intervening to aid Great Britain in 1941 or Greece in 1947. The world balance of power, they believed, was no longer working in favor of the United States. The use of jet planes made the western hemisphere vulnerable, and the revolutionary appeal of Communism could capture the imagination of the world's masses in a way that the legions of Hitler and Tojo could not. American engagement, as many old isolationists saw it, was no longer limited to constructing paper pacts or spending "rathole money"; the nation was taking a decisive stand in the language that "international Communism" best understood. To the majority of old isolationists, such erstwhile opponents of American involvement as Lawrence Dennis and the McCormick press merely revealed their eccentricity. The issue, most believed, was to win and to win quickly.

The Korean War could bring added dividends. It signified that the loss of China would not necessarily imply that all of Asia had to be written off. It could, in fact, lead to stronger American ties to both Japan and the Chiang government. Furthermore, MacArthur—a man long respected by isolationists—was the man directing military operations. The General might be able to reunite the Korean peninsula and, if this were the case, the United States would no longer have to worry about "holding the line"; it could take the initiative in "liberating" countries under Russian control. A natural patriotic response to a nation-in-arms appeared to go hand in hand with self-interest.

Such endorsements, of course, were by no means without reservations, and, in some ways, many old isolationists were fighting a different war from that of the Truman administration. Their own conflict was more strident: it discounted a nominal role for both European allies and the United Nations, boosted Chiang as an indispensable ally, and retained traditional hostilities toward presidential power and increased "socialization" at home. As long as the United States appeared to be winning, such reservations could be put aside. Only when the Chinese Communists suddenly and swiftly entered the struggle did most veteran isolationists begin to have second thoughts about the war itself.

At first American forces were almost driven off the peninsula. By August, however, they had staged an effective comeback. On September 15 MacArthur's troops landed at Inchon, a week later his forces took Seoul, and five days after that the Joint Chiefs permitted MacArthur to attack North Korea. Then, suddenly and without warning, the course of the war turned, for on October 26 South Korean and United States troops faced what military historian S. L. A. Marshall called "a phantom which casts no shadow." Chinese Communist forces had secretly crossed the Yalu River and entered North Korea, and MacArthur, who had failed to heed warnings, was soon facing a full-scale Communist offensive. As General George E. Stratemeyer, MacArthur's air chief, later commented, "Lo and behold, the whole mountain side turned out to be Chinese." With American troops again in rapid retreat, victory seemed as far away as ever.[20]

The administration's decision to invade North Korea had led to the Chinese Communist invasion, and had thereby radically changed the character of the conflict. Even before Truman and the Joint Chiefs had made their decision, a few old isolationists were apprehensive. Congressman Rich warned that "warmongering" efforts to conquer all of Korea might lead to war with China, with the United States holding "the biggest wildcat by the tail that you ever had in your life." Just two weeks before MacArthur ordered his major offensive into North Korea, Dennis declared that any rational person would soon expect to see Mao's forces enter directly. The *Chicago Tribune* asked whether either the Russians or the Chinese Communists could, with equanimity, accept the presence of American forces on their frontier.[21]

However, the unification of Korea was too tempting a goal for many old isolationists to resist. The United States, said Hoover in mid-October, would "successfully clean up the Korean aggression under General MacArthur's brilliant generalship and teach a lesson." Chamberlin praised America's firmness and courage: "Korea must set the pattern," he said. Taft, writing to a friend in January 1951, declared that he could not "see how we could permit an aggressor to retire behind his boundary and remain unpunished."[22]

Given the general American confidence, few in the country were prepared for the debacle to come. And once the debacle did come, most old isolationists blamed the administration, not MacArthur. Flynn and Hanighen stressed that the UN had commanded the General to cross the thirty-eighth parallel. Congressman Mason claimed that the international body had directed MacArthur to fight "with one hand tied behind his back." The *Chicago Tribune* accused government leaders of having "blood on their hands."[23]

Old isolationists continually assailed the country's policymakers. The *Chicago Tribune,* in calling for Truman's resignation, declared that "not even Franklin Roosevelt" had so wronged his country. It suggested that George Marshall was senile, for the Secretary of Defense had supposedly kept forgetting the names of his own generals and continually referred to "the war in Puerto Rico." Congressman Earl Wilson (Rep.–Ind.) commented, "The people of my district and I are sick to the teeth of this 'I love Harry who loves Dean who loves Alger who loves Stalin' business."[24]

As American troops were suddenly being routed, a few of the more ardent old isolationists began to suspect that Truman had entered the Korean conflict out of ulterior motives. Dennis claimed that the President had welcomed the war in order to avoid charges of pro-Communism as well as to avert economic depression. The *Chicago Tribune* pointedly remarked that politicians who create "garrison states pretty nearly have to go to war to justify the disorganization they have created." Flynn speculated that the President might have been drunk when he first ordered American combat troops to the peninsula.[25]

Veteran anti-interventionists of more liberal bent were equally appalled by the events in North Korea, although the nature of their anxiety was usually different. Norman Thomas regretted that the United Nations command had not promised more forcefully to respect the Yalu frontier. Harry Elmer Barnes called possible involvement with China "idiocy"; the United States could never win such a conflict. His fellow revisionist William L. Neumann was equally apprehensive: "That damn MacArthur will pull us into a good war with China yet."[26]

Several old isolationists even called for total withdrawal. The *Chicago Tribune*, the most vocal of all, claimed that the United States should call up the militia of the northern states ("where men are accustomed to heavy snow and intense cold") and train them to defend air fields in Alaska and northern Canada. Truman, it declared, was not justified in announcing a state of national emergency, because Russia lacked the surface navy and merchant marine to invade the United States. To Sterling Morton, the nation was fighting "a religious war," and one that lacked any realizable aim. The sheer expansionism of Communism, not American troops, would eventually cause its downfall. And since it was too late to follow the wisdom once suggested by the America First Committee, the country should reach an accord with Russia.[27]

Other old isolationists were even angrier. Hoffman, claiming that American troops were being driven out of Korea, said, "Let's keep them out." Burdick could only remark that if House colleagues had concurred with his opposition to military aid bills, "we would not be in Asia at all." Pettengill asked Acheson, "When in God's name are you and Truman and Marshall going to stop this insane course of pouring American blood and treasure into all the bottomless sinkholes of the earth? Who elected us to take sides in every civil war on this globe and uphold the status quo to the end of time for over two billion people?" For once, many old isolationists had the public on their side, for—by January 1951—two out of three Americans agreed to withdraw from Korea. The nation was ready for another Great Debate, the second within ten years.[28]

Administration efforts to strengthen ties with Europe added another dimension to the controversy. The armament of the Continent, the Truman government believed, needed to be speeded up, and speeded up rapidly. Acheson, in particular, pressed for a united European command and the inclusion of armed German units. The signers of the Atlantic Pact soon agreed, in principle, to German participation and created an integrated command structure with General Eisenhower at its head.[29] In order to accelerate European rearmament while alleviating anxieties over German involvement, the United States sent four divisions to Europe, bringing the total of its contribution to six. It was the sending of these four divisions, as well as the nature of the war in Korea, that led to the Great Debate. The argument involved large segments of the press, Congress, and the administration, and occasionally challenged the fundamentals of Cold War policy.

Joseph P. Kennedy was the first old isolationist to speak out.

A millionaire, prominent Roman Catholic layman, and former Ambassador to Great Britain, Kennedy had opposed United States entry into World War II. The conflict, he believed, would so ruin the centers of world capitalism that Communism was bound to spread. Even in England and America, the steps necessary for mobilization would necessitate a socialized dictatorship. Kennedy found the Nazi regime reprehensible, but did not see it as involving basic threats to the social and economic order.[30]

Addressing the Law School Forum of the University of Virginia on December 12, 1950, the former diplomat gave the most provocative speech of his long career. In words drafted by James M. Landis, Dean of Harvard Law School and a close personal friend, Kennedy revealed that he at least was one isolationist who had not changed. He called upon the United States to withdraw from "the freezing hills of Korea" and "the battle-scarred plains of Western Germany." "What business is it of ours," he asked, "to support the French colonial policy in Indo-China or to achieve Mr. Syngman Rhee's concepts of democracy in Korea?"

Similarly, Kennedy claimed that Europe was in no position to resist Communism. Britain was militarily weak, France racked with political turmoil, West Germany reluctant to start rearming, and Greece hardly able to police its own territory. Rather than attempt to hold frontiers on the Elbe, the Rhine, and Berlin, the United States, he declared, should build up hemispheric defenses. Fortunately for the nation, Russia's empire bore the seeds of its own decay: "It may be that Europe for a decade or a generation or more will turn Communistic. But in doing so, it may break itself as a unified force." Indeed, the more people under its yoke, the greater the possibilities for revolt.[31]

At first Kennedy's speech received relatively little attention; but, within two weeks, it became linked in the popular mind with the positions of Hoover and Taft. For on December 20, the day after Truman had announced that a sizable number of American troops would be sent to Europe, Hoover addressed the nation on radio. Like Kennedy, the former President opposed the stationing of United States forces in either Europe or Asia. Efforts to halt Communism by a land war, he said, would merely create a "graveyard" for "millions of American boys," and thereby exhaust "this Gibraltar of Western civilization." And, like the financier, Hoover called for total withdrawal from Korea; the world itself, he asserted, lacked forces adequate to repel the Chinese Communists. Differing from Kennedy by endorsing commitments beyond the Americas, Hoover advocated holding such "island nations" as Japan, Taiwan, and the Philippines (and Great Britain if it desired), encouraging Japanese independence and rearmament, and relying upon sea and air defenses.

Repeating a point that he had made two months earlier, Hoover questioned whether Europe possessed "the will to fight." The Continent, he claimed, was still haggling over the nature of German rearmament, had refused to permit Spain to join the North Atlantic Treaty Organization, and had within it well-organized Communist parties. Before the United States contributed "another man or another dollar" to its shores, the

Europeans should establish "organized and equipped divisions of such large numbers as would erect a sure dam against the Red flood."

Hoover branded the United Nations as "a forum for continuous smear on our honor" and pointed out that the United States had supplied ninety percent of the UN forces in Korea. For the UN to redeem itself, said the former President, it must declare Communist China an aggressor, refuse to admit Mao's government to its councils, and demand that all members embargo goods that would aid its war effort.[32]

Addressing the country again on February 9, 1951, Hoover slightly modified his position. This time he openly favored defending the Atlantic Pact nations, declaring that air and sea power—by depriving the Russians of "General Manpower, General Space, General Winter and General Scorched Earth"—would best protect Europe. While he still opposed administration plans to send ground troops, he now endorsed the shipment of munitions. He sought independence for Germany and Japan, asserting that for a century both countries had damned "the Russian-controlled hordes." Without West Germany's participation in NATO, in fact, there could be little defense of Europe itself. Again Hoover called for total withdrawal from Korea, approved the sending of American arms to Nationalist China, and claimed that he would permit Chiang "to do what he wishes in China." On February 27 Hoover, testifying before joint hearings of the Senate Foreign Relations and Armed Services committees, said that, if necessary, the hemisphere possessed the resources to stand alone. Challenging Governor Dewey's statement that the United States was dependent upon the world's resources, the ex-President declared that the Americas had an abundance of zinc, copper, cobalt, and uranium.[33]

The third major isolationist voice, Senator Taft, entered the Great Debate on January 5, 1951, with a major speech to the Congress. Suspecting that the administration had already made secret commitments, he opposed sending troops to Europe without congressional permission. The Atlantic Pact might have committed the United States to supplying arms, but it certainly did not involve ground forces. "The course which we are pursuing," he said, "will make war more likely." True, the Czech crisis of 1948 and the Korean invasion of 1950 had been part of a "determined plan," one first outlined by Lenin and then Stalin, "to communize the entire world." However, the Ohioan asserted that the Soviet Union was planning no war with the United States; rather, it relied solely upon satellite armies and local Communist parties to extend its power overseas. American foreign policy, he maintained, must center on "the liberty of our people," not efforts to "reform the entire world."

As with Hoover, Taft stressed air and sea power: such a strategy could guarantee "a reasonable alliance" with England, France, Holland, Australia, and Canada, while protecting such strategic areas as North Africa, Spain, the Suez Canal, Singapore, and the Malay peninsula. A strong air force, he said, could damage enemy bases, prevent retaliation, and "drop atom bombs where they might be decisive." In one area of Cold War tactics, Taft would even go beyond the administration. He called for aggressive propaganda, infiltration, and intelligence efforts, declaring that the United

States must "use the same methods which communism has adopted . . . or be swept away."

As far as Korea was concerned, Taft claimed that if American forces were truly jeopardized they should fall back to the "island nations" of Japan and Taiwan. Although he was against use of United States ground forces in China, he urged America to assist any mainland operations made by Chiang. The Senator did oppose dropping atomic bombs upon the Chinese Communists, declaring that they were a poor weapon to use against an army in the field.[34]

Taft, like Hoover, soon addressed himself to Truman's efforts to bolster NATO. He had originally favored the Wherry resolution, a proposal that would have made any sending of troops to Europe contingent upon congressional authorization. During testimony given on February 26 before the Senate Foreign Relations and Armed Services committees, Taft modified his position, endorsing sending the four divisions, or 100,000 men, that Eisenhower had requested and that Truman had already authorized. He claimed that further commitments, however, needed the permission of Congress. The Ohio Senator still insisted that the loss of Europe need not be fatal to the United States. Indeed, far greater danger could come from insufficient sea and air facilities and from the draining of raw materials. "Nothing can destroy this country," he said, "except the over-extension of our resources." Taft did differ with Hoover on one point: efforts to arm West Germany, he maintained, offered needless provocation to the Russians.[35]

A few old isolationists found Taft's commitments too risky. Dennis called most of Taft's January 5 speech a "magnificent contribution," but denied that the West was engaged in a gigantic struggle against world Communism. Both Russia and China, said Dennis, were fighting over such material resources as oil in the Middle East and land in Southeast Asia; a "smart tough elite" simply used Marxist ideology to help "bring home the bacon." Flynn held reservations about bases in Japan and Great Britain. Barnes declared that ten years earlier the Ohio Senator had opposed any assertion that America's frontier lay on the Rhine; in 1951, however, he was tacitly supporting this claim. Pacifist leader A. J. Muste noted that the Senator's commitments ranged to such far-flung areas as the Suez Canal and Southeast Asia: "For isolationists these Americans do certainly get around!"[36]

For the most part, however, the speeches of Kennedy, Hoover, and Taft refortified isolationist ranks. General Wood and ex-Senator Wheeler, in endorsing Kennedy's position, hoped for a revival of the America First Committee. The *Chicago Tribune* commented, "Mr. Hoover Speaks for the Nation," as it sought abolition of the draft, the recall of Eisenhower from Europe, and a defense line limited to the American Hemisphere's northern tier.[37]

Many old isolationists endorsed Taft's strategies, and in some cases went further. Lawrence H. Smith got 124 fellow Republicans in the House to sign "A Declaration of Policy" that demanded congressional participation in military decision-making, strong ocean frontiers, and peace treaties with

Germany, Austria, and Japan. Smith himself declared that United States demands for European rearmament were arrogant, serving only to depress Continent's living standards and invite Russian attack. Hoffman endorsed a report made by Congressman John F. Kennedy (Dem.–Mass.), son of the financier. After spending five weeks in Europe, young Kennedy claimed that the Continent needed to exert itself far more before it received American backing. Edwin C. Johnson warned that the United States was spreading itself too thin: "We must," he said, "get these friendly powers off our backs." Chamberlin, who usually supported strong NATO commitments, commented that Truman should send troops to Europe only after securing congressional approval.[38]

Hoover, Taft, and Joseph P. Kennedy had all made impressive points. The ground forces of the United States and Western Europe could not repel fully mobilized Russian troops. Most signers of the Atlantic Pact had been rearming slowly, and with the utmost reluctance. The inclusion of West Germany in the alliance undoubtedly increased Soviet rigidity. Walter Lippmann noted with much justice that Truman's arbitrary commitment of four divisions overseas did little to strengthen America's domestic system of "checks and balances."[39]

In addition, some attacks on the three old isolationists were unfair. The *Nation* declared that Hoover's policies "should set the bells ringing in the Kremlin as nothing has since the triumph of Stalingrad." The liberal journal warned that such "super-appeasers" might bargain away the freedom of others, promising American withdrawal from both Europe and Asia in return for Soviet aloofness from the western hemisphere and a continued supply of raw materials. The *New Republic* saw Stalin as sweeping onward "until the Stalinist caucus in the Tribune tower would bring out in triumph the first communist edition of the Chicago *Tribune.*" Interventionist columnists Joseph and Stuart Alsop wrote of "the craven voices, the squalid little men who would throw away the future for an hour's partisan success, the trembling gravediggers of freedom who would betray mankind for two more years' low taxes."[40]

Taft met with particular abuse. Senator Herbert H. Lehman (Dem.–N.Y.) noted that the Ohio Republican, by accusing the United States of fighting an illegal conflict in Korea, supported arguments made by Russian foreign minister Andrei Vyshinski. The *New York Post* claimed that Taft's views were "tediously recited day after day by the Communist propagandists." The *New York Times* played up *L'Humanité* and *Pravda* support for his claim that Russia did not intend to start war. These, and similar attacks, reveal that "McCarthyism" and "red-baiting" were not always one-sided.[41]

Opponents of Kennedy, Hoover, and Taft, however, also made legitimate points. The type of total withdrawal advocated by Kennedy bore heavy risks. Representative Eugene McCarthy (Dem.–Minn.) asserted that the financier was engaging in curious logic: "In order to bring about the downfall of communism we should encourage the Russian absorption of all Europe and Asia."[42] Even if Russia did not seek war, it could undoubtedly use both military and economic pressure to dominate the European continent. And even if its empire could not sustain itself forever, it still could make life extremely difficult for the United States. Comments about national self-sufficiency were more likely to frighten Americans than to reassure them.

Isolationist alternatives were often weak. The *Washington Post* doubted whether Hoover's strategy could have persuaded one single European nation to sign the Atlantic Pact; who, after all, would look forward to a "liberation" limited to bombs dropped by "an American air armada"? Senator Paul H. Douglas (Dem.–Ill.) asserted that the Korean War had shown that air attacks could not stop land armies. And, by destroying much of the Europe it sought to protect, Taft's strategy could hardly "win friends and influence people." It remained doubtful whether the Strategic Air Command could serve air bases and hold back initial land attacks made by effective ground troops.[43]

In December 1950, as over 200,000 Chinese troops pushed United Nations forces below the thirty-eighth parallel, MacArthur cabled the Joint Chiefs that he was facing an "entirely new war." To meet the Chinese Communist challenge, he wanted to blockade China's coast; bomb Chinese factories, depots, and troop assembly points; reinforce his own troops with Chiang's legions; and permit Nationalist diversionary action against mainland areas, with the latter activity (in MacArthur's own words) "possibly leading to counter-invasion." The General claimed that his recommendations would "severely cripple and largely neutralize China's capacity to wage aggressive war," while using only a small part of America's military potential.[44]

The Joint Chiefs, fearing a wider conflict, rejected MacArthur's suggestions. By February 1951 the situation had stabilized: General Matthew Ridgeway's Eighth Army had been able to repulse the Chinese offensive, the United Nations General Assembly had voted forty-seven to seven to condemn the Peking regime as aggressors, and the administration had renounced its goal of advancing beyond the thirty-eighth parallel. In the middle of March Truman decided to seek a cease-fire and peace negotiations. With the war becoming increasingly stalemated, MacArthur was ever more vocal in his demands for victory through escalation. Finally, on April 10, Truman removed the General from command, an action that precipitated still more impassioned debate over United States Asian policy. Ironically, Senator Vandenberg, whose bipartisan policies had been brought to ruin by the issues of China and Korea, died on the eve of MacArthur's defense before the Congress.

In some ways the firing of MacArthur was anticlimactic, for the administration had decided, several months before the General's dismissal, that under no circumstances would it permit an enlargement of the Korean War. No action of the Truman government, however, more infuriated the great majority of old isolationists.

For this majority, MacArthur's removal only revealed the folly of fighting with reluctant allies and under the auspices of a constraining international organization. They had welcomed the General's leadership, had rejoiced in his early victories, and, when the Chinese Communists entered the conflict, had supported his new proposals. To them, the cashiering of MacArthur was another major American setback in a long, twilight struggle that showed no real sign of ever ending. Heedless of their own past warnings against reckless intervention, they simply attributed the General's dismissal to the same interventionist "conspiracy" against which they had fought for so long.

Hence veteran isolationists contributed more than their share to national resentment. Congressman O. K. Armstrong called the firing the "greatest victory for the Communists since the fall of China." Publisher James H. Gipson compared MacArthur's removal to "the manager of the New York Yankees benching Babe Ruth at the height of his prowess when the score was tied and the Babe was coming to bat." Henry Regnery printed a pamphlet entitled "May God Forgive Us." Its author, candy manufacturer Robert Welch, was so outraged by American "appeasement" that he would organize the John Birch Society.[45]

World War II isolationists gave the General the most glowing of tributes. Dewey Short (perhaps reflecting his Methodist theological training) said immediately after MacArthur's address to Congress, "We saw a great hunk of God in the flesh, and we heard the voice of God." Herbert Hoover, although admitting privately that MacArthur was a bit overbearing, found him "a reincarnation of St. Paul." Conversely, militant old isolationists sought the removal of leading administration figures. The *Chicago Tribune*, for example, demanded Truman's departure as well as that of "his Svengali" Acheson. General Wood called for the firing of Secretary of Defense Marshall and Chief of Staff Omar Bradley; MacArthur, said the Sears executive, should become the new Secretary of State.[46]

For strong MacArthur partisans among the old isolationists, truce was out of the question. General Fellers declared that the enemy would exploit a cease-fire to stock forward landing fields, thereby gaining an advantage impossible to overcome. Congressman B. Carroll Reece (Rep.–Tenn.) agreed, fearing that the Communists could turn military stalemate into victory. Representative Leslie C. Arends (Rep.–Ill.) warned that the administration had been outmaneuvered at every peace conference thus far.[47]

Taft soon spoke out, using the occasion of MacArthur's dismissal to endorse many of the General's major proposals. The Ohio Senator called for the bombing of communications, supply depots, and industrial plants in Manchuria and China; sought to aid guerrillas on the Chinese mainland; and made the sweeping claim that "all South China today is apparently in a ferment." Cease-fire and American withdrawal from Korea, said Taft (perhaps overlooking his comments of January 5), would lead to Communist domination not only of the peninsula, but of Japan as well. The Senator privately conceded that MacArthur might not be entirely correct and, in September 1951, told the General that peace at the thirty-eighth parallel was probably better than a stalemated war. More important, however, he realized that MacArthur was politically popular and could gain votes for the Republican Party.[48]

A few old anti-interventionists were more reticent in their support. Even before MacArthur's dismissal, Usher Burdick feared that the General would embroil the United States "in an all-out war with China." William R. Castle admired MacArthur's address to Congress, but found it "touch and go" as to whether America could hold its position in East Asia. Sterling Morton believed MacArthur's dismissal "necessary from the standpoint of discipline" and opposed the bombing of mainland China. He said, "I do not think we can make friends of the Chinese by killing them by the millions." In addition, the Chicago industrialist sought recognition of Communist China on the grounds that it might soon fight the Russians. Chamberlin endorsed Truman's truce efforts: "Half a loaf is better than none." The pacifist Libby stressed the General's plea for higher living standards in Asia, while opposing MacArthur's strategy of bombing and blockades: "You do not cure hunger," he said, "by creating nationwide conditions of starvation." Morley found himself torn. He claimed that risk of "outright war with Russia" was well calculated to turn "thoughtful men" against MacArthur. Yet, to Morley, the General deservedly served as the rallying point for those opposed to "the whole sordid betrayal of Chinese nationalism that began at Yalta." Hanighen endorsed MacArthur's emphasis on sea and air strategy; he was less enamored of the General's call for a world crusade against Communism, a goal that he found threatening to "the stability of the economy."[49]

A handful of old isolationists found the General's policies worthless. The *Progressive* asserted that MacArthur's strategy would lead to "war with China for the rest of our lifetime." Norman Thomas said that MacArthur would have lost the United States "what non-Communist friends we have left in Asia and in all of Europe." Senator William Benton (Dem.–Conn.), domestic liberal and former America First backer, was so adamant about removing MacArthur that he had personally recommended the move to Truman a day before the official announcement. Dennis claimed to be more gladdened by the General's firing than by any news since the Great Crash of 1929. MacArthur's policies, said Dennis, were destructive: the bombing of Manchuria would lead to the "mass murder" of millions of innocent civilians; the blockading of China would sever vital trade from England; the sending of Chiang's "licked legions" to mainland China involved covering the Nationalist leader's inevitable errors with "a limitless supply of American cannon-fodder."[50]

At the outset, the Great Debate appeared to revive possibilities of an isolationism more far-reaching than any considered since the end of World War II. Early support for the war had turned to bitter disillusion, for by December 1950 the very survival of American forces in Korea was threatened. A good many old isolationists considered general withdrawal from all foreign commitments, and occasionally picked up some surprising support. At one stage of the Great Debate, Walter Lippmann endorsed much of Taft and Hoover's "island strategy." America, the columnist declared, must avoid commitments on both the Asian and European continents and rely upon an air-sea defense.[51]

By April 1951, however, many old isolationists were enthusiastically embracing MacArthur's policies. They had, in other words, taken merely four months to shift from an "island" defense to the bombing of China and Manchuria. Although such veteran isolationists were long calling for the "release" of Nationalist Chinese troops, they had seldom suggested blockading and bombing before the General had spoken out. Now they welcomed MacArthur's strategy with abandon. Joseph P. Kennedy, the most "extreme" of the parties to the Great Debate, lent MacArthur moral support in a radio address. Hoover, speaking to the nation in January 1952, combined a renewed plea for the withdrawal of ground forces from Korea with the comment that MacArthur's bombing and Formosa policies would have brought victory in Asia.[52]

This time it was the administration's turn to suggest limitations and constraints, and it wasted no time in stressing the risks involved in those very MacArthur proposals which many isolationists had received so enthusiastically. General Hoyt Vandenberg claimed that air strikes upon Chinese cities would be ineffective, for Communist China's main arsenal lay within the Soviet Union. The Air Force Chief of Staff commented that the effective bombing of Manchuria would require twice the number of planes available to the Strategic Air Command, and would leave the United States wide open to Russian attack. Admiral Forrest Sherman, Navy Chief of Staff, said that an economic blockade against China would have no impact because the country lacked the mature industries needed for such a tactic to succeed. Chiang's troops, according to the Joint Chiefs, offered little aid; they were poor fighters and in any event were needed to guard Taiwan.[53]

The administration also challenged MacArthur on other points. British trade with Communist China, a bane of the General's and an embarrassment to the Truman government, offered important markets for an island nation dependent upon exports for survival. On the crucial issue of escalation, MacArthur would not preclude the possibility of war with Russia. "You have to take risks," he told a Senate committee, although he acknowledged that Soviet resources and intentions remained "speculative."[54]

By the time MacArthur was removed, most old isolationists had abandoned their traditional position. Such veteran anti-interventionists as Taft had hoped that MacArthur's strategy would take pressure off American forces in Korea, but he willingly risked expanding the conflict. When his Senate colleague, Edwin C. Johnson, called in May 1951 for mutual withdrawal of American and Chinese troops from Korea and an armistice on the thirty-eighth parallel, only one old isolationist in Congress, Senator Langer, endorsed Johnson's proposal. Dennis, noting how many World War II isolationists had become "Asia Firsters," wrote Barnes: "They don't believe in neutrality. They just don't like one pattern of intervention and wish to replace it by their own."[55]

If demands for extensive Asian commitments could rally support from Americans frustrated by the fall of China and the Korean war, they revealed many old isolationists as people whose logic was faulty, military strategy highly risky, and cause intensely partisan. Isolationism, it seemed, was becoming a matter of convenience. To talk of a balanced budget while endorsing MacArthur's Korean strategy and committing the nation to such far-flung outposts as the Suez Canal was even more foolish, as was the rhetoric soon to come about total victory over Communism and the liberation of subject peoples.

Such contradictions were all too apparent. Senator Hubert Humphrey (Dem.–Minn.), in comparing Taft's skepticism concerning Western Europe with his enthusiasm for Formosa, said that the Ohio Senator deserved "a doctor of laws in inconsistency." Such criticism had merit. Taft had argued in January 1951 that a handful of American divisions in Europe might goad the Russians into war; within three months, he and many followers apparently believed that the Soviets would tolerate United States bombing near its Asian borders.[56]

In some ways MacArthur's own position merely added to the incongruity. Far from speaking, as he had in 1944, of Europe as a "dying system," the General appeared to endorse containment with a passion more akin to that of Henry R. Luce than to that of either the administration or the followers of Taft. Not only was Communism a "global problem," but "every place"—in Europe as well as in Asia—had to be held. Unlike Taft and Hoover, MacArthur opposed any congressional limitations upon troops to Europe.[57] The General could attack large-scale federal spending in one breath and promise to roll back the "bamboo curtain" and dominate the Pacific in another. Even, however, had MacArthur sought escalation in order to avoid stalemate, and with it the consequent financial drain and national insolvency, his proposals could only lead to massive federal spending.

If many conservatives among the old isolationists realized that MacArthur's dismissal worked to their political advantage, they were not alone. Several bipartisan supporters no longer remained so totally committed to administration policy. Congressman Edwin Arthur Hall, for example, claimed that the British had maneuvered the firing of MacArthur in order to preserve a thriving opium trade in Hong Kong. Lodge asserted that the General should have been consulted, not removed arbitrarily.[58]

Yet many old isolationists did not see themselves as forsaking their heritage of avoiding binding alliances and foreign commitments. Rather, they found MacArthur assailing a conspiracy that, they believed, had long existed. After his return to the United States, the General continually claimed that the nation's greatest danger came from "insidious forces working from within." And, for so many of his supporters, the Korean stalemate was the latest and most costly manifestation of America's continued betrayal—first Yalta and Potsdam, then China, and now the firing of the only military leader who saw "no substitute for victory." Such patterns, rooted as far back as Pearl Harbor, could not be accidental; they had to be the product of hidden and malevolent forces.[59]

For the overwhelming majority of old isolationists, the enemy did not simply reside in Moscow; it rested—at least in part—among America's own allies. Few would go as far as Lawrence H. Smith in wanting to nail a "For Sale" sign on the new UN headquarters in New York, or join Usher Burdick in accusing administration leaders of fostering the slogan "God Save the King." The sense of siege, however, remained real. George Bender—noting the loss of China, the stalemate in Korea, and newer threats to Indochina—could only comment, "We are everywhere on the defensive."[60] A limited war, in other words, was no war at all, and a good many isolationists intended to both expose and purge the nation's "traitorous" leadership.

## NOTES

1. Westerfield, *Foreign Policy*, pp. 353–54, 367; Vorys, *CR*, October 19, 1949, p. 15090.

2. Chiperfield, *CR*, January 19, 1950, pp. 639–940; Taber, *CR*, February 9, 1950, p. 1737; excerpt from minority report, House Foreign Affairs Committee, July 1, 1949, *CR*, January 19, 1950, p. 639; Rich, *CR*, February 7, 1950, p. 1608.

3. Spanier, *Truman-MacArthur Controversy*, pp. 26–30; Truman in Lloyd C. Gardner, "From Liberation to Containment, 1945–1953," in William Appleman Williams, ed., *From Colony to Empire: Essays in the History of American Foreign Relations* (New York: John Wiley, 1972), p. 371.

4. Dennis, *Appeal to Reason*, #222 (June 26, 1950) and #223 (July 1, 1950); "Korea" (editorial), *Chicago Tribune*. June 29, 1950; John O'Donnell, "Capitol Stuff," *New York Daily News*, June 28, 1950; C. C. Tansill to H. E. Barnes, June 27, 1950, Barnes Papers.

5. Crawford, *CR*, June 27, 1950, p. 9271.

6. Smith, *CR*, July 18, 1950, p. 10537; Shafer, *CR*, July 19, 1950, pp. 10640–41; Short, *CR*, June 27, 1950, p. 9290; Rich, *CR*, June 28, 1950, p. 9351. For popular expectations of a short war, see Matthew E. Mantell, "Opposition to the Korean War," Ph.D. diss., New York University, 1973, pp. 24 -26.

7. R. E. Wood to D. MacArthur, June 30, 1950, MacArthur Papers; R. E. Wood to L. Johnson, July 25, 1950, Box 3, Wood Papers; Vorys, *CR*, July 18, 1950, p. 10531; Thomas, "War and the Need for Positive Action," *Socialist Call* 17 (July 7, 1950): 8; "The Consequences of Korea" (editorial), *Progressive* 14 (August 1950): 2–4.

8. Taft, *CR*, June 28, 1950, pp. 9319–23; Goldman, *Crucial Decade*, p. 165.

9. Taft, *CR*, June 28, 1950, p. 9322; Patterson, *Mr. Republican*, p. 455.

10. "Anything to Destroy the Constitution" (editorial), *Chicago Tribune*, July 5, 1950; Hoffman, *CR*, July 17, 1950, p. 10444; Shafer, radio broadcast of July 16, 1950, in *CR*, p. A5224; Rich, *CR*, July 11, 1950, p. 9930.

11. Hoffman, *CR*, July 24, 1950, p. 10867; Short, *CR*, July 25, 1950, p. 10987.

12. Morgenstern, "Strategic Idiocy and Moral Principle," *Human Events* 7 (July 19, 1950); Flynn, "North Pacific," *Freeman* 1 (October 30, 1950): 72; S. Pettengill to S. Morton, October 16, 1950, Morton Papers.

13. Dondero, *CR*, July 19, 1950, p. 10644; Noah M. Mason, *CR*, July 24, 1950, p. 10869; D. A. Reed to L. Dean, September 20, 1950, Box 20, Reed Papers.

14. Curtis, *CR*, August 28, 1950, p. 13658; Smith, *CR*, July 18, 1950, p. A5191.

15. Burdick, *CR*, August 2, 1950, p. 11611; Dennis, *Appeal to Reason*, #242 (November 11, 1950). For an example of anxieties concerning sovereignty, see Arthur

Sears Henning, "H. T.'s Bypassing of Congress in Korean Action Stirs Fears," *Washington Times-Herald,* July 3, 1950.

16. Text of Hoover Address to American Newspaper Publishers Association, April 27, 1950, *New York Times,* April 28, 1950, p. 13; "Hoover Outlines a Road to Peace," *New York Times,* July 12, 1950, p. 16; Flynn, "After Korea, What?," radio broadcast #63 (July 16, 1950); Smith, "Senator William Langer," pp. 211–13.

17. "How to Lose a War" (editorial), *Chicago Tribune,* July 26, 1950; Taft, *CR,* August 10, 1950, pp. 12156–157; Reed in Bulkley, "Daniel A. Reed," p. 322.

18. Chamberlin, "A Line is Drawn in Asia," *Human Events* 7 (July 5, 1950); "The MacArthur Doctrine" (editorial), *Chicago Tribune,* August 31, 1950; Dennis, *Appeal to Reason,* #232 (September 2, 1950).

19. Pettengill, "Thoughts on the War" (unpublished memorandum), July 1950, in the Papers of Samuel B. Pettengill, University of Oregon Library; S. Morton to H. C. Bodman, July 10, 1950, Morton Papers; Henry Beston, "Soliloquy on the Airplane," *Human Events* 7 (October 18, 1950).

20. For accounts of the initial advance, see S. L. A. Marshall, *The River and the Gauntlet* (New York: William Morrow, 1953); David Rees, *Korea: The Limited War* (New York: St. Martin's Press, 1964), pp. 155–77. Marshall phrase on p. 1; quotation of George E. Stratemeyer in Rees, p. 155.

21. Rich, *CR,* July 19, 1950, p. 10634; Dennis, *Appeal to Reason,* #241 (November 4, 1950); "The Goal in Korea" (editorial), *Chicago Tribune,* August 21, 1950.

22. Hoover, address of October 19, 1950, *CR,* p. A7451; Chamberlin, "Korea Must Set the Pattern," *New Leader* 33 (October 30, 1950): 19; Taft in Patterson, *Mr. Republican,* p. 485.

23. Flynn, radio broadcast #85, "Fixing Blame for Korea" (December 17, 1950); Hanighen, "Not Merely Gossip," *Human Events* 7 (November 29, 1950); Mason, *CR,* December 14, 1950, p. A7696; "Blood on Their Hands" (editorial), *Chicago Tribune,* December 9, 1950.

24. "Truman Should Get Out" (editorial), *Chicago Tribune,* December 3, 1950; "What an Outfit to Run a War!" (editorial), *Chicago Tribune,* December 1, 1950; Earl Wilson, *CR,* August 30, 1950, p. 13919.

25. Dennis, *Appeal to Reason,* #259 (March 10, 1951); "How to Make a War Inevitable" (editorial), *Chicago Tribune,* December 11, 1950; J. T. Flynn to W. Trohan, December 28, 1950, Box 20, Flynn Papers.

26. Thomas, "The Liberal Failure," *Socialist Call* 17 (November 10, 1950): 8; H. E. Barnes to W. L. Neumann, December 7, 1950, Neumann Papers; W. L. Neumann to H. E. Barnes, November 29, 1950, Neumann Papers.

27. "What National Emergency?" (editorial), *Chicago Tribune,* December 13, 1950; Morton, speech to the Henry George School of Social Science, November 8, 1950, Morton Papers.

28. Hoffman, *CR,* December 20, 1950, p. 16855; Burdick, *CR,* December 28, 1950, p. A7924; S. Pettengill to D. Acheson, November 7, 1950, Pettengill Papers. Public sentiment can be found in Lawrence Wittner, *Cold War America* (New York: Praeger, 1974), p. 108.

29. Acheson, *Present at the Creation,* pp. 443–44; Ambrose, *Rise to Globalism,* p. 201.

30. For material on Kennedy, see the biographies by Koskoff and Whalen, and *Current Biography, 1940,* pp. 450–53. On March 29, 1941, R. Douglas Stuart, Jr., national director of America First, wrote General Wood that Kennedy was planning to contribute "through his son Jack." See Box 18, Stuart Folder, AFC Papers. A $100 contribution from John F. Kennedy is listed in the Large Contributors File of the America First Committee Papers.

31. Kennedy, address to the University of Virginia Law School, December 12, 1950, in *Vital Speeches* 17 (January 1, 1951): 170–73. Hoover too predicted that Communism

contained the seeds of its own decay. See Hoover to K. S. Wherry, May 9, 1950, Box 147, Hoover Papers.

32. Hoover, address to the nation, December 20, 1950, *CR*, pp. 17018–19. For Hoover's earlier speech, see address to the nation, October 19, 1950, *CR*, pp. A7451–52.

33. Hoover, address to the nation, February 9, 1951, *CR*, pp. A773–75; Hoover, testimony before Senate Foreign Relations and Armed Services Committee, February 27, 1951, *Assignment of Ground Forces in the European Area* (Washington, D.C.: U.S. Government Printing Office, 1951), pp. 734–37.

34. Taft, *CR*, January 5, 1951, pp. 55–68. Two days later Taft said that America definitely should withdraw from Korea and "fall back to a defensible position in Japan and Formosa." Patterson, *Mr. Republican*, p. 485.

35. Taft, testimony before the Senate Foreign Relations and Armed Services Committees, February 26, 1951, *Assignment of Ground Forces in the European Area*, pp. 603–66. The quotation is from p. 617. On April 2 Taft joined 37 other Republicans in voting for an amendment proposed by Senator John L. McClellan (Dem.–Ark.) to the Wherry Resolution. The amendment, which passed forty-nine to forty-three, declared that no more than four divisions could be sent to Europe without congressional approval. Among the old isolationists who supported the McClellan Amendment were Dworshak, Edwin C. Johnson, Dirksen, Butler, McCarran, Langer, Wiley, Case, Mundt, and Frank Carlson (Rep.–Kan.). Opposed were Lodge, Tobey, and Aiken. On April 12 Taft favored tabling the Wherry Amendment. See *CR*, April 2, 1951, p. 3096; Paterson, *Mr. Republican*, pp. 480–81.

36. Dennis, *Appeal to Reason*, #250 (January 6, 1951); J. T. Flynn to W. Jenner, March 26, 1951, Box 20, Flynn Papers; Barnes, review of Chamberlin's *America's Second Crusade* in *Current History* 19 (December 1950): 354; A. J. Muste, "The Global Picture—1951," *Fellowship* 17 (February 1951): 2.

37. B. K. Wheeler to R. E. Wood, January 5, 1951, Wood Papers; R. E. Wood to B. K. Wheeler, January 15, 1951, Box 7, Wood Papers; B. K. Wheeler to H. Hoover, December 21, 1950, Box 288, Hoover Papers; "Mr. Hoover Speaks for the Nation" (editorial), *Chicago Tribune*, December 22, 1950.

38. Smith, testimony before the Senate Foreign Relations and Armed Services Committees, February 20, 1951, *Assignment of Ground Forces in European Area*, pp. 289–300; idem, *CR*, August 16, 1951, p. 10155; Hoffman, *CR*, February 15, 1951, pp. 1301–02; Johnson, *CR*, March 22, 1951, p. 2845; Chamberlin, "No One Man Rule," *Wall Street Journal*, January 23, 1951.

39. Lippmann, "Mr. Taft and Mr. Truman," *New York Herald-Tribune*, January 9, 1951, p. 21.

40. "Hoover's Folly" (editorial), *Nation* 171 (December 30, 1950): 688–89; "Can We Save World Peace?" (editorial), *New Republic* 124 (January 1, 1951): 5; Joseph and Stuart Alsop, "Christmas in America," *New York Herald-Tribune*, December 25, 1950, p. 18.

41. Herbert H. Lehman, *New York Times*, January 7, 1951, p. 35. For excerpts from hostile newspapers, including the *New York Post*, see *New York Times*, January 7, 1951, p. 40. For stress upon *L'Humanité* and *Pravda*, see "Taft Talk 'Comforts' Red Press in Paris," *New York Times*, January 8, 1951, p. 7; "Taft Address Gets Big Play in *Pravda*," *New York Times*, January 9, 1951, p. 14.

42. Eugene McCarthy, *CR*, February 13, 1951, p. 1252.

43. "Mr. Hoover's Realities" (editorial), *Washington Post*, February 10, 1951; Paul H. Douglas, *CR*, January 15, 1950, p. 240. For the thinking of the NATO commanders, see Kaplan, "The United States," p. 313.

44. Spanier, *Truman-MacArthur Controversy*, pp. 137–40.

45. Armstrong, *New York Times*, April 12, 1951, p. 6; Gipson, speech of April 9, 1952

before Republican women of Spokane, CR, p. A2820; Robert Welch, "May God Forgive Us," pamphlet (Chicago: Regnery, 1952).

46. Short, *CR*, April 19, 1951, p. 4129; Hoover endorsement, *New York Times*, April 27, 1951, p. 14; Hoover's private reservations, Ronald J. Caridi, *The Korean War and American Politics: The Republican Party as a Case Study* (Philadelphia: University of Pennsylvania Press, 1968), p. 150; "Little Lies to Support the Big Lie" (editorial), *Chicago Tribune*, April 13, 1951; R. E. Wood to E. M. Dirksen, April 24, 1951, Box 1, Wood Papers.

47. B. Fellers to H. Hoover, July 22, 1951, Box 31A, Hoover Papers; B. Carroll Reece, *CR*, June 30, 1951, p. 7532; Leslie C. Arends, *CR*, July 9, 1951, p. 7804.

48. Taft, "The Korean War and the Dismissal of General MacArthur," Yale Club of New York, April 12, 1951, *CR*, pp. A2030–31; Taft, *CR*, April 27, 1951, pp. 4466–69; R. A. Taft to D. MacArthur, August 9, 1951, Box 898, Taft Papers; Radosh, *Prophets on the Right*, p. 186; Patterson, *Mr. Republican*, p. 491.

49. Burdick, *CR*, February 5, 1951, p. A565; W. R. Castle to H. Hoover, April 20, 1951, Box 14, Castle Papers; S. Morton to W. G. Wilcox, April 17, 1951, S. Morton to J. A. Warfel, August 3, 1951, S. Morton to E. E. Lincoln, July 27, 1951, Morton Papers; Chamberlin, "MacArthur Goes, The War Remains," *New Leader* 34 (June 4, 1951): 21; "Half a Loaf in Korea," *New Leader* 34 (July 23, 1951): 15; Morley, "The State of the Nation," *Nation's Business* 39 (June 1951): 20; Hanighen, "Not Merely Gossip," *Human Events* 8 (April 25, 1951).

50. "Truman or MacArthur" (editorial), *Progressive* 4 (May 1951): 3; Thomas, *New York Times*, June 2, 1951, p. 2; Benton, *CR*, May 8, 1951, p. 5031; Dennis, *Appeal to Reason*, #264 (April 14, 1951).

51. For Lippmann, see "Withdrawal and Reexamination," *New York Herald-Tribune*, December 11, 1950, p. 11, and "The Dewey and Hoover Theories," December 26, 1950, p. 29.

52. For Hoover, see address to the nation, January 27, 1952, in *Vital Speeches* 18 (February 15, 1952): 259–60. For Kennedy, see Koskoff, *Joseph P. Kennedy*, p. 357.

53. For Forrest Sherman and Hoyt Vandenberg, see Spanier, *Truman-MacArthur Controversy*, pp. 240–47.

54. For the issue of British trade, see Spanier, *Truman-MacArthur Controversy*, pp. 174–76. For MacArthur, see testimony before the Senate Foreign Relations and Armed Services Committee, May 3, 1951, *CR*, pp. 5046–47.

55. Johnson, *CR*, May 7, 1951, p. 5424; NBC radio interview, *CR*, May 28, 1951, pp. A3092–94; Langer in Mantell, "Opposition to the Korean War," p. 159; L. Dennis to H. E. Barnes, December 10, 1951, Barnes Papers. For Taft's underlying caution, see Patterson, *Mr. Republican*, p. 491.

56. Hubert Humphrey, *CR*, May 10, 1051, p. 5183. For an observation concerning Taft's strategic inconsistency, Patterson, *Mr. Republican*, pp. 481–82.

57. MacArthur on Europe, entry of November 22, 1944, *Forrestal Diaries*, p. 18; MacArthur testimony of May 3 and May 4, 1951, *CR*, pp. 5048, 5051; and Selig Adler, *The Isolationist Impulse: Its Twentieth-Century Reaction* (New York: Abelard-Schuman, 1957), p. 420.

58. Hall, *CR*, April 16, 1951, p. A2124; Lodge, address to Republican 21 Club of Worcester, Massachusetts, April 28, 1951, *CR*, pp. A2402–03.

59. For MacArthur conspiracy, see Graebner, *New Isolationism*, pp. 25; John M. Pratt, ed., *Revitalizing a Nation: A Statement of Beliefs, Opinions and Policies Embodied in the Public Pronouncements of General of the Army Douglas MacArthur* (Chicago: Heritage Foundation, 1952), p. 58.

60. Smith, *CR*, January 29, 1951, p. 755; Burdick, *CR*, January 24, 1951, p. 615; Bender, *CR*, July 11, 1951, p. 7996.

# 11

# "The Fight for America":
# McCarthyism and the Election of 1952

Given the severe setbacks in Korea and the firing of MacArthur, many old isolationists were no longer content to accuse the Truman government of mere bungling. Instead, they saw the administration acting as a conscious instrument of "the international Communist conspiracy." To them, the movement centering on Senator Joseph Raymond McCarthy did not involve the hounding of innocent diplomats and scholars, or the vilification of conscientious and able government servants. Rather, it concerned rescuing the United States from secret and powerful forces sworn to its destruction. It was, in the words of the Wisconsin Republican himself, "the fight for America."

These critics, by capturing the Presidency, hoped to prevent further "betrayal" of American interests. As the aging MacArthur's chances of gaining the Republican nomination were obviously slim, they sought the candidacy of Senator Taft. In their eyes, Taft's nomination was the country's "last, best hope"—a final opportunity to conduct a genuinely nationalistic foreign policy and one purified from all taint of "subversion." As Clarence Manion, dean of Notre Dame Law School and a strong backer of the Ohio Senator, later portrayed the issue, only Taft could have turned the nation's diplomacy in "the direction of American interests."[1] The battle at the 1952 Republican convention was a bitter one, and it took all the skill of political professionals to weld the party into a fighting instrument before the November elections. Despite a slow start, however, the two major factions formed a viable unit, and Robert A. Taft had the pleasure of seeing the party standard-bearer adopt many of his own positions.

Anti-Communist electoral appeals had long antedated McCarthy's rise to power. During the 1930s Republican campaigners had claimed that the New Deal was a major step on the road to collectivism. For example, in 1936 the vice-presidential candidate, Colonel Frank Knox, accused Roosevelt of "leading us toward Moscow." Then in 1944 Governor Dewey said that domestic Communists found FDR's reelection "essential" to their cause. Many GOP Congressional conservatives—people such as Taft, Taber, Mundt, and Hoffman—had stressed the "Communist" issue long before McCarthy appeared on the national scene.[2]

As early as 1945 various Congressmen, including some old isolationists, were talking less and less about "New Deal Communism," and more and more about the "Communistic elements" determining American foreign policy. Soon after the end of World War II, it became standard GOP fare to claim that Eastern Europe had been betrayed into Communist hands at Yalta, and that the administration was thoroughly infiltrated with subversives. By late 1945 George A. Dondero was calling for the investigation of State Department leaks to a small, bimonthly magazine, *Amerasia*. Paul W. Shafer charged that the Communist Party was plotting a series of strikes that ranged from the docks of New York to the movie studios of Hollywood. During the 1946 congressional elections, Taft accused the Democrats "of appeasing the Russians abroad and of fostering Communism at home." Their party, he continued, must choose "between Communism and Americanism." By 1947 Representative Karl Stefan (Rep.–Neb.) was seeking a probe of the entire State Department.[3]

It is hardly surprising to find so many old isolationists voicing such opinions. An internally purified nation, they believed, could free itself from any real Communist menace without the need for debilitating aid programs and alliances. By 1948 eastern interventionists were joining midwestern isolationists in stressing internal subversion, and both groups baited the Democrats with enthusiasm. Former Minnesota Governor Harold E. Stassen, long a target of conservative isolationists, called for banning the American Communist Party. Presidential candidate Dewey repeated his 1944 claim that the Democrats had abetted subversive inroads in government, and the vice-presidential candidate, Governor Earl Warren of California, accused the administration of "coddling" Communists.[4]

The Communist issue, however, involved more than partisan rivalries. Democrat Edwin C. Johnson was not above charging political enemies with harboring Communist sympathies; his party colleague Pat McCarran asserted that such leanings made many aliens unworthy of American citizenship. Furthermore, the President's loyalty proceedings, instituted in March 1947, and the exhortations of Attorney General J. Howard McGrath stressed the dangers of Soviet espionage and internal treason. Truman backers continually tried to link the supporters of Henry Wallace to the American Communist Party. Although enthusiasts of the President were usually not so extreme in their alarmism as were conservative Republicans, they were far from being innocent bystanders.[5]

Only a small minority among the veteran anti-interventionists resisted such an emphasis. By 1947 Oswald Garrison Villard mourned the "alarming anti-Red hysteria that is sweeping the country." The House Committee on Un-American Activities, he said, was installing "star chamber" proceedings and acting as "judges if not executioners." Chodorov, while criticizing the Truman Doctrine, saw "a 'red' witchhunt" already afoot in America. Dennis denied that "burning witches or lynching subversives" could save the nation from "the consequences of World War II or present policies." Commenting on the Alger Hiss espionage case, he said, "Any spy dumb enough to get caught by our F. B. I. is good riddance for the reds." William Henry Chamberlin had misgivings concerning the Smith Act, a bill used in 1949 to imprison eleven Communist leaders supposedly advocating the violent overthrow of the United States. The journalist warned that jailing everyone who sympathized with "Lenin's and Stalin's views on violent revolution" would be "an extravagant, self-defeating policy."[6]

This minority of critics particularly objected to the Mundt-Nixon registration bill and to the McCarran Act. The Mundt-Nixon bill, which passed the House in 1949 but not the Senate, would have required the registration of all "Communist political organizations" and their members. The McCarran Act, or the Internal Security Act of 1950, virtually outlawed all "Communist action" groups by establishing complicated machinery for registration. It also authorized preventive detention of suspected subversives in times of national emergency. It was passed by both houses in 1950, was vetoed by Truman, and was passed again over the President's veto.[7]

For those few liberals remaining among the old isolationists, such proposals were reprehensible. Chamberlin claimed that the Mundt-Nixon bill would suspend the Bill of Rights. Norman Thomas warned that the McCarran Act would "instill fear into reasonable debate." William L. Neumann asserted that the Internal Security Act of 1950 might put many new weapons in the hands of a ruthless state. Senator Langer, finding the McCarran bill striking at "the right of people to speak their minds," was so adamant in his support of Truman's veto that he collapsed on the Senate floor during a filibuster. He had to be rushed to Bethesda Naval Hospital.[8]

Langer's Dakota colleagues shared his aversion to "anti-subversive" legislation. William Lemke called the Mundt-Nixon bill "nickel-in-the-slot peanut politics." Far better, he said, to inform Americans that eighty percent of the Russian people "wear burlap for shoes and some wear burlap for underwear." Usher Burdick claimed that the McCarran Act was an effort to "strangle men who think, even though they think wrong," although he still announced with pride that only seventy-five known Communists lived in his home state of North Dakota.[9]

All previous debates, however, were minor when compared to the storm unleashed by Senator McCarthy. On February 9, 1950, in a Lincoln's Birthday speech at Wheeling, West Virginia, McCarthy declared that at least fifty-seven security risks remained in the State Department; they were, in fact, continuing the "traitorous" policies that had resulted in Chiang's demise and the Korean stalemate. Moving from one "exposé" to another before opponents could confront him effectively, McCarthy soon went as far as to claim that General Marshall's role in America's China policy made him part of "a conspiracy on a scale so immense as to dwarf any previous venture in the history of man."[10]

Ironically, in light of the fervent support he received from many old isolationists, McCarthy was never a strong opponent of intervention. In 1946, while campaigning in the Wisconsin Republican primary against "Young Bob" La Follette, he condemned his opponent for failing "to do a single thing to prepare us for World War II." La Follette, he said, was "playing into the hands of the Communists by opposing world cooperation." As Senator, McCarthy voted for such interventionist measures as the Truman Doctrine, the Marshall Plan, the Atlantic Pact, and MAP. In 1951 he questioned Hoover's "Gibraltar" strategy, although he did vote for the McClellan amendment limiting the number of American divisions that the President could send overseas. In March 1948 McCarthy opposed the presidential candidacy of General MacArthur, a favorite of many old isolationists, while lauding the qualifications of the interventionist Stassen. Even during the 1952 primary races, when the majority of old isolationists was fervently backing Taft, the Wisconsinite said little.[11]

McCarthy, however, was endorsed heartily by many old isolationists. He drew his strongest support from rural areas in the Midwest and Irish Catholic neighborhoods in eastern cities—both areas in which World War II isolationism had been strong. Certain of his sentiments had an anti-interventionist thrust. His hostility toward Great Britain was almost as great as his hatred of Russia, and he often assailed England's commerce with Communist China as "trading in blood money." He attacked "the bright young men who are born with silver spoons in their mouths," therein voicing a common theme among many veteran isolationists of his region. And, by reducing foreign policy issues to the simplistic dichotomy of "patriotism" versus "treason," McCarthy implied that a "purged" America could remain both aloof and secure.[12]

Hardly a conservative among the old isolationists opposed him. General Wood, while harboring a few unnamed misgivings about McCarthy's "methods," claimed that the Wisconsin Senator had "performed a great and valuable patriotic service to this country." Taft called him a "fighting Marine who risked his life to preserve the liberties of the United States." The Ohio Republican was quoted as saying that if McCarthy failed to substantiate one case, he should try another. Frank Chodorov mused that McCarthy did not go far enough. The Wisconsin Senator, he said, should have tried to abolish the government bureaucracy itself, because "a job of killing, not cleaning" was needed. In the meantime, the right-wing anarchist counted himself on McCarthy's side. Even the more liberal Langer, in defending McCarthy from attacks by Democratic Senators, said that McCarthy's attack on General Marshall was "one of the most important speeches that has ever been made on this floor."[13]

Words were matched by action. Robert Harriss often contributed ammunition to McCarthy's campaign against Marshall, sending him in one instance a letter from Harry Woodring in which the former Secretary of War accused Marshall of being capable of selling his own grandmother. Sterling Morton mailed him a hundred dollars to hire FBI men for his investigations. Devin-Adair published two of his books, *America's Retreat from Victory: The Story of George Catlett Marshall* (1951) and *McCarthyism: The Fight for America* (1952). Publishers Regnery and Garrity were among the signers of a "Declaration of Conscience" that accused the majority of the nation's press of treating McCarthy unfairly. Robert Young gave money and collected petition signatures on his behalf. Joseph P. Kennedy not only contributed to McCarthy's cause, but frequently entertained the Senator at his Hyannisport home.[14]

Few supporters were more ardent than Freda Utley, who revealed her zeal in the Lattimore case. She had once been befriended by the Far Eastern specialist Owen Lattimore—whom the Senator had called the "top Russian espionage agent" in the United States—and had cited Lattimore as a character reference on her personal vitae. Yet, embittered by the disapparance of her husband in the USSR and believing Lattimore too pro-Soviet, she wrote one of McCarthy's speeches attacking him. In testifying before a Senate investigating committee, Mrs. Utley denied his accusation that Lattimore was a Communist spy. Instead, she compared him to a "Judas cow," a stockyard animal that led others to the slaughter. "The Communist cancer," she said, "must be cut out if we are to survive as a free nation. Perhaps in this operation some healthy tissues on the fringe will be destroyed."[15]

In the Cold War struggle, McCarthy and his supporters even vilified an occasional old isolationist. For example, they attacked Philip C. Jessup, a distinguished international lawyer and U.S. Ambassador at Large, for having served as a character witness for Alger Hiss. Jessup had been a sponsor of the New York chapter of America First, a fact that caused the pro-McCarthy Frank Hanighen to muse that his record at the time was "curious and unclear." McCarthy's supporters also assailed William Benton, once a close adviser to the America First Committee, for introducing a resolution calling for the Wisconsinite's expulsion from the Senate. Morgenstern, for instance, accused Benton of committing political "immorality." In 1952 Flynn told Vivian Kellums, a right-wing isolationist manufacturer in Connecticut, that her third-party efforts for the Senate were not worth risking Benton's reelection. Even General Wood, a personal friend and business associate of the Connecticut Senator, refused to endorse him.[16]

An extremely small minority of veteran isolationists, usually more liberal on domestic policy, had little use for McCarthy. Philip La Follette, whose brother's Senate seat McCarthy had taken, said that he strongly disapproved of him and his tactics. Lindbergh too opposed his methods, although he did not consider the Senator a great danger. Barnes feared that McCarthy's reelection in 1952 probably meant "more pressure for an Asiatic war." Dennis claimed that both McCarthy and Taft were adopting Hitler's "smear techniques." By blaming "reds" and "pinks" for the country's woes, they were avoiding serious discussion of interventionist policies rooted as far back as the Presidency of Taft's own father.[17]

A thorough examination of McCarthyism would show that defamation was not one-sided and that the administration had itself baited many old isolationists. Truman called Republican opponents of his foreign policy "Kremlin assets," people committing national sabotage equal to shooting "our soldiers in the backs in a hot war." In 1950, as part of a concerted effort to vilify Taft, Ohio Democrats circulated a picture showing the Senator conversing with Communist party leader Earl Browder. The unidentified photograph had been taken in 1936, when Taft was debating Browder before the American Youth Congress. During the Great Debate of 1950 and 1951, the *New York Times* was playing up Soviet coverage of major isolationist speeches, and in 1952 diplomat W. Averell Harriman claimed that Taft would execute the foreign policy of Stalin. The tactic of anti-Communism, like so much else in the Cold War, was bipartisan.[18]

Although the McCormick press, Flynn, and many other old isolationists had been accused of being pro-Nazi in the 1940s, they usually possessed little sympathy for the victims of a different brand of slander. Flynn, long a McCarthy defender, had written a tract in 1947 opposing efforts to link his fellow isolationists with the Nazis. The title of his early pamphlet, ironic in light of his later position, was "The Smear Terror." Barnes, who personally opposed McCarthy, simply blamed the "war-mongers of 1937–41" for having created a crusading mentality that had finally backfired on them.[19]

More to the point, many old isolationists saw McCarthy as attacked by the same eastern elite that had fought Lindbergh, Wheeler, and Nye a decade earlier. To such individuals, people who had wrung their hands over the "smearing" of Acheson and Marshall merely had their facts confused. The Senator's critics ignored the reality of the "all-permeating conspiracy," hence confusing "persecutors" with "victims." If McCarthy's enemies (and more "neutral" observers as well) portrayed his movement as possessing immense power, his band of followers envisioned themselves as very much under siege.

McCarthyism helped to transform much of American isolationism, making it even more militant and chauvinistic. Like the cause of General MacArthur, it gave the movement a new lease on life. If, as many old isolationists hoped, America's leadership was again composed of genuine nationalists, there would be no further "sellouts" of non-Communist peoples. The country could remain both solvent and secure. With a citizenry alert to the subtle forms of subversion (and this could range from schoolbooks glorifying Robin Hood to clergymen endorsing national health plans), the American "Eden" could again resist foreign "contamination."

Only a small band of liberals among the old isolationists, as well as an occasional "maverick" such as Dennis, opposed McCarthy's movement. Such crusading, this minority believed, would retard needed domestic reform and lead to dangerous truculence overseas. For the great majority of veteran isolationists, however, the Wisconsin Senator, as well as the cause for which he stood, was a key to Republican victory in 1952, and to national purgation as well.

A truly nationalist triumph, most old isolationists believed, could come only with the presidential nomination of Senator Taft. If the Republicans again chose an interventionist, the country would forgo its final chance to pursue an independent destiny. And, in this regard, rumors concerning the budding candidacy of General of the Armies Dwight D. Eisenhower were far from reassuring.

Eisenhower often claimed that it was Taft's isolationism that had prompted his own entry into the 1952 presidential race. The General, meeting secretly with the Senator in 1951, failed to receive assurances that Taft firmly believed in collective security for Western Europe. Eisenhower had supposedly prepared a public statement renouncing all presidential ambitions but had torn it up once Taft had left. Of course the General obviously harbored presidential ambitions, and it was doubtful whether any interventionist policy statement by Taft could long restrain them. At the same time he undoubtedly feared that the Senator would so restrict America's commitments to Europe that the country's security would be threatened.[20]

In September 1951 Senator Lodge visited Eisenhower's NATO headquarters in Paris, there receiving tacit approval to promote the General's candidacy. Lodge had inherited both Vandenberg's leadership of the Republican interventionists and the Michigan's Senator's predisposition toward Eisenhower's nomination. ("Thank God for Eisenhower!", Vandenberg had said on his deathbed.) As soon as the General won the first Republican primary in March 1952, many Taft partisans realized that their man was in trouble.[21]

The efforts of Lodge and Governor Dewey on Eisenhower's behalf made many old isolationists furious. The General had no public reputation as a Republican, much less as an ardent nationalist; he had not even proclaimed himself as one until January 1952, when his name was filed in the New Hampshire primary. When his possible candidacy had been brought up in 1948, Eisenhower's leading backers had included liberal and interventionist Democrats out to replace Truman. He, in fact, had been the favorite of the Americans for Democratic Action, New York's Liberal Party, and such CIO leaders as James B. Carey of the International Union of Electrical, Radio, and Machine Workers. His career had been fostered almost entirely by such interventionist policymakers as Roosevelt, Marshall, and Truman, and his most recent post—commander of the NATO forces—epitomized the "Europe-first" strategy fostered by the administration. The General's decided conservatism on much domestic policy ("If all Americans want is security, they can go to prison," he once said in 1949) made little difference to those fearful of "entangling alliances."[22]

In 1952, with tensions over Korea remaining high, Taft's supporters were more furious than ever. The eastern Republicans, who formed the core of Eisenhower's strength, represented a faction of the party that had been defeated in three successive presidential elections. In their own campaigns such interventionist standard bearers as Willkie and Dewey had appeared visibly embarrassed by the more conservative and isolationist GOP congressional record. Then some of the more militant Eisenhower partisans, such as Clare Boothe Luce, seemed to go beyond the bounds of intra-party rivalry. Taft's nomination, claimed Mrs. Luce, "would give Stalin the only real political victory he has had in Europe since the formation of SHAPE [Supreme Headquarters Allied Powers, Europe] under Eisenhower."[23]

Old Guard Republicans, particularly if they considered themselves strong nationalists, saw "Ike's" candidacy as a conscious, calculated effort to prevent the United States from ever again being unable to determine its own fate. During the primary races of 1952, Eisenhower said baldly, "I'm running because Taft is an isolationist. His election would be a disaster." To the great majority of old anti-interventionists, the General's role was more than that of "spoiler"; it served to neutralize the party that might challenge administration policy in every part of the globe.[24]

For so many old isolationists, Eisenhower was neither a war hero nor a charismatic leader. To Congressman Jensen he was the instrument of "Eastern publishers and international financiers"; to General Fellers he was the candidate of "Fair Deal bureaucrats." Sterling Morton stressed that, as a military man, Eisenhower would always seek a military solution. Usher Burdick said that he would have preferred President Truman (a man who favored high subsidies to Burdick's Dakota farmers) to any Republican interventionist. Henry Regnery found Eisenhower a political opportunist. Although the Chicago publisher vaguely referred to possible positive qualities, he blamed the General for having called back American forces on their way to conquering Prague in 1945.[25]

To such people Eisenhower's candidacy was a fearsome prospect. Frank Gannett said that Eisenhower was no more a Republican than he, Gannett, was a "Chinaman." General MacNider praised his "magnificent record" as European commander, but found him too linked to Truman foreign policy to attack it effectively. Flynn accused Eisenhower of being as likely to surrender American sovereignty as such Democratic frontrunners as Harriman and Governor Adlai E. Stevenson of Illinois. Congressman Reece said that Eisenhower, while Chief of Staff in 1949, had so severely cut the air force budget that MacArthur lacked sufficient planes to bomb Manchuria.[26]

In light of Eisenhower's impending challenge, Taft found himself increasingly forced to articulate his foreign policy views. In a book entitled *A Foreign Policy for Americans* (1951), he reiterated familiar themes: the necessity of containing Russia, the ideological nature of the Cold War, the need for an all-powerful air deterrent, and the importance of MacArthur's strategy in Asia. Perhaps sensing that Republican interventionists were putting him on the defensive, he suggested that secret agents infiltrate Communist nations and promote liberation movements. While such activity, Taft readily admitted, was not in the American tradition, it could "give the Soviet government something to worry about behind the iron curtain itself." In an appendix, Taft defended his attitudes before Pearl Harbor.[27]

Because the book contained the most comprehensive statement yet articulated of Taft's views, it was hotly debated. MacArthur wholeheartedly endorsed the work, praising the Ohioan for clearing away "many of the cobwebs of uncertainty which are spun so carefully by . . . the invisible government." Mrs. Utley, on the other hand, accused Taft of failing to realize that war must continually be risked. Richard N. Current, a moderate World War II revisionist, endorsed his "forthright" attack on Truman's foreign policy, but regretted that the Senator's policies resembled the containment policy of George F. Kennan when a trenchant Beardian critique was needed. James Burnham warned that Taft's militancy in Asia could destroy American manpower, while leaving "the Soviet Empire" untouched. Several interventionist reviewers—ranging from *Time* magazine to geopolitician Robert Strausz-Hupé and Professor McGeorge Bundy of Harvard—accused him of lacking the needed "world vision."[28]

In 1952 Taft trod uneasily between militancy and caution. He attacked Truman for initiating truce talks in Korea with an enemy who, in the President's own words, could not "be trusted under any circumstances." At the same time he repeated his endorsement of MacArthur's strategy. A Nationalist invasion of the mainland, said Taft on February 12, offered the only chance of stopping a Communist assault on Southeast Asia. Two days later he claimed that he would use Nationalist troops to meet a Communist Chinese attack in Indochina. However, he soon mellowed on Korean truce talks. While not touching upon such sticky points as the prisoner-of-war issue, Taft asserted that he sought an armistice, to be followed by increased arms for the South Koreans and withdrawal of United States forces.[29]

At times Taft tried to turn the tables on his opponents. He accused the administration of housing "the new isolationists," for it would, he said, abandon most of Europe and Asia to Russia. His advocacy of air power intensified, and he declared just before the Republican convention that "the ability of our Air Force to deliver atom bombs on Russia should never be open to question." By June 1952 Taft was no longer talking the language of restraint; he was, without using the phrase, adopting in part the strategy of "massive retaliation." Denying that America's safety depended upon "begging bayonets from Germany and from France," he endorsed the plea of John Foster Dulles for the liberation of the iron curtain countries. As the party convention opened, the Senator hoped that he had been able to throw off the isolationist label.[30]

Despite Taft's more militant foreign policy, he remained the favorite of many old-time America Firsters. In the words of Congressman Noah Mason, "He is the Moses that can lead us out of the Truman wilderness." General Wood, serving as chairman of the Illinois Citizens for Taft, enlisted strong support among veteran isolationist industrialists. In other areas of the nation as well, businessmen who had been generous to the America First Committee gave to his campaign.[31]

Individual anti-interventionists felt even more strongly about Taft's candidacy in 1952 than they had in 1948. Louis Taber headed the Farmers' Taft Committee. Joseph P. Kennedy was so enthusiastic that his son John referred to him as "a Taft Democrat." Libby claimed that a ticket of Taft and MacArthur would have "great pulling power." Colonel McCormick briefly toyed with the candidacy of General Albert C. Wedemeyer, but soon went back to Taft. Dennis, who had been critical of the Senator's belief in air power and his Asia policy, endorsed him in a special issue of the *Appeal to Reason*. The Berkshire pamphleteer regretted that Taft had not been more unequivocal in opposing the Cold War, but found that the Ohioan's "moderate opposition" made "internationalist fanatics" brand him the equivalent of "a religious heretic." (Privately Dennis declared that he was so ardent in supporting Taft because some of his own financial backers, such as General Wood, favored the Senator.)[32]

Surprisingly enough, not all the editors of the *Freeman* favored the Ohio Senator. Rather, they were split among Taft, MacArthur, and the conservative Senator Harry F. Byrd (Dem.–Va.). A rightist journal edited by John Chamberlain and founded in 1950, the *Freeman* was publishing articles by such old isolationists as Flynn, Morley, Fellers, and Mrs. Utley. Leaning toward Taft, it claimed that Eisenhower's backers would permit the West to be "outflanked" in the "colonial" world, and thereby witness the imposition of a rigid military autarchy upon older industrial regions of Europe and America. Forrest Davis, one of the editors and a former aide of the Senator, contributed an article suggesting that Eisenhower had participated in "the fall of the United States from world authority."[33]

A few old isolationists hoped for MacArthur's nomination. Within a year of the convention, the General issued a statement declaring that he would not "shrink" from "accepting any public duty." In October 1951 Lansing Hoyt toured the South in an effort to drum up support from Democrats below the Mason-Dixon line. Robert Harriss attempted to organize American Legionnaires for MacArthur. Gannett, claiming that Taft lacked the necessary charisma, said that only MacArthur could carry the South and win Congress for the GOP. Tansill found the Ohio Senator too liberal on domestic and racial issues and endorsed the General. Francis H. Case, now a Senator, issued a statement just prior to the convention urging MacArthur as a compromise choice.[34]

A small minority of liberals favored quite different candidates. Both Barnes and the *Progressive* wanted Associate Justice William O. Douglas of the Supreme Court. In praising Douglas, the *Progressive* (which had backed Norman Thomas in 1948) pointed to the Justice's rejection of "our government's sterile, negative program of seeking to contain Communism almost solely by building up positions of military strength." Philip La Follette, a MacArthur leader in 1948, endorsed the candidacy of Earl Warren. When queried by General Wood, his former political ally, La Follette spoke vaguely of the California governor's "long administrative experience" and "unique vote-getting ability." La Follette had obviously set out to regain state control of the Republican Party from Thomas E. Coleman, a strong Taft backer, and his Warren slate was widely and accurately recognized as a screen for Eisenhower.[35]

The rivalry was fierce, both before and during the convention. Hamilton Fish tried to lead an insurgent Taft slate in upstate New York but lost the race. Hugh Butler personally cabled Eisenhower, urging him to withdraw. At one point during the convention, the pro-Taft Dirksen, who had become a Senator in 1950, pointed an angry finger at Governor Dewey and shouted, "We followed you before and you took us down the road to defeat."[36]

During the sessions at Chicago, the Taft forces played upon old isolationist esteem for MacArthur and Hoover. Possessing a firm majority on the Republican National Committee, the Senator's backers named MacArthur as keynoter. In his address the General told the party that a strong administration could have saved both Eastern Europe and continental Asia from Communist domination. MacArthur called for eventual "withdrawal of our ground garrisons from service abroad," claiming that the "free people of Asia and the Middle East" (but not Europe) sought only the military equipment needed to "turn the tide decisively against Communism." Early in the convention Taft had hopes that MacArthur would be his running mate; neither man, however, actually committed himself.[37]

Hoover, another Taft supporter, also addressed the assembly, telling it that frantic efforts to rearm Europe would accelerate financial ruin and fulfill "Stalin's greatest hope." Again proposing his "Gibraltar" strategy, Hoover claimed that the surest defense of London, New York, and Paris lay in "the fear of counterattack on Moscow from the air." Turning to Korea, the ex-President claimed that any halt at the thirty-eighth parallel would simply appease the Communists.[38]

Such voices had little impact on delegates, hungry for election victory, who nominated Eisenhower on the first ballot. Taft ascribed his defeat to "the power of the New York financial interests and a large number of businesses subject to New York," the opposition of four-fifths of the influential newspapers, and a majority of the governors. Coleman of Wisconsin, his floor manager, claimed that the industrialists of General Motors and Ford had forced Eisenhower upon their employees. Historian William L. Neumann speculated that big businessmen had been "sold on the continuous subsidization of their exports by the taxpayer under the guise of 'internationalism.'" Chodorov accused the corporate leadership of seeking to retain "the cocktail standard to which it has been accustomed by the New-Fair Deal."[39]

There was some justice to these remarks. The New York business orbit—based upon international commerce and finance—differed markedly from the manufacturing interests of Ohio and Illinois. The theologian and commentator Reinhold Niebuhr described the split in highly colored terms: midwestern isolationist industrialists, believing that Continental markets were sufficient for American prosperity, opposed the high taxes needed to underwrite "international responsibilities"; eastern internationalist businessmen, on the other hand, served as "proconsuls of our vast imperial commitments," and therefore supported a more "responsible" foreign policy.[40]

Yet Taft's defeat at the convention was not, as some partisans have claimed, the result of unfair machinations by the Eisenhower forces. Throughout the entire proceedings the Senator faced a familiar problem:

that of political weakness in the Northeast and on the Pacific coast. He had, in other words, failed the test of "political demography." Taft's foreign policy had offended the Easterners on two counts: it was too risky in Asia, too cautious in Europe. Even more important, however, the Republican delegates, both coastal and inland, yearned for a guaranteed winner and were convinced that they had one in Eisenhower. In this assumption they were probably correct. If a poll had been taken of all the Republicans in the nation, the General would probably have won. In this sense Taft's forces were probably overrepresented at the convention.[41]

All this did not stop many old isolationists from feeling crushed by Taft's defeat. Libby wrote to William H. Regnery, "You and I have lost the election already so far as I can see." To Barnes, the nomination marked "the point of no return." Flynn was not only hostile to Eisenhower but found the economic creed of the Republican vice-presidential nominee, Senator Richard M. Nixon (Rep.–Calif.), far too liberal. Dennis called Eisenhower's nomination "a victory for war," and, noting support given the General by McCarthy and the sensationalist columnist Walter Winchell, feared that "witchhunting will run riot." Hart denied that either presidential contender had "struck a patriotic note in any speech."[42]

Some Taft supporters were disappointed enough to consider a third party. Ever since the America First Committee had decided to endorse noninterventionist candidates in the 1942 congressional race, isolationists had considered establishing alternative political groups. The Republican Party appeared dominated by the Willkie-Dewey wing, the Democrats committed to the Roosevelt-Truman leadership. Many veteran isolationists found themselves without a national political vehicle, much less a clearing house for information and research. In 1944 General Wood hoped that Philip La Follette could lead a postwar political realignment. Old isolationists were prominent in the American Democratic National Committee of 1944, an effort led by Harry Woodring and Senator W. Lee ("Pappy") O'Daniel (Dem.–Texas) and organized to prevent Roosevelt's renomination. They also helped promote American Action, a group organized in February 1945 to rival the Political Action Committee of the CIO. The organization played a minor role in selected congressional races in 1946 and 1948, but never became a major political force.[43]

During the 1952 campaign Colonel McCormick tried to interest old isolationists in a third party. Initial plans were made when such Eisenhower foes as Gannett, Fish, Wedemeyer, Hart, O'Donnell, and Flynn gathered at the Harvard Club on August 18. Five days later the Colonel took to the air waves, attacking the slogan "I Like Ike" and calling for the formation of an American Party that could back conservatives and isolationists for Congress. In his address the Chicago publisher accused Eisenhower supporters of wanting "the continuation of the Marshall Plan, with money going to Europe and mink coats coming back." McCormick's call, however, received little support. Such conservatives as Butler endorsed the straight Republican ticket, and the more liberal Lodge publicly called the Colonel "something of a screwball."[44] Party ties, the smell of victory, hopes for patronage—all worked against the Colonel's efforts.

McCormick soon gave up the endeavor. He still attacked the interventionism of the Republican platform, declaring that—in his eyes—the UN, the Marshall Plan, and the NATO alliance had all been established "for purposes of graft." The GOP, he continued, went "along with Truman in pulling the threat of Russia—which nobody in Europe takes seriously—in order to scare people into voting for something they do not want." He indicated, however, that he might vote for Eisenhower, while still backing such independents as Vivian Kellems and Hamilton Fish in Senate races. The *Chicago Tribune* finally endorsed Eisenhower late in October; it denied that the General was well equipped for the Presidency but found Stevenson far worse.[45]

McCormick did not make the only third-party effort. Late in August Upton Close fostered the formation of the Constitution Party. Hoping to secure sufficient votes in the electoral college to select a team of MacArthur and Byrd, the party called for a return to isolationism and an end to "all international spending and boondoggling." The party had only a brief career, partially because both chairmen resigned almost immediately after its formation, and it was ignored by its supposed standard-bearer.[46]

In addition, Gerald L. K. Smith, an anti-Semitic propagandist, promoted MacArthur's candidacy on the Christian Nationalist ticket. Smith, like Close, found himself totally disregarded by MacArthur. The two parties were on the ballot in only eight states and received an infinitesimally small popular vote.[47]

A few liberal isolationists supported Adlai Stevenson. The *Progressive's* endorsement played up domestic issues, but criticized the Illinois Governor for not repudiating "the dominant note of military containment which is the heart of the Truman-Acheson position." Norman Thomas also backed Stevenson, declaring that Eisenhower was too ignorant to assume the Presidency. Langer, nominally a Republican, traveled with Truman across North Dakota on a whistle-stop campaign on Stevenson's behalf.[48]

Once the bitterness of the GOP convention began to fade, the great majority of old isolationists reluctantly began to back Eisenhower. Only a few, such as William Henry Chamberlin and Philip La Follette, were genuinely enthusiastic about the candidate. Sterling Morton, part of a delegation of Chicago businessmen visiting Eisenhower, returned solidly in the General's camp. The General had supposedly told Morton that he believed in hot pursuit of enemy planes across the Manchurian border and in bombing Manchurian factories. Most others couched their endorsements in far more cautious terms. General Wood claimed that Stevenson, a man whom he knew and liked personally, would "be a far more dangerous man in the White House than Truman because he has far more brains." Publisher James H. Gipson hoped to "infiltrate" the Eisenhower organization with "Libertarians" as well as with some of the "best and ablest men in the North—men like John Bricker and Joe McCarthy."[49]

Others came around more slowly. The *New York Daily News*, in calling for Eisenhower's election, accused the Democrats of "war-mongering." Clare E. Hoffman endorsed the General most reluctantly; Eisenhower, he said, was "an internationalist who wants to continue pouring millions and billions into aid to European countries and in arms expenditures."[50]

Eisenhower's meeting with Taft on September 12 helped muster more enthusiasm for the campaign. Embittered over his defeat, Taft had waited two months before meeting with the General. At the Eisenhower residence on Morningside Heights, the General accepted Taft's definition of the campaign as one of "liberty against creeping socialism." The Ohio Senator vaguely declared that he could not agree with all of Eisenhower's foreign-policy views, but claimed that differences were ones of degree. Taft privately doubted the wisdom of Eisenhower's call for the liberation of Eastern Europe, but felt no compunction about declaring that Stevenson, by limiting American action to containment, was making "a surrender to Communist policy."[51]

Taft's endorsement was followed by others. On October 18 Hoover, in praising Eisenhower, denied that the Republican Party was isolationist; unlike the Democrats, the GOP had always opposed alliance with Stalin and the spread of Communism. With Taft and Hoover now offering unequivocal support, Fish rallied to the colors. In fact the former New York Congressman now defined himself as "an internationalist in favor of a firm stand to stop Communist aggression in Europe and Asia no matter what it costs."[52]

Eisenhower, in fact, ended the campaign adopting much of Taft's foreign policy. In June he had upheld the policy of containment, refused to blame the Democrats for the loss of Korea, and backed the armistice negotiations at Panmunjon. By November the General was accusing the Democrats of having once "abandoned" Korea and China; he spoke in terms of "liberating captive nations," favored bombing on the Yalu, and attacked the truce talks. In addition he welcomed the support of McCarthy, declaring that he differed only with the Senator's "methods."[53]

There were, of course, limits to Eisenhower's shifts. The General never adopted Taft and MacArthur's Korean strategy and did not share their unqualified enthusiasm for air power. It was the General's promise to go to Korea, rather than his specific proposals concerning foreign policy, that helped him to clinch the 1952 race.[54] Until the President-elect visited the battlefront, and until the Eisenhower administration could develop its own foreign policy, the old isolationists could only wait and see.


Despite Eisenhower's militant campaign rhetoric, several veteran isolationists had mixed feelings about his victory, and in particular about his appointment of John Foster Dulles as Secretary of State. During the 1930s Dulles, an international lawyer with the firm of Sullivan and Cromwell, had been somewhat sympathetic to isolationism. His book *War, Peace and Change* (1939) called for concessions to such "have-not" nations as Germany, Japan, and Italy. He gave generously to Frederick J. Libby's National Council for the Prevention of War in 1940 and 1941, a time when the NCPW was devoting almost all its energies to fighting Roosevelt's foreign policy. Although he refused to join the America First Committee on the grounds that it was too isolationist, he opposed full-scale intervention before Pearl Harbor.[55]

During and after World War II, however, Dulles was an outspoken and articulate interventionist. He served as a major foreign policy adviser to the eastern wing of the Republican Party, in addition to carrying out such important administration assignments as the Japanese Peace Treaty of 1951. Despite such activities, Dulles never burned his bridges to the Taft faction. In the late spring of 1952 the Senator, who favored Dulles's stress on a sea-air strategy, made it clear that he wanted the prominent attorney to write the foreign policy plank for the Republican platform. Taft forces hinted that if the Senator were elected President, he would appoint Dulles Secretary of State. The New York lawyer was more sympathetic to Eisenhower's foreign policy and made no secret about his preference. When the President-elect chose Dulles for the post, however, Taft was delighted.[56]

A few old isolationists endorsed the appointment. Morton, for example, referred to Dulles as "a very able man, although somewhat on the stodgy side." Hanighen, sole editor of *Human Events* since 1950, claimed that Secretary was opposed to America's "ineffectual" policies in Europe and had urged the bombing of China. Having worked briefly on the Washington staff of America First, he recalled that Dulles had informally been very helpful to the Committee.[57]

Yet, to some old isolationists, the appointment of Dulles signified one thing: the ruinous interventionism of Roosevelt and Truman would now be continued under Republican auspices. When someone suggested earlier to McCormick that he back Dulles for the presidency, the Colonel replied that he would "just as soon support Judas Iscariot." Dennis asserted, "Nothing short of total global victory over red sin will satisfy Dulles." Neumann feared the Secretary's stress upon "liberation" of Eastern Europe, with American-trained *agent provocateurs* possibly triggering a world war. Flynn warned against the new President's closeness to Dulles, writing to General Wood that "We must . . . influence Eisenhower's mind as much as possible."[58]

For those already skeptical about any chance for major foreign policy changes, Eisenhower's inaugural address was particularly infuriating. Extremely interventionist in tone, it declared that the United States was "linked to all free peoples not merely by a noble idea but by a simple need." Tansill mourned that Truman policies would be continued. The *Chicago Tribune* declared that Eisenhower's speech "might have been written at Mr. Truman's order," for it amounted to "little more than an endorsement of the foreign policies of the outgoing regime." With such omens as these, Frederick C. Smith—now out of Congress—could only write, "Mr. Eisenhauer [*sic*] either doesn't understand the present trouble that afflicts our nation or does not care. Any way we must put our confidence in God, for there only lies any hope for America."[59]

To individuals who veered between withdrawal and militant unilateralism, and who strongly disliked America's allies, the ascendancy of Eisenhower and Dulles could not be reassuring. If most old isolationists ended up supporting the President-elect, they remained unconverted to his brand of interventionism. True, candidate Eisenhower had adopted much partisan rhetoric about administration "appeasement." It was, however, always questionable whether he could reverse Truman policy. The campaign might well, so old isolationists suspected, have changed nothing, and the General's victory could well have been the kiss of death. As Hanighen queried, "Our man won. But did *we* win?"[60]

# NOTES

1. Clarence E. Manion, *The Conservative American* (Shepherdsville, Ky.: Victor Publishing Company, 1966), p. 74.

2. Frank Knox and Thomas E. Dewey cited in Richard M. Fried, "Electoral Politics and McCarthyism: The 1950 Campaign," in Robert Griffith and Athan Theoharis, eds., *The Specter: Original Essays on the Cold War and the Origins of McCarthyism* (New York: New Viewpoints, 1974), p. 193. Other old isolationists in this category include Capehart, Curtis, Dondero, Halleck, Mason, Rankin, Shafer, and Lawrence H. Smith. See Theoharis, *Seeds of Repression*, p. 14.

3. Dondero, *CR*, November 28, 1945, pp. 11150–51; Shafer, CR, November 6, 1945, p. A4730; Taft in Patterson, *Mr. Republican*, p. 313; Stefan in Griffith, *Politics of Fear*, pp. 40–41.

4. Stassen, Dewey, and Warren, in Griffith, *Politics of Fear*, p. 46.

5. Johnson and McCarran in Griffith, *Politics of Fear*, pp. 45–46; J. Howard McGrath in Theoharis, *Seeds of Repression*, p. 136. For attacks on Wallace, see Allen Yarnell, *Democrats and Progressives: The 1948 Presidential Election as a Test of Postwar Liberalism* (Berkeley: University of California Press, 1974).

6. Villard to *Peace News* (London), November 12, 1947, Villard Papers; Chodorov, "A Byzantine Empire of the West," *analysis* 3 (April 1947): 3; Dennis, *Appeal to Reason*, #125 (August 14, 1948); Chamberlin, "Outlaw the Communists?," *New Leader* 32 (October 29, 1949): 16. Chamberlin did endorse the House Committee on Un-American Activities. He claimed that it had made mistakes in methods and procedures, but had focused needed attention on Communist infiltration. W. H. Chamberlin to O. G. Villard, October 22, 1948, Villard Papers.

7. For provisions and history of both bills, see William R. Tanner and Robert Griffith, "Legislative Politics and 'McCarthyism': The Internal Security Act of 1950," in Griffith and Theoharis, *The Specter*, pp. 172–89.

8. Chamberlin, "Civil Liberties and Communist Conspiracy," *Human Events* 5 (August 11, 1948); Thomas in Johnpoll, *Pacifist's Progress*, p. 263; W. L. Neumann to H. E. Barnes, September 29, 1950, Neumann Papers; Smith, "Senator William Langer," p. 58.

9. Lemke, *CR*, May 19, 1948, p. 6114; Burdick, *CR*, August 29, 1950, p. 13768.

10. Joseph R. McCarthy, Wheeling address, *CR*, February 20, 1950, p. 1953, and on Marshall, June 14, 1951, p. 6602. Hanighen suggested that the speech was written by journalist Forrest Davis. See "Not Merely Gossip," *Human Events* 8 (June 20, 1951).

11. *Madison Capital Times*, June 16, 1946; McCarthy on La Follette, ibid., June 10, 1946; McCarthy on MacArthur in Jack Anderson and Ronald D. May, *McCarthy: The*

Man, The Senator, the "Ism" (Boston: Beacon, 1952), pp. 235–36; McCarthy on 1952 fight and before in Patterson, *Mr. Republican*, p. 530, and Thomas E. Coleman to R. A. Taft, December 26, 1951, Box 881, Taft Papers.

12. For the implicit tie between McCarthyism and isolationism, see Hans J. Morgenthau, *The Purpose of American Politics* (New York: Vintage, 1960), p. 144.

13. R. E. Wood to W. Benton, August 9, 1951, Box 1, Wood Papers; Taft in Patterson, *Mr. Republican*, p. 446; Griffith, *Politics of Fear*, p. 73; Chodorov, "McCarthy's Mistake," *Human Events* 9 (November 12, 1952); Langer, *CR*, February 12, 1951, pp. 1221–22; Richard Rovere, *Senator Joe McCarthy* (New York: Meridian, 1959), pp. 174–75. Langer was not always so enthusiastic about McCarthy. In 1954 McCarthy sent regrets to the Dakota Senator for not being able to campaign in his state. Langer replied that McCarthy was welcome to campaign, but only for his opponent in the primary! Smith, "Senator William Langer," pp. 59–60.

14. Robert Harriss, item in *Watertown* (N.Y.) *News*, November 30, 1954, and "McCarthy—Has the Senate Had Enough?" (editorial), *New Republic* 131 (August 16, 1954): 3; S. Morton to J. R. McCarthy, May 24, 1950, Morton Papers; Joseph R. McCarthy, *America's Retreat from Victory: The Story of George Catlett Marshall* (New York: Devin-Adair, 1951); McCarthy, *McCarthyism: The Fight for America* (New York: Devin-Adair, 1952); Regnery and Garrity in Lately Thomas, *When Even Angels Wept: The Senator Joseph McCarthy Affair—A Story Without a Hero* (New York: William Morrow, 1973), pp. 304–5; Young in Borkin, *Robert R. Young*, p. 8; Kennedy in Koskoff, *Joseph P. Kennedy*, p. 364, and Whalen, *Founding Father*, p. 427.

15. Freda Utley, *Odyssey of a Liberal*, p. 278; Utley, undated vita, Villard Papers; Utley testimony, *New York Times*, May 2, 1950, p. 1, and Griffith, *Politics of Fear*, pp. 86–87.

16. F. Hanighen to J. T. Flynn, March 24, 1950, Flynn Papers; Morgenstern, "On Political Morality," *Human Events* 8 (October 17, 1951); J. T. Flynn to V. Kellums, September 2, 1952, Box 18, Flynn Papers; R. E. Wood to J. Howe, September 26, 1950, Box 1, Wood Papers.

17. P. La Follette to W. Evjue, April 13, 1951, Philip La Follette Papers; Lindbergh in Cole, *Lindbergh*, pp. 236–37; H. E. Barnes to W. L. Neumann, September 11, 1952, Neumann Papers; Dennis, *Appeal to Reason*, #210 (April 1, 1950).

18. Truman quoted in Thomas, p. 169, and in Theoharis, "The Politics of Scholarship: Liberals, Anti-Communism, and McCarthyism," in Griffith and Theoharis, *The Specter*, p. 278; Taft photo in Patterson, *Mr. Republican*, p. 466; *New York Times*, January 5, 1951, p. 7, and January 9, 1951, p. 14; Harriman, *New York Times*, July 11, 1952, p. 5.

19. John T. Flynn, "The Smear Terror" (pamphlet), (New York: published by the author, 1947); H. E. Barnes to W. L. Neumann, January 29, 1949, Neumann Papers. For an example of an old isolationist who saw no incongruity between opposing vilification of himself in the 1940s and his support of McCarthy in the 1950s, see Cole, *Nye*, p. 222.

20. Dwight D. Eisenhower, *The White House Years*, vol. 1: *Mandate for Change, 1953–1956* (New York: Signet, 1963), p. 39; Eisenhower, *At Ease: Stories I Tell to Friends* (Garden City, N.Y.: Doubleday, 1967), pp. 371–72; Patterson, *Mr. Republican*, pp. 483–84.

21. Vandenberg to Clare Boothe Luce (unsent), February 10, 1951, in *Private Papers*, p. 576. Among the old isolationists in the Eisenhower camp were Congressmen Hugh D. Scott, Jr., of Pennsylvania, Clifford Hope of Kansas, Charles Halleck of Indiana, and Senator Frank Carlson of Kansas.

22. For Eisenhower's liberal backing in 1948, see Mary S. McAuliffe, "The Red Scare and the Crisis in American Liberalism," Ph.D. diss., University of Maryland, 1972, pp. 89–98; Clifton Brock, *Americans for Democratic Action: Its Role in National Politics* (Washington, D.C.: Public Affairs Press, 1962), pp. 91–95. For his conservatism,

see Herbert S. Parmet, *Eisenhower and the American Crusades* (New York: Macmillan, 1972), p. 36.

23. Willkie and Dewey in Mayer, *Republican Party*, pp. 482–83; Mrs. Luce in Swanberg, *Luce and His Empire*, p. 323.

24. For Eisenhower on Taft, see Divine, *Presidential Elections*, vol. 2: *1952–1960*, p. 31.

25. Ben Jensen to General Douglas MacArthur, June 2, 1952, copy in the Papers of Hanford MacNider, Hoover Presidential Library; B. Fellers to H. Hoover, March 1, 1951, Box 31A, Hoover Papers; S. Morton to C. A. Evans, May 5, 1952, Morton Papers; Burdick, "Political Bee Bites Ike," *CR*, January 17, 1952, pp. A223–24; H. Regnery to Mrs. G. Patton, Jr., April 22, 1952, Box 80, copy in Hoover Papers.

26. F. Gannett to R. E. Wood, January 22, 1952, Box 19, Wood Papers; H. MacNider to W. E. Hall, March 14, 1952, MacNider Papers; J. T. Flynn, draft of letter to J. H. Gipson, no date, Box 18, Flynn Papers; Reece, *CR*, June 19, 1952, p. 7626.

27. Robert A. Taft, *A Foreign Policy for Americans* (Garden City, N.Y.: Doubleday, 1951), p. 119. For the appendix, see pp. 122–27.

28. Douglas MacArthur to R. A. Taft, November 19, 1951, MacArthur Papers; review of Utley, *Economic Council Review of Books* 9 (January 1952); review of Current, *Progressive* 16 (February 1952): 34; James Burnham, *Containment or Liberation?: An Inquiry into the Aims of United States Foreign Policy* (New York: John Day, 1953), p. 111; *Time* (review) 58 (November 26, 1951): 23–24; review of Robert Strauz-Hupé, *New Leader* 34 (December 10, 1951): 15–17; review of McGeorge Bundy, *Reporter* 5 (December 11, 1951): 37–39.

29. Taft, speech to the Women's National Republican Club of New York, January 26, 1952, *CR*, p. A869, and address over NBC radio, June 1, 1952, pp. A3410–11; Taft favoring use of Nationalist troops, *New York Times*, February 13, 1952, p. 21, February 15, 1952, p. 11; Taft on prisoners in Divine, *Presidential Elections*, 2: 10. For a critique of Taft's wavering on Indochina, see Arthur M. Schlesinger, Jr., "The New Isolationism," *Atlantic* 189 (May 1952): 34.

30. Taft, NBC radio address, *Congressional Record*, pp. A3410–11; *United States News and World Report* 32 (June 13, 1952): 98–101; idem, address to Zach Chandler Republican Club, Lansing, Michigan, April 16, 1952, *CR* p. A2549; Divine, *Presidential Elections*, 2: 10, 24, 30.

31. Mason, *CR*, Jan. 31, 1952, p. 729. The Illinois Citizens for Taft included such prominent contributors to the America First Committee as Lawrence Armour (who served as treasurer of the group), Edward A. Cudahy, Wade Fetzer, Jr., Clay Judson, Sterling Morton, and Edward L. Ryerson. Compare letterhead, Morton Papers, with Large Contributors File, AFC Papers. Among the national America First backers were B. K. Leach, Edwin S. Webster, Colonel Archie S. Roosevelt, and Robert H. Morse. Ernest Weir was in a decided minority among the old isolationists in contributing to the Eisenhower campaign. Boxes 979–980, Taft Papers; Barrow Lyons, "The Men Behind the Money," *Nation* 175 (July 5, 1952): 6–9. For the popular base of Taft's strength, see Lubell, *Future of American Politics*, p. 222.

32. Taber, interview, Columbia Oral History Collection, p. iii; Kennedy in Koskoff, *Joseph P. Kennedy*, p. 367; and Whalen, *Founding Father*, pp. 424–25; F. J. Libby to W. H. Regnery. June 30, 1952, NCPW Papers; McCormick in Trohan, *Political Animals*, pp. 272–77; Dennis, *Appeal to Reason*, #318 (April 26, 1952); L. Dennis to H. E. Barnes, July 7, 1952, Barnes Papers.

33. "Facing the Convention" (editorial), *Freemen* 2 (July 14, 1952): 683; "Who Likes Ike?" (editorial), ibid., 2 (April 21, 1952) 543–54; Forrest Davis, "Bob Taft's Dilemma," ibid.,2 (May 19, 1952): 527–30. For a brief history of the *Freeman*, see Nash, *Conservative Intellectual Movement*, pp. 27–28, 146–47.

34. MacArthur statement in Divine, *Presidential Elections*, 2: 11; Hoyt in *New York Times*, October 4, 1951, p. 36; Harriss's work discussed in R. E. Wood to F. Gannett, November 19, 1951, Box 19, Wood Papers; F. Gannett to D. MacArthur, January 21, 1952, copy in Wood Papers, Box 19; C. C. Tansill to H. E. Barnes, July 4, 1952, Barnes Papers; Case in Paul T. David, Malcolm Moos, and Ralph M. Goldman, *Presidential Nominating Politics in 1952*, vol. 4: *The Middle West* (Baltimore, Md.: The Johns Hopkins University Press, 1954), p. 264.

35. "First Choice" (editorial), *Progressive* 16 (April 1952): 3; J. H. Holmes to H. E. Barnes, May 27, 1952, Barnes Papers, acknowledges support for Douglas of both men. For Philip La Follette, see his letter to R. E. Wood, February 29, 1952, Philip La Follette Papers, and David, et al., *Presidential Nominating*, 4: 136.

36. Fish efforts in *New York Times*, January 1, 1952, p. 14, and April 24, 1952, p. 27; Butler in Paul, "Political Career," p. 362; Dirksen, *New York Times*, July 10, 1952, p. 12.

37. MacArthur's speech in *New York Times*, July 8, 1952, p. 18; Divine, *Presidential Elections*, 2: 33; MacArthur-Taft relations in Paterson, *Mr. Republican*, p. 549; Trohan, *Political Animals*, p. 280.

38. Hoover, "The Freedom of Men," *Vital Speeches* 18 (July 15, 1952): 583–86.

39. Taft, "Analysis of the Results of the Chicago Convention" (undated memorandum to prominent supporters), in MacArthur Papers; Coleman in Patterson, *Mr. Republican*, p. 550; W. L. Neumann to H. E. Barnes, July 15, 1952, Neumann Papers; Chodorov, "The July Verdict," *Human Events* 9 (April 9, 1952).

40. Reinhold Niebuhr, "The Republican Split on Foreign Policy," *New Leader* 35 (May 12, 1952): 16–17.

41. For material on the comparative strength of Taft and Eisenhower, see Patterson, *Mr. Republican*, p. 560; Divine, *Presidential Elections*, 2: 37; David, et al., *Presidential Nominating Politics in 1952*, Vol. 1: *The National Story*, p. 234.

42. F. J. Libby to W. H. Regnery, July 14, 1952, NCPW Papers; H. E. Barnes to W. L. Neumann, July 18, 1952, Neumann Papers; J. T. Flynn, rough draft of letter to J. H. Gipson, no date, Box 18, Flynn Papers; Dennis on witchhunting, letter to H. E. Barnes, October 6, 1952, Barnes Papers; Hart, "The Roots of Communism," *Economic Council Letter*, #298 (November 1, 1952).

43. Cole, *America First*, pp. 178–88; R. E. Wood to I. La Follette, December 18, 1944, Box 3, Wood Papers; American National Democratic Committee in *P.M.*, August 20, 1944, and October 19, 1944; minutes and contributors of American Action, testimony of Edward A. Hayes, October 15, 1946, *Hearings before the House Committee to Investigate Campaign Expenditures* (Washington, D.C.: U.S. Government Printing Office, 1946), pp. 210–19, 240–45. For the political role of American Action, R. E. Wood to J. T. Flynn, March 1, 1946, Box 20, Flynn Papers; R. E. Wood to S. Morton, March 26, 1947, and E. A. Hayes to S. Morton, July 14, 1948, Morton Papers.

44. H. Fish to W. Trohan, August 6, 1952, Box 4, Trohan Papers; *New York Times*, August 24, 1952, p. 1. The text of McCormick's speech is found in Waldrop, *McCormick of Chicago*, pp. 298–303. For Lodge, see *Chicago Daily News*, August 25, 1952. For third-party sentiment among the old isolationists, projected either before or after the election, see R. Harriss to R. R. McCormick, August 19, 1952, copy in Wood Papers, Box 4; Hanighen, "Not Merely Gossip," *Human Events* 9 (October 29, 1952); J. T. Flynn to R. E. Wood, September 9, 1952, Box 20, Flynn Papers; R. E. Wood to J. T. Flynn, September 15, 1952, Box 2, Wood Papers.

45. *New York Times*, September 5, 1952, p. 13, and October 26, 1952, p. 72.

46. Ibid., September 1, 1952, p. 8. Among the candidates endorsed by the Constitution Party were Senators McCarthy, Bricker, and William E. Jenner (Rep.–Ind.), and Congressman John F. Kennedy (Dem.–Mass.). The party was chaired by Mrs. Suzanne Silvercruys Stevenson and Percy L. Greaves, Jr. Mrs. Stevenson headed a small ultra-

nationalist group called the Minute Women of the U.S.A. Greaves, an economist by profession, had been minority counsel during the congressional investigation of Pearl Harbor. Mrs. Stevenson claimed that some of the national committee objected to her because she was a Roman Catholic and born overseas. Ibid., September 2, 1952, p. 17.

47. For material on the MacArthur movement, see Milton Friedman, "MacArthur Patriots," *Nation* 175 (July 19, 1952): 40; Hannah Bloom, "That MacArthur Draft," *Nation* 175 (October 4, 1952): 284; Arnold Forster and Benjamin R. Epstein, *Cross-Currents* (Garden City, N.Y.: Doubleday, 1956), pp. 54–61; Roy, *Apostles of Discord*, p. 21–24.

48. Morris Rubin, "Adlai, Warts and All" (editorial), *Progressive* 16 (October 1952): 3–5; Thomas in Johnpoll, *Pacifist's Progress*, p. 259; Smith, "Senator William Langer," p. 43.

49. Chamberlin, "Convention Bared Deep Split in GOP," *New Leader* 35 (July 21, 952): 18; memorandum from radio station WIBA, October 22–23, 1953, Philip La Follette Papers; S. Morton to H. F. Wade, August 18, 1952, Morton Papers; R. E. Wood to J. T. Flynn, September 15, 1952, Box 20, J. H. Gipson to J. T. Flynn, August 2, 1952, Box 18, J. H. Gipson to P. L. Greaves, Jr., August 2, 1952, copy in Flynn Papers, Box 18.

50. *New York Daily News*, July 11, 1952; Hoffman, *New York Times*, August 16, 1952, p. 6.

51. Patterson, *Mr. Republican*, pp. 577–79.

52. Hoover, *New York Times*, October 19, 1952, pp. 1, 78; Fish, *New York Times*, November 3, 1952, p. 24.

53. Divine, *Presidential Election*, 2: 50–51, 70–71; Graebner, *New Isolationism*, pp. 99–101; Parmet, *Eisenhower and the American Crusades*, p. 132.

54. Divine, *Presidential Elections*, 2: 82–85; Parmet, *Eisenhower and the American Crusades*, pp. 142–143; Caridi, *Korean War*, p. 207.

55. For Dulles and "have-not" nations, see John Foster Dulles, *War, Peace and Change* (New York: Harper, 1939), pp. 141–51. For Dulles and the NCPW, see the Dulles file, NCPW Papers. For Dulles and America First, see J. F. Dulles to W. R. Castle, November 8, 1940, Castle Papers. His wife, Janet, gave to the America First Committee. See Large Contributors File, AFC Papers.

56. For the Taft-Dulles relationship, see Divine, *Presidential Elections*, 2: 26–27; Elson, *World of Time Inc.*, 2: 305–6; *Eisenhower and the American Crusades*, p. 122; Richard Goold-Adams, *The Time of Power: A Reappraisal of John Foster Dulles* (London: Weidenfeld and Nicholson, 1962), p. 63; Patterson, *Mr. Republican*, p. 583.

57. S. Morton to G. L. Eskew, November 25, 1952, Morton Papers; Hanighen, "Not Merely Gossip," *Human Events* 9 (November 16, 1952). For Hanighen's own role with America First, see R. D. Stuart, Jr. to R. E. Wood, March 12, 1941, Box 18, Stuart Folder, AFC Papers.

58. McCormick in Trohan, *Political Animals*, p. 288; Dennis, *Appeal to Reason*, #348 (November 22, 1952); W. L. Neumann to H. E. Barnes, January 17, 1953, Neumann Papers; J. T. Flynn to R. E. Wood, December 18, 1952, Box 20, Flynn Papers.

59. Eisenhower inaugural, January 20, 1953, in *Vital Speeches* 19 (February 1, 1953): 252–54; C. C. Tansill to H. E. Barnes, February 30, 1953, Barnes Papers; "Inaugural Address" (editorial), *Chicago Tribune*, January 21, 1953; F. C. Smith to G. H. Cless, Jr., July 18, 1953, Box 20, the Papers of Frederick C. Smith, Ohio Historical Society.

60. Hanighen, "Not Merely Gossip," *Human Events* 9 (November 5, 1952).

# 12

# A Permanent Loss:
# The Advent of Eisenhower, 1953-1954

Despite the apprehension of such people as Hanighen, some actions of the new government could not help but gratify the followers of Senator Taft. In his first State of the Union Address, Eisenhower announced the removal of the United States Seventh Fleet from the Straits of Taiwan. It was a symbolic gesture, but one that appeared to aid any Nationalist military campaign on the Chinese mainland. Then, as if to confirm McCarthy's charges of Communist infiltration, the new administration doggedly pursued Owen Lattimore, dismissed China specialist John Paton Davies from the diplomatic service, and vigorously prosecuted an executive order aimed at clearing the State Department of "security risks."[1]

The Eisenhower government also gave the impression of altering defense policies. In December 1953 Dulles—sounding a bit like Hoover during the Great Debate—issued a solemn warning: unless the European alliance integrated West Germany into its ranks, the United States might be forced into an "agonizing reappraisal" of its commitments. A month later the Secretary stressed that any new aggression would be met by "massive retaliatory power." Although Dulles was merely reiterating Truman policy, and specifically denied that limited aggression would be met by general war, his stress upon air and sea power seemed, at first glance, to fulfill the strategic visions of both Hoover and Taft.[2]

For many old isolationists, there could be other reasons for enthusiasm. To please Taft, Eisenhower appointed Admiral Arthur Radford, a strong exponent of the air-sea strategy, as Chairman of the Joint Chiefs. The President's "New Look" in defense strategy combined strong superiority in nuclear weapons with cutbacks in the number of ground troops. If it appeared to limit American options to a response of "all or nothing," it promised (so pundits said) "more bang for the buck." Domestically Taft exerted such control over the new Republican Congress, placing his followers in the most crucial spots, that it looked as if Eisenhower's election victory in 1952 might have been a Pyrrhic one.[3]

Yet most old isolationists had little reason to remain jubilant. Foreign aid, high taxes, conscription, an unbalanced budget—all indicated that the Eisenhower Presidency might simply be continuing the most "destructive" policies of the Truman regime. Although Taft had agreed to serve as the administration's "first mate," he still demanded that Europeans contribute far more to their own defense and that American forces bomb Manchuria and blockade China.[4]

Eisenhower's election weakened much opposition to the executive. Such legislators as Dirksen, Bender, and Taber radically shifted their position, Taber going so far as to support the President on over seventy-five percent of all roll calls.[5] Indeed, in light of Eisenhower's growing hold on the Republican party, conservatives among the old isolationists were, at best, merely winning a few last skirmishes. On major issues they spoke out with little chance of being heard: they might warn that the Korean truce of 1953 betrayed the entire American war effort and contained seeds of further aggression; they might attempt to prevent Senate censuring of Senator McCarthy; they might seek to organize a nationalist action group; they might promote Senate adoption of the Bricker Amendment, a measure that, they believed, could curtail future inroads on the country's sovereignty; and they might speak out against possible military involvement in Indochina. In each of these efforts, however, they were either ignored or unsuccessful. And in opposing American action in Southeast Asia, veteran isolationists constituted such a small part of the general opposition that it remains doubtful whether they had any distinctive impact. With their ranks diminished by age and electoral defeat, they were losing, and losing rapidly.

The new administration first sought to end the Korean War. The President-elect, returning from the battlefront in December 1952, called for meeting the enemy with "deeds—executed under circumstances of our own choosing." Then, during the truce negotiations, Dulles spoke of giving the Chinese "one hell of a licking" and hinted about Chiang's return to the mainland. In May 1953 the Secretary issued a warning to Peking: America would use atomic weapons if the Chinese Communists continued to stall on the disputed prisoner issue. Dulles's threat, a more modified United States position concerning the prisoners, the death of Stalin—all undoubtedly played some role in the Communist desire to end the fighting. By late July a military armistice was signed.[6]

Even before the truce was made, several old isolationists feared an "appeasement peace." Langer assailed America's allies for opposing action beyond the Yalu. Mrs. Utley compared Eisenhower unfavorably to Neville Chamberlain: whereas at Munich the British Prime Minister had merely given Sudeten Germans the right to self-determination, the President—she said—was delivering half of Korea to the aggressors. In Taft's last public address, written less than a month and a half before his death, the Ohio Senator found the pending settlement "extremely unsatisfactory." Although he reluctantly endorsed a truce, he warned that such a peace would sanction the artificial division of Korea, create continued instability, and release a million Chinese soldiers for use against Formosa or Indochina. And since the United Nations had failed in Korea, America must in the future reserve "a completely free hand" in Asia.[7]

Other old isolationists, however, expressed relief that the war was coming to an end. Widening the conflict, said Morley, would merely increase casualties. Bender called the peace "welcome news": notice had been successfully served that aggression would be resisted. "We have," commented Vorys, "taught the Communists a bloody lesson in Korea."[8]

A few others among the old isolationists were more ambivalent. Gratification that the war was finally over was mixed with bitterness and fear. The truce, establishing a demilitarized zone slightly north of the thirty-eighth parallel, appeared too unstable, too ambivalent. Dewey Short maintained that the United States could still have gained a military victory. Sterling Morton called the Korean armistice "one of the most unsavory documents our country has ever been called on to sign." The *Washington Times-Herald* felt forced to ask: "We have tied ourselves up in combat for 3 years, sacrificed the blood of some of the finest of America's young men, and wasted $15 billion. For what?" To Congressman Shafer, Korea was "a tragic and ignominious defeat."[9]

To many old isolationists, the fate of Senator McCarthy was equally worrisome. Herbert Hoover spoke for far more than himself when he called McCarthy's reelection to the Senate in 1952 "a victory for the American people." General Wood had financed a nationally televised speech in which McCarthy predicted that Governor Stevenson would continue the "suicidal Kremlin-directed policies of this nation." Flynn endorsed the Senator's attacks upon British trade with Communist China, telling radio listeners: "God bless Joe McCarthy."[10]

As the Wisconsin Senator faced increasing attack from the Eisenhower administration, and finally censure from the Senate, various old isolationists rallied behind him. Morley, Hanighen, Chodorov, O'Donnell, and Trohan signed petitions accusing the press of bias. Henry Regnery printed a defense of McCarthy by two young journalists, William F. Buckley, Jr., and L. Brent Bozell. The National Economic Council served as a clearing house for contributions offered by McCarthy backers. Far more veteran isolationists among the Senate Republicans voted against the censure than voted for it. (All Democrats, including such World War II isolationists as Edwin C. Johnson and Gillette, voted for censure.)[11]

Wood, Fish, MacNider, Flynn—these and others came to McCarthy's defense. Wheeler compared McCarthy's efforts to his own exposé of Teapot Dome almost thirty years earlier: "When you are dealing with crooks and spies, you have to be tough." Even the pacifist Libby vaguely asserted that the Senator had "rendered the country an important service." Occasionally his cause manifested symbolic continuity with the isolationism of 1940 and 1941, as shown by the "America First" signs prominent at one pro-McCarthy rally in New York. A reporter noted many in the audience who had been active in the America First Committee.[12]

A minority of old isolationists remained suspicious of McCarthy. Dennis had found the Senator effective in disrupting national unity, and hence one who weakened possibilities for renewed war. Later, however, he claimed to share Barnes's "contempt and loathing for the late Joe." Morley said that McCarthy, once zealous in fighting subversives, was tending "to regard himself as judge, jury, and lord high executioner." Morton feared that Eisenhower was adopting the "New Deal socialist point of view," but asserted that the Senator was stupid to have attacked the President directly. William R. Castle noted numerous resignations from the government and claimed that McCarthy had done "infinite harm here and abroad." Bender, reflecting a growing impatience among the leadership of his party, called McCarthyism "a synonym for witch-hunting, star-chamber methods and the denial of those civil liberties which have distinguished our country in its historic growth."[13]

It was, however, General Wood who probably represented the majority of old isolationists when he mourned the loss of McCarthy, who died in 1957. The Senator, wrote Wood to his widow, had been "a patriotic and courageous American"; his passing signified "a great loss to our country."[14] Such veteran isolationists would still support occasional efforts to "cleanse" the nation of "subversion," but never again would the attempt to "purge" be so intense or so passionate.

The Eisenhower victory, followed by the Korean truce and the administration attack on McCarthy, caused staunch conservatives to foster a new nationalistic organization. In December 1952 Colonel McCormick, finding the President "as bad as we expected," called for an action committee with the working title "The Committee for the American Form of Government." A year later General Wood saw a new party as the only solution, and early in 1954 Flynn suggested a right-wing "Politbureau" composed of a few people "schooled" in new methods of "social warfare."[15]

On May 7, 1954, McCormick announced the formation of a group entitled For America. The organization was extremely conservative in domestic policy, stressing the themes of limited government and states rights, and was isolationist in overseas affairs. "Enlightened nationalism," its initial manifesto proclaimed, was far superior to "our costly, imperialistic foreign policy of tragic super-interventionism, and policing the world single-handed with American blood and treasure." Although the body sought armed forces sufficient in strength "to protect our sovereignty and rights of our citizens throughout all the world," it opposed "so-called preventive wars, or 'police actions.'" "Our American boys," it continued, should not have to "fight all over the world without the consent of Congress." One brochure of For America pleaded its cause: "If our sons and daughters are to be saved from compulsory military service and death in the rice paddies of Asia or the bloody plains of Europe, we—today—will have to save them."[16]

A skeleton organization was established, with General Wood and Dean Clarence Manion of Notre Dame Law School named co-chairmen, and with such longtime isolationists as Flynn on the organizing committee. In November the group selected General Fellers as director. Initial blueprints were grandiose, with provision made for women, labor, and youth divisions. Further plans included autonomous state units (patterned after the Veterans of Foreign Wars and the Daughters of the American Revolution), a central policymaking board, research divisions in Chicago and Washington, a speakers' bureau, films, field workers, billboards, radio broadcasts, and a book club.[17]

Within a month after it was organized, For America received over 5,000 telegrams and letters from prospective members as well as an equal number of telephone calls. Soon afterwards Fellers outlined a foreign policy program that included air supremacy, counterinsurgency within the Soviet Union, full reliance upon hemispheric resources, and avoidance of all regional wars.[18]

The group, however, soon suffered from personality conflicts and faltering leadership, and made relatively little impact upon the country. Sterling Morton resigned from For America's national committee on the grounds that he was never consulted; Manion, he said, was more concerned with speaking against the "socialist menace" than with tending to vital details of organization. Burton K. Wheeler, whose wife was on the national committee, commented that McCormick had been singularly inept in administering the *Washington Times-Herald,* which the Chicago publisher had bought in 1947. Hence he, Wheeler, was suspicious of any organization the Colonel sponsored. Hamilton Fish soon broke from For America, declaring that its renunciation of political activity made it "totally useless." The organization, he declared, involved only "a few rich men" who contributed "large sums of tax-exempt money to finance this educational organization." Fish's own efforts to establish a conservative, isolationist group, to be called the American Political Action Committee, fared no better.[19]

Fish's judgment might have been a bit harsh. The group supplied Congressman Otto Passman (Dem.–La.), a powerful House figure, with arguments against foreign aid, promoted the Bricker Amendment, and was almost solely responsible for the presidential nomination of T. Coleman Andrews of Virginia in 1956 on the States Rights ticket. To be sure, For America, as Dean Manion himself later commented, was staffed with far more "Chiefs" than "Indians" and fell far short of the dreams of its founders.[20]

Far more concerted isolationist efforts centered on the Bricker Amendment, first introduced into the Senate in 1951 by Senator John Bricker. As Governor of Ohio from 1939 to 1945, Bricker had been able to skirt much of the debate over intervention. In 1940 and 1941 he confined his comments on foreign policy to uncontroversial demands for a strong national defense. Handsome, silver-haired, and an excellent orator, Bricker was chosen as Dewey's running mate in 1944, at which point he accused the Democrats of covering up the Pearl Harbor issue.[21] Elected to the Senate in 1946, Bricker supported the Marshall Plan and the Atlantic Pact, but opposed the Truman Doctrine and MAP. In 1951 he voted to limit the number of American troops that the President could send to Europe.

The formal history of the Bricker Amendment is complicated, for a highly technical debate over the status of treaty law was soon turned into an impassioned controversy over the entire course of the country's foreign policy. When presented to the Senate in January 1953, the Amendment bore the sponsorship of some sixty-four Senators. It sought to restrict presidential authority in policymaking and had three main features: no part of any treaty that overrode the Constitution would be binding upon Americans; treaties would become law only "through legislation which would be valid in the absence of a treaty"; and Congress would have the authority to impose the same restrictions upon presidential executive agreements that it did upon treaties. The legislation had originally been drafted by Frank E. Holman, Seattle attorney and president of the American Bar Association in 1948–49. Because Holman particularly feared the United Nations Covenant of Human Rights, which contained a worldwide call for welfare measures, Eisenhower mused that the bar leader seemed determined to "save the United States from Eleanor Roosevelt."[22]

To many old isolationists, the Bricker Amendment transcended academic speculation; it involved restoring political autonomy to the nation. Once the Amendment passed, so they argued, the country could no longer surrender its sovereignty. Both the Constitution and the Bill of Rights would remain inviolate. Dean Manion, a leading proponent of the Amendment, later claimed that it would have served as "a visible shield against the direct or indirect management of our domestic affairs by foreign governments." With such issues at stake, Bricker's proposal—in Manion's eyes—became "the hottest question since the Civil War."[23]

The Bricker Amendment was debated for well over a year. It underwent several versions, with Senators Watkins and Walter George (Dem.–Ga.) offering drafts favored by isolationists and Senators Knowland and Ferguson presenting versions sponsored by the administration. Eisenhower and Dulles, acting in the hope that opposition could be quelled, supported innocuous forms of the Amendment. Both men, however, strongly opposed any hint that Congress should pass on executive agreements; neither believed that individual states of the Union should validate a treaty in order for it to serve as internal law. Langer, chairman of the Senate Judiciary Committee, tried to straddle the isssue, but to no avail.[24]

The Amendment was finally defeated in February 1954, but only by a one-vote margin. It was never voted upon again and, after Bricker failed to be reelected in 1958, the issue was dropped.

Bricker's proposal alarmed interventionists. Dana Converse Backus, chairman of the committee on international law of the New York City Bar

Association, argued that such an amendment would have blocked the 1783 treaty ending the Revolutionary War, and would also have outlawed the Baruch Plan over 150 years later. It could still, warned Backus, restrict defense coordination with Canada, and restrict it even if the hemisphere was invaded. Wiley called the Amendment "pro-Communist," for it served, he claimed, to incapacitate the President.[25]

Such defenders as Dean Manion accused the administration of deliberately misrepresenting its terms. For example, he denied that the Amendment required treaties to be ratified by all forty-eight states. Bricker's proposal, he continued, gave no new powers to the states; it neither affected the war powers of Congress nor impaired congressional action in such areas as atomic energy or narcotics. The President reserved his prerogatives as Commander-in-Chief of the armed forces and therefore could still have initiated the Berlin airlift, administered the occupation of Japan and Germany, and made a truce in Korea.[26]

To some of the more extreme among the old isolationists, the power of the United Nations alone revealed the need for such legislation. The world organization, as they saw it, was part of a global plot designed to destroy American sovereignty. Garet Garrett, who wrote isolationist editorials for the *Saturday Evening Post* in 1941, feared that a race riot in Detroit or the lynching of an American black would hold the United States accountable before an international court. Colonel McCormick accused the UN of seeking to enforce polygamy in the United States, going so far as to claim that the UN Convention on Genocide, which sought to outlaw mass extermination of entire nationalities, would render such literature as the New Testament illegal. Congressman Usher Burdick agreed, asserting that any American who made a derogatory remark about any minority group might find himself facing trial outside the nation.[27]

The debate over the Bricker Amendment only added to anti-UN hostility. Morley, finding similarities between the UN Declaration of Human Rights and the Russian Constitution of 1936, claimed that Communists were indirectly trying to write American laws. Senator McCarran told his colleagues that he would regret voting for the UN Charter as long as he lived. The United Nations, of course, was not the only source of contention, for memories of the Crimean conference and Potsdam still rankled. Dirksen, for example, boasted that the Amendment, by requiring Congress to ratify all executive agreements, could prevent future Yaltas.[28]

Old isolationists pointed frequently, and with much alarm, to the Supreme Court decision of *Missouri* vs. *Holland* (1920), in which Justice Oliver Wendell Holmes, in ruling on a case of migratory birds from Canada, declared that treaty law transcended the enumerated powers of Congress. Senator Wiley mused, "Today I heard a great flow of words from our distinguished friend from Illinois. When he was through, I saw that bird flying out from Louisiana, over various states, through Missouri, and, behold, it was shot. I heard the gun." Also disturbing was the case of *United States* vs. *Pink* (1942). Here the Supreme Court held that certain executive agreements could be enforced as internal law. In addition, there were the so-called Status-of-Forces agreements, a series of treaties that permitted the occasional trial of American servicemen in foreign courts. An ambitious federal government, isolationists feared, could use treaty law as an instrument to gain unlimited power. As William Henry Chamberlin expressed the issue, "Treaties can be traps."[29]

Veteran isolationists fought hard for the Bricker Bill. The Committee for Constitutional Government, a foe of lend-lease in 1941, issued "Spotlight" bulletins by Garrett and Chodorov. For part of his argument, Chodorov pointed to the Greek Ionian League as evidence that "an internationalist government must be absolutist in character." Barnes criticized the American Civil Liberties Union for opposing the Amendment. Dean Manion announced his resignation as chairman of Eisenhower's Commission on Intergovernmental Relations, a group designed to eliminate waste in federal-state affairs, and, in so doing, Manion claimed that he had been fired because he had been vocal in supporting the Amendment. Hart suggested that the President was surrounded by a secret band of internationalists who were plotting against both the Amendment and the Constitution. General Wood felt so strongly about the need for it that he endorsed a pro-Amendment tract by the anti-Semitic pamphleteer Elizabeth Dilling. Dennis, in endorsing the proposal, commented, "Anything to obstruct or paralyze American world leadership into a Third World War we are inclined to favor."[30]

On the surface, the sentiment for the Bricker Amendment marked the peak of Cold War anti-interventionism. Never again would the aging group of old isolationists be so able to mobilize its forces with such strength and passion. The debate itself, however, involved much shadowboxing, revealing more than anything else the desire to "punish" and "repudiate" the Roosevelt administration. The United States never ratified the Genocide Convention, the isolationists' classic example of a foreign pitfall. Although Amendment proponents stressed the need to preserve the powers of the legislative branch, the Senate—as was seen in the League fight of 1919–20— had not always been docile as far as treaties were concerned. Manion himself admitted that the Amendment left many presidential powers intact. Even had it passed, the Bricker Amendment might have been only a small and symbolic victory.

Already, as For America was being planned and as the Bricker Amendment was being debated, Communist forces were gaining power in Southeast Asia. During the spring of 1954 the crisis remained relatively small, with most old isolationists concurring with their fellow countrymen in opposing direct United States participation.

America's long and painful involvement with Vietnam had begun during the Truman administration. As early as 1946 the United States was supplying military equipment to French troops fighting the guerrilla forces of Ho Chi Minh. In February 1950 the National Security Council reported that the fall of Indochina would place all Southeast Asia in grave peril. Although the Korean War accelerated American aid, it soon became obvious that the

United States could not prevent the French from being routed. By early 1954 Vietminh insurgents controlled over half the countryside, and Washington appeared to be moving toward war. On April 3, in a secret conference with selected congressional leaders, Dulles and Admiral Radford sought a resolution authorizing the use of American air and naval power. Radford and the Air Chief of Staff, General Nathan Twining, spoke in terms of massive air strikes, including the use of 60 B-29s, 150 fighter escorts, and three small tactical atomic bombs. Two days later the National Security Council endorsed "nothing short of military victory in Indochina" and, within two weeks, Vice President Richard M. Nixon commented that the nation should risk "putting our boys in."[31]

Eisenhower, however, opposed involvement and the United States took no substantive action. After another month the major French fortress of Dien Bien Phu fell and in mid-July, at the Geneva Conference, the defeated French recognized Ho's control over northern Vietnam. The United States did not sign the agreements; instead it unilaterally endorsed free elections and vaguely vowed to oppose any renewal of aggression. In September 1954 the United States sponsored the South East Asia Treaty Organization (SEATO), an eight-power pact that—among other pro-visions—pledged each member to consider a direct attack upon Vietnam as a danger to its own "peace and safety." No major Asian power signed the agreement, which was limited to the United States, Britain, France, Australia, New Zealand, Thailand, the Philippines, and Pakistan. After Dulles assured the Senate that American forces could be used only after Congress observed all "constitutional processes," the Senate approved the treaty eighty-two to one. The war scare had been a brief one. For the moment the Indochina crisis appeared to reveal an administration success-fully committed to both containment and peace.[32]

Even before the Korean War broke out, a few old isolationists had been wary of possible commitments to Indochina. In May 1950 Congress-man Hoffman warned that the State Department was going to conscript United States troops for Southeast Asia. Bruce Barton, pointing to the Vietnamese Emperor Bao Dai, said, "We are hooked up with a rascal whom no self-respecting American would trust for 5 minutes with his daughter or his dough." Once the Korean conflict began Flynn feared that untold dollars and lives would be lost to stop "an ex-communist agent named Ho Chi Minh," and in October 1950 Dennis warned that "Indo-China is now beckoning thousands of Americans to fresh dug graves." Morton compared the Vietminh forces to the beleaguered colonial armies of George Washington, with the Chinese Communists who aided them playing a part similar to Lafayette's and Rochambeau's. Although in February 1952 Taft had hinted at diversionary action in Indochina, he always opposed the use of United States troops. As he entered a New York hospital just before his death, he left a note on his desk that read: "No Indo-China—Except in case of emergency invasion by the Chinese."[33]

During the crisis of April 1954 several old isolationists began voicing the fear that the United States would soon be fighting in Southeast Asia. John O'Donnell commented, "Hold your hats, boys and girls; it looks as if we are starting on another ride." Flynn favored giving Dulles "a gun and sending him over there." Pettengill called the Republicans "the new war party." General MacNider wrote his old friend, Senator Hickenlooper, "Keep us out of Indo-China, for God's sakes, unless we are willing to put on an all-out atomic bomb war against the Chinese and some selected Soviet centers."[34]

Eisenhower and Dulles, so such old anti-interventionists argued, were behaving similarly to Roosevelt in the months before Pearl Harbor. Chodorov, now editor of the *Freeman,* saw "the return of 1940." Neumann feared more talk of "all steps short of war." Barnes declared that "the Indo-China mess is reviving Frankie's old formula." Libby accused Dulles of risking "the final war of our civilization" in hopes of destroying China. Although Dulles had once contributed generously to the NCPW, Libby called for the Secretary's resignation.[35]

To such veteran isolationists, involvement was both ruinous and futile. Senator Butler asked, "If three years of fighting in Korea resulted in a stalemate, how many years of fighting would be required to drive all the Communists out of Indochina?" The *Progressive* cited John F. Kennedy, now Democratic Senator from Massachusetts, who warned of hostility from the indigenous population. When General Charles A. Willoughby, a former MacArthur aide, spoke about ways of securing Southeast Asia, Dennis claimed that such a topic could just as well be entitled "How to Hold North America for the British Crown." Congressman Lawrence Smith declared that war in Indochina could well mark "the end of the Republican Party." Smith's own alternative to the Indochinese war included the severing of all trade and diplomatic relations with Russia and Communist China. Hanighen—fearing that the United States would gradually be drawn into the "fruitless quagmire" of "another Korea"—mused, "Why couldn't the State Department have chosen a temperate zone for a change?"[36]

To some old isolationists, the Indochina war was fundamentally a colonial struggle and, as such, symbolized the very Old World oppression that America had long opposed. As in the case of their opposition to the British loan almost a decade earlier, the theme of "anti-imperialism" took precedence over "anti-Communism." The United States, said Congressman Burdick, would be "fighting against the people who are struggling for liberty." Garrett found the United States siding with Britain and France, "the two most hated colonial powers in Asia," and reminded readers of *Human Events* that "the white man" was already defeated on that continent. America, commented Dennis, was bound to lose any conflict with the "colored world." "We can't pick the winner," he said, "for the winner will not pick us." Similarly, as Eisenhower spoke of falling dominoes, Flynn remarked, "How silly can politicians get? The Reds already have Asia." Tansill, fearing another "police action," claimed that it would be hard to justify French colonial administration if France itself would not really fight.[37]

No old isolationist stressed the colonial issue more than Edwin C. Johnson. "American GI's," he declared, should not be sent "into the mud and muck of Indochina on a blood-letting spree to perpetuate colonialism and white man's exploitation in Asia." Such a war, said Johnson, would be "the most foolhardy venture in all American history," involving 500,000 casualties, costing $100 billion, and lasting ten years. Eventually "the brown and Malay races" would be driven into the arms of the Communists, and a collective assault upon the white race would "destroy all civilization."[38]

In addition some veteran isolationists denied that Southeast Asia was vital, either economically or ideologically, to the United States. Clare E. Hoffman could not understand why "the most productive, most powerful nation . . . sends its Armed Forces halfway around the world to participate in a defensive war." Of course, the Michigan Congressman caustically remarked, an Indochinese war would eliminate America's productive surplus as well as provide business for casket-makers. "I think," said General MacNider, "we can manage to get along without the benighted corner of the world." Flynn queried, "I would like to know who in Asia is going to cross the Pacific Ocean and attack us." Chodorov found it ridiculous to assume that the Vietnamese carried "an ideological germ that threatens our way of life." America, he said, should work at "killing" the idea of Communism (which he defined as the right of the individual to own property), but let "all natives live." General Fellers feared that the United States had overextended itself at the Geneva conference, and warned that efforts to guarantee the 17th parallel involved "a heavy commitment a long way from home in a hostile country."[39]

Frank Hanighen went so far as to deny that a non-Communist Indochina could prevent Communist infiltration of Burma and Thailand, for the Communists, he said, already controlled Tibet and had in India's Prime Minister Nehru "a docile spokesman." Challenging the argument that the United States needed the resources of Southeast Asia, Hanighen maintained that America already possessed large reserves of both rubber and tin.[40]

These critics found SEATO involving equally serious risks. Flynn called the agreement "as crazy a scheme as has ever been invented for mischief." The alliance, he said, would commit American "military and naval forces to guarantee the colonial grabs of England and France." General Fellers called the pact a "white man's collective security arrangement" at a time when "all Asia is sick of white domination." Langer, the one Senator to vote against SEATO, feared that some "trigger-happy, warmongering, fascist" President would send troops to the "swamps and jungles" of Southeast Asia; the United States would merely have turned over the initiative to Communists, who would continually generate crises throughout the world.[41]

A few old isolationists offered alternatives. Hanighen suggested large-scale military aid to Chiang. If Communist China still threatened Southeast Asia, the editor called for blockading the Chinese coast and ominously pointed to "something else." (Atomic diplomacy apparently was far from dead.) Far better, commented Fellers, to have a "Free Asia Treaty Organization" headed by the Philippine leader Ramon Magsaysay and including South Korea, Nationalist China, and Japan.[42]

The Indochina crisis signified one of the few times that many old isolationists were in accord with their fellow countrymen. Debates on the

Senate floor indicated little popular enthusiasm for open involvement in Vietnam. Congressional leaders meeting with Dulles and Radford on April 3, including Senate minority leader Lyndon B. Johnson (Dem.–Tex.), stressed that full-scale intervention must be contingent upon total independence for France's colonial wards and their own ability to continue the fight.[43] Such veteran isolationists, no longer enamored of risky Asian involvements, had simply drawn from their traditional ideology in order to reinforce the nation's sentiments. They had seen their country "burned" in Korea, and they had no desire to see it burned again. As in the case of the Atlantic Pact, the remaining handful of liberal isolationists joined with conservatives to oppose the Indochina involvement. The *Progressive* and Harry Elmer Barnes were as staunch in their opposition as Congressman Hoffman and John T. Flynn. For a brief period the dying breed of World War II isolationists—both left and right—had all returned home.

The Indochina crisis, the debate over the Bricker Amendment, the abortive efforts to organize For America—these were the last concerted efforts of many old isolationists. The death of Taft in July 1953 cost them their most powerful and articulate leader; the death of Colonel McCormick in April 1955 deprived them of their strongest voice in the world of newspaper publishing. After the elections of 1952 only five veteran isolationists still remained in the Senate, and by 1954 only three of these five survived.[44]

Similarly, fewer than forty veteran isolationists stayed in the House. If some of those remaining in Congress still fought administration trade and mutual security programs, they could little alter the fundamental direction of American foreign policy. And if some denounced their President and titular head of their party as a "false Republican" and one lacking the "proper" nationalism, they knew full well that they could never prevent Eisenhower's renomination. The President—by purging McCarthy with skill, promoting conservative domestic policies, and avoiding international confrontations—had reduced their already dwindling ranks even further.

A few old isolationists occasionally spoke out. Some, such as Freda Utley and William Henry Chamberlin, opposed Eisenhower's efforts to reach some accommodation with the Communists. Others, such as Lawrence Dennis and Ernest T. Weir, endorsed that very accommodation. Weir commented, "It is not the mission of the United States to go charging about the world to free it from bad nations and bad systems of government." Activities were sporadic. General Wood attempted to raise money for underground operations within Russia, suggesting that a total of $40,000, given by ten corporate leaders, could initiate an internal revolution! General Fellers wrote a book finding peace dependent upon atomic weapons and "our air ramparts." Conservative isolationists were prominent in a score of small organizations designed to promote rightist domestic policies and a strident nationalism—the Campaign for the 48 States, the Committee of Endorsers, America's Future, Inc., the Congress of Freedom,

Facts Forum, the Citizens Foreign Aid Committee, and lesser groups that seldom got past drafting a letterhead.[45]

Yet, as they weakened in ranks and power, protests from old isolationist voices became increasingly scattered. During the 1955 crisis over China's offshore islands, Morton asked: "What business is it of ours whether Chiang or Mao rules Formosa?" Langer was so apprehensive over the Taiwan issue that he asked that it be entrusted to the very United Nations he had condemned four years before. In 1956 a few remaining veteran isolationists opposed American involvement in the Middle East crisis of 1956. When McCarthy supported Britain, France, and Israel in their invasion of Egypt, Flynn cabled the Senator: "I feel we have lost a great captain." Dennis called the Eisenhower Doctrine of 1957—pledging military support for Middle East states—a "really fool-proof dependable formula for perpetual war." The outbreak of the Berlin crisis in 1961 led Hamilton Fish to call for a disarmed and neutralized Germany with free access to Berlin. (Fish did, however, believe that Fidel Castro's control of Cuba threatened hemispheric security and sought his overthrow.)[46]

Survivors among the old isolationists, following through on warnings dating back to 1952, pointed to the Vietnam conflict of the 1960s as the logical consequence of continued intervention. Nye invoked Washington's Farewell Address against "one of the nastiest wars of all time." Wheeler, finding the costly involvement resulting only in "contempt and ridicule" for the United States, claimed that the majority of Americans remained isolationists. Barnes called Vietnam "criminal idiocy," a "hypocritical and sugar-coated" attempt to maintain the "white man's burden." In 1968 the revisionist historian endorsed Senator George S. McGovern for President, reasoning that the South Dakota Democrat took a stronger anti-war position than did Senator Eugene McCarthy. General MacNider saw the Indochina war as the latest example of American "meddling"; the United States, he said, should either "stomp hell out of them and get it over with, or get out." To Dennis, Vietnam marked the final reckoning. After a "long and brilliant record of success" in empire-building, America's time had come.[47]

Some comparisons may be drawn between many conservative isolationists and the Goldwater movement of the 1960s. Both groups shared a belief in limited government and a unilateral foreign policy. Both possessed much support in the rural Middle West (with Goldwater far stronger in the South) and among small businessmen. Both shared an antipathy toward the cultural values and commercial ties of the eastern seaboard. In 1952 Senator Barry Goldwater (Rep.–Ariz.) had personally favored Taft's nomination. However, as a delegate to the Chicago convention, he voted for Eisenhower on the grounds that Arizona's pro-Taft faction had acted in a high-handed manner. In Congress Goldwater backed the Bricker Amendment, called for overwhelming air superiority, and claimed that the United Nations and European allies hampered America's Cold War efforts.

In both 1960 and 1964, Goldwater's bid for the Presidency received the support of a good number of conservatives among the remaining old isolationists.[48]

Such mutuality, however, should not hide strong differences, for Goldwater was far more militant in foreign policy than most old isolationists had been. He ardently supported NATO, opposed United States "retreat" anywhere in the world, and pointedly asked, "Why not victory?" His rhetoric did not center on insulating the United States from global commitments; rather, it denoted defending an outer perimeter that encircled the globe. For example, Goldwater wrote in 1960, "We must always try to engage the enemy at times and places, and with weapons, of our own choosing." Dennis could only note with irony that Goldwater's interventionism "would have gone over big before World War II."[49]

Distinctions also existed between many old isolationists and William F. Buckley, Jr., editor of *National Review*. Buckley came from an outspoken isolationist family and had supported America First as a youth. When *National Review* was founded in 1955 such veteran isolationists as Mrs. Utley, Chamberlin, and Chodorov wrote for the journal. Buckley, however, was far more influenced by the conservative political scientist Willmoore Kendall and the former Trotskyist commentator James Burnham. Dennis noted that the young editor had no use for the doctrine of absolute neutrality; Morley claimed that such ideologues as Burnham were so absolutist that if they ever gained power they would simply substitute one form of totalitarianism for another. When Flynn submitted an article criticizing "the military racket," he soon found Buckley returning his manuscript.[50]

As with Buckley, there was occasional continuity between some old isolationists and the John Birch Society. Robert Welch, the candy manufacturer who founded the Society in 1958, had been sympathetic to the America First Committee. An ardent nationalist, he strongly admired General MacArthur and in 1952 wanted Taft as President. One national committeeman of America First, Dean Manion, served on the national council of the John Birch Society. Such old isolationists as General Fellers, Gipson, and Hart were listed among the Society's Committee of Endorsers. The Society, a far weaker organization than America First, stressed several themes that had been voiced by many veteran isolationists: recall of NATO troops from Europe, hostility toward the United Nations, an end to massive foreign aid programs, Pearl Harbor revisionism, and the purging of "subversives" and "communist sympathizers." However, as with the followers of Goldwater and Buckley, its ideology differed considerably from that of World War II isolationism. The Society denied all possibility of coexistence between a Communist and "Christian-style" civilization. "The struggle between them must end," it said, "with one completely triumphant and the other completely destroyed." Welch claimed that "no marching of our troops in Europe," and "no hostile step we take no matter how drastic," could provoke the Soviets into war.[51]

Slightly better comparisons might be made to a group of writers, far more liberal in domestic policy, who, beginning in the mid-1960s, sought large-scale curtailment of overseas commitments. These publicists often reflected a general popular suspicion of foreign involvements so acute that by June 1974 only forty-eight percent of those polled approved using an American military force to help Western Europe. Senator J. William Fulbright (Dem.–Ark.) attacked America's "arrogance of power," political scientist Hans Morgenthau insisted that the nation distinguish between the "desirable" and "essential," retired diplomat George F. Kennan sought a return to the "balance of power," and journalist Ronald Steel hoped for a restoration of "spheres of influence." Steel, more impassioned than most, wrote that Americans had been cruelly used by "political leaders who have squandered their wealth and stolen the lives of their children to fight imperial wars." Their skepticism concerning United States intervention was, if anything, far more consistent than those old isolationists who by 1951 were demanding widespread Asian commitments and a strategy based totally upon air power.[52]

Although these writers were soon branded "neo-isolationists" by more ardent interventionists, they vehemently denied such kinship. They pointed with pride to their own endorsements of containment in the 1940s and the 1950s and stressed that they still favored economic aid, international trade and investment, cultural ties, and technical assistance. They were far less suspicious of the United Nations and saw international arms limitation as an absolute necessity. Their urban social base and centrist ideology gave them little resemblance to followers of Colonel McCormick or Robert A. Taft. Yet their similarity to veteran isolationists was stronger than they wanted to admit. Like many old isolationists, they emphasized domestic priorities (although obviously quite different ones), opposed unrestricted presidential power, sought to curb military spending, and denied that the Soviet Union sought military conquest.

One of these commentators, political scientist Robert W. Tucker, did not shy away from advocating what he called a "new isolationism." Going beyond arguments for a new balance of power, Tucker claimed that the United States should intervene only when its own institutions were directly threatened. Old-style anti-Soviet and anti-Chinese alliances, he said, had become liabilities, no longer needed in a multi-polar, pluralistic world. Claiming that he was no descendant of the old anti-interventionists, Tucker remarked that "an isolationist America would not be an isolated America." The similarity, however, is closer than he wanted to recognize. Echoing comments made by Hoover in 1941 and again in 1951, he declared that the nation—by care and sacrifice—could remain remarkably self-sufficient.[53]

Even strong isolationist attitudes were adopted by the loose radical coalition of the late 1960s that went under the general ideological label *New Left*. Believing that "imperialist" America at times acted as *the* major repressive force on the globe, intellectuals on the New Left called as much for the world's isolation from the United States as for United States aloofness from the world. The historian Christopher Lasch went so far as to fear that the country might become "a kind of super-South Africa, a reactionary, racist, outlaw power of frightening proportions, armed with instruments of universal destruction."[54]

The two groups, of course, differed in ideology and social vision. Many old isolationists had found interventionism strengthening the very social trends that they believed were already causing the demise of the small businessman and farmer. To such New Left pamphleteers as Carl Oglesby, an American power elite was exploiting impoverished minorities at home while inflicting "U.S. Marines, cool plunder and the napalm fist" overseas.[55] Pictures of the good society were hardly alike: the great majority of old isolationists sought to restore the days of a pristine individualism that, they maintained, had existed before the New Deal; the New Left often spoke in terms of a "humanistic socialism" and "communal" control of production.

Both groups, however, had much in common. Both believed that the nation had abandoned its moral moorings, both saw global withdrawal as a necessary precondition of internal renewal, and both expressed a yearning for a lost autonomy. Both denied that the country's prosperity and security should depend upon overseas commitments made surreptitiously by power elites. To both, a narrow spectrum of the society was bleeding the populace, squandering both lives and money overseas while depriving the people of essential liberties at home.

Then some in each camp, though by no means all, accepted a conspiratorial interpretation of certain events in American history. The older revisionists indicted presidential mendacity at Pearl Harbor and Yalta. The New Left revisionist Gar Alperovitz accused the Truman administration of dropping the atomic bomb on Hiroshima in order to frighten the Russians. Joyce and Gabriel Kolko claimed that the United States, not North Korea, was secretly responsible for the outbreak of the war in 1950. True, New Left historians usually paid far more attention to broad social factors than to the offenses of the historical actors, although they gave no more attention than did the old isolationist Lawrence Dennis.[56]

In both cases, however, major events could result not from accident or contingency, but from conscious—if hidden—design, and for both groups, conventional analyses could hide reality, not illuminate it. The majority of Americans, many in both groups believed, lived like the chained prisoners in Plato's parable of the cave, with the world of "shadows" confused with a genuine reality lying beyond their range of vision. Hence it is quite understandable for several New Left historians to have found Beard a noble ancestor, and at least one historian has included in the same category Barnes and Tansill as well.[57]

Given this common outcome, it is hardly surprising that both old isolationists and partisans of the New Left—each in their own way— challenged the traditional picture of the Cold War. Both groups occasionally denied the reality of any Soviet "menace"; rather, both claimed that the administration deliberately orchestrated war scares in order to gain appropriations. Given such an interpretation, such individuals as Taft, Villard, Dennis, and Flynn were no longer pariahs but "prophets on the right," people who served as "conservative critics of American globalism." Ronald Radosh, in fact, goes so far as to call Dennis "our earliest and most consistent critic of the Cold War." Similarly Carl Oglesby, once president of Students for a Democratic Society, calls upon his countrymen to reread

Garet Garrett and Frank Chodorov. After several decades, when isolation-ism had increasingly become an ideology for conservatives, it has again taken a form of radicalism unfamiliar to it since the middle of the 1930s.[58]

The legacy left by the isolationist survivors is a mixed one. If many of them opposed economic and military aid to Europe on the narrow grounds of a balanced budget and "anti-socialism," they wisely cautioned against overcommitment. If they propounded a conspiratorial form of revisionism, they levied needed, and occasionally thoughtful, challenges to "official" history. If their proposals could weaken presidential action in an emergency, they often betrayed a healthy distrust of executive power and administration rhetoric. If their political base, lying in rural and small-town areas, might be isolating them from the dominant American culture, it is doubtful whether they could have been more ignorant of social change than those "best and brightest" who led the country into the Vietnam war. And if some of them stubbornly believed in a pastoral Eden forever lost to reality, they could—at least until 1950—claim that they opposed extend-ing this Eden by force.

Other aspects of their ideology are, of course, far less defensible. The support many of them gave to McCarthy, the obsession with air strategy, and the irresponsible "Asialationism" still prove embarrassing to most defenders, for these policies betray the worst in moralism, political expediency, and international recklessness.

Continual setbacks in recent American foreign policy have caused a reexamination of the old isolationists. One respected commentator has argued that American participation in World War II was not needed to protect the country's security; another has claimed that Russia presented little military threat during the early Cold War years.[59] An examination of the diverse paths taken by old isolationists is now less likely to seem either supercilious or patronizing. Their heritage, like that of the administra-tions they so passionately criticized, contains wisdom as well as folly, prophetic elements as well as foolish ones. The bequest must remain ambivalent, but it is not one without either vision or insight.

# NOTES

1. For security practices, see Graebner, *New Isolationism*, p. 141.

2. For Dulles's strategy, see Michael A. Guhin, *John Foster Dulles, A Statesman and His Times* (New York: Columbia University Press, 1972), pp. 211–39.

3. For Arthur Radford and the New Look, see Ambrose, *Rise to Globalism*, p. 222–24, 296; Graebner, *New Isolationism*, p. 131. For Taft's new power, see Richard Rovere, *Affairs of State: The Eisenhower Years* (New York: Farrar, Straus, and Cudahy, 1956), entry of March 22, 1953, pp. 102–4.

4. For Taft's protests, see *New York Times,* February 9, 1953, pp. 1, 4; Patterson, *Mr. Republican,* p. 591.

5. Henderson, "Congressman John Taber," p. iv.

6. Caridi, *Korean War,* p. 23; Parmet, *Eisenhower and the American Crusades,* pp. 298–99, 313; Ambrose, *Rise to Globalism,* pp. 226–27.

7. Langer, *CR,* June 30, 1953, p. 7667; F. Utley to H. Hoover, June 15, 1953, Box 141, Hoover Papers; Taft, "United States Foreign Policy," address before the National Conference of Christians and Jews, May 26, 1953, in *Vital Speeches* 19 (June 15, 1953): 529–31. For endorsements of Taft, see Burdick, *CR,* June 19, 1953, p. A3343; Lawrence Smith, *CR,* June 4, 1953, pp. 6114–15.

8. Morley, "The State of the Nation," *Nation's Business* 41 (March 1953): 18; Bender, *CR,* July 27, 1953, pp. A4932–33; Vorys, *CR,* July 27, 1953, p. A4669.

9. Short in Parmet, *Eisenhower and the American Crusades,* p. 315; S. Morton to E. P. Farley, July 31, 1953, Morton Papers; "Three Years—For What?" (editorial), *Washington Times-Herald,* June 11, 1953; Shafer, *CR,* June 11, 1953, p. A3415.

10. H. Hoover to J. R. McCarthy, November 5, 1952, Box 73, Hoover Papers; Wood activity noted in "McCarthy: A Documented Record," *Progressive* 18 (April 1954): 67–68. For Flynn's contribution to the McCarthy campaign, letter of acknowledgment, J. R. McCarthy to J. T. Flynn, November 28, 1952, Box 20, Flynn Papers. For Flynn comments on McCarthy, see "Asia and Joe McCarthy," radio broadcast #206 (April 13, 1953).

11. Petition noted in "Not Merely Gossip," *Human Events* (April 8, 1953); other protesters found in George Seldes, "New War on the Press—'Reform' from the Right," *Nation* 180 (February 5, 1955): 113–16; William F. Buckley, Jr., and L. Brent Bozell, *McCarthy and His Enemies: The Record and Its Meaning* (Chicago: Regnery, 1954); National Economic Council in *Brooklyn Eagle,* May 2, 1954. Among the old isolationists who voted for censure were Senators Carlson, Case, and Aiken. Opponents of censure included Dworshak, Dirksen, Langer, and Mundt. *CR,* December 2, 1954, p. 16392.

12. R. E. Wood to J. William Fulbright, August 13, 1954, Box 2, Wood Papers; Fish, *New York Times,* September 29, 1954, p. 18; Hanford MacNider to B. Hickenlooper, January 3, 1955, MacNider Papers; Flynn, "Joe McCarthy: His War on American Reds, and Those Who Oppose Him" (pamphlet) (New York: America's Future, 1954); Wheeler, *Helena Independent Herald,* December 31, 1953; F. J. Libby to S. Morton, January 15, 1954, NCPW Papers; McCarthy rally, *New York Times,* November 30, 1954, pp. 1, 22.

13. Dennis, *Appeal to Reason,* #411 (February 8, 1954); L. Dennis to H. E. Barnes, June 10, 1957, Barnes Papers; Morley, "The State of the Nation," *Nation's Business* 42 (July 1954): 16; S. Morton to J. E. Crane, December 30, 1954, and W. R. Castle to S. Morton, March 11, 1955, Morton Papers; Bender quoted in Griffith, *Politics of Fear,* p. 264.

14. Cable of R. E. Wood to Mrs. J. R. McCarthy, May 3, 1957, Box 4, Wood Papers.

15. R. R. McCormick to F. A. Virkus, December 6, 1952, copy in Box 4, Wood Papers; R. E. Wood to J. K. Herr, December 4, 1953, Box 2, Wood Papers; J. T. Flynn to R. Harriss, March 24, 1954, Box 18, Flynn Papers.

16. "The Story of For America" (undated pamphlet), the Papers of Clarence Manion, Chicago Historical Society. For a hostile description of the group, but one that includes verbatim sections of its program, see Anti-Defamation League of B'nai B'rith, *Facts* 9 (June-July, 1954): 17–18.

17. "Basic Plan of For America"; B. Fellers to R. E. Wood, December 18, 1954, copy in Manion Papers. The National Committee included such old isolationists as Gannett, Chodorov, Mrs. Burton K. Wheeler, Pettengill, and Sterling Morton. See *New*

*York Times*, November 14, 1954, p. 42; S. Morton to R. E. Wood, November 26, 1954, Morton Papers.

18. Statement of For America, June 5, 1954, Manion Papers; "Basic Plan of For America"; B. Fellers to R. E. Wood, December 18, 1954, copy in Manion Papers.

19. S. Morton to R. E. Wood, November 26, 1954, and S. Morton to F. Heide, March 19, 1955, Morton Papers; B. K. Wheeler to J. T. Flynn, June 1, 1954, Box 20, Flynn Papers; Fish, *New York Times*, September 22, 1954, p. 20; mimeographed copy of letter of H. Fish to R. E. Wood and C. Manion, September 21, 1954, Manion Papers.

20. Clarence Manion to author, October 7, 1974.

21. For Bricker in 1944 campaign, see Divine, *Presidential Elections,* 1: 146.

22. In 1946, as a member of a commission of the American Bar Association dealing with the United Nations, Frank E. Holman began to fear that the United Nations would interfere with racial segregation in the United States. See Youngnok Koo, "Dissenters from American Involvement in World Affairs: A Political Analysis of the Movement for the Bricker Amendment," Ph.D. diss., University of Michigan, 1966, pp. 23–29. For Eisenhower on Holman, see Parmet, *Eisenhower and the American Crusades,* p. 312.

23. Manion, *Conservative American,* p. 117–18.

24. Smith, "Senator William Langer," p. 65. For summaries of the debate over the Bricker Amendment, see Eisenhower, *Mandate for Change,* pp. 340–48; Parmet, *Eisenhower and the American Crusades,* pp. 305–12; Congressional Quarterly, *Congress and the Nation, 1945–1964: A Review of Government and Politics in the Postwar Years* (Washington, D.C.: Congressional Quarterly Service, 1965), pp. 110–13.

25. Statement of Dana Converse Backus, *CR*, June 20, 1953, p. A4503; Wiley, *CR*, June 24, 1953, p. 7160.

26. Manion, address to the Foundation for the Study of Treaty Law, January 26, 1954, in Manion, *Conservative American,* pp. 119–24.

27. Garet Garrett, *CR*, July 12, 1951, p. A4315. Both Garrett and McCormick cited the decision of an Appellate Court in California, *Fujii* vs. *State* (1950). The court held that a state law barring Japanese from owning real estate in California had been outlawed by the United Nations Charter.

28. Morley, "Treaty Law and the Constitution—A Study of the Bricker Amendment," *CR*, August 3, 1953, pp. 10991–98; McCarran in Parmet, *Eisenhower and the American Crusades,* p. 308; Dirksen in Theoharis, *The Yalta Myths: An Issue in U.S. Politics 1945–1955* (Columbia: University of Missouri, 1970), p. 180.

29. Wiley, *CR*, February 1, 1954, p. 1069; Chamberlin, "Treaties Can be Traps," *Human Events* 9 (May 28, 1952)).

30. Garrett, "Nullification by Treaty," *Spotlight* (C-222); Chodorov, "Again the Issue is Freedom," *Human Events* 10 (May 13, 1953), and "Freedom is Close to Home," ibid., 11 (February 3, 1954); H. E. Barnes to R. Baldwin, October 27, 1954, Barnes Papers; Manion's letter of resignation, *CR* February 17, 1954, p. 1913; Hart, "Now, After Adjournment," *Economic Council Letter,* #317 (August 15, 1953); R. E. Wood to E. Dilling, February 25, 1954, Box 1, Wood Papers; Dennis, *Appeal to Reason,* #408 (January 16, 1954).

31. "Report by the National Security Council on the Position of the United States with Respect to Indochina," February 27, 1950, in *The Pentagon Papers,* vol. 1, Senator Gravel ed. (Boston: Beacon, 1971), pp. 361–62. For accounts of the impending crisis, see Walter LaFeber, *America, Russia, and the Cold War, 1945–1975,* 3d ed. (New York: Wiley, 1976), pp. 161–65; Parmet, *Eisenhower and the American Crusades,* pp. 375–76; Richard M. Nixon in Graebner, *New Isolationism,* pp. 163–65.

32. For the fall of Dien Bien Phu and SEATO, see Parmet, *Eisenhower and the American Crusades,* pp. 376–79; 392–96; LaFeber, *America, Russia,* pp. 163–65.

33. Hoffman, *CR*, May 11, 1950, p. 6942; Barton, "Why We Are Losing," *Washington Star*, June 11, 1950; Flynn, "Who is Next on Stalin's List?," radio broadcast #65

(July 30, 1950); Dennis, *Appeal to Reason*, #239 (October 23, 1950); S. Morton to C. A. Evans, November 3, 1950, Morton Papers; Taft in Patterson, *Mr. Republican*, p. 611.

34. O'Donnell cited in Flynn radio broadcast, #M-10 (April 4, 1954); Flynn radio broadcast, #M-11 (April 11, 1954); S. B. Pettengill to J. Taber, May 19, 1954, Box 138, Taber Papers; H. MacNider to B. Hickenlooper, April 29, 1954, MacNider Papers.

35. Chodorov, "The Return of 1940" (editorial), *Freeman* 5 (September 1954): 81–82; W. L. Neumann to H. E. Barnes, February 27, 1954, and H. E. Barnes to W. L. Neumann, March 2, 1954, Neumann Papers; Libby, "You Should Help in Momentous Decision," *Peace Action* 20 (May 1954): 1; F. J. Libby to D. Eisenhower, July 2, 1954, NCPW Papers.

36. Butler, radio address, June 22, 1954, *CR*, p. 8567; "The Trouble in Indo-China," *Progressive* 18 (May 1954): 3–4; Dennis, *Appeal to Reason*, #428 (June 5, 1954); Lawrence Smith, *CR*, April 29, 1954, p. 5777, and April 14, 1954, p. 5178; Hanighen, "Not Merely Gossip," *Human Events* 11 (April 21, 1954).

37. Burdick, *CR*, April 15, 1954, p. 5255; Garet Garrett, "Exit the White Man," *Human Events* 11 (July 21, 1954); Dennis, *Appeal to Reason*, #421 (April 17, 1954); Flynn, radio broadcast #M-11 (April 11, 1954); C. C. Tansill to H. E. Barnes, April 16, 1954, Barnes papers.

38. Johnson, *CR*, April 19, 1954, p. 5281, and April 26, 1954, p. 5477.

39. Hoffman, *CR*, April 7, 1954, p. 4830; H. MacNider to B. Hickenlooper, April 29, 1954, MacNider Papers; Flynn, radio broadcast #M-17 (May 23, 1954); Chodorov, "Reds Are Natives," *Freeman* 5 (August 1954): 45–46; Fellers, "A Program for Asia," *Human Events* 11 (August 4, 1954).

40. Hanighen, "Not Merely Gossip," *Human Events* 11 (May 19, 1954).

41. Flynn, radio broadcasts #M-34 (September 19, 1954) and #M-37 (October 10, 1954); Fellers, "A Program for Asia"; Smith, "Senator William Langer," pp. 220–21.

42. Hanighen, "Not Merely Gossip," *Human Events* 11 (September 1, 1954); Fellers, "A Program for Asia."

43. Parmet, *Eisenhower and the American Crusades*, pp. 366–69.

44. The five were Edwin C. Johnson, Dworshak, Langer, Taft, and Butler. The latter two died by 1954.

45. Utley, "Was It Planned That Way?," *Human Events* 12 (January 1, 1955); Chamberlin, "The Great Conference Obsession," *Human Events* 12 (February 17, 1954); Ernest Weir, "Leave Emotions Out of Our Foreign Policy," *Faith and Freedom* 5 (April 1954): 8; Dennis, Appeal to Reason, #486 (July 16, 1955); R. E. Wood to R. E. Wilson, July 8, 1954, Box 1, Wood Papers; Fellers, *Wings for Peace: A Primer for a New Defense* (Chicago: Regnery, 1953), p. 248. Among the veteran isolationists who were members of the Citizens Foreign Aid Committee were Harriss, Morton, Nye, Pettengill, Tansill, Wheeler, Wood, and Manion. General Fellers was national director. For a hostile account of such action groups, see Arnold Forster and Benjamin R. Epstein, *Danger on the Right* (New York: Random House, 1964).

46. S. Morton to A. Landon, February 7, 1955, Morton Papers; Langer in Wilkins, "Non-Ethnic Roots," p. 217; J. T. Flynn to J. R. McCarthy, November 23, 1956, Box 20, Flynn Papers; Dennis, *Appeal to Reason*, #571 (March 2, 1957); Fish on Berlin, letter to *New York Times*, October 17, 1961, p. 38; Fish on Cuba, letter to *New York Times*, March 5, 1966, p. 26.

47. Nye, "Interventionist Madness," *American Mercury* 103 (Fall 1966): 26–29; Wheeler, "The Majority of Americans Are Isolationists," *New York Times*, November 26, 1971, p. 37; H. E. Barnes to W. L. Neumann, April 24, 1965, and H. E. Barnes to W. L. Neumann, August 14, 1968, Neumann Papers; Dennis, *Operational Thinking for Survival* (Colorado Springs, Colo., Ralph Myles, 1969), p. 126.

48. For Goldwater at the 1952 convention, see Edwin McDowell, *Barry Goldwater: Portrait of an Arizonan* (Chicago: Regnery, 1964), p. 101. For examples of early

support for Goldwater, see B. Fellers to S. Morton, January 8, 1960, and S. Morton to B. Fellers, February 1, 1960, Morton Papers; Chodorov obituary, *New York Times,* December 29, 1966, p. 28; M. K. Hart to B. Goldwater, July 7, 1960, Hart Papers; Cole, *Nye,* p. 223; General Wood obituary, *Chicago Sun-Times,* November 7, 1969; Fish, *New York Times,* November 14, 1964, p. 28; Manion, *Conservative American,* pp. 203–8.

49. Barry Goldwater, *The Conscience of a Conservative* (New York: Hillman Books, 1960), p. 122; Dennis, *Appeal to Reason,* #788 (September 19, 1964). For stress on the differences between Goldwater and the old isolationists, see Jonas, *Isolationism in America,* pp. 285–87.

50. L. Dennis to H. E. Barnes, September 1, 1952, Barnes Papers; F. Morley to R. C. Cornelle, June 17, 1954, Morley Papers; William F. Buckley, Jr., to J. T. Flynn, October 22, 1956, Box 17, Flynn Papers. For ties of the Buckley family to America First, see William F. Buckley, Jr., to S. Morton, November 13, 1959, Morton Papers; Mrs. William F. Buckley, Sr., to America First Committee, November 3, 1940, Box 36, AFC Papers; cable of William F. Buckley, Sr., to General Wood, December 10, 1941, Box 119, AFC Papers. For a discussion of Buckley's ideology and the role of varied associates affiliated with *National Review,* see Ronald Lora, *Conservative Minds in America* (Chicago: Rand McNally, 1971), pp. 195–215; George H. Nash, *Conservative Intellectual Movement,* pp. 86–87, 123–30, 256–73, 377 n. 197; Diggins, *Up from Communism,* pp. 402–11; and Justus D. Doenecke, "Conservatism: The Impassioned Sentiment," *American Quarterly* 28 (Winter 1975): 601–9.

51. The name of Welch's wife was filed among those who wanted to start an America First Committee chapter. See Box 60, AFC Papers. For Welch and America First, see Robert Welch to J. T. Flynn, June 29, 1953, Box 20, Flynn Papers. Welch notes his support for Taft in *The Blue Book of the John Birch Society,* 12th printing (Belmont, Mass.: John Birch Society, 1961), p. 114. For Committee of Endorsers, see "The John Birch Society," in Anti-Defamation League of B'nai B'rith, *The Facts* 14 (November-December, 1961): 227–28. For interventionist statements by Welch, see "General Beliefs and Principles of the John Birch Society," *CR,* June 12, 1962, p. A4292, and *Blue Book,* §1, p. v.

52. J. William Fulbright, *The Arrogance of Power* (Cambridge, Mass.: Harvard University Press, 1966); Hans J. Morgenthau, *A New Foreign Policy for the United States* (New York: Praeger, 1969); "Interview with George F. Kennan," *Foreign Policy* 7 (Summer 1972): 5–21; Ronald Steel, "A Sphere of Influence Policy," *Foreign Policy* 5 (Winter 1971–1972): 107–18. The Steel quotation is from p. 117. For a critique of the above positions, see Walter Laqueur, *Neo-Isolationism and the World of the Seventies* (New York: Library Press, 1972). For the poll showing isolationist sentiments, "Polls Find U. S. Isolationism on Rise, Hope at Ebb," *New York Times,* June 16, 1974, p. 3.

53. Robert W. Tucker, *A New Isolationism: Threat or Promise?* (New York: Universe, 1972).

54. Christopher Lasch, foreword to Gar Alperovitz, *Cold War Essays* (Garden City, N.Y.: Anchor, 1970), p. 22.

55. Carl Oglesby, "Vietnamese Crucible: An Essay on the Meanings of the Cold War," in Carl Oglesby and Richard Shaull, *Containment   and Change* (New York: Macmillan, 1967), p. 107.

56. For a New Left interpretation of Hiroshima, see Alperovitz, *Atomic Diplomacy.* For a New Left interpretation of the Korean War that stresses conspiracy, see Joyce and Gabriel Kolko, *The Limits of Power,* chap. 21.

57. For praise of Beard, see William Appleman Williams, "Charles Austin Beard: The Intellectual as Tory-Radical," in Harvey Goldberg, ed., *American Radicals: Some Problems and Personalities* (New York: Monthly Review Press, 1957), pp. 295–308, and Ronald Radosh, "America's Entry into World War II," *Left and Right: A Journal of*

*Libertarian Thought* 3 (Autumn 1967): 31–38. For ties between Barnes, Tansill, Beard, and New Left historians, see Alperovitz, *Cold War Essays*, p. 104; Justus D. Doenecke, "Harry Elmer Barnes: Prophet of a 'Usable' Past," *History Teacher* 8 (February 1975): 265–76. For an analysis of the New Left using the cave analogy found in Plato's *Republic*, see Ole R. Holsti, "The Study of International Politics Makes Strange Bedfellows: Theories of the 'Old Right' and the 'New Left'," *American Political Science Review* 68 (March 1974): 218.

58. Radosh, *Prophets of the Right*, p. 332; Oglesby, "Vietnamese Crucible," p. 166.

59. Bruce M. Russett, *No Clear and Present Danger: A Skeptical View of the U. S. Entry into World War II* (New York: Harper, 1972); Adam B. Ulam, *The Rivals.*

# Bibliography of Sources and Works

*Manuscripts*

The Papers of the America First Committee, Library of the Hoover Institution on War, Revolution and Peace, Stanford University

The Papers of Harry Elmer Barnes, University of Wyoming Library

The Papers of William R. Castle, Hoover Presidential Library, West Branch, Iowa

The Papers of Lawrence Dennis, in the possession of Mr. Dennis, Garnerville, New York

The Papers of John T. Flynn, University of Oregon Library

The Papers of Frank Gannett, Cornell University Library

The Papers of Merwin K. Hart, University of Oregon Library

The Papers of Herbert Hoover, Hoover Presidential Library

Materials related to the Keep America Out of War Congress, Socialist Party Collection, Duke University Library

The Papers of Philip La Follette, Wisconsin State Historical Society, Madison, Wisconsin

The Papers of Robert M. La Follette, Jr., Library of Congress

The Papers of Douglas MacArthur, Douglas MacArthur Memorial Library, Norfolk, Virginia

The Papers of Hanford MacNider, Hoover Presidential Library

The Papers of Clarence Manion, Chicago Historical Society

The Papers of Verne Marshall, Hoover Presidential Library

The Papers of Felix Morley, Hoover Presidential Library

The Papers of Sterling Morton, Chicago Historical Society

The Papers of the National Council for the Prevention of War, Swarthmore College Peace Collection

The Papers of William L. Neumann, University of Wyoming Library

The Papers of Samuel B. Pettengill, University of Oregon Library

The Papers of Daniel Reed, Cornell University Library

The Papers of Frederick C. Smith, Ohio State Historical Society, Columbus, Ohio

The Papers of John Taber, Cornell University Library

The Papers of Robert A. Taft, Library of Congress

The Papers of Walter Trohan, Hoover Presidential Library

The Papers of Harry S. Truman, Truman Presidential Library, Independence, Missouri

The Papers of Oswald Garrison Villard, Houghton Library, Harvard University

The Papers of John M. Vorys, Ohio State Historical Society

The Papers of Robert E. Wood, Hoover Presidential Library

*Oral History Collections*

Transcript of interview with Lawrence Dennis, 1967, Oral History Collection, Butler Library, Columbia University

Transcript of interview with Louis Taber, 1952, Oral History Collection, Butler Library, Columbia University

*Public Documents*

*Congressional Record.*

Department of State. *Bulletin.*

Department of State. *Peace and War: United States Foreign Policy, 1931–1941.* Washington, D.C.: U.S. Government Printing Office, 1943.

United States House of Representatives. Committee on Banking and Currency. *Anglo-American Financial Agreement.* Washington, D.C.: U.S. Government Printing Office, 1946.

United States House of Representatives. Committee on Foreign Affairs. *Assistance to Greece and Turkey.* Washington, D.C.: U.S. Government Printing Office, 1947.

United States House of Representatives. Special Committee to Investigate Campaign Expenditure. *Hearings.* Washington, D.C.: U.S. Government Printing Office, 1946.

United States House of Representatives. Committee on Foreign Affairs. *United States Foreign Policy for a Post-War Recovery Program.* Washington, D.C.: U.S. Government Printing Office, 1948.

United States Senate. Committees on Foreign Relations and Armed Services. *Assignment of Ground Forces in the European Area.* Washington, D.C.: U.S. Government Printing Office, 1951.

United States Senate. Committee on Foreign Relations. *Foreign Relief Aid: 1947.* Historical series. Washington, D.C.: U.S. Government Printing Office, 1973.

United States Senate. Committee on Foreign Relations. *Legislative Origins of the Truman Doctrine.* Historical series. Washington, D.C.: U.S. Government Printing Office, 1973.

United States Senate. Committee on Foreign Relations. *North Atlantic Treaty.* Washington, D.C.: U.S. Government Printing Office, 1949.

United States Senate. Committee on Foreign Relations. *Report on European Recovery Program.* Washington, D.C.: U.S. Government Printing Office, 1948.

United States Senate. Committee on Foreign Relations. *The Vandenberg Resolution and the North Atlantic Treaty.* Historical series. Washington, D.C.: U.S. Government Printing Office, 1973.

United States Senate and House of Representatives. Joint Committee on the

Investigation of the Pearl Harbor Attack. *Pearl Harbor Attack: Hearings and Report*. Washington, D.C.: U.S. Government Printing Office, 1946.

*Memoirs*

Acheson, Dean. *Present at the Creation: My Years in the State Department*. New York: Norton, 1969.

Chamberlin, William Henry. *Confessions of an Individualist*. New York: Macmillan, 1940.

Chodorov, Frank. *Out of Step: The Autobiography of an Individualist*. New York: Devin-Adair, 1962.

Dobney, Frederick J., ed. *The Selected Papers of Will Clayton*. Baltimore, Md.: The Johns Hopkins University Press, 1971.

Drury, Allen. *A Senate Journal, 1943–1945*. New York: McGraw-Hill, 1963.

Eisenhower, Dwight D. *At Ease: Stories I Tell to Friends*. Garden City, N.Y.: Doubleday, 1967.

———. *The White House Years*. Vol. I: *Mandate for Change, 1953–1956*. New York: Signet, 1963.

Grew, Joseph C. *Ten Years in Japan*. New York: Simon and Schuster, 1944.

Hull, Cordell. *Memoirs*. Two vols. New York: Macmillan, 1948.

Kennan, George F. *Memoirs*. Vol. 1: *1925–1950*. Boston: Little, Brown, 1967.

Kimmel, Husband E. *Admiral Kimmel's Story*. Chicago: Regnery, 1955.

Libby, Frederick J. *To End War: The Story of the National Council for the Prevention of War*. Nyack, N.Y.: Fellowship Publications, 1969.

Lindbergh, Charles A. *The Wartime Journals of Charles A. Lindbergh*. New York: Harcourt Brace Jovanovich, 1970.

MacArthur, Douglas. *Reminiscences*. New York: McGraw-Hill, 1964.

Millis, Walter, ed. *The Forrestal Diaries*. New York: Viking, 1951.

Nock, Albert Jay. *Memoirs of a Superfluous Man*. New York: Harper, 1943.

Stimson, Henry L., and Bundy, McGeorge. *On Active Service in Peace and War*. New York: Harper, 1948.

Trohan, Walter. *Political Animals: Memoirs of a Sentimental Cynic*. Garden City, N.Y.: Doubleday, 1975.

Truman, Harry S. *Memoirs*. Vol. 1: *Year of Decision*. Vol. 2: *Years of Trial and Hope*. Garden City, N.Y.: Doubleday, 1955.

Vandenberg, Arthur H. Jr., and Morris, Joe Alex, eds. *The Private Papers of Senator Vandenberg*. Boston. Houghton Mifflin, 1952.

Wheeler, Burton K., with Healy, Paul F. *Yankee from the West*. Garden City, N.Y.: Doubleday, 1962.

*Newspapers*

*Brooklyn Eagle*
*Caldwell* (Idaho) *Tribune*
*Chicago Daily News*
*Chicago Sun-Times*
*Chicago Tribune*
*Daily Press New Dominion*
*Detroit Times*
*Elmira* (N.Y.) *Advertiser*
*Helena* (Mont.) *Independent Herald*
*Kansas City* (Mo.) *Times*
*Madison* (Wis.) *Capital Times*
*New York Daily News*

*New York Herald Tribune*
*New York Journal-American*
*New York Times*
*Wall Street Journal*
*Washington Post*
*Washington Star*
*Washington Times-Herald*
*Watertown* (N.Y.) *News*

*Periodicals*

*American Affairs;* a publication of the National Industrial Conference Board
*American Mercury*
*analysis;* monthly edited by Frank Chodorov
*Annals of the American Academy of Political and Social Science*
*Appeal to Reason;* a newsletter edited by Lawrence Dennis
*Atlantic*
*Battle*; a publication of the Friends of Democracy
*Business Week*
*Catholic World*
*Christian Century*
*Closer-Ups;* a newsletter edited by Upton Close
*Collier's*
*Common Sense*
*Commonweal*
*Congressional Digest*
*Current History*
*Economic Council Letter*; a publication of the National Economic Council
*Economic Council Papers*; publications of the National Economic Council
*Economic Council Review of Books;* a publication of the National Economic
    Council
*Faith and Freedom;* a publication of Spiritual Mobilization
*Facts*; a publication of the Anti-Defamation League of B'nai B'rith
*Fellowship*; a publication of the Fellowship of Reconciliation
*Fortune*
*Freeman*
*Free World*
*Harpers*
*Human Events*
*Inside Your Congress*; a newsletter edited by Samuel Pettengill
*Left and Right: A Journal of Libertarian Thought*
*Life*
*Nation*
*National Review*
*Nation's Business*
*New Leader*
*New Republic*
*Newsweek*
*New Yorker*
*Peace Action*; a publication of the National Council for the Prevention of War
*Peace News* (London)
*Prevent World War III;* a publication of the Society for the Prevention of World
    War III

*Progressive*
*Reader's Digest*
*Reporter*
*Saturday Review of Literature*
*Scribner's Commentator*
*Social Forces*
*Socialist Call*
*Spotlight;* a publication of the Committee for Constitutional Government
*Time*
*Town Meeting: The Bulletin of America's Town Meeting of the Air*
*Today's World;* a monthly edited by Hamilton Fish
*United States News and World Report*
*Vital Speeches*

*Contemporary Books*

Allen, Robert S., and Shannon, William V. *Truman Merry-Go-Round.* New York: Vanguard, 1950.

Anderson, Jack, and May, Ronald D. *McCarthy: The Man, the Senator, the "Ism."* Boston: Beacon, 1952.

Bailey, Thomas A. *The Man on the Street: The Impact of American Public Opinion on Foreign Policy.* New York: Macmillan, 1948.

Barnes, Harry Elmer, ed. *Perpetual War for Perpetual Peace: A Critical Examination of the Foreign Policy of Franklin D. Roosevelt and its Aftermath.* Caldwell, Idaho: Caxton, 1953.

Beard, Charles A. *American Foreign Policy in the Making, 1932–1940: A Study in Responsibilities.* New Haven, Conn.: Yale University Press, 1946.

———. *President Roosevelt and the Coming of the War, 1941: A Study in Appearances and Realities.* New Haven, Conn.: Yale University Press, 1948.

Belgion, Montgomery. *Victor's Justice.* Chicago: Regnery, 1949.

Blackett, P. M. S. *Fear, War, and the Bomb: Military and Political Consequences of Atomic Energy.* New York: Whittlesey House, 1949.

Buckley, William F., and Bozell, L. Brent. *McCarthy and His Enemies: The Record and its Meaning.* Chicago: Regnery, 1954.

Burnham, James. *Containment or Liberation?: An Inquiry into the Aims of United States Foreign Policy.* New York: John Day, 1953.

———. *The Struggle for the World.* New York: John Day, 1947.

Carlson, John Roy [pseud. Avedis Derounian]. *Under Cover: My Four Years in the Nazi Underworld of America.* New York: Dutton, 1943.

Chamberlin, William Henry. *America: Partner in World Rule.* New York: Vanguard, 1945.

———. *America's Second Crusade.* Chicago: Regnery, 1950.

———. *The German Phoenix.* New York: Duell, Sloan and Pearce, 1963.

Chiang Kai-shek, *China's Destiny.* New York: Macmillan, 1947.

Current, Richard N. *Secretary Stimson: A Study in Statecraft,* New Brunswick, N.J.: Rutgers University Press, 1954.

Davis, Forrest, and Lindley, Ernest K. *How War Came: An American White Paper.* New York: Macmillan, 1942.

Dennis, Lawrence. *The Dynamics of War and Revolution.* New York: Weekly Foreign Letter, 1940.

———. *Operational Thinking for Survival.* Colorado Springs, Colo.: Ralph Myles, 1969.

Dulles, John Foster. *War, Peace and Change.* New York: Harper, 1939.

Feis, Herbert. *The Road to Pearl Harbor: The Coming of War Between the United States and Japan.* Princeton, N.J.: Princeton University Press, 1950.

Fellers, Bonner. *Wings for Peace: A Primer for a New Defense.* Chicago: Regnery, 1953.

Fink, Reuben. *America and Palestine.* New York: American Zionist Emergency Council, 1944.

Fish, Hamilton. *The Challenge of World Communism.* Milwaukee, Wis.: Bruce, 1946.

———. *The Red Plotters.* New York: Domestic and Foreign Affairs, 1947.

Flynn, John T. *The Lattimore Story.* New York: Devin-Adair, 1953.

———. *The Road Ahead: America's Creeping Revolution.* New York: Devin-Adair, 1949.

———. *The Roosevelt Myth.* New York: Devin-Adair, 1948.

———. *While You Slept: Our Tragedy in Asia and Who Made It.* New York: Devin-Adair, 1951.

Fulbright, J. William. *The Arrogance of Power.* New York: Praeger, 1969.

Goldwater, Barry. *The Conscience of a Conservative.* New York. Hillman Books, 1960.

Gollancz, Victor. *In Darkest Germany.* Chicago: Regnery, 1947.

———. *Our Threatened Values.* Chicago: Regnery, 1946.

Grenfell, Russell. *Unconditional Hatred: German War Guilt and the Future of Europe.* New York: Devin-Adair, 1953.

Gunther, John. *Inside U.S.A.* New York: Harper, 1947.

Hankey, Lord Maurice. *Politics: Trials and Errors.* Chicago: Regnery, 1950.

Johnson, Walter. *The Battle Against Isolation.* Chicago: University of Chicago Press, 1944.

Jones, Joseph Marion. *The Fifteen Weeks.* New York: Viking, 1955.

Langer, William L., and Gleason, S. Everett. *The Challenge to Isolation: The World Crisis of 1937–1940 and American Foreign Policy.* New York: Harper, 1952.

———. *The Undeclared War, 1940–1941: The World Crisis and American Foreign Policy.* New York: Harper, 1953.

Laqueur, Walter. *Neo-Isolationism and the World of the Seventies.* New York: Library Press, 1972.

McCarthy, Joseph R. *America's Retreat from Victory: The Story of George Catlett Marshall.* New York: Devin-Adair, 1952.

———. *McCarthyism: The Fight for America.* New York: Devin-Adair, 1952.

Manion, Clarence E. *The Conservative American.* Shepherdsville, Ky.: Victor, 1966.

Millis, Walter. *This is Pearl! The United States and Japan—1941.* New York: Morrow, 1947.

———. *Viewed Without Alarm: Europe Today.* Boston: Houghton Mifflin, 1937.

Morgenstern, George. *Pearl Harbor: The Story of the Secret War.* New York: Devin-Adair, 1947.

Morgenthau, Hans. *A Foreign Policy for the United States.* New York: Praeger, 1969.

Morley, Felix, and Hanighen, Frank, eds. *A Year of Human Events.* Chicago: Human Events, 1945.

Oglesby, Carl, and Shaull, Richard. *Containment and Change.* New York: Macmillan, 1967.

Pettengill, Samuel B. *Smoke Screen.* New York: Southern Publishers, 1940.

Pratt, John M., ed. *Revitalizing a Nation: A Statement of Beliefs, Opinions and Policies Embodied in the Public Pronouncements of General of the Army Douglas MacArthur.* Chicago: Heritage Foundation, 1952.

Rauch, Basil. *Roosevelt from Munich to Pearl Harbor: A Study in the Creation of a Foreign Policy.* New York: Creative Age, 1950.

Rothfels, Hans. *The German Opposition to Hitler.* Hinsdale, Ill.: Regnery, 1948.

Rovere, Richard. *Affairs of State: The Eisenhower Years.* New York: Farrar, Straus and Cudahy, 1956.

Sanborn, Frederic R. *Design for War: A Study of Secret Power Politics, 1937–1941.* New York: Devin-Adair, 1951.

Sherwood, Robert E. *Roosevelt and Hopkins: An Intimate History.* New York: Harper, 1948.

Stout, Rex. *The Illustrious Dunderheads.* New York: Knopf, 1943.

Taft, Robert A. *A Foreign Policy for Americans.* Garden City, N.Y.: Doubleday, 1951.

Tansill, Charles Callan. *Back Door to War: The Roosevelt Foreign Policy, 1933–1941.* Chicago: Regnery, 1952.

Theobald, Robert A. *The Final Secret of Pearl Harbor.* New York: Devin-Adair, 1954.

Thomas, Norman. *Appeal to the Nations.* New York: Holt, 1947.

Tucker, Robert W. *A New Isolationism: Threat or Promise?* New York: Universe, 1972.

Utley, Freda. *The China Story.* Chicago: Regnery, 1951.

———. *The Dream We Lost: Soviet Russia Then and Now.* New York: John Day, 1940.

———. *The High Cost of Vengeance.* Chicago: Regnery, 1949.

———. *Last Chance in China.* Indianapolis, Ind.: Bobbs-Merrill, 1948.

Veale, F. J. P. *Advance to Barbarism.* Appleton, Wis.: C. C. Nelson, 1953.

Welch, Robert. *The Blue Book of the John Birch Society.* 12th printing. Belmont, Mass.: John Birch Society, 1961.

Willkie, Wendell L. *One World.* New York: Simon and Schuster, 1943.

*Secondary Books and Monographs*

Adler, Selig. *The Isolationist Impulse: Its Twentieth-Century Reaction.* New York: Abelard-Schuman, 1957.

Alperovitz, Gar. *Atomic Diplomacy: Hiroshima and Potsdam; The Use of the Atomic Bomb and the American Confrontation with Soviet Power.* New York: Simon and Schuster, 1965.

———. *Cold War Essays.* Garden City, N.Y.: Anchor, 1970.

Ambrose, Stephen E. *Rise to Globalism: American Foreign Policy, 1938–1970.* Baltimore, Md.: Penguin, 1971.

Bailyn, Bernard. *The Ideological Origins of the American Revolution.* Cambridge, Mass.: Belknap Press, 1967.

Barnet, Richard J. *Intervention and Revolution.* New York: New American Library, 1968.

Beisner, Robert L. *Twelve Against Empire: The Anti-Imperialists, 1898–1900.* New York: McGraw-Hill, 1968.

Bell, Daniel, ed. *The Radical Right.* Garden City, N.Y.: Doubleday, 1964.

Bensman, Joseph, and Vidich, Arthur J. *The New American Society: The Revolution of the Middle Class.* Chicago: Quadrangle, 1971.

Borkin, Joseph. *Robert R. Young: The Populist of Wall Street.* New York: Harper and Row, 1969.

Brock, Clifton. *Americans for Democratic Action: Its Role in National Elections.* Washington, D.C.: Public Affairs Press, 1962.

Buhite, Russell D. *Patrick J. Hurley and American Foreign Policy.* Ithaca, N.Y.: Cornell University Press, 1973.

Burns, James MacGregor. *Roosevelt: The Soldier of Freedom, 1940–1945.* New York: Harcourt Brace Jovanovich, 1970.

Campbell, Thomas M. *Masquerade Peace: America's UN Policy, 1944–1945.* Tallahassee: Florida State University Press, 1973.

Caridi, Ronald J. *The Korean War and American Politics: The Republican Party as a Case Study.* Philadelphia: University of Pennsylvania, 1968.

Chatfield, Charles. *For Peace and Justice: Pacifism in America, 1914–1941.* Knoxville: University of Tennessee Press, 1971.

Cole, Wayne S. *America First: The Battle Against Intervention, 1940–1941.* Madison: University of Wisconsin Press, 1953.

———. *Charles A. Lindbergh and the Battle Against American Intervention in World War II.* New York: Harcourt Brace Jovanovich, 1974.

———. *An Interpretive History of American Foreign Relations.* Rev. ed. Homewood, Ill.: Dorsey, 1974.

———. *Senator Gerald P. Nye and American Foreign Relations.* Minneapolis: University of Minnesota Press, 1962.

Congressional Quarterly. *Congress and the Nation, 1945–1964: A Review of Government and Politics in the Postwar Years.* Washington, D.C..: Congressional Quarterly Service, 1965.

Conner, Paul W. *Poor Richard's Politicks: Benjamin Franklin and His New American Order.* New York: Oxford University Press, 1965.

*Current Biography.* Annual. New York: H. W. Wilson.

David, Paul T.; Moos, Malcolm; and Goldman, Ralph M. *Presidential Nominating Politics in 1952.* 4 vols. Baltimore, Md.: The Johns Hopkins Press, 1954.

Diggins, John P. *Up From Communism: Odysseys in American Intellectual History.* New York: Harper and Row, 1975.

Divine, Robert A. *Foreign Policy and U.S. Presidential Elections.* Vol. 1: *1940–1948.* Vol. 2: *1952–1960.* New York: New Viewpoints, 1974.

———. *The Reluctant Belligerent: American Entry into World War II.* New York: Wiley, 1965.

———. *Roosevelt and World War II.* Baltimore, Md.: The Johns Hopkins University Press, 1969.

———. *Second Chance: The Triumph of Internationalism in America during World War II.* New York: Atheneum, 1967.

Doenecke, Justus D. *The Literature of Isolationism: A Guide to Non-Interventionist Scholarship, 1930–1972.* Colorado Springs, Colo.: Ralph Myles, 1972.

Eckes, Alfred E. *A Search for Solvency: Bretton Woods and the International Monetary System, 1941–1971.* Austin: University of Texas Press, 1975.

Edwards, Jerome E. *The Foreign Policy of Col. McCormick's Tribune, 1929–1941.* Reno: University of Nevada Press, 1971.

Elson, Robert T. *The World of Time Inc.: The Intimate History of a Publishing Enterprise.* Vol. 2: *1941–1960.* New York: Atheneum, 1973.

Feis, Herbert. *The Atomic Bomb and the End of World War II.* Princeton, N.J.: Princeton University Press, 1966.

———. *From Trust to Terror: The Onset of the Cold War.* New York: Norton, 1970.

Fleming, Denna. *The Cold War and Its Origins.* Volume 1: *1917–1950.* Garden City, N.Y.: Doubleday, 1961.

Forster, Arnold and Epstein, Benjamin R. *Cross-Currents*. Garden City, N.Y.: Doubleday, 1956.
————. *Danger on the Right*. New York: Random House, 1964.
Freeland, Richard M. *The Truman Doctrine and the Origins of McCarthyism: Foreign Policy, Domestic Politics, and Internal Security, 1946–1948*. New York: Schocken, 1971.
Gaddis, John L. *The United States and the Origins of the Cold War*. New York: Columbia University Press, 1972.
Gardner, Lloyd C. *Architects of Illusion: Men and Ideas in American Foreign Policy, 1941–1949*. Chicago: Quadrangle, 1970.
Gardner, Richard N. *Sterling Dollar Diplomacy: The Origins and Prospects of Our International Economic Order*. New, expanded ed. New York: McGraw-Hill, 1969.
Goldman, Eric F. *The Crucial Decade—and After*. New York: Vintage, 1960.
Goold-Adams, Richard. *The Time of Power: A Reappraisal of John Foster Dulles*. London: Weidenfeld and Nicholson, 1962.
Graebner, Norman A. *The New Isolationism: A Study in Politics and Foreign Policy since 1950*. New York: Ronald Press, 1956.
Graham, Otis L., Jr. *An Encore for Reform: The Old Progressives and the New Deal*. New York: Oxford University Press, 1967.
Griffith, Robert. *The Politics of Fear: Joseph R. McCarthy and the Senate*. Lexington: University of Kentucky Press, 1970.
Guhin, Michael A. *John Foster Dulles: A Statesman and His Times*. New York: Columbia University Press, 1972.
Halle, Louis J. *The Cold War as History*. New York: Harper and Row, 1967.
Hero, Alfred O., Jr. *American Religious Groups View Foreign Policy: Trends in Rank-and-File Opinion, 1937–1969*. Durham, N.C.: Duke University Press, 1973.
Hofstadter, Richard. *The Progressive Historians: Turner, Beard, Parrington*. New York: Knopf, 1968.
James, D. Clayton. *The Years of MacArthur*. Vol. 1: *1880–1941*. Vol. II: *1941–1945*. Boston: Houghton Mifflin, 1970, 1975.
Johnpoll, Bernard K. *Pacifist's Progress: Norman Thomas and the Decline of American Socialism*. Chicago: Quadrangle, 1970.
Johnson, Roger T. *Robert M. La Follette, Jr. and the Decline of the Progressive Party in Wisconsin*. Madison: Wisconsin State Historical Society, 1964.
Jonas, Manfred. *Isolationism in America, 1935–1941*. Ithaca, N.Y.: Cornell University Press, 1966.
Keeley, Joseph. *The China Lobby Man: The Story of Alfred Kohlberg*. New Rochelle, N.Y.: Arlington House, 1969.
Kennedy, Thomas C. *Charles A. Beard and American Foreign Policy*. Gainesville: University of Florida Press, 1975.
Kimball, Warren F., ed. *Franklin D. Roosevelt and the World Crisis, 1937–1945*. Lexington, Mass.: Heath, 1973.
Koen, Ross T. *The China Lobby in American Politics*. New York: Harper and Row, 1974.
Kolko, Joyce, and Kolko, Gabriel. *The Limits of Power: The World and the United States Foreign Policy, 1945–1954*. New York: Harper and Row, 1972.
Koskoff, David E. *Joseph P. Kennedy: A Life and Times*. Englewood Cliffs, N.J.: Prentice-Hall, 1974.
LaFeber, Walter. *America, Russia, and the Cold War, 1945–1975*. 3d ed. New York: Wiley, 1976.

Levin, N. Gordon, Jr. *Woodrow Wilson and World Politics: America's Response to War and Revolution.* New York: Oxford University Press, 1968.

Lochner, Louis P. *Herbert Hoover and Germany.* New York: Macmillan, 1960.

Lora, Ronald. New York: *Conservative Minds in America.* Chicago: Rand McNally, 1971.

Liston, Robert A. *Sargeant Shriver: A Candid Portrait.* N.Y.: Farrar, Straus, 1964.

Lubell, Samuel. *The Future of American Politics.* 3d ed., rev. New York: Harper, 1965.

McCoy, Donald R. *Landon of Kansas.* Lincoln: University of Nebraska Press, 1966.

McDowell, Edwin. *Barry Goldwater: Portrait of an Arizonan.* Chicago: Regnery, 1964.

Marshall, S. L. A. *The River and the Gauntlet.* New York: William Morrow, 1953.

Marx, Leo. *The Machine in the Garden: Technology and the Pastoral Ideal in America.* New York: Oxford University Press, 1964.

Matusow, Allen J., ed. *Joseph R. McCarthy.* Englewood Cliffs, N.J.: Prentice-Hall, 1970.

Mayer, Arno J. *The Politics and Diplomacy of Peacemaking: Containment and Counterrevolution at Versailles.* New York: Knopf, 1967.

Mayer, George H. *The Republican Party,* 2d ed. New York: Oxford University Press, 1967.

Miller, William J. *Henry Cabot Lodge: A Biography.* New York: James H. Heineman, 1967.

Morgenthau, Hans J. *The Purpose of American Politics.* New York: Vintage, 1960.

Nash, George H. *The Conservative Intellectual Movement in America Since 1945.* New York: Basic Books, 1976.

O'Connor, Raymond G. *Diplomacy for Victory: FDR and Unconditional Surrender.* New York: Norton, 1971.

Parmet, Herbert S. *Eisenhower and the American Crusades.* New York: Macmillan, 1972.

Paterson, Thomas G. *Soviet-American Confrontation: Postwar Reconstruction and the Origins of the Cold War.* Baltimore, Md.: The Johns Hopkins University Press, 1973.

Patterson, James T. *Mr. Republican: A Biography of Robert A. Taft.* Boston: Houghton Mifflin, 1972.

————, *Congressional Conservatism and the New Deal.* Lexington: University of Kentucky Press, 1967.

*The Pentagon Papers.* Senator Gravel ed. 4 vols. Boston: Beacon, 1971.

Pilat, Oliver. *Drew Pearson: An Unauthorized Biography.* New York: Pocket Books. 1973.

Pinson, Koppel S. *Modern Germany: Its History and Civilization.* 2d ed. New York: Macmillan, 1966.

Polenberg, Richard. *War and Society: The United States, 1941–1945.* Philadelphia: Lippincott, 1972.

Radosh, Ronald. *Prophets on the Right: Profiles of Conservative Critics of American Globalism.* New York: Simon and Schuster, 1975.

Rees, David. *Korea: The Limited War.* New York: St. Martin's Press, 1964.

Rieselbach, Leroy N. *The Roots of Isolationism: Congressional Voting and Presidential Leadership in Foreign Policy.* Indianapolis, Ind.: Bobbs-Merrill, 1966.

Rovere, Richard. *Senator Joe McCarthy.* New York: Meridian, 1959.

Roy, Ralph Lord. *Apostles of Discord: A Study of Organized Bigotry and Disruption on the Fringes of Protestantism.* Boston: Beacon, 1952.

Russett, Bruce M. *No Clear and Present Danger: A Skeptical View of the U.S. Entry into World War II.* New York: Harper, 1972.

Sanford, Charles S. *The Quest for Paradise: Europe and the American Moral Imagination.* Urbana: University of Illinois Press, 1961.

Schlesinger, Arthur M., Jr. *The Politics of Upheaval.* Boston: Houghton Mifflin, 1960.

Schroeder, Paul W. *The Axis Alliance and Japanese-American Relations.* Ithaca, N.Y.: Cornell University Press, 1958.

Seidler, Murray. *Norman Thomas: Respectable Rebel.* 2d ed. Syracuse, N.Y.: Syracuse University Press, 1967.

Sherwin, Martin J. *A World Destroyed: The Atomic Bomb and the Grand Alliance.* New York: Knopf, 1975.

Shewmaker, Kenneth E. *Americans and Chinese Communists, 1927–1945: A Persuading Encounter.* Ithaca, N.Y.: Cornell University Press, 1971.

Shils, Edward A. *The Torment of Secrecy.* Glencoe, Ill.: Free Press, 1956.

Smith, Henry Nash. *Virgin Land: The American West as Symbol and Myth.* New York: Vintage, 1950.

Smith, Geoffrey S. *To Save a Nation: American Countersubversives, the New Deal, and the Coming of World War II.* New York: Basic Books, 1973.

Spanier, John W. *The Truman-MacArthur Controversy and the Korean War.* Cambridge, Mass.: Belknap Press, 1959.

Stenehjem, Michele Flynn. *An American First: John T. Flynn and the America First Committee.* New Rochelle, N.Y.: Arlington House, 1976.

Swanberg, W. A. *Luce and His Empire.* New York, New York: Scribners, 1972.

Theoharis, Athan G. *Seeds of Repression: Harry S. Truman and the Origins of McCarthyism.* Chicago: Quadrangle, 1971.

———. *The Yalta Myths: An Issue in U.S. Politics, 1945–1955.* Columbia: University of Missouri Press, 1970.

Thomas, Bob. *Winchell.* Garden City, N.Y.: Doubleday, 1971.

Thomas, Lately. *When Even Angels Wept: The Senator Joseph McCarthy Affair—A Story Without a Hero.* New York: William Morrow, 1973.

Tompkins, C. David. *Senator Arthur H. Vandenberg: The Evolution of a Modern Republican, 1884–1945.* East Lansing: Michigan State University Press, 1970.

Tsou, Tang. *America's Failure in China, 1941–1950.* Chicago: University of Chicago Press, 1963.

Ulam, Adam B. *The Rivals: America and Russia since World War II.* New York: Viking, 1971.

Waldrop, Frank C. *McCormick of Chicago: An Unconventional Portrait of a Controversial Figure.* Englewood Cliffs, N.J.: Prentice-Hall, 1966.

Ward, John William. *Andrew Jackson: Symbol for an Age.* New York: Oxford University Press, 1955.

Westerfield, H. Bradford. *Foreign Policy and Party Politics: Pearl Harbor to Korea.* New Haven, Conn.: Yale University Press, 1955.

Whalen, Richard J. *The Founding Father: The Story of Joseph P. Kennedy.* New York: New American Library, 1964.

Whiting, Charles. *Incident at Malmédy.* New York: Stein and Day, 1971.

Wilson, Joan Hoff. *Herbert Hoover: Forgotten Progressive.* Boston: Little, Brown, 1975.

Wittner, Lawrence. *Cold War America*. New York: Praeger, 1974.
———. *Rebels Against War: The American Peace Movement*. New York: Columbia University Press, 1969.
Wolfe, Harold. *Herbert Hoover: Public Servant and Leader of the Loyal Opposition*. New York: Exposition, 1956.
Yarnell, Allen. *Democrats and Progressives: The 1948 Presidential Election as a Test of Postwar Liberalism*. Berkeley: University of California Press, 1974.
Young, Roland. *Congressional Politics in the Second World War*. New York: Columbia University Press, 1959.
Zink, Harold. *The United States in Germany, 1944–1955*. New York: Macmillan, 1957.

## Scholarly Articles

Adams, Henry M. "World War II Revisionist." In *Harry Elmer Barnes: Learned Crusader*, edited by Arthur Goddard. Colorado Springs, Colo.: Ralph Myles, 1968, pp. 288–313.
Beard, Charles A. "Neglected Aspects of Political Science." Presidential address to the American Political Science Association, Washington, D.C., December 29, 1947, *American Political Science Review* 42 (April 1948): 211–22.
Bemis, Samuel Flagg. "First Gun of a Revisionist Historiography for the Second World War." *Journal of Modern History* 19 (March 1947): 55–59.
Berger, Henry W. "Senator Robert A. Taft Dissents from Military Escalation." In *Cold War Critics: Alternatives to American Foreign Policy in the Truman Years*, edited by Thomas G. Paterson. Chicago: Quadrangle, 1971, pp. 167–204.
Bernstein, Barton J. "The Quest for Security: American Foreign Policy and International Control of Atomic Energy, 1943–1945." *Journal of American History* 60 (March 1974): 1003–44.
Billington, Ray Allen. "The Origins of Middle Western Isolationism." *Political Science Quarterly* 60 (March 1945): 44–64.
Borchard, Edwin M. "The Charter and the Constitution." *American Journal of International Law* 39 (October 1945): 767–772.
———. "The Impractability of 'Enforcing' Peace." *Yale Law Journal* 55 (August 1946): 966–73.
———. "International Law and International Organization." *American Journal of International Law* 41 (January 1947): 106–8.
———. "United States Foreign Policy." *American Journal of International Law* 43 (April 1949): 333–35.
Carleton, William G. "Isolationism and the Middle West." *Mississippi Valley Historical Review* 32 (December 1946): 377–90.
Current, Richard N. "How Stimson Meant to 'Maneuver' the Japanese." *Mississippi Valley Historical Review* 40 (June 1953): 67–74.
Divine, Robert A. "The Cold War and the Election of 1948." *Journal of American History* 59 (June 1972): 100–108.
Doenecke, Justus D. "Conservatism: The Impassioned Sentiment," *American Quarterly* 28 (Winter 1976): 601–9.
———. "Harry Elmer Barnes." *Wisconsin Magazine of History* 56 (Summer 1973): 311–23.
———. "Harry Elmer Barnes: Prophet of a 'Usable' Past." *History Teacher* 8 (February 1975): 265–76.

————. "General Robert E. Wood: The Evolution of a Conservative." *Journal of the Illinois State Historical Society* 71 (August 1978), 162–175.

————. "Lawrence Dennis: Cold War Revisionist." *Wisconsin Magazine of History* 55 (Summer 1972): 275–86.

————. "Isolationism of the 1930's and 1940's: An Historiographical Survey." In *American Diplomatic History: Issues and Methods,* edited by Robert W. Sellen and Thomas A. Bryson. Carrollton, Ga.: West Georgia College Studies in the Social Sciences, 1974, pp. 5–40.

————. "The Isolationists and a Usable Past: A Review Essay." *Peace and Change* 5 (Spring 1978), 67–73.

————. "Non-Interventionism of the Left: The Keep America Out of War Congress, 1938–41." *Journal of Contemporary History* 12 (April 1977): 221–36.

————. "Power, Markets, and Ideology: The Isolationist Response to Roosevelt Policy, 1940–1941." In *Watershed of Empire: Essays on New Deal Foreign Policy,* edited by Leonard Liggio and James J. Martin. Colorado Springs, Colo.: Ralph Myles, 1976, pp. 132–64.

————. "Protest Over Malmédy: A Case of Clemency." *Peace and Change* 4 (Spring 1977): 28–33.

————. "Verne Marshall's Leadership of the No Foreign War Committee." *Annals of Iowa* 41 (Winter 1973): 1153–72.

Fensterwald, Bernard, Jr., "The Anatomy of American 'Isolationism' and Expansion." *Journal of Conflict Resolution* 2 (June 1958): 111–39 and (December 1958): 280–307.

Ferrell, Robert H., and McLellan, David. "Dean Acheson: Architect of a Manageable World Order." In *Makers of American Diplomacy: From Benjamin Franklin to Henry Kissinger,* edited by Frank J. Merli and Theodore A. Wilson. New York: Scribner's, 1971, pp. 523–57.

Fried, Richard M. "Electoral Politics and McCarthyism: The 1950 Campaign." In *The Specter: Original Essays on the Cold War and the Origins of McCarthyism,* edited by Robert Griffith and Athan Theoharis. New York: New Viewpoints, 1974, pp. 190–223.

Gaddis, John Lewis. "Harry S. Truman and the Origins of Containment." In *Makers of American Diplomacy: From Benjamin Franklin to Henry Kissinger,* edited by Frank J. Merli and Theodore A. Wilson. New York: Scribner's, 1971, pp. 493–522.

Gardner, Lloyd C. "From Liberation to Containment, 1945–1953." In *From Colony to Empire: Essays in the History of American Foreign Relations,* edited by William Appleman Williams. New York: Wiley, 1972, pp. 337–84.

Gitlin, Todd. "Counter-Insurgency: Myth and Reality in Greece." In *Containment and Revolution,* edited by David Horowitz. Boston: Beacon, 1967, pp. 140–81.

Graff, Henry P. "Isolationism Again, With a Difference." *New York Times Magazine,* May 16, 1965, pp. 27–27, 99.

Hess, Gary R. "The Iranian Crisis of 1945–46 and the Cold War." *Political Science Quarterly* 89 (March 1974): 117–46.

Holsti, Ole R. "The Study of International Politics Makes Strange Bedfellows: Theories of the 'Old Right' and the 'New Left.'" *American Political Science Review* 68 (March 1974): 217–42.

Johnston, Paul E. "Caxton Printers, Ltd., Regional Publishers." *Pacific Northwest Quarterly* 48 (July 1957): 100–105.

Jonas, Manfred. "Internationalism as a Current in the Peace Movement: A

Symposium." In *Peace Movements in America,* edited by Charles Chatfield. New York: Schocken, 1973, pp. 174–79.

————. "Pro-Axis Sentiment and American Isolationism." *Historian* 29 (February 1967): 221–37.

Kaplan, Lawrence S. "The United States and the Atlantic Alliance: The First Generation." In John Braeman, Robert H. Bremner, and David Brody, eds. *Twentieth-Century American Foreign Policy.* Columbus: Ohio State University Press, 1971, pp. 294–342.

"Kennan, Interview with George F.," *Foreign Policy* 7 (Summer 1952): 5–21.

Mayer, Arno J. "The Lower Middle Class as Historical Problem." *Journal of Modern History* 47 (September 1975): 409–36.

Morison, Samuel Eliot. "Did Roosevelt Start the War?: History Through a Beard." *Atlantic* 182 (August 1948): 91–97.

Nobleman, Eli E. "American Military Government Courts in Germany." *Annals of the American Academy of Political and Social Science* 267 (January 1950): 87–97.

Rovere, Richard. "Arthur Hays Vandenberg: New Man in the Pantheon." In *The American Establishment and Other Reports, Opinions, and Speculations,* edited by Richard Rovere. New York: Harcourt, Brace and World, 1962, pp. 182–91.

Schlesinger, Arthur M., Jr. "The New Isolationism." *Atlantic* 49 (May 1952): 34–38.

Schonberger, Howard B. "The General and the Presidency: Douglas MacArthur and the Election of 1948." *Wisconsin Magazine of History* 57 (Spring 1975): 201–19.

Sears, Louis Martin. "Historical Revisionism Following the Two World Wars." In *Issues and Answers: Studies in Twentieth Century American Diplomacy,* edited by George L. Anderson. Lawrence: University of Kansas Press, 1959, pp. 127–46.

Steel, Ronald. "A Sphere of Influence Policy." *Foreign Policy* 5 (Winter 1971–72): 107–18.

Tanner, William R., and Griffiths, Robert. "Legislative Politics and 'McCarthyism': The Internal Security Act of 1950." In *The Specter: Original Essays on the Cold War and the Origins of McCarthyism,* edited by Robert Griffith and Athan Theoharis. New York: New Viewpoints, 1974, 262–80.

Wilkins, Robert P. "The Non-Ethnic Roots of North Dakota Isolationism." *Nebraska History* 44 (September 1963): 205–22.

Williams, William Appleman. "Charles Austin Beard: The Intellectual as Tory-Radical." In *American Radicals: Some Problems and Personalities,* edited by Harvey Goldberg. New York: Monthly Review Press, 1957, pp. 295–308.

Wood, Gordon S. "Rhetoric and Reality in the American Revolution." *William and Mary Quarterly* 23 (October 1966): 3–32.

*Unpublished Manuscripts*

Backstrom, Charles H. "The Progressive Party of Wisconsin, 1943–1946." Ph.D. dissertation, University of Wisconsin, 1956.

Bryniarski, Joan Lee. "Against the Tide: Senate Opposition to the Internationalist Foreign Policy of Presidents Franklin D. Roosevelt and Harry S. Truman, 1943–1949." Ph.D. dissertation, University of Maryland, 1972.

Bulkley, Peter B. "Daniel A. Reed: A Study in Conservatism." Ph.D. dissertation, Clark University, 1972.

Chasteen, Robert J. "American Foreign Aid and Public Opinion." Ph.D. dissertation, University of North Carolina, 1958.

Dalstrom, Harl A. "Kenneth S. Wherry." Ph.D. dissertation, University of Nebraska, 1966.

Darilek, Richard E. "A Loyal Opposition in Time of War: The Republican Party and the Politics of Foreign Policy from Pearl Harbor to Yalta." Ph.D. dissertation, Princeton University, 1973.

Doenecke, Justus D. "The Making of a 'Seditionist': The *Realpolitik* of Lawrence Dennis." Paper delivered at the Duquesne History Forum, Pittsburgh, November 1, 1973.

Ekirch, Arthur, Jr. "William L. Neumann: A Personal Recollection and Appreciation." Paper delivered at the joint session of the Conference on Peace Research in History and the Organization of American Historians, Washington, D.C., April 6, 1972.

Frey, Richard C., Jr. "John T. Flynn and the United States in Crisis, 1928–1950." Ph.D. dissertation, University of Oregon, 1969.

Guinsburg, Thomas N. "Hiram Johnson: Paragon of Isolationism." Paper delivered at the Duquesne History Forum, Pittsburgh, November 1, 1973.

———. "Senatorial Isolationism in America, 1919–1941." Ph.D. dissertation, Columbia University, 1969.

Henderson, Cary S. "Congressman John Taber of Auburn: Politics and Federal Appropriations, 1923–1962." Ph.D. dissertation, Duke University, 1964.

Honhart, Frederick L. "Charles Callan Tansill: American Diplomatic Historian." Ph.D. dissertation, Case Western Reserve University, 1972.

Kemp, Virginia M. "Congress and China, 1945–1949." Ph.D. dissertation, University of Pittsburgh, 1966.

Kent, Alan E. "Portrait in Isolationism: The La Follettes and Foreign Policy." Ph.D. dissertation, University of Wisconsin, 1956.

Koo, Youngnok. "Dissenters from American Involvement in World Affairs: A Political Analysis of the Movement for the Bricker Amendment." Ph.D. dissertation, University of Michigan, 1966.

Libby, Justin H. "The Irresolute Years: American Congressional Opinion Towards Japan, 1937–1941." Ph.D. dissertation, Michigan State University, 1971.

Mantell, Matthew E. "Opposition to the Korean War." Ph.D. dissertation, New York University, 1973.

McAuliffe, Mary S. "The Red Scare and the Crisis in American Liberalism." Ph.D. dissertation, University of Maryland, 1972.

Myers, Robert H. "William Henry Chamberlin: His Views of the Soviet Union." Ph.D. dissertation, Indiana University, 1973.

Paterson, Thomas G. "The Economic Cold War: American Business and Economic Policy, 1945–1950." Ph.D. dissertation, University of California at Berkeley, 1968.

Paul, Justus F. "The Political Career of Senator Hugh Butler." Ph.D. dissertation, University of Nebraska, 1966.

Philipose, Thomas. "The 'Loyal Opposition': Republican Leaders and Foreign Policy, 1943–1946." Ph.D. dissertation, University of Denver, 1972.

Poole, Walter S. "The Quest for a Republican Foreign Policy, 1941–1951." Ph.D. dissertation, University of Pennsylvania, 1968.

Ribuffo, Leo. "Protestants on the Right: William Dudley Pelley, Gerald B. Winrod, and Gerald L. K. Smith." Ph.D. dissertation, Yale University, 1976.

Sarles, Ruth. "A Story of America First." Manuscript; undated and on deposit in AFC papers.

Skettering, John R. "Republican Attitudes Toward the Administration's China Policy, 1945–1949." Ph.D. dissertation, Iowa State University, 1952.
Smith, Glenn H. "Senator William Langer: A Study in Isolationism." Ph.D. dissertation, University of Iowa, 1968.
Weiner, Bernard. "The Truman Doctrine: Background and Presentation." Ph.D. dissertation, Claremont College, 1967.
Yavenditti, Michael J. "American Reactions to the Use of Atomic Bombs on Japan." Ph.D. dissertation, University of California at Berkeley, 1970.

*Interviews*

Davidson, Eugene. Chicago, June 29, 1974.
Fellers, General Bonner. Washington, D.C., June 12, 1973.
Finucane, James. Washington, D.C., June 17, 1973.
MacKenzie, Gladys. Swarthmore, Pennsylvania. July 30, 1971.
Neumann, William L. Lutherville, Maryland. July 19, 1971.

# Index

Acheson, Dean: on eastern Mediterranean, 84; Delta Council address, 138; on Atlantic Pact, 154, 156, 163–64; on MAP, 156; on negotiations with the Russians, 165; on Chinese civil war, 172–73; attacks on policies of, 181, 191–92, 195–96, 202, 216, 223

Addams, Jane, 28–29

*Advance to Barbarism* (Veale), 142–43

AEC (Atomic Energy Commission), 68

Africa, 118, 122

Aiken, George D.: on UN Charter, 44; on Bretton Woods, 69 n. 2; on British loan, 64; joins interventionists, 66; on ECA, 129 nn. 40, 42; on Atlantic Pact, 157, 159; on troops-to-Europe, 208 n. 35; on McCarthy censure, 248 n. 11

Air power; strategy of, advocated, 161–65, 198, 201, 218–19, 221, 235, 243, 245; administration reliance on, 165; and Eisenhower, 224, 231; appraisal of, 247. *See also* Air–sea strategy; Atomic diplomacy; Massive retaliation

Air–sea strategy: advocated, 197–99, 225; debated, 199–200, 203–4; evaluated, 200–201; and Eisenhower administration, 231. *See also* Air power: strategy of, advocated; Atomic diplomacy

Alaska, 179, 196

Allen, Robert S., 98

Alperovitz, Gar, 246

Alsop, Joseph, 200

Alsop, Stuart, 200

*Amerasia*, 212

*America: Partner in World Rule* (Chamberlin), 41

America First Committee (as group): and negotiated peace, 30, 145; and the *Progressive*, 34 n. 25; attempted justification of, 98; and College Committee for Defense First, 109 n. 23; opposition of, to centralized planning, 165; and Sino-Japanese conflict, 181; close after Pearl Harbor, 9; and 1942 elections, 222; and *Human Events*, 51 n. 10; hopes for revival of, in 1949, 157; in 1950, 192, 196, 199; support of backers, for Taft in 1948, 125; in 1952, 219, 228 n. 31; support of backers, for McCarthy, 233–34

America First Committee (as individuals): Armour, L., 228 n. 31; Barrows, A. S., 138; Benton, W., 203; Blodgett, J. W., Jr., 101; Bowles, C., 145; Buckley family, 244; Capehart, H., 122; Castle, W. R., 28; Chamberlin, W. H., 41; Cudahy, E. A., 228 n. 31; Dulles, Janet, 230 n. 55; Dulles, John Foster, 224–25; Fellers, B., 161; Fetzer, W., Jr., 288 n. 31; Flynn, J. T., 29, 93; Ford, G. R., 21; Garrity D. A., 109 n. 23; Hammond, T., 51 n. 10; Hanighen, F., 39–40, 215; Hoover, H., 137; Jessup, P., 215; Judson, C., 51 n. 10, 228 n. 31; Kennedy, John F., 21, 207 n. 30; La Follette, R. M., Jr., 28; Leach, B. K., 228 n. 31; Leeds, Morris, 51 n. 10; Libby, F. J., 43, 157; Lindbergh, C. A., 9, 51 n. 10; McCormick, R. R., 51 n. 10; Manion, C., 241; Morley, F., 39; Morse, R. S., 228 n. 31; Morton, S., 51 n. 10, 68, 196, 228 n. 31; Mundt, K., 74; Otis, J. S. 51 n. 10; Pennypacker, I., 51 n. 10; Regnery, Henry, 98–99; Regnery, William H. 51 n. 10; Roosevelt, A. S., 228 n. 31; Ryerson, E. L., 228 n. 31; Shriver, R. S., 21; Taber, L., 24; Utley, F., 185 n. 19; Webster, E. S., Jr., 51 n. 28, 228 n. 31; Weir, E. T., 78, 228 n. 31; Welch, R., 244; Wood, R. E., 9, 26, 51 n. 10; Young, R., 67

269

# Index

opposed, 38, 50, 98, 141; evaluated, 42

*Undeclared War, The* (Langer and Gleason), 104

*Under Cover* (Carlson), 20

Unilateralism: isolationist proclivity toward, 10, 12, 83; threatened by Atlantic Pact, 158, 160. *See also* Air power; Air-sea strategy; Europe: demands for total withdrawal from

United Kingdom. *See* Great Britain

United Nations: preliminary plans for 13, 39; isolationist reactions to Charter of, 42, 44–50, 80, 237; and Atomic Energy Commission, 67; and Baruch Plan, 67–68; and Iran crisis, 63, 84; suggested role of, in Greek–Turkish crisis, 73, 82, 84–85; suggested role of, in Marshall Plan, 121–22; and debate concerning Atlantic Pact, 155, 160–61; substitute proposed for, 163; and Spain, 162; and Communist China, 183; enters Korean War, 190; role of, in Korean War attacked, 192–96, 198, 233; Hoover on, 193; condemns Peking regime, 201; McCormick, on, 222; Goldwater on, 243; and Formosa crisis of 1955, 243; and Covenant on Human Rights, 236; and Declaration of Human Rights, 237; and Convention on Genocide, 237–38; Holman on, 249 n. 22; treaty law issue, 249 n. 27; John Birch Society on, 244; and neo-isolationists, 245

United Nations Monetary and Financial Conference. *See* Bretton Woods

United States of Europe. *See* Europe: federation of, advocated

*United States* vs. *Pink*, 237–38

UNNRA (United Nations Relief and Rehabilitation Administration), 37

Utley, Freda: background of, 176; on Nazi Germany, 30, 185 n. 19, 176; on Taft, 124–25, 219; on postwar Germany, 135–36, 142; on Malmédy, 144; and Neumann, 176; on Chinese civil war, 175–76, 179, 183; on Lattimore case, 215; and the *Freeman*, 220; on Korean truce, 232; on Eisenhower policy, 242; and the *National Review*, 244

Vandenberg, Arthur H.: background of, 45; on Pearl Harbor, 92; and MacArthur movement of 1944, 45, 124; Asia-first strategy of, 37; on unconditional surrender, 38; "conversion" of, to interventionism, 11, 19, 45–46,

65–66; postwar influence of, 10; on Poland, 40; proposed three-power treaty, 42; on UN Charter, 45–46; on atomic monopoly, 67; on British loan, 66, 71 n. 38; on Truman Doctrine, 74–75, 84–85; on Marshall Plan, 115–16, 123; in 1948 election, 125, 130 n. 53; on dismantling German factories, 139; Vandenberg Resolution, 153–54; on MAP request, 156, 164; on Atlantic Pact, 160; on fate of China, 177–78, 184 n. 2; on Butterworth appointment, 183; on Eisenhower candidacy, 217; death of, 201

Vandenberg, Hoyt, 204

Van Roden, Edward LeRoy, 143, 144, 150 n. 50, n. 52

Vansittart, Robert, 38, 132

Veale, F. J. P., 143

Veteran isolationists, defined, 11

Veterans of Foreign Wars, 235

*Victor's Justice* (Belgion), 142

Vietminh, 239

Vietnam, conflict in, 11, 238–43. *See also* Indochina

Villard, Oswald Garrison: German background of, 145; cooperates with isolationists, 11, 24; and the *Progressive*, 29, 34 n. 25; on allied food council, 42; on UN Charter, 46–47; on aid to Turkey, 77; on 1948 emergency, 118; on Potsdam, 132, 135; on German starvation, 134; on occupation of Germany, 136, 138; on Nuremberg, 141; on Chiang regime, 173; and Manchurian Petition, 175, 185 n. 16; on subversion issue, 212; and New Left, 246

Vincent, John Carter, 175

Vinson, Fred, 57

Vorys, John M.: background of, 177; and peace offensive in 1941, 74, 177; on British loan, 60, 64; on Churchill "iron curtain" speech, 63; on Truman Doctrine, 33 n. 9, 74; on Marshall Plan, 123; on MAP appropriation, 156, 162; on aid to China, 162, 172, 177–78, 180, 183; on aid to South Korea, 189–90; on Korean War, 191, 233

Wade, Mason, 103

Wadsworth, James, 115

Waldrop, Frank C., 82–83, 132

Walker, Richard L., 179

Wallace, Henry A., 65, 212

Wall Street, isolationist opposition to, 21–22, 24–28, 33 n. 16, 45, 93, 109 n. 22, 117

## DATE DUE

|  |  |  |  |
|---|---|---|---|
| 4 '81 | | | |

MAY 01

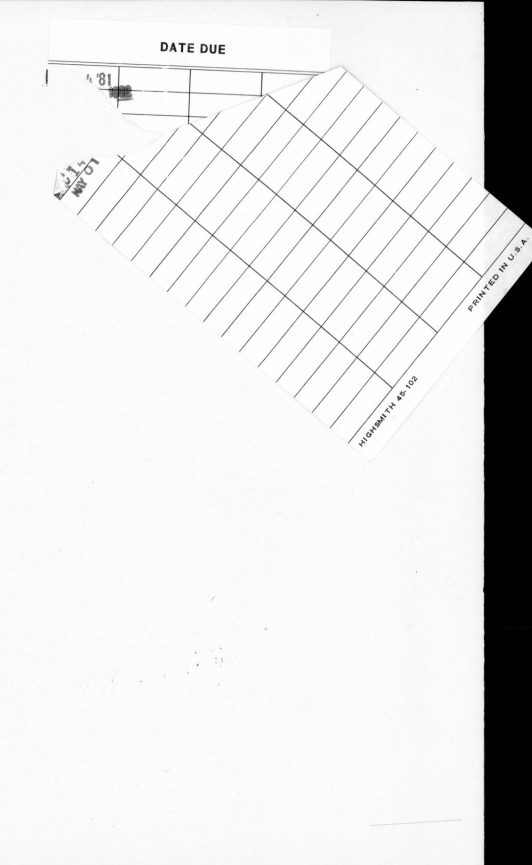

HIGHSMITH 45-102

PRINTED IN U.S.A.